D1682149

BOOK HISTORY

Book History

Volume 11

2008

Edited by

Ezra Greenspan
Southern Methodist University

Jonathan Rose
Drew University

The Pennsylvania State University Press
University Park, Pennsylvania

Graduate Student Essay Prize

Book History offers an annual prize to the outstanding graduate student essay submitted to our journal. The competition is open to anyone pursuing a course of graduate studies at the time of submission. The winning author will receive an award of $400, and the essay will be published in *Book History*. Articles should be submitted to either of the editors at the addresses below.

The Graduate Student Essay Prize for 2008 is awarded to Joanne Filippone Overty for her article "The Cost of Doing Scribal Business: Prices of Manuscript Books in England, 1300–1483."

ISSN 1098-7371
ISBN 978-0-271-03418-8

Copyright © 2008 The Society for the History of Authorship, Reading and Publishing
All rights reserved
Printed in the United States of America
Published by The Pennsylvania State University Press
University Park, PA 16802-1003

The Pennsylvania State University Press is a member of the Association of American University Presses.

It is the policy of The Pennsylvania State University Press to use acid-free paper. This book is printed on Natures Natural, containing 50% post-consumer waste, and meets the minimum requirements of American National Standard for Information Sciences—Permanence of Paper for Printed Library Materials, ANSI Z39.48–1992.

Book History is the annual journal of the Society for the History of Authorship, Reading and Publishing, Inc. (SHARP). Articles dealing with any part of the American hemisphere, Judaica, or the Middle East should be submitted to Professor Ezra Greenspan, Department of English, Southern Methodist University, Dallas, TX 75275-0435, USA, egreensp@smu.edu. All other articles should be submitted to Professor Jonathan Rose, Department of History, Drew University, Madison, NJ 07940, USA, jerose@drew.edu.

Book History is sent to members of SHARP and to institutions holding subscriptions. For information on membership in SHARP, see www.sharpweb.org or contact members@sharpweb.org. For information on institutional subscriptions, contact the Journals Department, the Pennsylvania State University Press, Suite C, 820 North University Drive, University Park, PA 16802-1003.

CONTENTS

The Cost of Doing Scribal Business: Prices of Manuscript Books in England, 1300–1483   1
Joanne Filippone Overty

"Books for the Use of the Learned and Studious": William London's *Catalogue of Most Vendible Books*   33
Margaret Schotte

Marketing Longitude: Clocks, Kings, Courtiers, and Christiaan Huygens   59
Nicole Howard

"Patron of Infidelity": Scottish Readers Respond to David Hume, c. 1750–c. 1820   89
Mark R. M. Towsey

Cadell and the Crash   125
Ross Alloway

Authorship, Ownership, and the Case for *Charles Anderson Chester*   149
David Faflik

From Private Journal to Published Periodical: Gendered Writings and Readings of a Late Victorian Wesleyan's "African Wilderness"   169
Lize Kriel

In the Margins: Regimental History and a Veteran's Narrative of the First World War   199
Janice Cavell

In Search of the Collective Author: Fact and Fiction from the Soviet 1930s   221
Mary A. Nicholas and Cynthia A. Ruder

Designing John Hersey's *The Wall*: W. A. Dwiggins, George Salter, and the Challenges of American Holocaust Memory   245
Robert Franciosi

The Women in Print Movement: History and Implications   275
Trysh Travis

The History of the Book in New England: The State of the Discipline   301
Matt Cohen

Contributors   325

ADVISORY EDITORS

Michael Albin
Library of Congress (emeritus)

John Bidwell
The Pierpont Morgan Library

Fiona Black
Dalhousie University

Hortensia Calvo
Tulane University

✓ Scott E. Casper
University of Nevada, Reno

Richard W. Clement
University of Kansas

John Y. Cole
Center for the Book, Library of Congress

✓ Robert Darnton
Harvard University

Donna Farina
New Jersey City University

Richard Fine
Virginia Commonwealth University

Francis Galloway
University of Pretoria

Abhijit Gupta
Jadavpur University

✓ Philip Gura
University of North Carolina at Chapel Hill

David Scott Kastan
Columbia University

Perter Kornicki
University of Cambridge

Beth Luey
Arizona State University (emerita)

Martyn Lyons
University of New South Wales

Leah Price
Harvard University

Christopher A. Reed
Ohio State University

James A. Secord
University of Cambridge

Sydney J. Shep
Victoria University of Wellington

David Shneer
University of Denver

Iain Stevenson
City University

Andie Tucher
Columbia University

Adriaan van der Weel
University of Leiden

James Wald
Hampshire College

The Cost of Doing Scribal Business

Prices of Manuscript Books in England, 1300–1483

Joanne Filippone Overty

> No dearness of price ought to hinder a man from the buying of books, if he has the money that is demanded for them.
> —Richard de Bury, *Philobiblon*

Since the 1970s, scholars of medieval manuscripts have increasingly focused on issues of production and use.[1] An outgrowth of the wider examination of lay literacy and its effect on the rapid proliferation and copying of texts in the fifteenth century, work in these areas has been conducted primarily by scholars of English literature, who have sought to link demand for vernacular literature with increased professionalization and specialization of the urban book trade.[2] While this work has proved invaluable for understanding the relationship between literacy and the demand for manuscripts, less attention has been devoted to quantitative analyses of the book trade as a whole. Consequently, supply-and-demand-side issues, most notably the costs associated with manuscript production, have often been overlooked.[3] Yet this information is vital for understanding not only the ability of the book trade to meet the demands of an increasingly literate society, but also the ability of institutions and individuals to obtain manuscript books at affordable prices.

It is with these costs in mind that this study will explore manuscript prices and valuations in England during the period 1300–1483, when manuscript production shifted from ecclesiastical institutions, such as monasteries, to more professional urban-based organizations.[4] Three questions in particular will be addressed: Were labor or materials more significant in

---

I owe a debt of gratitude to Maryanne Kowaleski for first suggesting that I study book prices, and patiently reading several drafts of this paper. I would also like to thank Mary C. Erler for her insightful comments. All calculations were performed by me and thus errors are mine alone.

determining a manuscript's price? How did fluctuations in the availability of professional scribes affect production costs, and thus prices of manuscript books, especially after the Black Death? And did increased demand and subsequent specialization in manuscript production (that is, a shift toward economies of scale) lower the price of manuscript books?

The arguments presented in this paper rely primarily on several library inventories compiled between 1300 and 1483 that provide manuscript valuations. The majority were assembled by F. M. Powicke from two fourteenth-century library catalogs of Merton College, Oxford: a catalog of philosophical works compiled between 1320 and 1340, and a catalog of theological works completed around 1360. Together, these inventories include the valuations of over three hundred works.[5] R. A. B. Mynors and R. M. Thomson's modern catalog of medieval manuscripts in the famous "chained" library of Hereford Cathedral provide additional data, including a series of valuations written into forty-three manuscripts by a single scribe in about 1300.[6] Remarkably, thirty-three of these valuations were updated early in the fifteenth century, again by a single scribe, providing a rare glimpse into the appreciation of a specific set of manuscripts. Finally, a 1483 inventory of some fifty manuscripts valued at Oxford by the university stationer Thomas Hunt, recovered from the flyleaf of a later manuscript, yields additional valuations.[7]

Medieval book prices are not easily quantifiable, by virtue of a manuscript's nature as a unique hand-produced item. The book trade before the advent of printing was a bespoke trade, where buyers would likely contract with several different practitioners of the book arts (such as a parchment maker, scribe, illuminator, and binder), either directly or through a stationer, to purchase products that precisely met their specifications and budget.[8] Thus any examination of manuscript prices can often take on the clichéd difficulty of comparing apples and oranges, since scripts, illumination, parchment, and binding may differ considerably between manuscripts compared in a single data series.

Despite these problems, comparisons can be attempted with data that reflect similar attributes. The inventories and valuations of manuscripts used in this survey were, for the most part, assigned value based on a common system, having been compiled by librarians in response to lending privileges at medieval institutions. For example, students of medieval universities who could not afford books of their own were permitted to borrow one of the many copies owned by the university. (The most valuable copy of a manuscript was often chained in the main library for common use, while less expensive copies were loaned out to individual borrowers to use for study.)[9] As a result, the value placed on them was intended to gauge the student's responsibility in accepting the loan. If the volume was lost, the student would be responsible to the university chest for paying the valuation amount, which would then be used to purchase a new volume similar in content and appearance to the lost item.[10] Additionally, based on information of how a manuscript was valued, general assumptions can be made about their overall quality. One can reasonably expect that these "borrowed" manuscripts assigned valuations were well-thumbed copies, not lavishly illustrated, and evidenced the ordinary wear that modern library editions often exhibit.

However, inventory valuations were arguably higher than market prices, and must therefore be used with caution. A university statute of 1439 suggests that valuations of library manuscripts were regularly inflated to encourage the borrower to take special care of the volume.[11] As a result, one would wish to avoid comparisons between prices and valuations, since their differences (market value alone versus market value plus "penalty cost") would make them difficult to evaluate equally. Yet valuation sets, based on similar rules for assigning value and consisting of manuscripts of comparable quality, could provide a fairly accurate comparison as to the percentage increase or decrease in book prices during this period. But it must be stressed that the intention of this paper is not to assign average or specific market prices to the manuscripts analyzed here. Rather, the aim is to gauge the fluctuations in manuscript valuations in the period covered, as these may well imply similar movements in market prices.

By far the most regular comparisons can be attempted from the Hereford Cathedral Library data series, which is remarkable in that it provides a fairly accurate portrait of manuscript inflation within a relatively stable environment. The Hereford data (Table 1) reveal a considerable increase in valuation of 174 percent between the first (c. 1300) and second (c. 1400) valuations; thus the majority of manuscripts in the Hereford Cathedral Library data series almost tripled in value in a span of only a hundred years.[12] What could account for such a dramatic increase? To explore a possible answer to this question, we must begin by considering the components which together constitute a manuscript's value, or, in the case of books produced for direct sale, a manuscript's price.

The manufacture of a manuscript book is by necessity labor intensive. In addition to the industry of a variety of independent craftsmen, such as scribes, bookbinders, and illuminators, the production of manuscripts in the later Middle Ages required such materials as parchment, ink, pigments, gold leaf, and leather.[13] But approximately what percentage of a manuscript's cost was determined by labor, and what percentage by materials?

While this question may seem relatively straightforward, it is very difficult to address, since detailed records accounting for all phases in a manuscript's production have rarely survived in England.[14] The few extant

Table 1. Books Valued at Hereford Cathedral Library, 1300–1400, in Pence

Manuscript	Valuation c. 1300	Valuation c. 1400	Change 1300–1400	% Change 1300–1400
Collectio Lanfranci of the Pseudo-Isidorean Decretals	360	480	+120	33
Book of Kings, glossed	320	48	−272	−85
Commentary on the Gospel of Mark	240	480	+240	100
Moralia, Part 1	240	240	0	0
Book of Numbers and Deuteronomy, glossed	160	240	+80	50
Augustine, Confessions	120	320	+200	167
Dionysius, *De Caelesti Hierarchia* with commentary; Hugh of St. Victor, *Speculum Ecclesiae*	120	80	−40	−33
Dionysius, *De Caelesti Hierarchia*; Hugh of St. Victor, *Speculum Ecclesiae*	120	160	+40	33
Gospel of John, glossed	120	24	−96	−80
Liber Officialis	120	240	+120	100
Patristica	120	240	+120	100
Acts of the Apostles, Canonical Epistles, and Apocalypse glossed	80	240	+160	200
Augustine, various works	80	240	+160	200
12 Minor Prophets, glossed	80	240	+160	200
12 Minor Prophets, glossed	80	240	+160	200
Book of Numbers, glossed	60	240	+180	300
Ezechiel and Daniel, glossed	60	120	+60	100
Gospel of Luke, glossed	60	120	+60	100
Jeremiah, glossed, with others	60	120	+60	100
Leviticus, glossed	60	240	+180	300
Paralipomena, with others, glossed	60	240	+180	300
Psalter, glossed	60	320	+260	433
Psalter, glossed	60	240	+180	300
Psalter, glossed, with Canticles	60	320	+260	433
Gospel of Luke, glossed	48	120	+72	150
John Chrysostom, Homilies	48	80	+32	67
Book of Job, glossed	36	120	+84	233
Epistles of Paul, glossed	36	160	+124	344

Table 1. (Continued)

Manuscript	Valuation c. 1300	Valuation c. 1400	Change 1300–1400	% Change 1300–1400
Exodus, glossed	36	120	+84	233
Gospel of Mark, glossed	36	80	+44	122
Apocalypse with Canticles, glossed	24	80	+56	233
Exodus, glossed	24	120	+96	400
Jerome, with others	24	120	+96	400
Average	**97**	**196**	**+99**	**174**

SOURCE: Data compiled from *Catalogue of the Manuscripts of Hereford Cathedral Library*, ed. R. A. B. Mynors and R. M. Thomson (Cambridge: D. S. Brewer, 1993). The total number of manuscripts valued in 1300 and revalued in 1400 is 33. Valuations were converted to pence to facilitate calculations.

records, however, can yield useful results. These accounts include late fourteenth-century payments for two illuminated antiphoners created for the Chapel of St. Thomas Becket located on London Bridge; the accounts of John Prust, canon of Windsor, for the production of a late fourteenth-century evangelarium; and five fifteenth-century university manuscripts from Peterhouse, Cambridge, which contain comprehensive accounts of their production written on the flyleaves of the manuscripts.

The London Bridge antiphoners, like most liturgical books intended for display, were of the highest quality: total payments for the two volumes amounted to some £24 5s 2d.[15] A breakdown of the manuscripts' costs reveals that labor accounted for 74 percent of the manuscript's price and materials only 26 percent (Table 2).

An analysis of the accounts from five fifteenth-century manuscripts from Peterhouse, Cambridge, yields similar results (Table 3). Their costs were approximately 83 percent for labor versus only a little over 17 percent for materials. Given that materials for the binding process were not specified, the labor percentage may be slightly inflated, bringing it more in line with the London Bridge antiphoners' 74 percent.

Several problems arise in attempting to quantify the data so far presented. First, the costs pertaining to writing, illumination, and binding frequently omit many of the materials used in their execution, such as ink, pigments, shell gold, gold leaf, leather, and metal clasps.[16] However, it is reasonable to assume that the absence of the breakdown of these materials in both the Peterhouse and London Bridge payment records would have a relatively mild impact on overall cost, as these supplies were relatively inexpensive and easy to obtain. For example, a scribe requires merely a goose quill pen and ink, both of which could be either made by a scribe

Table 2. Production Costs, London Bridge Antiphoners

	Cost			% of Total Cost
Labor				
Writing	£13	10s	11d	56
Text	£10	4s	3d	
Musical Notation	£ 3	6s	8d	
Illumination	£ 3	6s	8d	14
Binding	£ 0	20s	0d	4
Total	£17	17s	7d	74
Materials				
For Binding/Finishing MS	£ 1	10s	6d	6
Parchment	£ 4	17s	1d	20
Total	£ 6	7s	7d	26
Total	£24	5s	2d	100

SOURCE: Data compiled from C. Paul Christianson, *Memorials of the Book Trade in Medieval London: The Archives of Old London Bridge* (Cambridge: D. S. Brewer, 1987): 14–15.

NOTE: Materials used in the binding process included four clasps and tissues of silk for 12s, two deerskins and ten goatskins plus eight large knots with silk tassels for 18s, and two "chaptrells" of bone with markers of red leather for 6d.

Table 3. Production Costs, Peterhouse Manuscripts, Fifteenth Century

	Materials	Labor			Total Cost
MS No.	Parchment	Writing	Illumination	Binding	of MS
88	19s 6d	65s 0d	1s 0d	2s 6d	£4 0s 8d
110	6s 9d	36s 0d	8d	2s 0d	£2 5s 5d
114	6s 9d	36s 0d	6d	2s 0d	£2 5s 3d
142	8s 3d	44s 0d	1s 0d	2s 0d	£2 15s 3d
192	7s 3d	38s 8d	1s 0d	2s 0d	£2 8s 11d
Total	£2 8s 6d	£10 19s 8d	4s 2d	10s 6d	£14 2s 10d
%	17	78	1	4	100
Total %	17	83			100

SOURCE: Data compiled from Montague Rhodes James, *A Descriptive Catalogue of the Manuscripts in the Library of Peterhouse* (Cambridge: Cambridge University Press, 1899), 105, 128, 133, 169, 226.

NOTE: The scribe's rate is often listed per quire; for example, the rate for MS 88 is 20d per quire for 39 quires, for MS 110 16d per quire for 27 quires; for MS 114 16d per quire for 27 quires, for MS 142 16d per quire for 33 quires, and for MS 193 16d per quire for 29 quires.

with easily obtainable materials or purchased for a small sum. Illuminators could acquire gold leaf relatively inexpensively. Pigments (depending on those used) could be quite expensive, but such luxuries were usually restricted to the most costly of commissions.[17] While bindings for luxury volumes could be elaborate (precious and nonprecious metal bosses and clasps, and sometimes even semiprecious gemstones were used), it has been suggested that average bindings of this period were generally not costly.[18] The most common consisted of oak boards covered in leather or parchment, which could be dyed different colors according to the commissioner's taste.[19]

Wages, especially those of the scribe and illuminator, may be underreported in surviving accounts, as artisans were often given clothing (sometimes worth as much as 20s) and even room and board for the duration of their employ, in addition to cash payments.[20] This practice was common in the post–Black Death period, when payments in kind were often used to circumvent the Statute of Laborers of 1349, which mandated wage ceilings for certain forms of work.[21] Allowing for these factors would, of course, only increase our estimates of scribal labor costs.

A useful case in point is the account of payments by John Prust, canon of Windsor, for the production of an evangelarium in the early 1380s (Table 4). The accounts clearly distinguish between the scribe's wages and the expenditure for meals given to him for the duration of his employ, and the amount is not insignificant: food and drink accounted for over half of the scribe's total compensation package. In addition, ink and vermilion, used in rubrication, are also reported. Even in this fuller account of manuscript production, the total cost of labor outweighs that of supplies, accounting for 76 percent of the final cost.

If labor indeed accounted for upwards of three-quarters of manuscript production costs, it stands to reason that those costs would be especially sensitive to severe fluctuations in the labor market, as was the case in late fourteenth-century England. The late Middle Ages have been called the "Golden Age of the Laborer," as real wages (i.e., nominal wages deflated by prices) for most artisans and laborers rose considerably. The Black Death of 1347–48 wiped out a large proportion of laborers, and subsequent waves of plague (in 1360, 1369, and 1375) kept long-term population recovery at bay, rendering labor scarce and wages high. But how far did wages rise?

David Farmer, the preeminent historian of medieval English prices, has argued that artisans' nominal wages in the fifty years following the Black Death increased by roughly 60 percent.[22] Artisans frequently clustered in major urban centers to facilitate trade, and plague mortality is suspected to have been higher in urban areas than in the countryside, the result of inadequate sanitation and overcrowded living and working conditions.[23] By the

Table 4. Production Costs, *Evangeliarium*, Collegiate Church of St. George, c. 1379–85

	Cost			% of Total Cost
Labor				
writing	£1	8s	4d	37
stipend		13s	4d	
food & drink		15s	0d	
rubrics & correction		3s	0d	4
illumination		3s	4d	4
binding	£1	3s	4d	31
binding		3s	4d	
goldsmith	£1	0s	0d	
Total	£2	18s	0d	76
Materials				
ink & vermilion		1s	11d	3
bottle to hold ink			10d	1
parchment		12s	8d	17
smaller items & transport		2s	3d	3
Total		17s	8d	24
TOTAL	£3	15s	8d	100

SOURCE: Data compiled from an extract of the accounts reproduced in J. Henry Middleton, *Illuminated Manuscripts in Classical and Medieval Times: Their Art and Their Technique* (Cambridge: Cambridge University Press, 1892), 220–22.

late Middle Ages, bubonic plague was viewed by contemporaries as primarily an urban disease; large commercial centers such as London, Norwich, York, and Leicester were reported to have been especially hard hit.[24] The death rates of master craftsmen from the many guilds of London bear witness to the severity of the plague for the urban artisan class, whose losses included wardens from the goldsmiths, hatters, shearmen, and cutters.[25] The demise of so many skilled artisans in a short period must have had serious repercussions on the transmission of craft skills to future generations, as master craftsmen were the main repository of trade secrets, which were usually imparted through long-term apprenticeships. Indeed, it could be said that a craftsman's greatest asset was his skill and accumulated knowledge, not his equipment.[26] Yet while Farmer's 60 percent increase in artisan's wages is certainly significant, it does not come close to accounting for the 174 percent increase noted in the Hereford Cathedral Library manuscript valuations. What could explain such an enormous increase?

Several factors appear to have rendered the scribal labor pool particularly vulnerable to the effects of plague, making their wages disproportionately high relative to those of other artisans. First, demographic studies have suggested that clerics, the members of society most likely to be engaged in scribal activities, had a higher mortality rate from plague than the general population. (Scribes were often university-trained men in clerical orders, as their education enabled them to both read and write Latin.)[27] For example, J. C. Russell and A. H. Thompson, tracing the vacancy rate of benefices recorded in bishops' registers, have argued that clerical death-rates exceeded 40 percent for the first year of the plague.[28] Additional studies have yielded even higher death rates of upwards of 45 percent, although the registers used to reach these conclusions are generally thought to be less reliable. The extremely high 60 percent of Lincoln clergy that were replaced after the plague could suggest that the higher numbers are generally correct.[29] But why were clergy more likely to succumb to plague? While no consensus exists, scholars have suggested that clergy were probably on average far older than the general population, and thus more susceptible to death from the plague, especially by contamination through deathbed duties. Although the exact percentage of England's clerical population felled by plague continues to be a topic of debate, a majority of historians now agree that beneficed clergy (with the notable exception of the high clergy) were especially vulnerable to the effects of plague in the fourteenth century.[30] Unfortunately, no study has yet yielded reliable results of the plague death rates of unbeneficed clergy, yet there is nothing to indicate that they would have died at a lower rate than their beneficed colleagues.[31]

Contemporary accounts also point to a growing shortage of priests in the Black Death period. A 1349 letter from the Bishop of Bath and Wells bemoaning the lack of qualified priests is an oft-cited example; indeed, the shortage was considered so remarkable that the bishop allowed confessions of persons dying of plague to be heard by anyone, even a woman, if no priest could be found.[32] These accounts of the plague's severe impact on clergy have been bolstered by more recent studies that indicate that educated clerics in minor orders were encouraged to advance to major orders to secure benefices left vacant by the Black Death. Such men would thus capitalize on the opportunity to secure the good living that such a benefice provided, and forsake other types of employment (such as scribal work) usually open to educated but poorly supported clergy.[33] R. A. Davies has shown that vacant benefices in the diocese of Coventry and Lichfield in the early days of the Black Death were filled rather quickly, on average in about three weeks. This early surplus of available candidates (likely the most educated) was soon to run dry, so that after a relatively short period (roughly three months) there was a considerable lapse of time before a suitable candidate was found.[34]

Of course, not all who took clerical orders in English universities went on to become priests, so a high death rate for parish clergy would not provide an exact correlation to a lack of scribes. That most scribes were university trained, however, can also in itself suggest high plague mortality, as contemporary accounts suggest that educated men, like parish clergy, did not fare well as a group in Black Death England.[35] As late as 1363 Simon Islip, Archbishop of Canterbury, expressed concern that the transmission of knowledge had been irreparably damaged by the loss of learned men in the plague of 1348 and subsequent epidemics. Endowments to both Cambridge and Oxford Universities in the immediate post-plague period reflect patrons' concerns that the supply of educated men had dwindled to historic lows, with gifts specifying a particular wish to increase the number of educated clergy and state officials.[36] An increase in schoolmasters' wages and the extension of their contract periods after 1350 also suggests just such a shortage, in evidence around 1370, at least twenty years after the first onset of plague.[37] Schoolmasters proficient in Latin were considered especially scarce and thus highly valued. This last point, a proficiency in Latin, finds particular resonance with the data series examined in this study, as the work of most scribes (especially those employed in the copying of university texts) required a knowledge of Latin.

Thus, the sharp increase in manuscript book valuations after the Black Death, as illustrated by the data set from Hereford Cathedral Library, seems directly related to a shortage of scribes. As labor constituted approximately three-quarters of a medieval manuscript's production cost, any contraction of the supply of scribes would sharply increase prices. Spurred by unusually high death rates among both clergy and educated men—the groups most likely to engage in scribal activities—and the greater plague mortality in urban areas where most manuscript production took place, manuscript prices may have increased as much as 174 percent, outpacing increases in wages for other skilled workers. Men with enough education to function as scribes who survived the epidemics were able to advance themselves through the pursuit of lucrative and recently vacated job opportunities, and were less likely to engage in the drudgery of part-time scribal work.

But what of more long-term trends in manuscript prices in the late Middle Ages? To this end, we must now expand our data set to include manuscript valuations from Oxford University.

The Oxford University series comprises over three hundred manuscript valuations found in two fourteenth-century library catalogs from Merton College, and a 1483 inventory of fifty manuscripts valued by the university stationer, Thomas Hunt. An analysis of these data reveal a marked decrease in valuations from the earliest manuscript inventories (those completed before 1340) to the later Oxford inventory of 1483 (figure 1). On average, the valuation of late fifteenth-century manuscripts examined are nearly 40 percent lower than their early fourteenth-century predecessors (Appendix

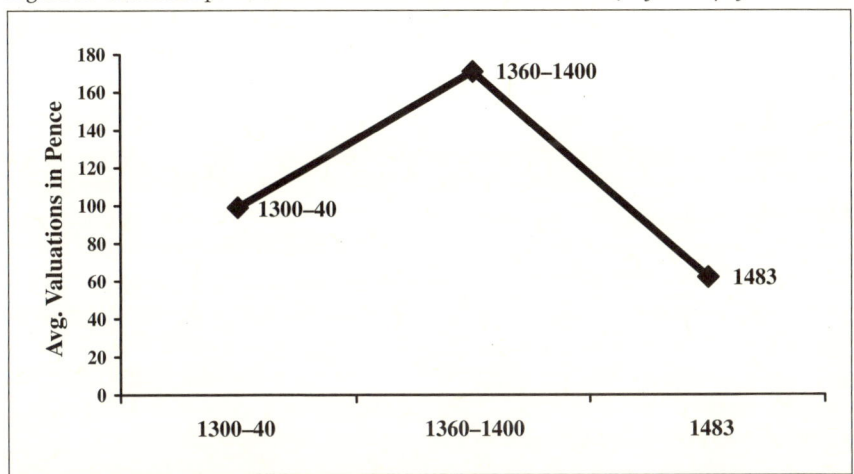

Figure 1. Manuscript valuations from Oxford and Hereford, 1300–1483.

SOURCE: Data compiled from Appendices A–C.
NOTE: Valuations were converted to pence to facilitate calculations.

A).[38] These calculations suggest that a manuscript book purchased in 1483 would cost roughly half the price of a manuscript book purchased before 1360.

Several factors may underlie this precipitous drop. First and foremost, the late-medieval increase in demand for manuscript books, long noted by scholars, promoted economies of scale.[39] Part of a wider post–Black Death transformation in consumer spending, this increased demand for a variety of commodities was considered radical enough by contemporaries to trigger treatises against luxury and waste, legislation governing leisure pursuits, and sumptuary laws.[40] The catalyst for this "consumer revolution" was a general increase in standards of living for large portions of the population. Population contraction caused by numerous waves of plague had the effect of both increasing real wages and lowering prices, and thus greatly increasing disposable income among the survivors.[41] Wages for skilled building workers, for example, rose 82 percent from circa 1300 to 1400, while prices for consumables (such as grain, meat, and cloth) decreased by 8 percent in the same period.[42] Luxuries that would have been unthinkable in the early fourteenth century, such as hand-produced books, were now within reach for new sections of the literate public, who utilized manuscript books as both symbols of recently acquired status and objects of value.[43]

The rise in disposable income would also enable a larger portion of the population to send their children to school and thus acquire the ability to read and write, especially in the vernacular.[44] This newly literate laity, who increasingly relied on the written word for bookkeeping, communication, and entertainment, formed the basis of a new market for vernacular writing, challenging the older definition of *literatus* as one who was proficient in Latin alone.[45] Derek Pearsall speculates that the typical members of this new literate laity might have included rich merchants, lawyers, and country gentlemen: people who enjoyed prosperity but were anxious to acquire prestige, partly through the ownership of books.[46] Not only were Latin works translated into the vernacular, but for the first time original works were composed in vernacular languages on a large scale, creating a climate ripe for the introduction of the printing press in the fifteenth century.[47] Besides literary works, devotional works were highly prized; indeed demand was great enough to lead to the importation of Flemish books of hours for the English market. "Do-it-yourself" books proliferated as well, covering such subjects as personal health and veterinary medicine.[48]

The late-medieval urban book trade met the challenges of increased demand with more efficient methods of production. Medieval book artisans were most often paid by their labor, not their time, and therefore they worked fast.[49] Some scholars theorize that the standardization in layout, decoration, and design of fifteenth-century vernacular manuscripts was instituted by artisans to accelerate production.[50] To keep up with demand, each of the book arts developed time-saving techniques, such as tracing designs through parchment and dividing text into sections (quires) that were farmed out to multiple scribes and illuminators.[51] It is possible that several scribes found it useful to retain in-house exemplars to produce multiple copies of popular works, although this has been the subject of much academic debate.[52]

Scholars have noted new patterns of organization in manuscript book production from roughly the middle of the fourteenth century until the advent of printing. The late-medieval development of the stationer, who often functioned as both an independent craftsman and a mediator between customers and other book artisans, increased the output of codices.[53] The writing of a single manuscript thus often became a cooperative enterprise among book artisans, allowing a collective response to spikes in demand through collaboration on unusually large works or orders.[54] These combined efforts necessitated that those engaged in the trade work in close proximity, sometimes within the same building.[55] Book artisans in England clustered most often in major towns and university centers, primarily in the south, with London as the epicenter.

Among London booksellers a more robust trade enabled certain shops to specialize in specific types of work. For example, C. Paul Christianson has identified what could be called a "specialty line" of very small books of hours produced by a London stationer in the late fifteenth century.[56] The well-known London copyist John Shirley possibly specialized in the works of the fifteenth-century vernacular poet John Lydgate, as he may have known the poet personally and is the sole authority for thirty of Lydgate's minor poems.[57] Some of these shops may have been so successful that they gambled on speculative work, for cases of blank spaces left for coats of arms or other heraldic devices have been found in several otherwise completed works.[58]

In addition to the book trade's improved production techniques, the sharply reduced cost of raw materials in the late medieval period helped to keep the prices of most finished goods, including books, relatively low. Increased pastoral husbandry lowered the prices of hides, which could be used for parchment or bookbinding, and the introduction and wider use of paper for both manuscripts and printed books in the latter half of the fifteenth century further decreased the costs of manuscript production.[59] (I intend to examine the prices of these materials and their effect on manuscript production in a later work.)

To sum up, the Black Death had both short-term and long-term impacts on book prices, in very different directions. The immediate impact was to increase the replacement cost of books—by as much as 174 percent over a hundred years in the case of valuations from Hereford Cathedral. The plague sharply depleted the pool of educated men most likely to engage in scribal activities—clerics and university graduates—perhaps proportionally more than the general population. That contraction in the labor market for educated men resulted in higher wages and greater benefits, and those increased costs were passed along to book consumers. In the long run, however, the rise of vernacular literacy among the increasingly well-to-do laity expanded demand to historic levels, and the book trade met these challenges with more efficient methods of production. The ultimate result, as suggested by the statistical evidence presented in this paper, was a sharp decrease in the price of manuscript books, by perhaps as much as 50 percent, from the early fourteenth century until the beginning of printing activity in the late fifteenth century.

Appendix A:
Inventory of Books Valued at Merton College, Oxford, and Hereford Cathedral Library, c. 1300–1340

Data compiled from *The Medieval Books of Merton College*, ed. F. M. Powicke (Oxford: Clarendon Press, 1931); and *Catalogue of the Manuscripts of Hereford Cathedral Library*, ed. R. A. B. Mynors and R. M. Thomson. (Cambridge: D. S. Brewer, 1993.)

MC = Merton College
HC = Hereford Cathedral

	Title	Date of Valuation	Valuation (in pence)	Source
1	Acts, Canonical Epistles, Apocalypse, glossed	1300	80	HC
2	Almagest	1320–40	96	MC
3	Analytics, Prior and Posterior	1320–40	6	MC
4	Apocalypse, with Canticles, glossed	1300	24	HC
5	Book of Job, glossed	1300	36	HC
6	Book of Numbers and Deuteronomy, glossed	1300	160	HC
7	Book of Numbers, glossed	1300	60	HC
8	City of God	1300	720	HC
9	Collectio	1300	360	HC
10	Collectio Lanfranci	1300	240	HC
11	Commentaries on the De Caelo, De Sensu, De Anima, De Generatione, etc.	1320–40	180	MC
12	Commentaries on the Physics and Parva Naturalia	1320–40	192	MC
13	Commentary on the De Caelo and the De Causis	1320–40	192	MC
14	Commentary on the De Caelo et Mundo	1320–40	84	MC
15	Commentary on the Epistles of Paul	1300	160	HC
16	Commentary on the Gospels of Mark, with Other Works	1300	240	HC
17	Commentary on the Metaphysics	1320–40	192	MC
18	Commentary on the Metaphysics and De Anima	1320–40	216	MC
19	Commentary on the Physics	1320–40	288	MC
20	Confessions	1300	120	HC
21	De Anima, and the Shorter Naturales	1320–40	36	MC
22	De Animalibus	1320–40	20	MC

	Title	Date of Valuation	Valuation (in pence)	Source
23	De Animalibus in New Translation	1320–40	240	MC
24	De Caelesti Hierarchia and Speculum Ecclesiae	1300	120	HC
25	De Generatione, et al.	1320–40	36	MC
26	Epistles of Paul, glossed	1300	36	HC
27	Ethics	1320–40	48	MC
28	Ethics and the Liber de Causis	1320–40	48	MC
29	Exodus, glossed	1300	36	HC
30	Exodus, glossed	1300	24	HC
31	Exposition of the De Caelo	1320–40	8	MC
32	Exposition (probably on Aquinas)	1320–40	7	MC
33	Exposition of the Meteorology of Peter of Auvergne	1320–40	36	MC
34	Exposition of the Meteorology, with Expositions of the Bona Fortuna	1320–40	20	MC
35	Exposition on Politics	1320–40	96	MC
36	Ezechiel and Daniel, glossed	1300	60	HC
37	Four Books of Kings, glossed	1300	320	HC
38	Generation	1320–40	18	MC
39	Geometria and Algorismus Demonstratus	1320–40	36	MC
40	Gospel of John, glossed	1300	120	HC
41	Gospel of John, glossed	1300	36	HC
42	Gospel of Luke, glossed	1300	60	HC
43	Gospel of Luke, glossed	1300	48	HC
44	Gospel of Mark, glossed	1300	36	HC
45	Gospel of Matthew, glossed	1300	48	HC
46	Great and Small Priscian	1320–40	48	MC
47	Grecismi et Boicii	1320–40	18	MC
48	Homilies, with Others	1300	48	HC
49	Jeremiah, with Others, glossed	1300	60	HC
50	Jerome, with Others	1300	24	HC
51	Leviticus, glossed	1300	60	HC
52	Liber Astronomie	1320–40	8	MC
53	Liber Officialis	1300	120	HC
54	Metaphysics	1320–40	40	MC
55	Metaphysics	1320–40	36	MC
56	Metaphysics and Nicomachean Ethics	1320–40	72	MC
57	Metaphysics and Other Works in Old Translations (i.e. 12/13th c.)	1320–40	24	MC
58	Metaphysics et al.	1320–40	48	MC
59	Meteorology	1320–40	42	MC
60	Meteorology	1320–40	18	MC

	Title	Date of Valuation	Valuation (in pence)	Source
61	Meteorology and Other Works	1320–40	60	MC
62	Minor Prophets, glossed	1300	84	HC
63	Minor prophets, glossed	1300	80	HC
64	Moralia, part 1	1300	240	HC
65	On Constructions	1320–40	6	MC
66	On Constructions with Commentary of Peter Helias	1320–40	24	MC
67	On the Metaphysics	1320–40	120	MC
68	On the Planisphere with the Almagest	1320–40	120	MC
69	On the Seven Arts	1320–40	6	MC
70	Optics	1320–40	48	MC
71	Panormia and Sermons	1300	120	HC
72	Paralipomena, with Others, glossed	1300	60	HC
73	Passional, November to January	1300	480	HC
74	Patristica	1300	120	HC
75	Physics and Meteorology in the Old Translation	1320–40	24	MC
76	Physics and Other Libri Naturales	1320–40	7	MC
77	Physics and Other Libri Naturales and the Pseudo-Aristotelian Liber de Prob.	1320–40	320	MC
78	Postils on the Psalter	1320–40	360	MC
79	Psalter with Canticles, glossed	1300	60	HC
80	Psalter, glossed	1300	60	HC
81	Questiones	1320–40	6	MC
82	Questions on the Metaphysics and Other Aristotelian Texts	1320–40	12	MC
83	Questions on the Meteorology	1320–40	6	MC
84	Sermons "de verbis domini et apostoli"	1300	360	HC
85	Tables of Toledo with a Work on the Astrolabe	1320–40	6	MC
86	The Meteorology	1320–40	30	MC
87	The New Logic	1320–40	24	MC
88	The Old and New Logic	1320–40	120	MC
89	The Old Logic	1320–40	48	MC
90	The Old Logic	1320–40	24	MC
91	The Old Logic	1320–40	12	MC
92	The Old Logic, Beginning with the Categories, and The New Logic	1320–40	48	MC
93	Theorica Planetarum cum Tabluis Equacionum	1320–40	6	MC
94	Timaeus with the Martialis	1320–40	24	MC
95	Twelve Minor Prophets, glossed	1300	80	HC

	Title	Date of Valuation	Valuation (in pence)	Source
96	Unknown	1320–40	48	MC
97	Various Works	1300	80	HC
98	Various Works by Jerome and the Other Fathers, with Glosses on Aristotle	1320–40	480	MC
	Average Valuation		99	

Appendix B:
Inventory of Books Valued at Merton College, Oxford, c. 1360

Data compiled from *The Medieval Books of Merton College*, ed. F. M. Powicke (Oxford: Clarendon Press, 1931).

	Title	Date of Valuation	Valuation (in pence)
1	12 Minor Prophets, glossed	1360	48
2	83 questiones	1360	120
3	Acts of the Apostles, glossed	1360	20
4	Acts of the Apostles, glossed	1360	6
5	Acts, the Canonical Epistles, and the Apocalypse, glossed	1360	80
6	Bede on Canonical Epistles and Haymo on the Apocalypse	1360	120
7	Brito, Expositiones Super Prologos Bible	1360	60
8	Canonical Epistles, Song of Songs and Lamentations, glossed	1360	12
9	Chronicle	1360	40
10	Chronicle	1360	40
11	City of God	1360	480
12	City of God	1360	288
13	City of God	1360	240
14	City of God	1360	240
15	City of God	1360	192
16	City of God	1360	60
17	Commentary on the First Book of the Sentences	1360	120
18	Commentary on the Fourth Book of the Sentences	1360	320
19	Commentary on the Third Book of the Sentences	1360	120
20	Commentary on the Third Book of the Sentences	1360	96
21	Commentary, First and Second Books of Sentences	1360	48
22	Commentary, First Book of Sentences	1360	60
23	Commentary, First Book of Sentences	1360	24
24	Commentary, First Book of the Sentences	1360	60
25	Commentary, First Book of the Sentences	1360	12
26	Commentary, Fourth Book of the Sentences	1360	320
27	Commentary, Fourth Book of the Sentences	1360	240
28	Commentary, Fourth Book of the Sentences	1360	180
29	Commentary, Fourth Book of the Sentences	1360	160
30	Commentary, Fourth Book of the Sentences	1360	120

	Title	Date of Valuation	Valuation (in pence)
31	Commentary, Fourth book of the Sentences	1360	60
32	Commentary, on Genesis ad Literam	1360	312
33	Commentary, on Genesis ad Literam	1360	288
34	Commentary, on Genesis ad Literam	1360	124
35	Commentary, on Genesis ad Literam	1360	120
36	Commentary, on Genesis ad Literam	1360	120
37	Commentary, on Genesis ad Literam, etc.	1360	360
38	Commentary, on Genesis ad Literam, etc.	1360	288
39	Commentary, on the Trinity	1360	480
40	Commentary, on the Trinity	1360	120
41	Commentary, on the Trinity	1360	96
42	Commentary, on the Trinity	1360	96
43	Commentary, on the Trinity and Others	1360	360
44	Commentary, Psalms	1360	1600
45	Commentary, Second and Fourth Books of the Sentences	1360	156
46	Commentary, Second and Third Books of the Sentences	1360	156
47	Commentary, Second Book of the Sentences	1360	80
48	Commentary, Second Book of the Sentences	1360	72
49	Commentary, Second Book of the Sentences	1360	60
50	Commentary, Sentences	1360	360
51	Commentary, Sentences	1360	160
52	Commentary, Sentences	1360	144
53	Commentary, Sentences	1360	120
54	Commentary, Sentences	1360	96
55	Commentary, Sentences	1360	80
56	Commentary, Sentences	1360	72
57	Commentary, Sentences	1360	60
58	Commentary, Sentences	1360	36
59	Commentary, Third and Fourth Books of Sentences	1360	120
60	Commentary, Third and Fourth Books of Sentences	1360	96
61	Commentary, Third and Fourth Books of the Sentences	1360	96
62	Commentary, Third and Fourth Books of the Sentences, with Others by Crosby	1360	60
63	Commentary, Third Book of the Sentences	1360	48
64	Confessions	1360	240
65	Confessions, with Many More of His Works	1360	720
66	Contra Gentiles	1360	160
67	Contra Gentiles	1360	160
68	Contra Gentiles	1360	96

	Title	Date of Valuation	Valuation (in pence)
69	Cronica	1360	156
70	De Bono et Malo	1360	120
71	De Bono Virginale, with Others	1360	240
72	De Causa Dei Contra Pelagios	1360	480
73	De Consolatione, with Other Items	1360	18
74	De Doctrina Cordis, etc.	1360	156
75	De Fide ad Petrum, etc.	1360	120
76	De Fide et Symbolo	1360	96
77	De Fide Rerum Invisibilium	1360	24
78	De Fide, de Spiritu Sancto, and De Incarnatione Domini	1360	156
79	De Ordine ad Sinobium	1360	120
80	De Spiritu et Anima	1360	240
81	De Veritate	1360	120
82	De Veritate	1360	120
83	De Veritate	1360	72
84	De Virginitate, with others	1360	288
85	De Vita Beate Virginis	1360	18
86	Dialogues	1360	144
87	Dialogues, with Other Works	1360	160
88	Epistle of James, glossed	1360	12
89	Epistles of Paul, glossed	1360	360
90	Epistles of Paul, glossed	1360	240
91	Epistola ad Lucilium	1360	40
92	Epistolae	1360	240
93	Epistolae, with works of Augustine	1360	320
94	Exodus, glossed	1360	40
95	Four Major Prophets, glossed	1360	60
96	Genesis and Exodus, glossed	1360	144
97	Genesis and Others, glossed	1360	144
98	Gloss on the Epistles of Paul	1360	156
99	Gospels of Mark, Matthew, and John glossed	1360	24
100	Gospels with Gregory's homilies	1360	80
101	Gospels, glossed	1360	800
102	Gospels, glossed	1360	360
103	Gospels, glossed	1360	96
104	Half of the Psalter, glossed	1360	48
105	Hierarchia, with Other Items	1360	40
106	Historia Ecclesiastica	1360	240
107	Historia Scholastica	1360	480
108	Historia Scholastica	1360	240
109	Historia Scholastica	1360	240
110	Historia Scholastica	1360	216
111	Historia Scholastica	1360	160
112	Historia Scholastica	1360	160

	Title	Date of Valuation	Valuation (in pence)
113	Historia Scholastica	1360	96
114	Historia Scholastica with Allegories	1360	360
115	Historia Scholastica with Allegories	1360	264
116	Historie Ecclesiastice	1360	80
117	Homilies	1360	216
118	Homilies on Ezekiel with 89 Sermons of Augustine	1360	240
119	Homilies on the Gospel of Mark	1360	360
120	Hugh of St. Victor, On the Sacraments	1360	240
121	Hugh of St. Victor, On the Sacraments	1360	156
122	Hugh of St. Victor, On the Sacraments, with Other Works of Hugh and Anselm	1360	360
123	Isaiah, glossed	1360	72
124	Job, Minor Prophets, with Others, glossed	1360	120
125	Job, Proverbs with Others, glossed	1360	120
126	Kings and Chronicles, glossed	1360	80
127	Letters, with Many Other Works	1360	360
128	Leviticus, Numbers and Deuteronomy, glossed	1360	160
129	Luke and John, glossed	1360	160
130	Major Prophets, glossed	1360	192
131	Mark and Matthew, gloss on the Evangelists	1360	36
132	Meditations	1360	12
133	Minor Prophets, glossed	1360	60
134	Moralia	1360	720
135	Moralia	1360	480
136	Moralia	1360	480
137	Moralia	1360	240
138	Moralia, book 1	1360	156
139	Numbers and Deuteronomy, glossed	1360	160
140	Numbers and Deuteronomy, glossed	1360	40
141	On Christian Doctrine	1360	360
142	On Christian Doctrine with Many Other Works	1360	160
143	On Clemency, with Other Works	1360	120
144	On Free Will, with Many Other Works	1360	480
145	On Infant Baptism, Against the Donatists	1360	96
146	On Maccabees	1360	160
147	On the Nature of God, with Other Writings	1360	192
148	On the Properties of Things	1360	360
149	On the Properties of Things	1360	120
150	On the Pseudo-Dionysius the Areopagite	1360	288
151	On the Sermon on the Mount	1360	120
152	On the Value of the Psalms	1360	144
153	Pastoralia	1360	80

	Title	Date of Valuation	Valuation (in pence)
154	Pastoralia	1360	36
155	Pastoralia	1360	24
156	Pastoralia, with Other Works	1360	24
157	Paul's Epistles, Canonical Epistles, Acts and Apocalypse, glossed	1360	84
158	Paul's Epistles, glossed	1360	240
159	Pentateuch, glossed	1360	160
160	Postil on Ecclesiastes	1360	60
161	Postil on Matthew and Others	1360	18
162	Postils on Ecclesiasties and Wisdom	1360	96
163	Postils on Genesis	1360	120
164	Postils on Genesis	1360	40
165	Postils on Hosea with Others	1360	24
166	Postils on Isaiah	1360	80
167	Postils on Isaiah	1360	24
168	Postils on John and Luke	1360	80
169	Postils on John and part of the Psalter	1360	24
170	Postils on Luke the Evangelist	1360	240
171	Postils on Luke with the Works of Hugh of St. Victor	1360	18
172	Postils on Proverbs and the Apocalypse	1360	40
173	Postils on Proverbs, Ecclesiastes and the Song of Solomon	1360	80
174	Postils on the Book of Wisdom	1360	160
175	Postils on the Books of Wisdom	1360	80
176	Postils on the Books of Wisdom	1360	60
177	Postils on the Canonical Epistles	1360	84
178	Postils on the Canonical Epistles	1360	48
179	Postils on the Gospel of John	1360	40
180	Postils on the Minor Prophets	1360	144
181	Postils on the Pentateuch	1360	240
182	Postils on the Pentateuch	1360	120
183	Postils on the Song of Solomon	1360	120
184	Postils on the Song of Solomon	1360	8
185	Prophets, glossed	1360	120
186	Psalter, gloss of	1360	24
187	Psalter, glossed	1360	240
188	Psalter, glossed	1360	180
189	Psalter, glossed	1360	160
190	Psalter, glossed	1360	160
191	Psalter, glossed	1360	120
192	Psalter, glossed	1360	120
193	Psalter, glossed	1360	84
194	Psalter, glossed	1360	60
195	Questiones de Veritate	1360	120

	Title	Date of Valuation	Valuation (in pence)
196	Retractations, with Others	1360	360
197	Retractations, with Others	1360	160
198	Richard of St. Victor on the Trinity, with Many Writings of Anselm	1360	96
199	Sentences	1360	320
200	Sentences	1360	312
201	Sentences	1360	240
202	Sentences	1360	240
203	Sentences	1360	156
204	Sentences	1360	144
205	Sentences	1360	144
206	Sentences	1360	144
207	Sentences	1360	120
208	Sentences	1360	120
209	Sentences	1360	120
210	Sentences	1360	120
211	Sentences	1360	96
212	Sentences	1360	96
213	Sentences	1360	60
214	Sentences, Chart or Analysis	1360	120
215	Sermons	1360	120
216	Sermons, with Calendar	1360	120
217	Summa i	1360	192
218	Summa ii	1360	240
219	Summa ii	1360	240
220	Summa ii	1360	180
221	Summa ii	1360	160
222	Summa Theologica	1360	240
223	Summa, Part i	1360	160
224	Summa, Part i	1360	156
225	Summa, Part i	1360	120
226	Table, Sentences	1360	80
227	Works by Anselm	1360	240
228	Works by Anselm and Augustine	1360	120
229	Works by Anselm, with the Questions of Aquinas on Evil	1360	144
230	Works of Anselm with Other Items	1360	400
231	Writings of Anselm	1360	120
232	Writings of Anselm and Augustine	1360	240
233	Writings of Anselm in 3 gatherings	1360	40
234	Writings of Bernard with Others	1360	480
	Average Valuation		**168**

Appendix C:
Books Valued at Oxford University by Thomas Hunt, University Stationer (c. 1483)

Data compiled from *Collectanea*, first series, ed. C. R. L. Fletcher (Oxford: Clarendon Press for the Oxford Historical Society, 1885).

	Title	Date of Valuation	Valuation (in pence)
1	Albertus ab Eyb, *Margarita Poetica*	1483	108
2	Albertus Magnus, *De Secretis Mulierum*	1483	8
3	Angelus de Gambilionibus, *Super Instituta*	1483	192
4	Antonius de Parma, *Sermons*	1483	44
5	Aristotle, *De Animalibus*	1483	84
6	Boethius, *De Consolatione*	1483	48
7	Duns Scotus, *Omnia Opera Scotj in Communi Forma cum Quodlibetis*	1483	76
8	Duns Scotus, *Quodlibeta Scoti in Communi Forma*	1483	48
9	Dyonysius Areopagita, *Epistole Dyonisij*	1483	32
10	Eusebius, *De Viris Illustribus*	1483	12
11	*Flores Poetarum (de Virtutibus et Vitiis)*	1483	16
12	*Formularius Advocatorum et Procuratorum Curiae Romanae*	1483	52
13	*Formularius Instrumentorum ad Usum Curiae Romanae*	1483	48
14	Gaetanus, *De Anima*	1483	50
15	Godfredus, *Summa Godfredi*	1483	44
16	Gulielmus Durandus, *Rationale Divinorum Officiorum*	1483	96
17	Henricus de Piro, *Super Instituta*	1483	52
18	Henricus de Zoemeren, *Dyalogi Henrici de Zömeren*	1483	44
19	Hugo de Vienna (Hugo de S. Caro), *Super Quatuor Evangelia*	1483	288
20	Johanes de Vassolis, *Commentary on the Four Books of Sentences*	1483	56
21	Johannes de Capestranis, *Tractatus de Cupiditate*	1483	24
22	Johannes de Imola, *Super Clementinas*	1483	204
23	Johannes de Turnout, *Casus Juris Civilis*	1483	76
24	Johannes Gerson, *Sex Lectiones*	1483	12
25	Johannes Herolt, *Sermones Discipuli de Tempore et Sancts cum Promptuario*	1483	120
26	Johannes Nicolaus de Milis, *Repertorium Juris*	1483	72
27	Juvenalis, *Decimus Junius*	1483	16

	Title	Date of Valuation	Valuation (in pence)
28	Laurentius Valla, *De vero Bono*	1483	24
29	Lovanium, *Declamatio Louvaniensium*	1483	3
30	Marcus Tullius Cicero, *De Officiis cum Commento*	1483	80
31	*Marcus Valerius*	1483	36
32	Martin Luther, *De Potestate Pape*	1483	10
33	Ovid, *De Vetula*	1483	16
34	Ovid, *Methamorphoses*	1483	48
35	Ovid, *Omnia Opera*	1483	120
36	Petrus de Alliaco, *De Imagine Mundi*	1483	48
37	Petrus de Crescentiis, *Opus Ruralium Commodorum*	1483	52
38	*Processus Juris*	1483	48
39	Publius Afer Terentius, *Terentius cum Donato*	1483	72
40	*Quinque Specula* (?)	1483	40
41	*Sermones ad Omnes Status (hominem)*	1483	44
42	*Sermones Tredecim*	1483	16
43	*Sextus Liber Decretalium*	1483	144
44	Soccus, *Sermones Socci de Sanctis*	1483	54
45	St. Thomas Aquinas, *Contra Gentilles*	1483	60
46	*Summarii Casus Super Instituta Justiniani*	1483	16
47	Tedeschi, Nicolas, *Abbas tantum in Parva Forma*	1483	72
48	Thomas Wallensis, *Super Psalterium*	1483	64
49	*Vita Apiani* (?)	1483	24
	Average Valuation		62

Notes

1. For example, see A. I. Doyle and M. B. Parkes, "The Production of Copies of the *Canterbury Tales* and the *Confessio Amantis* in the Early Fifteenth Century," in *Medieval Scribes, Manuscripts & Libraries: Essays Presented to N. R. Ker*, ed. M. B. Parkes and Andrew G. Watson (London: Scolar, 1978), 163–210; Derek Pearsall, "Texts, Textual Criticism, and Fifteenth-Century Manuscript Production," in *Fifteenth-Century Studies: Recent Essays*, ed. Robert F. Yeager (Hamden, Conn.: Archon, 1984), 121–36; and Richard H. and Mary Rouse, *Manuscripts and their Makers: Commercial Book Producers in Medieval Paris, 1200–1500* (Turnhout, Belgium: Harvey Miller, 2000).

2. See, for example, Margaret Connolly, *John Shirley: Book Production and the Noble Household in Fifteenth-Century England* (Aldershot: Ashgate, 1998); A. S. G. Edwards, "Beinecke MS 661 and Early Fifteenth-Century English Manuscript Production," *Yale University Library Gazette* 66 (1991): 181–96; A. S. G. Edwards and Derek Pearsall, "The Manuscripts of the Major English Poetic Texts," in *Book Production and Publishing in Britain 1375–1475*, ed. Jeremy Griffiths and Derek Pearsall (Cambridge: Cambridge University Press,

1989), 257–69; and George R. Keiser, "Lincoln Cathedral MS. 91: Life and Milieu of the Scribe," *Studies in Bibliography* 32 (1979): 158–79.

3. The most notable exceptions are H. E. Bell, "The Price of Books in Medieval England," *The Library* 4th ser., 17 (1936–37): 312–32; C. Paul Christianson, *Memorials of the Book Trade in Medieval London: The Archives of Old London Bridge* (Cambridge: D. S. Brewer, 1987), and "The Rise of London's Book-Trade," in *The Cambridge History of the Book in Britain*, vol. 3, 1400–1557, ed. Lotte Hellinga and J. B. Trapp (Cambridge: Cambridge University Press, 1999), 128–47; R. Malcolm Hogg, "Some Thirteenth-Century English Book Prices," in *Thirteenth Century England V: Proceedings of the Newcastle upon Tyne Conference 1993*, ed. P. R. Coss and S. D. Lloyd (Woodbridge: Boydell, 1995), 179–94; and Wilbur Lang Schramm, "The Cost of Books in Chaucer's Time," *Modern Language Notes* 48, no. 3 (1933): 139–45. Christianson's exemplary studies of English manuscript production are confined mainly to London, and Bell's study, while still the most often cited by scholars, is more of a survey of manuscript prices, rather than a comprehensive analysis. Additionally, Hogg and Schramm are concerned primarily with book prices in the thirteenth and fifteenth centuries, respectively, and thus avoid drawing conclusions about the fluctuation of prices over more extended periods in the Middle Ages. While full-scale treatments of book prices are rare, scholars have often touched upon various commodities as components of manuscript production. For example, James E. Thorold Rogers explored the prices of parchment and paper in his monumental text, *A History of Agriculture and Prices in England*, vol. 4, 1401–1582 (Oxford: Clarendon Press, 1882), and Jonathan J. G. Alexander, Christopher De Hamel, D. C. Greetham, and Ernest A. Savage have used prices to examine the cost of scribes, illumination, and parchment. See J. J. G. Alexander, *Medieval Illuminators and their Methods of Work* (New Haven: Yale University Press, 1992); Christopher De Hamel, *Medieval Craftsmen: Scribes and Illuminators* (Toronto: University of Toronto Press, 1992); D. C. Greetham, *Textual Scholarship: An Introduction* (New York: Garland, 1992); and Ernest A. Savage, *Old English Libraries: The Making, Collection, and Use of Books during the Middle Ages* (Chicago: A. C. McClurg & Co., 1912).

4. Most books in England were copied in monasteries or ecclesiastical institutions from the early Middle Ages until roughly the end of the twelfth century. C. Paul Christianson ("Evidence for the Study of London's Late Medieval Manuscript Book Trade," in *Book Production and Publishing in Britain 1375–1475*, ed. Jeremy Griffiths and Derek Pearsall [Cambridge: Cambridge University Press, 1989], 89) suggests that the period of greatest commercial manuscript activity in London was between 1390 and 1490, after which it declined due to the introduction of printed books. See also Alexander, *Medieval Illuminators*, 20–22, and A. I. Doyle, "Book Production by the Monastic Orders in England (c. 1375–1530): Assessing the Evidence," in *Medieval Book Production: Assessing the Evidence; Proceedings of the Second Conference of The Seminar in the History of the Book to 1500, Oxford, July 1988*, ed. Linda L. Brownrigg (Los Altos Hills, Calif.: Red Gull Press/Anderson-Lovelace, 1990), 1.

5. *The Medieval Books of Merton College*, ed. F. M. Powicke (Oxford: Clarendon Press, 1931), 47–60.

6. *Catalogue of the Manuscripts of Hereford Cathedral Library*, ed. R. A. B. Mynors and R. M. Thomson (Cambridge: D. S. Brewer, 1993).

7. The inventory was transcribed by F. Madan in *Collectanea*, first series, ed. C. R. L. Fletcher (Oxford: Clarendon Press for the Oxford Historical Society, 1885), 141–43.

8. The concept of "workshop" production in medieval England has stimulated much debate over the years. For a good overview of the debate and their views in context, see Doyle and Parkes, "Production of Copies," 163–210; Laura Hibbard Loomis, "The Auchinleck Manuscript and a Possible London Bookshop of 1330–1340," *PMLA* 57, no. 3 (1942): 595–627; Linne R. Mooney and Lister M. Matheson, "The Beryn Scribe and His Texts: Evidence

for Multiple-Copy Production of Manuscripts in Fifteenth-Century England," *The Library* 7th ser., 4, no. 4 (2003): 347–70; and Timothy A. Shonk, "A Study of the Auchinleck Manuscript: Bookmen and Bookmaking in the Early Fourteenth Century," *Speculum* 60, no. 1 (1985): 71–91.

9. This was a common practice in universities on the Continent as well, and is thought to have descended from monastic practice; see Arthur F. Leach, "Wykeham's Books," in *Collectanea*, 3rd ser. (Oxford: Clarendon Press for the Oxford Historical Society, 1896), 218; see also Francis Wormald, "The Monastic Library," in *Gatherings in Honor of Dorothy E. Miner*, ed. Ursula E. McCracken (Baltimore: Walters Art Gallery, 1974), 100.

10. Leach, "Wykeham's Books," 218.

11. Ibid.: "and for the better custody of the said books every of them shall be priced appreciably beyond the true value, which value every one taking one of the books on loan shall, if he lose it, be bound to pay to the chest, and with the sum so received another book shall be provided of like binding and shape, as soon as possible." This practice was followed in both institutional libraries and private libraries such as the library of Richard de Gravesend (Bishop of London). See also Bell, "Price of Books," 324–25; and Savage, *Old English Libraries*, 168. R. Malcolm Hogg ("Some Thirteenth-Century English Book Prices") devotes considerable attention to inflation of manuscript valuations in his examination of thirteenth-century book prices, notably their use in securing loans of lesser value.

12. The valuations of a few of the Hereford Cathedral Library manuscripts remained the same or even decreased in this period, perhaps because they were damaged through misuse, outdated, or no longer in fashion.

13. C. Paul Christianson has extensively studied the cost of doing business for booksellers in London in the later Middle Ages, most notably rents and arrangements between different practitioners of the book arts. For a recent contribution to the subject, see Christianson, "Rise of London's Book-Trade," 130–31.

14. C. Paul Christianson, "A Community of Book Artisans in Chaucer's London," *Viator* 20 (1989): 213.

15. Christianson, *Memorials of London Book Trade*, 15.

16. A fascinating account of the methods and materials used in late medieval painting and manuscript illumination was written by the fifteenth-century Florentine artist Cennino d'Andrea Cennini, *The Craftsman's Handbook "Il Libro dell'Arte,"* trans. Daniel V. Thompson Jr. (New York: Dover, 1960).

17. The two types of ink most commonly used in the medieval period were made from iron and carbon, whose components were readily available through lampblack or oak galls mixed with an adhesive, usually gum arabic. For accounts of the materials used to make ink in the Middle Ages, see Leila Arvin, *Scribes, Script and Books: The Book Arts from Antiquity to the Renaissance* (Chicago: American Library Association; London: British Library, 1991), 213–15; De Hamel, *Medieval Craftsmen*, 32; Greetham, *Textual Scholarship*, 66; and J. H. Middleton, *Illuminated Manuscripts in Classical and Mediaeval Times: Their Art and Their Technique* (Cambridge: Cambridge University Press, 1892), 230–38. While entries for ink are found in medieval accounts, their quantities are seldom listed. The proliferation of ink recipes in both medieval and early modern manuscripts may suggest that the purchase of ready-made ink was the exception rather than the rule. For one such recipe from sixteenth-century England, see *A Booke of Secrets: Shewing Diuers Waies to Make and Prepare all Sorts of Inke, and Colours*, trans. W. Phillip of Ettliche Küntse (London: A. Islip for E. White, 1596). James Thorold Rogers occasionally found references to the price of ingredients for ink making; for example, in 1418 three pounds of oak galls were 2d, and three pounds of copperas were 4d. See James E. Thorold Rogers, *A History of Agriculture and Prices in England*, vol. 3, 1401–1582 (Oxford: Clarendon Press, 1882), 547. The most expensive pigment by far was ultrama-

rine, made from lapus lazuli imported from Afghanistan. Surviving accounts suggest that its value was more than twice its weight in gold; as a result, it was often supplied to the illuminator by the commissioner of the manuscript. Its value is further substantiated by the fact that ultramarine was occasionally scraped off manuscripts for reuse: see Middleton, *Illuminated Manuscripts,* 240–42. For an excellent overview of all medieval pigments, see Daniel V. Thompson, *The Materials and Techniques of Medieval Painting* (New York: Dover Publications, 1996). Gold leaf was made by hammering a piece of gold (usually a coin) into extremely thin sheets. An astonishing amount of gold leaf could be acquired through this method from one coin; Cennino Cennini asserts that goldsmiths in fifteenth-century Italy produced 145 sheets of gold leaf from a single gold ducat. See Avrin, *Scribes, Script and Books,* 214; and Cennini, *Craftsman's Handbook,* 84.

18. Bell, "Price of Books," 321–22. For a more detailed description of English bookbinding practice, see Mirjam Foot, "English Decorated Bookbindings," in *Book Production and Publishing in Britain, 1375–1475,* ed. Jeremy Griffiths (Cambridge: Cambridge University Press, 1989), 65–85. Note that even in the accounts of the two luxury commissions examined here, the London Bridge antiphoners and Collegiate Church of St. George evangelarium, the costliness of the binding materials had a fairly negligible effect on overall prices, because the costs of labor far outweighed those of materials.

19. Middleton, *Illuminated Manuscripts,* 257.

20. See Bell, "Price of Books," 316. Additional payments of these kinds were not confined to the book arts. Christopher Dyer has suggested that an urban craftsman's chief expenditures were food and clothing; thus their inclusion in their overall wage would be especially rewarding. See Christopher Dyer, *Standards of Living in the Later Middle Ages: Social Change in England c. 1200–1520* (Cambridge: Cambridge University Press, 1989), 205, 221.

21. John Hatcher, "England in the Aftermath of the Black Death," *Past & Present* 133 (1994): 11; and Simon Penn and Christopher Dyer, "Wages and Earnings in Late Medieval England: Evidence from the Enforcement of the Labour Laws," *Economic History Review* n.s. 43, no. 3 (1990): 357, 366. For additional information on the Statute of Laborers and various other post–Black Death methods of price and wage controls, see David Farmer, "Prices and Wages, 1350–1500," in *The Agrarian History of England and Wales,* vol. 3, 1348–1500, ed. Edward Miller (Cambridge: Cambridge University Press, 1991), 483–90.

22. Based on Farmer's calculations of the day wages of carpenters from 1300 to 1410. See Farmer, "Prices and Wages, 1350–1500," 471. The wages of building workers, such as carpenters, are used most often by historians because they are the only group paid on a per diem basis for whom enough usable evidence has survived. For a thorough discussion, see Dyer, *Standards of Living,* 220.

23. See Richard Britnell, "The Black Death in English Towns," *Urban History* 21, no. 2 (1994): 202–3.

24. Dyer, *Standards of Living,* 192. See additionally William J. Dohar, "'Since the Pestilence Time': Pastoral Care in the Later Middle Ages," in *A History of Pastoral Care,* ed. G. R. Evans (London: Cassell, 2000), 175–60.

25. See Barbara E. Megson, "Mortality among London Citizens in the Black Death," *Medieval Prosopography* 19 (1998): 128; and Britnell, "Black Death in English Towns," 205.

26. Dyer, *Standards of Living,* 172. With regard to the book arts, art historians have noted this breakdown in training in the marked decrease in standards of illumination in both England and on the Continent in the years following the Black Death. See Middleton, *Illuminated Manuscripts,* 120. Francis Aidan Gasquet argued that the extent of plague activity in a particular region could often be inferred from the quality of its record keeping; see Francis Aidan Gasquet, *The Great Pestilence* (London: Simpkin Marshall, Hamilton, Kent & Co., 1893), 81, 83.

27. Regarding clerics as scribes, see A. I. Doyle, "The English Provincial Book Trade before Printing," in *Six Centuries of the Provincial Book Trade in Britain,* ed. Peter Isaac (Winchester: St. Paul's Bibliographies, 1990), 15. Regarding examples of professional scribes, such as Thomas Hoccleve and William Ebesham, see Doyle and Parkes, "Production of Copies," 198; and A. I. Doyle, "The Work of a Late Fifteenth-Century English Scribe, William Ebesham," *Bulletin of the John Rylands Library* 39 (1956–57): 298–325.

28. Josiah Cox Russell, *British Medieval Population* (Albuquerque: University of New Mexico Press, 1948), 216, 218, 220–22. As with other epidemics and disease, the groups that suffered the greatest mortality were the young and the very old. Russell estimates that plague morality in 1348–50 was 33 percent for those under the age of five, 33 percent for those thirty-six to forty, 34 percent for those fifty-one to fifty-five, and 46 per cent for those fifty-six and older. See also A. H. Thompson, "The Registers of John Glynwell, Bishop of Lincoln, for the years 1347–50," *Archaeological Journal* 68 (1911): 317.

29. See John Hatcher, *Plague, Population and the English Economy 1348–1530* (London: Macmillan, 1977), 21–22; and R. A. Davies, "The Effect of the Black Death on the Parish Priests of the Medieval Diocese of Coventry and Lichfield," *Historical Research* 62 (1989): 85–90. High clerical death rates during the plague were not limited to England: see also Richard F. Gyug, "The Effects and Extent of the Black Death of 1348: New Evidence for Clerical Mortality in Barcelona," *Mediaeval Studies* 45 (1983): 385–98. Gyug's study, which utilizes information from benefices, takes into account pluralists but still concludes that clerical death rates must have been at least 40 percent.

30. W. J. Courtenay, "The Effect of the Black Death on English Higher Education," *Speculum* 55, no. 4 (1980): 703.

31. Jo Ann Hoeppner Moran, "Clerical Recruitment in the Diocese of York, 1340–1530: Data and Commentary," *Journal of Ecclesiastical History* 34, no. 1 (1983): 26.

32. For an excerpt of this letter, see Francis Aidan Gasquet, *The Great Pestilence,* 81–83.

33. See Courtenay, "Effect of the Black Death," 713; Moran, "Clerical Recruitment," 32; and Dyer, *Standards of Living,* 21–22. That unbeneficed clergy often resorted to scribal work is supported by a provision of the company of text writers in York (founded in 1377), which prevented priests with a salary over 8 marks from working in the industry; see Alexander, *Medieval Illuminators,* 31.

34. Davies, "Effect of the Black Death," 88–89. The need for unbeneficed clergy to find additional sources of income before the Black Death has been documented throughout Europe. According to one pre-plague commentator, there were so few lucrative benefices for educated clergy that many turned to criminal behavior rather than part-time work (such as scribal work) to supplement their income. This underemployed "wandering clerical element" was prone to vagabondage. See Bronislaw Germek, *The Margins of Society in Late Medieval Paris* (Cambridge: Cambridge University Press, 1987), 144; and Barbara Hanawalt, *Crime and Conflict in English Communities, 1300–1348* (Cambridge: Harvard University Press, 1979), 136. Vacated benefices were not the only employment for learned men after the plague of 1348, who pursued other opportunities as well. Clergy with smaller stipends who were unable to secure a vacated benefice sometimes deserted their parishes, as their specialized skills in the plague-altered labor market enabled them to pursue more lucrative job opportunities. Additionally, significant numbers of priests with university backgrounds ended up in newly endowed chantries which proliferated in the post–Black Death period to pray for souls of the dead. See Dohar, "Since the Pestilence Time," 177; and Courtenay, "Effect of the Black Death," 713.

35. Anna Campbell, *The Black Death and Men of Learning* (New York: Columbia University Press, 1931), 146. Courtenay's more recent study ("Effect of the Black Death," 696–714) questions the impact of the Black Death on higher learning, especially at Oxford University, but one should take into account the time of year that the plague hit Oxfordshire.

36. Campbell, *Black Death*, 151–54.

37. Ibid., 151, 176, cites examples from both York and Winchester, where schoolmasters were appointed for much longer terms than had previously been granted, sometimes even for life.

38. The average valuation of a pre-1340 manuscript from the data set is approximately 8s 3d (99d), while the average valuation from the 1483 inventory is 5s 2d (62d).

39. Consumer demand for books was driven not only by individual patrons, but also by corporate entities, such as churches, schools, and royal commissions. See Christianson, "Evidence for the Study," 99.

40. Maryanne Kowaleski, "A Consumer Economy," in *A Social History of England, 1200–1500*, ed. Rosemary Horrox and W. Mark Ormrod (Cambridge: Cambridge University Press, 2006), 239.

41. See J. L. Bolton, *The Medieval English Economy 1150–1500* (London: J. M. Dent; Totowa, N.J.: Rowman & Littlefield, 1980), 47.

42. Henry Phelps Brown and Sheila V. Hopkins, "Seven Centuries of Prices of Consumables Compared with Builders' Wage Rates," in *A Perspective of Wages and Prices*, ed. Henry Phelps Brown (London: Methuen, 1981), 28. Brown and Hopkins's "composite unit of consumables" included grains (wheat, rye, and barley), peas, meat, fish, butter, cheese, drink (malt and hops), fuel, and textiles.

43. J. B. Friedman, "Books, Owners and Makers in Fifteenth-Century Yorkshire: The Evidence from Some Wills and Extant Manuscripts," in *Latin and Vernacular: Studies in Late-Medieval Texts and Manuscripts*, ed. A. J. Minnis (Cambridge: D. S. Brewer, 1989), 112; Derek Pearsall, *John Lydgate* (Charlottesville: University Press of Virginia, 1970), 72. Carol M. Meale suggests that it is an oversimplification to tie the consumption of books as status symbols only to the newly rich in the fifteenth century, as the English gentry were also major commissioners and owners of books. See Meale, "The Politics of Book Ownership: The Hopton Family and Bodleian Library, Digby MS 185," in *Prestige, Authority and Power in Late Medieval Manuscripts and Texts*, ed. Felicity Riddy (Woodbridge: York Medieval Press, 2000), 103–31.

44. Kowaleski, "Consumer Economy," 256–57.

45. Keiser, "Lincoln Cathedral Library MS. 91," 158; Christopher De Hamel, *A History of Illuminated Manuscripts* (London: Phaidon, 1994), 13; and J. Hoeppner Moran, "Literacy and Education in Northern England, 1350–1550: A Methodological Inquiry," *Northern History* 17 (1981): 1–23. For an overview and examples of manuscripts used by the literate laity during this period, see Barbara A. Shailor, *The Medieval Book* (Toronto: University of Toronto Press, 1994), 88–98.

46. Pearsall, *John Lydgate*, 72. Scholars have observed increased trade in the second-hand book market as evidence of changes in demand. See Kate Harris, "Patrons, Buyers and Owners: the Evidence for Ownership and the Rôle of Book Owners in Book Production and the Book Trade," in *Book Production and Publishing in Britain 1375–1475*, ed. Jeremy Griffiths and Derek Pearsall (Cambridge: Cambridge University Press, 1989), 172; and Christianson, "Rise of London's Book-Trade," 132–34.

47. The fifteenth century in particular witnessed a need for practical literacy, and many merchants used Latin for recordkeeping, as it provided a useful medium for international fairs. See Marjorie Plant, *The English Book Trade: An Economic History of the Making and Sale of Books* (London: George Allen & Unwin, 1974), 36. Questioning the need for vernacular literacy among literate males, given the fact that educational institutions were run by ecclesiastical authorities who conducted their business in Latin, scholars have suggested other catalysts for this linguistic revolution. As men were usually the only beneficiaries of a Latin-based education, it has been argued that women played an important role in the development of vernacular

translations and original literary texts. Indeed, evidence suggests that women's ownership of manuscript books, both in Latin and the vernacular, increased dramatically in the fourteenth and fifteenth centuries. Additionally, books of hours were often used by women to teach their children reading and devotionary lessons. See Susan Groag Bell, "Medieval Women Book Owners," in *Women and Power in the Middle Ages*, ed. Mary Erler and Maryanne Kowaleski (Athens: University of Georgia Press, 1988), 149–87; Patricia Callum and Jeremy Goldberg, "How Margaret Blackburn Taught her Daughters: Reading Devotional Instruction in a Book of Hours," in *Medieval Women: Texts and Contexts in Late Medieval Britain. Essays in Honour of Felicity Riddy*, ed. Jocelyn Wogan-Browne, Rosalynn Voaden, Arlyn Diamond, Ann Hutchinson, Carol Meale, and Lesley Johnson (Turnhout: Brepols, 2000), 217–36; Mary Carpenter Erler, *Women, Reading and Piety in Late Medieval England* (Cambridge: Cambridge University Press, 2002); and Carol M. Meale, "'Alle the bokes that I haue of latyn, englisch and frensch': Laywomen and their Books in Late Medieval England," in *Women and Literature in Britain, 1150–1500*, ed. Carol M. Meale (Cambridge: Cambridge University Press, 1996), 128–58.

48. Kowaleski, "Consumer Economy," 256–57.

49. Michael Gullick, "How Fast Did Scribes Write? Evidence from Romanesque Manuscripts," in *Making the Medieval Book: Techniques of Production*, ed. Linda L. Brownrigg (Los Altos Hills, Calif.: Anderson-Lovelace; London: Red Gull Press, 1995), 41. See additionally De Hamel, *Scribes and Illuminators*, 62.

50. Edwards, "Beinecke MS 661," 182. Mass-production techniques have been observed in other sectors of the late-medieval English economy, including the earthenware and pewterware trades. See Kowaleski, "Consumer Economy," 258.

51. Joan A. Holladay, "The Willehalm Master and His Colleagues: Collaborative Manuscript Decoration in Early-Fourteenth-Century Cologne," in *Making the Medieval Book: Techniques of Production*, ed. Linda L. Brownrigg (Los Altos Hills, Calif.: Anderson-Lovelace; London: Red Gull Press, 1995), 69; see also De Hamel, *Scribes and Illuminators*, 41. For an example of an exemplar likely partitioned out among different scribes for more rapid copying, see Doyle and Parkes, "Production of Copies," 164. For a description of various time-saving techniques to illuminate late-medieval manuscripts, including the importation of single-leaf miniatures, see Alexander, *Medieval Illuminators*, 49–51, 126.

52. For example, see Doyle and Parkes, "Production of Copies," 163–210; Edwards, "Beinecke MS 661," 181–96; and Mooney and Matheson, "The Beryn Scribe," 347–70.

53. Rowan Watson, *Illuminated Manuscripts and their Makers* (London: Harry N. Abrams for V&A Publications, 2003), 12. Perhaps the most famous fifteenth-century stationer in London was John Shirley, who held the lease on a tenement where he combined the activities of scribe, bookseller, publisher, and lending library. For a full account of Shirley's career, see Connolly, *John Shirley*.

54. Holladay, "Willehalm Master," 74.

55. Christianson, "Evidence for the Study," 89–90, 96. Using fifteenth-century Bridge House Accounts in London, Christianson notes that fifteenth-century artisans may have worked independently in small shops, often comprising only a single room, yet in close proximity to one another, evident in the clustering of members of the London and Oxford book trades into designated areas within the city. He further observes close ties and personal relationships between artisans of different bookmaking crafts; for example, of the forty members of book crafts he cites as working within the immediate vicinity of St. Paul's, thirty-eight were named by their fellow artisans as either witnesses, executors, overseers or beneficiaries of wills. See also M. A. Michael, "English Illuminators c. 1190–1450: A Survey from Documentary Sources," *English Manuscript Studies 1100–1700* 4 (1993): 63.

56. Christianson, "Rise of London's Book-Trade," 135.

57. See, for example, Connolly, *John Shirley,* and A. I. Doyle, "More Light on John Shirley," *Medium Aevum* 30 (1961): 93–101. See also Stephen R. Reimer, "Differentiating Chaucer and Lydgate: Some Preliminary Observations," in *Computer-Based Chaucer Studies,* ed. Ian Lancashire (Toronto: University of Toronto Centre for Computing in the Humanities, 1993), 163; and Pearsall, *John Lydgate,* 74.

58. Harris, "Patrons, Buyers and Owners," 183.

59. See Kowaleski, "Consumer Economy," 249; and R. J. Lyall, "Materials: The Paper Revolution," in *Book Production and Publishing in Britain, 1375–1475,* ed. Jeremy Griffiths and Derek Pearsall (Cambridge: Cambridge University Press, 1989), 11–29.

"Books for the Use of the Learned and Studious"

William London's *Catalogue of Most Vendible Books*

Margaret Schotte

If Books be the Spectacles we see through to all Learning, let's then use them so; branch them forth, and spread their Knowledge.[1]

Newcastle-upon-Tyne bookseller William London produced his pioneering bibliographical text, *A Catalogue of the Most Vendible Books in England*, between 1657 and 1660.[2] London's work was one of the earliest attempts to catalog all English-language books, at a time when booksellers and readers alike were scrambling to keep up with the output of printed matter. In his extended preface, London explained that he was offering his audience a new means of harnessing this typographic flood, a treasure map that would ensure that books did not end up buried in obscurity. To date scholars have largely limited their discussion of this catalog to these bibliographic contributions.[3] However, as London makes clear in his introduction, he considered books to be far more than repositories of intangible learning; rather, they offered access to an important new kind of functional knowledge. London intended his catalog not only to convey information about the latest printed material to a broad audience—one that he would play a role in creating—but also to promote the very idea of knowledge as a practical tool.

Little is known about William London's life beyond a few details from 1649 to 1660, the period when he was active in the book trade in Newcastle.[4] However, a close examination of the *Catalogue of Most Vendible Books* can shed light on both his business practices and his intellectual interests. Dedicated to readers in "the Northern Counties of Northumberland, Bppk. of Durham, Westmerland and Cumberland," and prefaced by a forty-nine-page "Introduction to the Use of Books," London's catalog is notable in conception, scale, and content. The 1657 *editio princeps* of *A Catalogue of the Most Vendible Books* contains 3,284 titles arranged under seven subject headings, while the two supplementary installments of 1658 and 1660 added 510 additional books.[5] More than half of the 1657 work is devoted to "Divinity Books" (1,698), a proportion slightly greater than the average over the period.[6] The "Physick and Chyrurgery" and "Mathematicks"[7] sections contain 152 and 241 titles respectively, or approximately one-eighth of the total, a significant proportion for any seventeenth-century library or book list.[8] In addition to sizeable sections on "History with other pieces of humane learning intermixed, alphabetically digested" (479) and "Common and Civil Law" (155), London had a separate list of 261 "Romances Poems and Playes" and concluded with 298 "Hebrew, Greek, and Latin bookes Such as falls not directly under the heads of divinity, physick, or law, &c. but are properly usefull for schooles and scholars." London planned to issue annual supplements to keep his customers updated on "what Books are daily prest for their service," but only succeeded at this in 1658 and 1660.

London displayed an enthusiastic familiarity with the books in his catalog, as well as a basic facility for Latin and other languages.[9] In his introduction he referenced at least thirty of the most popular texts of the day. (After the Bible, the most frequently cited works are those of Francis Bacon, an English translation of Montaigne's essays, Robert Burton's *Anatomy of Melancholy*, and Thomas Stanley's *History of Philosophy*.)[10] This obvious love for books and reading has earned his catalog comparisons to Richard de Bury's canonical *Philobiblon*.[11]

London produced his catalog at a time when the English book trade was inventing new vehicles to disseminate information about printed works. The *Catalogue of Most Vendible Books* and the handful of other systematic lists that appeared in the first half of the seventeenth century met a clear need, particularly in regions some distance from London. Between 1557 and 1662 English book publishing was essentially limited to London, Oxford, and Cambridge, and further constrained by the 1643 Licensing Order. As a result, even in sizeable provincial towns readers and booksellers had to place orders with London publishers. These limits aside, F. J. Levy has shown that, thanks to an efficient distribution network, the circulation of printed matter in the provinces was brisk and affordable.[12] London's catalog was a novel tool that served both booksellers and their clients.

In his survey of early printed catalogs, which calls attention to the dichotomous system of urban wholesalers and rural booksellers, Graham Pollard describes William London's work as a "Reference work for booksellers."[13] London's catalog emerged alongside three other near-contemporary attempts at comprehensive bibliographies, Andrew Maunsell's *Catalogue of English Printed Books* (1595), William Jaggard's *Catalogue of Such English Bookes, as Lately Haue Bene, and Now are in Printing for Publication* (1618), and the series compiled by Robert Clavel(l) known as "Term Catalogues" (1668–1711).[14] These three works—and the ways in which they differ from London's catalog in organization and audience—bear examination.

Maunsell, a draper who became a bookseller in the early 1570s, completed two parts of his catalog, "Divinitie" and "Mathematicke, Physicke, and Surgerie," leaving a planned "Humanity" section unfinished at his death. His "Tables" follow a loose alphabetical arrangement that alternates between subject and author, with frequent cross-references. Maunsell meticulously listed the printer or publisher and date of each work, a signal that he intended his catalog to be used by fellow booksellers; by providing the imprint information, Maunsell made it possible for each dealer to contact the publisher directly to obtain the most favorable trade discount.[15]

The next attempt to catalog current English books came in 1618, when the Stationers' Company of London selected William Jaggard to print *A Catalogue of Such English Bookes*.[16] Despite the plan for biannual installments, only one appeared. Within two broad categories ("Divinity" and "History"), Jaggard arranged the books according to their publishers, disregarding format or specific subject. This type of catalog, which facilitated access to producers rather than information retrieval, once again served booksellers rather than browsing customers.[17]

Shortly after the fire of London, Robert Clavel stepped in where William London had left off in 1660.[18] Clavel, originally working in partnership with John Starkey, issued 159 catalogs of English imprints on a quarterly basis between 1668 and 1711, and published four cumulative lists in 1673, 1675, 1680, and 1696. Starkey was a publisher/wholesaler, while Clavel held a position with the Post Office before becoming a bookseller and then Master of the Stationers' Company. As primary editor, Clavel's policies for these cumulative catalogs evolved over the years: he organized the catalogs by format, including prices in most editions, and publishers' names in some. While Starkey hoped that readers would place all their orders through his shop—and thus did not want to provide imprint information—Clavel had the twin goals of increasing postal revenues (by splitting up orders that might otherwise be consolidated through Starkey) and obtaining stock from the publishers he represented in exchange for listing their names.[19]

Maunsell considered his catalog an expressly professional tool: in his prefatory letter to the Master of the Stationers' Company, he compared it to "the Apothecarie his *Dispensatorium*, or the Schoole-master his *Dictionarie*."[20] Clavel, on the other hand, saw his lists as a marketing aid; while Maunsell listed a handful of books in which he had a share, the Term Catalogues contain a substantial number of the books "printed for or sold by R. Clavel." Jaggard's work on behalf of the Stationers Company was a serviceable promotional instrument; in the absence of even a prefatory note, the title page conveyed what the commercial buyer needed to know. William London's motivations seem more complicated: he did not include imprint information in his entries, which suggests that his primary audience was not fellow booksellers but the end consumer, yet he was not focused solely on attracting clients to his shop. His efforts to promote reading more broadly represent a significant development within the catalog genre.

William London's substantial prefatory essay—which has been heralded as the most "excellent treatise . . . [to ever] accompany any bookseller's catalogue"[21]—effectively transports his catalog beyond the merely commercial. With his "Introduction to the Use of Books," he invited an examination of social status and pedagogical philosophy. London explained that he intended his catalog to be a place where "Books [were] treasured up and set in order for the use of the *Learned* and *studious*."[22] He aimed to organize and improve access to information, with the hope of promoting both personal betterment and the greater good. London recognized that the public needed "Books set in order" to help manage the increasing tide of information flowing from the early modern print revolution.[23] Rather than abandoning readers to "seek for [books] in an empty store-house,"[24] he offered "this reducement of Many into One" as an antidote to the confusion and obscurity that were brought on by a lack of guidance: "It was this which made that Honourable Sr. Wa[lter] Raleigh his voyage [to Guyana] so unfortunate; in that he knew there was a mine, but knew not how to find it: and there seems to be no less, then as great need of a Register of Books, which else may be buried with their Authors."[25] As an author, businessman, and would-be educator, London expressed horror not only at futile quests but at under-advertised books: "Much of the ignorance in many places may be attributed to the want of Books, but in this Nation for want of their use; and many a good Book lies asleep as not known."[26] His catalog was more than a Maunsell-style reference for professionals, it was a useful map for the adventurous, teaching them how to navigate unknown territory and locate treasures.[27]

In terms of organizing his "Register of Books," London had several precedents to follow, including manuscript inventories of private and monastic libraries. While Gabriel Naudé's influential *Advis pour dresser une bibliothèque* (1627) was not yet available in English, both he and London were writing at a moment when knowledge was being organized in increasingly systematized ways.[28] The *Catalogue of Most Vendible Books* conforms well to the goals outlined by the eighteenth-century librarian Paolo Maria Paciaudi, who defined a catalog as "a concrete form of collected and systematized knowledge, arranged to be accessible by both content and form," created in order to insure that "the individual does not drown in a sea of boundless information."[29] London attempted to meet similar objectives.

Displaying what might be called a nascent empirical approach, he echoed Maunsell's model of listing authors alphabetically by "Sir name" rather than "Christen name," and subdividing the contents by subject rather than format.[30] By contrast, Clavel's cumulative catalogs were hybrids, preserving the traditional format groupings within subject headings. (Both of London's addenda preserved almost all of the same subject headings, but the 1658 supplement did away with alphabetization, perhaps due to the exigencies of rushing the text to press.)

Ever focused on improving the reader's experience with books, London wished to correct a "general defect . . . in Catalogues" by listing complete titles. While they occasionally tend toward the excessive (the separately identified fascicles of one of William Fenner's books occupy more than one-and-a-half text columns), he wished to prevent his readers from being "cosen'd by a short title, that when they expected a Book to treat of one thing, it hath the clean contrary."[31] For him, supplying full titles meant that "all books [were] brought to you lying open; shops open'd in your studies; and to me it lookes like a walking Library."[32] This "walking" or portable library, miraculously keeping up with the reader wherever he might be, symbolized the epitome of convenience for the bookseller-author. Just as striking is the notion that all of his readers would have dedicated studies in their homes: despite the egalitarian sympathies London displayed throughout his catalog, he obviously hoped that the majority of his "candid and ingenious readers" would have substantial accommodations and disposable incomes to match.[33]

As for the criteria by which he selected the "most vendible" books for his catalog, London provided frustratingly little information.[34] What would make some books more vendible than others? Was their degree of salability based on perceived popularity or some other inherent value? London purported to be extremely tolerant of heterodox political and religious content—at least in comparison to Maunsell—but were there books which he would deem simply unsalable?[35] He certainly aspired to objectivity, not just "insert[ing] only such as please my own humour." While he recognized the impossibility of "a Catalogue compleat; yet this I dare promise, that there is no choice Book omitted, but the best and most Books printed in England are here inserted."[36]

In light of the dearth of evidence regarding his shop at the foot of Newcastle's bridge across the Tyne, it remains an open question whether London actually owned copies of the nearly 3,700 titles listed in the *Catalogue* and its appendices, or whether he was instead describing an imaginary "ideal stock." On the basis of the title page of the 1657 *Catalogue*, which proclaimed that the listed books were "All to be sold . . . at his Shop in New-

Castle," C. J. Hunt believes that William London "probably had the most extensive stock of any North of England bookseller before the eighteenth century."[37] John Barnard, Maureen Bell, and András Kiséry are skeptical of this, positing that the list was an abstract assemblage on a national scale. Aligning it with Andrew Maunsell (and even Konrad Gesner), Kiséry contends that London conceived his catalog as "an organized and classified account of the learning amassed in English language books."[38]

London may have been the proprietor of a modest bookshop who merely concatenated his catalog from books that had crossed his path over a period of several years, augmenting it with those titles available from London printers of his acquaintance. However, the structure and content of the lengthy list support the idea that London was working primarily from books on his premises: his philosophy of including complete titles for each work would have been very difficult to accomplish unless he was working with the books themselves. (During the period, it became common for publishers to include a list of their recent editions on extra leaves at the end of books. While London could feasibly have assembled his catalog from such advertisements, a survey of lists from selected publishers reveals differing word order and spelling, as well as substantially more detailed titles on London's part, indicating that he almost certainly had copies of the physical books.)[39]

Despite his claim that "no choice book" was excluded, London's list was far from comprehensive. The idiosyncratic distribution of works, particularly the sparse coverage of Latin works, further supports the idea that he worked from stock he had on hand. His omission of the six Latin editions of Camden's *Britannia*—he mentioned only two in English (f. Vv)—reinforces the hypothesis that he was not attempting to list every edition he was aware of, but rather those that he had in stock (or could at least obtain easily through publishers with whom he was acquainted in the capital).[40]

On the final page of the mathematics section (f. Ee2), London eschewed full titles for more generic summaries, yet these still evidently describe specific works in his possession: "All sorts of books for teaching to write shorthand or Charracters," "A book of Beasts, lively drawn," and "A book of habits and fancies, of Hollare."[41] A handful of books are puzzlingly listed in duplicate, appearing in two different sections of the catalog with slightly variant spellings or authorship attributions.[42] These inexact repetitions may suggest that London relied on an assistant to read titles aloud to him, resulting in phonetic spellings; that the catalog was compiled over a lengthy period, during which time London changed his mind on the best category for a particular book; that he supplemented transcriptions made from his actual stock with lists of inaccurate abbreviated titles; or that he wished certain volumes to appear in more than one category to attract multiple audiences.

Understanding the *Catalogue of Most Vendible Books* as an actual representation of a substantial provincial bookshop enables fruitful analysis of London's marketing tactics. It becomes apparent that London provided his customers with numerous options regarding format, price, illustrations, and language. He carried the same title in several sizes to appeal to different pocketbooks (e.g., three editions of the London pharmacopoeia, appearing in different years and formats, f. Aa*v*), promoted illustrated volumes (unlike several small English-language editions of Ovid, the Latin folios featured "Cuts," ff. [Ee4]*v*–F[f]), and offered several titles in both English and Latin editions. His efforts at marketing were uneven, however: while he strategically included every imaginable topic within the *Catalogue*'s subject headings, he chose not to have his name printed on the 1660 supplement (although London's name did not appear on the title page of the 1657 *Catalogue*, he did sign the dedicatory epistle, f. B2), and those books he financed or authored were listed anonymously.[43]

It is clear that William London's business stood out from his neighbors in the regional trade. Accepting the premise that London's catalog was based principally upon the books on his shelves, his Newcastle establishment would have "had the largest stock in the north of England."[44] As F. J. Levy documents, the financial viability of most provincial book shops—which served as distributors for London publishers—was marginal, and the majority of dealers expanded their stock to include writing materials, school supplies, and other paper goods.[45] London carried more than just printed texts, advertising "All sorts of Globes, Mapps of the World or in Parts ... French and Duch Pictures and Landskips; Paper of all sorts from 5^s to 5^{lb} a Reame: The best perfumed India, and English Wax, &c." on the title page of the *editio princeps*.[46] He may have taken up the mantle of a "full-service stationer" not because his enterprise was as tenuous as other regional bookshops, but because he was the most successful figure in the region. Over the course of six years (1653–59), he was able to finance at least seven publications, having them printed either in the capital or on Stephen Bulkley's local press, which moved between Newcastle and Gateshead (Gateside).[47] London's ability to stock a sizeable inventory while investing repeatedly in topical titles (primarily anti-Catholic and anti-Quaker theological skirmishes) suggests that, during the mid-1650s at least, business was steady and profitable.

It cannot be doubted that London's project, like those of Maunsell and Clavel, had a financial incentive; as he candidly noted: "we all know there's no action whose Naturall tendency is not to *Meum, Tuum, or both*."[48] Obviously, in publishing his catalog and highlighting the benefits that reading could bring to others, he was hoping to increase the number of customers in the economically tenuous enterprise of provincial bookselling. Throughout the work, he slipped between rapturous metaphors and commercial terms—he referred to the "merchandize of Knowledg," advised that "the more a man hath of it, he is wisely ambitious to purchase more," and tellingly closed his introduction with these words: "There's nothing comparable to the purchase of Knowledg, and when ever men begin to taste it, they will say I speak truth with a witness."[49]

His tendency toward commodification notwithstanding, London protested that his main objective was not financial: "I do not alwaies expect to sell what I so greatly value, I am more ambitious to read then to sell them; but the chief end is to Invite men to value the means of knowledge above trifles, which cannot be better improved, nor more prudently expended then in such a purchase."[50] The stationers in the capital ascribed similarly selfless goals to the technology that they were simultaneously promoting and profiting from: the "first and greatest end of order in the Presse is the advancement of wholesome knowledge."[51] Despite the temptation to dwell on financial motivations Adrian Johns reminds us that booksellers were "no mere dupes of avarice."[52] While undoubtedly a rhetorical trope, London's admission of intellectual ambition introduced the message undergirding his entire catalog: in his ideal world, learning would be valued more than monetary wealth.

In his prefatory essay, London laid out clear reasons for "men to value the means of knowledge above trifles," all the while hoping that, once thus convinced, they would end up making their "prudent purchases" from him. From this perspective London was fortunate in the location of his business: Newcastle could realistically have supported a shop of this size in the mid-seventeenth century. Many studies of the city focus on its publishing boom in the eighteenth century, when it became a major locus of production for chapbooks and periodicals, "the most important printing center in England outside of London and the university towns," in the view of Helen Berry.[53] However, the city's literary tradition dates back far earlier: a library was established by 1597, booksellers were admitted into a guild in 1675, and there was a market for used books by the 1680s, when at least one private library was sold at auction.[54] All of this bibliophilic activity was supported and fostered by the intellectually inclined citizens in the region, including several generations of dukes and duchesses of Newcastle, and Lady Anne Clifford, who retired to her family castles in Durham and Westmorland.

London addressed his "Epistle Dedicatory" to the gentry not only of Northumberland but also the neighboring counties of Cumberland, Durham, and Westmorland, yet the region's bookselling industry was unquestionably concentrated in Newcastle. There, records of paper merchants *cum* stationers date back to the first decade of the sixteenth century; booksellers and printers had established a continuous presence by the later seventeenth century.[55] The other northern counties, by contrast, supported no more than four or five booksellers or stationers over the course of the seventeenth century.[56] During the 1650s readers across the region would have looked to Newcastle for new books.

The average bookseller located in a town some distance from London typically catered to (and was primarily supported by) schoolteachers and clergy; William London, however, aimed at a broader audience. Clergymen would no doubt find an ample number of doctrinally relevant texts among the more than 1,600 theological titles,[57] and teachers and students alike would be well served by the final section of the catalog, which featured those books that "Are properly usefull for Schooles and Scholars." However, as Barnard and Bell point out, London clearly also wished to sell books to gentry, and was well positioned to do so.[58] He opened his dedicatory epistle by flattering the "extracted Quintessence of true nobleness," and the "Learning, Generosity, Urbanity, Knowledg, &c." of "Gentry, Ministers of the Gospel and others of a Peculiar Choice, . . . in the Northern Counties."[59] In courting such prominent, moneyed men (and a few women) London tapped into a market that was increasingly likely to own "at least a small library."[60] After elaborating upon the benefits of reading, and the honor and glory they would inevitably accrue "by *Study, Reading,* and converse with Discreet and Wise men," he then highlighted the depravity of those who did not read, those "Tinkers and vulgar Brains, [who] drown and soak their meaner wits and conceptions, in draining a Country Alehouse."[61]

Here London reiterated a message that had emerged a century earlier among English humanist writers, "condemning the practical equation between English gentility and ignorance and urging gentlemen to take to their studies."[62] London drew his nuanced conception of gentility from three early modern models of gentlemanly conduct. Stephen Shapin identifies these as a "secular, knightly code which laid great stress upon blood, individual honor, and reputation," a partly secular humanist culture of virtue (embodied by Henry Peacham's 1622 *The Compleat Gentleman*), and a newer Puritan interpretation of proper conduct (exemplified by Richard Braithwait's 1630 *The English Gentleman*). For this last "Christian gentleman"—who was paradoxically intent on upward social mobility—honor came from virtuous behavior rather than exclusively from money and birth. London quoted both Peacham and Braithwait, and listed six of their books in the history section of the catalog.[63] His theory of gentility varied depending on his audience, but when addressing members of the established upper class he emphasized virtuous behavior for the greater good. Returning to his earlier point that the ample numbers of books in England were embarrassingly underused, he urged his gentle readers to do battle against ignorance and to promote learning on every occasion.[64]

To convince these local gentry as well as the wider public to develop their reading habits, William London celebrated their northern home throughout the catalog. In an effort to support an intellectual community in Newcastle, he dedicated his catalog to the "use of the northern provinces," and drew attention to the achievements of fellow northerners—particularly in the field of mathematics.[65] (He expressed only rhetorical concern that his cataloguing project might be hindered by being "so distanced" from "the mint of Books," although he indeed fell silent after issuing his second supplement.)[66] London included the majority of titles printed by Stephen Bulkley, Newcastle's preeminent midcentury printer. A controversial figure who styled himself "Printer to the King's most Excellent Majesty," Bulkley printed the first editions of all the titles financed by William London. Whether London shared Bulkley's royalist feelings is uncertain, as is the degree to which the business association between the two men was pragmatic or ideological.[67]

By placing particular emphasis on northern authors and publishers, London combined regional pride with savvy marketing, and probably thus stimulated local business. While Kiséry suggests that London reissued his catalog in 1658 to tap into the larger market of the capital—resetting the title page and removing any reference to his physical bookshop—the ideology behind the main project remained unchanged: the *Catalogue of Most Vendible Books* brought new works (with a northern flavor) to the attention of nascent readers in Newcastle, London, and beyond.[68]

London's promotion of local imprints stopped short of advertising for his competitors. He neglected to list Thomas Tillam's *Banners of Love*, which was ostensibly "to be had at the stationers in Newcastle."[69] Nor did he include many Edinburgh publications, despite his northern boosterism.[70] Instead, he focused his attention on local authors. The divinity section includes a range of works by theologians associated with the region. There are several polemical pamphlets against papal authority by Bishop Mourton, a moderate Calvinist whose career ended ignominiously at Durham Cathedral (1632–41);[71] new books by Bishop Bramhall (f. L2), whose debate with Thomas Hobbes was made public by the Duke of Newcastle;[72] a sermon preached by Mr. Cole of Newcastle at a local funeral (f. [L4]*v*); as well as works by Cuthbert Sydenham, "teacher to a Church of Christ at Newcastle upon Tine," and several York theologians (ff. [L4]*v*, M*v*). A folio edition of the "Poems and fancies by the Lady Marg. Newcastle" (second f. F) appears among the "Romances, Poems, and Playes," reaching a local audience despite her temporary exile to Antwerp.

In his introduction, London proudly draws attention to mathematicians born in the north.[73] While he does not specify names, it is possible to identify a small circle of contemporary local mathematical practitioners, including the renowned Sir Jonas Moore (1617–79) who was born in Brancepeth, Durham county, and studied with William Milbourne (fl. 1620–43), parson of Brancepeth. (Milbourne's friend Elias Ashmole purchased his library after his death.) Milbourne also taught the Westmorland astronomer George Wharton (1617–81), another friend of Ashmole's. Surprisingly, Moore is the only one of these men to appear as an author in the mathematics section: his 1650 *Arithmetick* is listed, but neither Wharton's contentious almanacs nor Milbourne's sole theological title appear.[74] By expanding his purview to Yorkshire, London is able to include mathematicians Jeremy Shakerley (*Tabulae Brittanica, Mathematicall Recreations,* and *Mathematicall Magick,* f. Dd2), Henry Briggs (*Trigonometria Britanica* and *Arithmetica logarithma,* f. Dd*v*), and Edmund Wingate (six titles on f. [Cc4*v*]).

William London's passion for mathematics was more than just an intellectual enthusiasm. Among his own stock of books, London found support for the idea that scientific knowledge was of particular value to a country's development. He cited Robert Gentili's translation of *La Chemin Abregé; or, A Compendious Method for the Attaining of Sciences,* a fervent argument for public scientific education. The author proposed a national program for improving the sciences in France, and wished to see youth "study Mathematicks and Philosophy, . . . which [would make] them more capable and fitting for publick employments."[75] London also cited Cornwallis, who mentioned in his *Essays* that "the Sciences well managed, adde a marvellous luster to one in Government."[76] On a practical level, London reiterated that such learning "fit men for the Government of themselves, and their Country, either Millitary or Civill," particularly "publick affairs in City or Commonwealth."[77] Disdainful of those who had "learning without wisdom and sound knowledg," London quoted Montaigne's condemnation of those "Letter-strucken-men" who "ha[d] been lopt off from publique imployment" and failed to contribute anything to society.[78] He viewed the *Catalogue of Most Vendible Books* as his personal contribution to "*knowledg,* which the whole Nation may reap."[79] Acting out of a combination of civic involvement and patriotism, he willingly invested time and money: "I once more adventure my own fortune, to repair and careen my countries."[80] Contributions to the public good outweighed the allure of personal finances in London's conception of a gentleman.

While good business practices required London to seek approbation from the gentry in the "Epistle Dedicatory," a closer reading of the prefatory material reveals that his sympathies lay with those untitled individuals addressed in the "Epistle to the Reader." London addressed his catalog not only to influential gentry and learned professionals but also to self-made men, those merchants, artisans, and autodidacts whose straitened finances or family circumstances closed the doors of formal education to them. When he laid out the benefits to be had from reading in the introduction,

London drew a significant distinction between learning and knowledge, equating the first with conventional university education, whereas the second could be acquired in less traditional ways. He mentioned paradoxical situations where supposedly learned men lacked "wisdom and sound knowledg," as well as inspirational cases of "Wise men . . . [who] want[ed] the Education of Learning."[81] He then reached the unsurprising conclusion that individuals without formal education could easily "improve [their abilities] by the study and habit of Books."[82] His comments in the "Epistle to the Reader"—that he lacked "the parings of Learning" and was only qualified to analyze it from a distance—may not have been merely a conventional display of authorial modesty, but perhaps also a tacit intimation that he himself lacked a formal education.[83] London's dissatisfaction with the privilege inherent in social hierarchies grew increasingly evident throughout the introduction, as he railed against educational inequalities:

> [W]ee see how fortune distributes unequally, in giving advantages to empty braines, whereby those that are best fitted for the greatest Improvements, and Imployments, wants the help, which others have too much of . . . if aptness, and fitness, were dived into, wee should not have so pitifull effects, by forcing of mens minds to be scholars, because rich; when those whom nature ha's adopted to be frank engrossers of all learning, should be stifled, and crush't in their ripe conceptions; and because young brothers by birth, they must be alwaies, and in all things, kept so.[84]

One wonders if the well-read provincial bookseller of uncertain financial stature was thinking of himself when describing those "frank engrossers of all learning, stifled and crush't." The sparseness of biographical information does not permit us to confirm that London was himself a younger son, but this impassioned statement reveals strong sympathies with those trapped by heredity.

During the seventeenth century, an emphasis on national improvement in concert with the development of Puritan ideology resulted in significant changes to the English pedagogical system. As Ken Arnold explains, the traditional university curriculum was no longer sufficient for the growing range of military, naval, or court careers, and "the demise of the clerical monopoly on culture produced the need to groom lay administrators and professional men with different skills and knowledge."[85] The gentry began to aspire to the polymathic erudition of "virtuosi," enrolling in the new grammar schools and universities in substantial numbers during this period. An increasingly powerful mercantile and artisanal population also demanded new educational services. Mathematical practitioners began to teach in dedicated schools and lecture to the general public.[86] London's catalog reflected all of these changes, listing a large number of the myriad technical and practical manuals—on arithmetic, geometry, navigation, astronomy, medicine, and more—that were published during this period.[87] While stigma persisted against the utilitarian knowledge of the "Mechanicks" (Peacham's courtly definition of gentility excluded anyone who labored for a living), the boundaries were increasingly contested.[88] Figures like Jonas Moore, who made a considerable fortune as a practical mathematician, helped to improve the perception and broaden the scope of certain scientific fields. Frances Willmoth notes that "patrons from among the gentry, who were unlikely to risk tarnishing their gentility by personally practicing manual arts for gain, were nevertheless keen to study them."[89]

In the spirit of employing this new functional knowledge himself, London leavened the *Catalogue* with metaphors drawn from his favorite subjects: mathematics and other sciences, travel and exploration, and commerce. He promised to "steere a new course" with his catalog, and "(to speak in the dialect of Arithmetick) [to] make an Intiger the product of fractions."[90] Seeing that "Wisdom and Knowledg . . . are the very Loadstones and Attractives of all Honour," he felt that the customer "that gets Books for his money, has in my mind as good a bargain as our Mariners, who trade with the Indians, and get Gold for Knives, Rattles, Glasses, &c." Though one's fortune might be "shipwrackt," one could still return with more treasures from books then from the Indies.[91] The *Catalogue*, and by extension London's inventory, included a substantial number of books related to the New World (in the history section), as well as a range of navigation textbooks (in the mathematics section, ff. Dd3–4).[92] Even London's commercial metaphors about the "merchandize of Knowledg" can be read not only as the *leitmotif* of an entrepreneur but as an acknowledgment of the merchants who would be purchasing the account books, advice on bills of trade, and titles such as *The Merchant's Avizo* and the *Treasure of Traffick; or, A Discourse on Forreign Trade* that conclude the mathematics section (ff. [Dd4]v–Ee).

Given London's desire to promote what he saw as a new type of knowledge, it is unsurprising that he carried seventeenth-century imprints exclusively and favored books hot off the press. (In contrast, a considerable number of Maunsell's titles had been printed more than fifty years prior to the catalog's issuance.) London did not provide specific publication dates, but he identified those books printed between 1650 and 1655 with an asterisk, and those that had come off the press within the past two years with a visually striking pointing hand (☞).[93] More than 40 percent of the list comprises these new works, though the proportion of recent titles varies by category. The divinity section is the most current, with 42 percent of the titles appearing in the previous seven years. "Physick" (medicine) and "History" are also heavily weighted to new books; "Physick" has the largest proportion of 1656–57 titles in the catalog (28.3 percent). The "Mathematics" and "Law" books are less topical (30.2 percent and 25.7 percent of those titles appeared between 1650 and 1657), while less than 10 percent of the school texts were printed after 1650. While no dates are noted for the "Romance" titles, the emphasis on current works persists there.

In light of the prevalence of contemporary political and theological works in London's catalog, one would expect to find a large number of pamphlets, the fuel of the late seventeenth-century press.[94] However, aside from the admittedly copious number of ephemeral sermons, the anti-Quaker screeds published by London himself, and a group of Richard Baxter's explicitly titled octavo "sheets" in the 1660 *New Catalogue* (f. Hh3), broadsheets and political pamphlets do not overwhelm the inventory. As such materials were typically very topical and brief, London may have decided not to list those he had in stock during the period he was preparing the *Catalogue*, although they almost certainly comprised a sizeable percentage of his merchandise.

London's project to promote knowledge as a constructive tool coincided with the trend privileging vernacular publishing in England.[95] While London did include "some few Latine Books," since they were "usually sold in most places of repute in the Country" (a category evidently including his own shop), his business focused predominantly on English-language works.[96] The *Catalogue* contains approximately five hundred Latin titles (including twenty-three in the supplements), or 13.3 percent of all books. Half of these are found in the "Hebrew, Greek and Latin Bookes" category (257 titles, or 86 percent of the section), and a further 145 among the divinity titles (8.5 percent). The medical section has the second highest percentage (26 titles, or 17 percent), while History and Romance have the lowest (4.2 percent and less than 5 percent respectively). If the schoolbooks are excluded from the analysis, Latin works constitute 7 percent of the total titles in the three editions.[97] While a certain percentage of theological books continued to be printed in Latin, by the mid-seventeenth century the non-university presses were increasingly catering to a vernacular readership. Popular works on science and medicine began to appear in English, while more technical Latin treatments of those subjects were imported from the continent.[98] This is reflected in the *Catalogue*'s law and scholastic sections, where reference works remained in Latin (or French), while the medical and mathematical categories include a high proportion of newer English-language titles aimed at a nonprofessional audience.

Working under the assumption that all English-language books in the *Catalogue* would have been printed in England, one finds that a survey of the Latin titles can offer insight into how much business William London conducted with continental publishers. The majority of the Latin publications in the *Catalogue* were in fact written by English authors, many of whom had vernacular titles listed as well; these tended to be published in London, Cambridge, or Oxford. However, we do find a small number of Latin texts that were never published in England and must therefore have been imported.[99] While several of these books were published in the first quarter of the seventeenth century, a substantial proportion saw new editions in the 1650s. This suggests that London may have obtained the newer titles during a recent purchasing trip to the capital. He could have obtained the more dated foreign volumes from another bookseller who wished to unload old stock upcountry.

The small number of foreign Latin works are diverse in their origins: titles from Geneva and Amsterdam are listed alongside more unusual imprints, such as Franeker, Herborn, Middleburg, and Modena.[100] The divinity section includes works from a range of Protestant confessions: three titles from the German (Ramist) theologian Johannes Piscator, all printed at Herborn, where he taught at the university (f. [P4]*v*); three volumes by the French Huguenot André Rivet, published in Geneva (1625, 1644) (f. Q2*v*); Petri Ravanelli's Christian dictionary, *Uticensis Occitani Bibliotheca Sacra* (Geneva, 1650 or 1654) (f. Q4*v*); and the Briton Anthony Wotton's *De reconciliatione peccatoris* (Basel, 1624), seemingly never published in England (f. [S4]). Additional imported works in the other sections are dominated by Low Country printing: four legal texts by Johannes Corvinus (Amsterdam), works by Boxhorn and Cluver (Leiden), Jacob Golius's *Lexicon Arabico-Latinum* (Amsterdam or Leiden, 1653), and *Historia belgica* (Antwerp or Ingolstadt).

While London expressed a fervent interest in mathematics and other sciences, and demonstrated a modicum of competency with Latin throughout his introduction, he did not position himself as an importer of the latest sophisticated continental natural philosophy. Foreign Latin titles remained a specialized subdivision of his stock; in this situation, his personal interests were subordinate to those of his market.

The *Catalogue* also includes a small but significant stock of works in continental vernaculars, published in London for the domestic market. William London was versed in French authors, citing Montaigne and Richelieu, and offering translations of romances such as Mme. de Scudéry's *Clelia* (1656) and a new edition of Marguerite de Navarre's *Heptameron* (1654). But the *Catalogue* contains very few titles produced in France (Fanelli's *Varie architeture* may have been printed in Paris, but Descartes's *Meditationes* was more likely to have been one of the numerous Amsterdam editions). The romance and poetry titles seem to be exclusively domestic productions, although they include several French and Spanish works in translation. While Greek and Hebrew texts are largely confined to the scholarly reference category, multilingual dictionaries appear in almost every section, some devoted to common vernacular tongues and others to ancient languages (Syriac, Chaldean). Toward the end of the mathematics section, accompanying the works aimed at international traders, London includes *An Introduction to the French Tongue* and seven other titles for those interested in learning the language, and well as an Italian phrasebook (ff. Dd4v–Ee) and, in the 1660 continuation, a *Dutch Tutor* (f. C4v).

Returning to Shapin's discussion of seventeenth-century English gentility, we find two contrasting "cultural repertoires": "one repertoire (understandably underrepresented in literate culture) defiantly identified gentility with 'pleasure,' recognizing a gentleman by his birth, wealth, repute, and quarrelsomeness, and the traditional avocations (hunting, hawking, gambling, visiting) structuring his day."[101] Having skewered just such "vulgar" idlers, London clearly wished to propagate the second repertoire, which "celebrated knowledge and its presumed product, virtue."[102] His desire to improve the status of reading permeated his catalog and is echoed in the encomium for ancient military strategists who earned fame thanks to their study of philosophy, one that might just as well be applied to London and his fellow aspiring readers: "minted out of the rubbish of the world, [they] received the stamp of Honour, as a due debt to their Learning and Wisdom."[103]

William London represents an example of a man of modest means, distanced from the capital yet very much a part of the country's changing intellectual environment. His catalog and the newly founded Royal Society can be seen as manifestations of the same trend toward more accessible information, at a moment when the distinctions between the humanities and sciences were still fluid.[104] According to Thomas Sprat, the Royal Society's first historian, one of the society's "primary goal[s] was to make public knowledge out of what had previously been locked up in 'the closets of Physicians, or the Work-houses of Mechanicks.'"[105] While Steven Shapin has demonstrated that members of the Royal Society placed great importance on social status, seeing gentility and wealth as prerequisites to objectivity, William London offered a more inclusive concept, based fundamentally on the principles of knowledge rather than heredity, a model that held benefits on both a national and personal level.

London clearly regarded books as tools—or even scientific instruments—to be utilized in the noble project of spreading wisdom: "If Books be the Spectacles we see through to all Learning, let's then use them so; branch them forth, and spread their Knowledge."[106] More than just an optional accessory, books, like eyeglasses, were capable of bringing important concepts into focus. London's metaphor was well-chosen for an age when scientific equipment and empirical experiences were garnering more respect, and lively minds across England and Europe were calling for information to be disseminated more broadly. In the end, London was interested not simply in raising the status of the self-made man, but in raising the status of the knowledge that he embodied. Through his catalog London ingeniously demonstrated that all readers could easily participate in this endeavor for national, local, and personal improvement, simply by buying and reading books.

Notes

1. William London, *A Catalogue of the Most Vendible Books in England, Orderly and Alphabetically Digested, Under the heads of Divinity, History, Physick and Chyrurgery, Law, Arithmetick, Geometry, Astrology, Dialling, Measuring Land and Timber, Gageing, Navigation, Architecture, Horsmanship, Faulconry, Merchandize, Limning, Military Discipline, Heraldry, Fortification and Fire-works, Husbandry, Gardening, Romances, Poems, Playes, &c. with Hebrew, Greek and Latine for Schools and Scholars. The like Work never yet performed by any. Also, All sorts of Globes, Mapps of the World or in Parts . . . All to be sold by the author at his shop in New-Castle.* (London: n.p., 1657) f. F3. Cited in Donald G. Wing et al., *Short-title Catalogue of Books Printed in England, Scotland, Ireland, Wales, and British America, and of English Books Printed in Other Countries, 1641–1700* 3 vols., 2nd ed. (New York: Modern Language Association of America, 1972–88) (hereafter "Wing"), L2849.

2. Only three extant copies of the 1657 first issue are documented in major libraries: Bodleian, Cambridge University, and University of Pennsylvania. All citations in this paper refer to the Bodleian copy reproduced on Early English Books Online/EEBO (accessed 16 March 2007); see also the facsimile edition: William London, *A Catalogue of the Most Vendible Books in England (1657, 1658, 1660)* (London: Gregg Press, 1965).

3. The significance of London's work is analyzed by Graham Pollard and Albert Ehrman, *The Distribution of Books by Catalogue from the Invention of Printing to A.D. 1800* (Cambridge: Roxburghe Club, 1965), 124–33; Richard A. Hunter and John F. Fulton, "A Lesser Tercentenary: William London's *Catalogue of the Most Vendible Books in England* (1657)," *Journal of the History of Medicine* 14 (January 1959): 74–78; John Feather, *The Provincial Book Trade in Eighteenth-Century England* (Cambridge: Cambridge University Press, 1985), 45; C. J. Hunt, *The Book Trade in Northumberland and Durham to 1860: A Biographical Dictionary* (Newcastle: Thorne's Students' Bookshop for History of the Book Trade in the North, 1975), 60. See also P. J. Wallis, *The Book Trade in Northumberland and Durham to 1860: A Supplement to C. J. Hunt's Biographical Dictionary* (Newcastle: Thorne's Students' Bookshop for History of the Book Trade in the North, 1981).

4. His "parentage, education, and private life are obscure" (Marja Smolenaars, "William London [fl. 1653–1660]," in *Oxford Dictionary of National Biography* [http://www.oxforddnb.com/view/article/16958, accessed 20 March 2007]). See also Adolf Growoll, *Three Centuries of English Booktrade Bibliography* (London: Holland Press, 1964), 45; H. R. Plomer, *Dictionary of the Booksellers and Printers Who Were at Work in England, Scotland, and Ireland from 1641–1667* (London: Bibliographical Society, 1907), 119; Hunter and Fulton, "Lesser Tercentenary"; Hunt, *Book Trade in Northumberland*, 60. William Osler debunks an

earlier "absurd" attribution to William Juxon, Bishop of London, in *Bibliotheca Osleriana* (Oxford: Clarendon Press, 1929), 7179.

5. The 1658 edition of the *Catalogue* (London: [n.p.], printed in the year 1658; Wing L2850) is a reissue of the 1657 *editio princeps* with a new title page and an additional five-leaf supplement. (All copies of the 1657 and 1658 issues examined online and in person contain the same crooked letter 'h' in the catchword "whose" on f. E.) The twenty-four-page 1660 supplement (Wing L2848), entitled *A Catalogue of New Books, by Way of Supplement to the Former. Being such as have been printed from that time, till Easter-Term* (London: printed by A. M. and are to be sold by Luke Fawn at the Parrot in Pauls Church-yard, and Francis Tyton at the three Daggers in Fleetstreet, 1660), seems to have been sold appended to the 1658 issue. The numbers reported by Hunter and Fulton ("Lesser Tercentenary," 75–76) have been corrected here, but are still smaller than the inflated estimate of "approximately 4500 titles" claimed by Smolenaars in "William London."

6. Divinity books constituted 30.4 percent of the total entries and 41.8 percent of *new* titles in the Term Catalogues (1668–1709); John Barnard and D. F. McKenzie, eds. *The Cambridge History of the Book in Britain*, vol. 4, 1557–1695 (Cambridge: Cambridge University Press, 2002), 788.

7. "Viz. Arithmatick, geometry, musick, astronomy, astrology, dialling, measuring of land and timber, gageing vessels, navigation, architecture, &c. Also of horsemanship, faulconry, merchandize, limning, millitary discipline, herauldry, fire-works, husbandry, &c." (London, f. [Cc3]).

8. While Barbara Shapiro slightly overestimates the proportion of books in London's *Catalogue* that deal with scientific subjects (it is not quite "one of every six books listed") she correctly recognizes its position as a bellwether of English interest in the sciences. Barbara Shapiro, "The Universities and Science in Seventeenth-Century England," *Journal of British Studies* 10, no. 2 (1971): 79.

9. London pitied gentlemen who did not "know other Languages then their own," f. [A4]*v*.

10. Bacon's *The Twoo Bookes . . . of the Proficience and Advancement of Learning* (London: for Henry Tomes, 1605); see Alfred W. Pollard, *A Short-Title Catalogue of Books Printed in England, Scotland, & Ireland and of English Books Printed Abroad, 1475–1640*, 2nd ed. (London: Bibliographical Society, 1963) (hereafter "STC"), 1164; *Essaies* (London: J. Beale, 1612), STC 1141, and multiple other editions; Montaigne/John Florio, trans. *The Essayes or Morall, Politike and Millitarie Discourses of Lo: Michaell de Montaigne* (1603/32), STC 18041/3, or *Essays Written in French by Michael Lord of Montaigne* (1613), STC 18042; Robert Burton, *The Anatomy of Melancholy what it is. With all the kindes, causes, symptomes, prognostickes, and seuerall cures of it . . .* (Oxford: J. Lichfield and J. Short, for Henry Cripps, 1621), STC 4159; Thomas Stanley, *The History of Philosophy, in eight parts* (London: For Humphrey Moseley and Thomas Dring, 1656), Wing S5237/8.

11. Written in 1345 and first printed in Cologne in 1473, Latin editions of *Philobiblon* appeared in Oxford in 1598 and 1599. It is difficult to hypothesize whether London would have been familiar with de Bury's work; he does not list it in the *Catalogue*. See Richard de Bury, *The Philobiblon*, ed. Archer Taylor (1345; Berkeley: University of California Press, 1948).

12. F. J. Levy, "How Information Spread among the Gentry, 1550–1640," *Journal of British Studies* 21, no. 2 (1982): 11–34. See also John Barnard and Maureen Bell, "The English Provinces," chap. 32 in *The Cambridge History of the Book in Britain*, vol. 4, 1557–1695, ed. John Barnard and D. F. McKenzie (Cambridge: Cambridge University Press, 2002), 677–78.

13. Pollard and Ehrman, *Distribution of Books by Catalogue*, ch. 6.

14. Andrew Maunsell, *The Catalogue of English Printed Books* (London: printed by John

Windet for Andrew Maunsell, 1595; repr. London: Gregg Press, 1965). William Jaggard, *A Catalogue of Such English Bookes, as lately have bene, and now are in Printing for Publication. From the ninth day of October, 1618. untill Easter Terme, next ensuing* (London, 1618), STC 14341. Robert Clavel, *The Term Catalogues, 1668–1709 A.D.: With a Number for Easter Term, 1711 A.D.*, ed. from the Quarterly Lists by E. Arber. 3 vols. (London: E. Arber, 1903–6).

15. Printed prices did not become ubiquitous in sales catalogues until the eighteenth century. See n.30, below, for more on faculty-based subject headings.

16. Growoll, *English Booktrade Bibliography*, 35.

17. Another near-contemporary catalogue of recent English imprints, issued in 1631, adopted none of these organizing principles; the anonymous *A Catalogue of Certaine Bookes Which haue Beene Published, and (by Authoritie) Printed in England, Both in Latine and English, since the Yeare 1616. vntil November this Present Yeare 1631. Now published for supply since the intermission of the English Catalogue, with intention hereafter to publish it exactly every yeare* (London: [J. Dawson], 1631), STC 9979, did not arrange the titles either by subject, format, or publisher, although it did provide printers' and publishers' names. This brief discussion necessarily focuses on those catalogues that aimed at bibliographic comprehensiveness for English-language books, termed "trade lists" by Graham Pollard, "Bibliographical Aids to Research—IV. General Lists of Books Printed in England," *Historical Research* 12, no. 36 (1935): 166. For further examination of other varieties within the genre, such as fair lists, specific subject lists, inventories of personal collections, and printer's catalogues, see Pollard and Ehrman, *Distribution of Books by Catalogue*, and E. Arber, "Contemporary Printed Lists of Books Produced in England," *Bibliographica* 3 (1897): 173–91.

18. John Feather (*Provincial Book Trade*, 45) hypothesizes about the influence London's work may have had upon the Term Catalogues.

19. See Pollard and Ehrman, *Distribution of Books by Catalogue*, 129–30, for an account of Clavel's problematic partnership with John Starkey.

20. Maunsell, f. [4].

21. Thomas More, *Utopia*, ed. T. F. Dibdin (1808) 2:284; cited by Hunter and Fulton, "Lesser Tercentenary," 75. London's own assertion that his catalogue was an "*opus sine exemplo*" has been corroborated by a more objective voice: "London's claim to have produced the earliest catalogue of any bibliographical pretensions is fully justified" (Osler, *Bibliotheca Osleriana*, 7179).

22. London, f. C3v.

23. Growoll discusses various estimates of the number of books published in England in the seventeenth century, calculating that more than 10,108 "editions" are listed between the catalogues of Maunsell, London, and Clavel (*English Booktrade Bibliography*, 74). This, in conjunction with the statistics found in the *Cambridge History of the Book* (vol. 4, Appendix I) contradict E. G. R. Taylor's assertion that "during the Civil War book production came nearly to a standstill" (Taylor, *The Mathematical Practitioners of Tudor & Stuart England* [Cambridge: Institute of Navigation/University Press, 1954], 84).

24. London, ff. B2v, C2v. J. Spencer (1658) employed a similar metaphor of books as "Store-house of things old and new"; cited by Werner Oechslin, "'Mentalmente architettato'—Thoughts in Physical Form: Immutable or Dynamic? The Case of the Library," in *Collection, Laboratory, Theater: Scenes of Knowledge in the Seventeenth Century*, ed. Helmar Schramm et al. (Berlin: W. de Gruyter, 2005), 128.

25. London, f. B2v. London lists seven of Raleigh's books in the history section, f. Yv.

26. London, f. B3.

27. London also described books as containing treasures themselves: "*Books*, which are the Cabinets of these rare Jewels [Knowledge and Learning]" (f. I2), a turn of phrase he may have borrowed from Thomas Nicols's *Arcula Gemmea; or, A Cabinet of Jewels* (1653), which

appeared on the final page of the mathematics section (f. Ee2); or Mr. Cooper's *Cabinet of Spiritual Jewels* (f. M), in the divinity section.

28. As the first English translation of Naudé's *Advis*, John Evelyn's *Instructions concerning Erecting of a Library*, was not published until 1661, London was unlikely to have read it before writing his *Catalogue*.

29. Paolo M. Paciaudi, *Memoria ed Orazione* (Parma: Bodoniani, 1815), 60; cited by Oechslin, "'Mentalmente architettato,'" 125–26.

30. For a discussion of classification systems, see Paul Nelles, "Three Audiences for Religious Books in Sixteenth-Century France," in *The Sixteenth-Century French Religious Book*, ed. Philip Conner et al. (Aldershot: Ashgate, 2001), 256–85. Modifying the traditional tripartite arrangement according to academic faculties (divinity, medicine, and law), William London included a final section devoted to those books that "fall not directly under the Heads of Divinity, Physick, or Law, &c. *but* Are properly usefull for Schooles and Scholars" (f. [Ff2]). András Kiséry identifies London as the first cataloguer to treat fiction as a classificatory category (Kiséry, "'They are Least Usefull of Any': Catalogues, Booksellers, and the Invention of Literature in Seventeenth-Century England," paper delivered at the February 2005 Graduate Student Conference, Princeton University Center for the Study of Books and Media, p. 28).

31. London, ff. [M4*v*], C*v*.

32. London, f. C*v*.

33. See Ian Roy, "The Libraries of Edward, 2nd Viscount Conway, and Others: An Inventory and Valuation of 1643," *Bulletin of the Institute of Historical Research* 41, no. 103 (1968): 43 and Appendix, for statistics regarding the average value of private seventeenth-century libraries as a percentage of annual income; *Cambridge History of the Book*, 4:575, on the rise of private libraries within residences.

34. Cf. "vendible"; when coupled with *more*, or *most*, "denoting the readiness with which a thing can be sold" (*Oxford English Dictionary Online* [accessed 2 August 2007]; hereafter *OED Online*). See Kiséry, "They are Least Usefull of Any," 33, on the erroneous yet enlighteningly transposed version of the title—"A Catalogue of most Books vendible in England, of Divinity, History, Law, &c. 4°."—which appears in an advertisement of books printed by Francis Tyton (Richard Baxter, *A Holy Commonwealth; or, Political Aphorisms*, 1659), Wing B1281.

35. In reference to Maunsell's blanket prohibition of books written by suspected Catholics (f. [3*v*]), London proclaimed "I like not his resolution and opinion, that lately thrust out a Catalogue in print, and out of a comendable Zeale, refuses to insert Heterodox Books, as unfit to be sold (to some indeed they are so)." Then, ostensibly playing the part of neutral middleman, while simultaneously flattering the intelligence and virtue of his potential buyers, he explained that "I am against selling [pernicious Pieces] to such as may be seduced by them, yet will I not hinder their acquaintance to such as may confute them" (f. C2). He evidently recognized the axiomatic relationship between censoring books and their increased popularity. (On the variety of theological works in the catalogue, see n. 57, below.)

36. London, ff. C*v*, C.

37. London, f. [A]. Hunt, *Book Trade in Northumberland and Durham*, 60.

38. Barnard and Bell, *Cambridge History of the Book*, 4:674; Kiséry, "They are Least Usefull of Any," 11.

39. In the case of Fenner's *Works* (Wing F680, F709, F710), London devotes nearly an entire page to recording each fascicle of the contents (f. [M4]*v*); here London must have copied not simply from the book's title page, but from its actual table of contents. For evidence of London diverging from the publisher's advertising materials, compare the final leaves in two works by Cuthbert Sydenham, both printed by W. Hunt for Richard Tomlins in 1654 (*The*

Greatnes of the Mystery of Godlines, Wing S6296, and *Hypocrisie Discovered in its Nature and Workings,* Wing S6300).

40. While nothing is known of William London's early career, it is likely that he followed the typical pattern of apprenticing in the capital and then returning to his home town to establish a business. See *Cambridge History of the Book,* 4:665 and 677, for the province-capital supply network.

41. Wenceslaus Hollar, *Ornatus muliebris Anglicanus; or, The Severall Habits of English Women, from the nobilitie to the contry woman, as they are in these times* ([London]: Sold by H. Overton at the White Horse without Newgate ..., 1640) STC 13599.5.

42. Edmund Gayton's *Pleasant Notes upon Don Quixot* (f. [V4]*v* in the history section) is listed anonymously under romances as *Pleasant Notes on Don Quickset* (f. [Ee4]), and the author of *Tractatus duo Mathematici . . . de globis Caelestibus & Terrestribus* (Oxford, 1651) is recorded as "Mr Hewes" in the mathematics section (f. Dd) but "A. R. Hues" among the textbooks (f. Gg*v*). London enters one work in the medical section under its full title, albeit quirkily spelled, and also offers a précis of the books' contents in the history section: Alexander Ross's *Arcana microcosmi; or, The Hid Secrets of Man's Body Discovered; in an anatomical duel between Aristotle and Galen concerning the parts thereof: as also, by a discovery of the strange and marveilous diseases, symptomes & accidents of man's body. With a refutation of Doctor Brown's vulgar errors, the Lord Bacon's Natural history, and Doctor Harvy's book De Generatione, comenius, and others; whereto is annexed a letter from Doctor Pr. to the author, and his answer thereto, touching Doctor Harvy's book De Generatione. By A. R.* (London: T. Newcomb . . . , 1652), Wing R1947 (f. Aa2*v*) is synopsized and cross-referenced as "Against Ld Bacon, Dr. Harvey, Mr Brown, &c. as at large in catalogue of physick books, an advertisement to the jury men of England, and touching witches" (f. Y2).

43. Only one title in the entire mathematics section (ff. [Cc3]–Ee2, see n.7, above) is on fireworks, and topics such as "faulconry" and "gageing" are almost as scarce. Kiséry ("They are Least Usefull of Any," 16) questions why the author-bookseller's name does not feature more prominently in the 1658 edition. London produced two starkly anti-Catholic texts only a short time before: *The Civil Wars of France, during the Bloody Reign of Charls the Ninth: wherein is shewed, the sad and bloody murthers of many thousand Protestants . . .* (London: printed by H. H. for W. London, 1655), Wing L2851, and *Clamor Sanguinis Martyrum; or, The Bloody Inquisition of Spain . . .* (London: printed by A. M. for Fr. Tyton at the three Daggers in Fleet street, 1656), Wing C4403. Translated and compiled from various sources, he published these anonymously—the French work attributed to "a true Protestant, and friend to the common-wealth of England," the Spanish to "a friend to the Protestant interest." Although he may have originally intended to be cautiously discreet about the authorship of these polemical texts, by 1657 his tentative marketing ambitions won out, and he listed them in the history section (f. V2) as being "By the Authour of this Catalogue." On the texts financed by London, see n.47, below, and Kiséry, "They are Least Usefull of Any," 13–21.

44. Feather, *Provincial Book Trade,* 45.

45. See ibid., 80 and chap. 5 passim; Levy, "How Information Spread," 20, 34.

46. London, f. [A].

47. Kiséry, "They are Least Usefull of Any," 19n.38; and n.67, below, for more on Bulkley. Books printed "for Will[iam] London": Wing C4403, C5045, H623bA, G769, L2851, W1266, W1268.

48. London, f. B3*v*.

49. London, ff. F2*v*, [C4]*v*, I2.

50. London, f. [B4].

51. [H. Parker], *The Humble Remonstrance of the Company of Stationers,* London (Lon-

don, 1643), cited in Adrian Johns, *The Nature of the Book: Print and Knowledge in the Making* (Chicago: University of Chicago Press, 1998), 188.

52. Johns, *Nature of the Book*, 187.

53. Helen Berry, "Promoting Taste in the Provincial Press: National and Local Culture in Eighteenth-Century Newcastle-upon-Tyne," *British Journal for Eighteenth-Century Studies* 25 (2002): 1. After the 1662 Licensing Act was repealed nineteen years later, regional printing became viable, with Newcastle developing into one of the most flourishing locales.

54. Barnard and Bell, *Cambridge History of the Book*, 4:331, 665; Feather, *Provincial Book Trade*, 29; see also Hunt, *Book Trade in Northumberland*; Peter John Wallis, "The North-east Book Trade to 1860: Imprints and Subscriptions" (Newcastle, 1977–81), PHIBB 153, 268a. *A Catalogue of Choice Books, consisting of divinity, history, phylosophy, physick, mathematicks, poetry, curious collections of prints, &c.: most of them fairly bound, which will be sold by way of auction, in the Flesh Market at New-Castle upon Tyne, on Monday the first day of August, 1687; at which place catalogues will be distributed gratis: and likewise at Durham* ([Newcastle: n.p.], Printed in the year 1687), Wing C1298A.

55. The British Book Trade Index (BBTI; available at http://www.bbti.bham.ac.uk/) records more than a dozen book merchants active in Newcastle between 1505 and 1511, at least fifteen later in the sixteenth century, and ten family enterprises during the seventeenth century in addition to William London's. Northumberland's first printer, Thomas Gibson, was active in Morpeth in 1562; Robert Barker and possibly John Leggatt printed works in Newcastle c. 1639; and Stephen Bulkley (see n.67, below) resided intermittently there and in Gateshead between 1646 and 1662.

56. According to the BBTI, the cathedral city of Durham supported just one bookselling enterprise in the mid-seventeenth century, the Hutchinson family firm, and by the 1690s only three additional sellers: William Worden, William Freeman, and Abraham Ashworth. In Cumberland, Robert Scott was the sole bookseller in Carlisle in the mid-seventeenth century (1656–59), with four booksellers and one stationer in various Cumberland towns toward the end of the century. Kendal, Westmorland, had four booksellers over the course of the seventeenth century. Newcastle's figures are, however, dwarfed by the fifty booksellers active in York over the course of the sixteenth and seventeenth centuries. See John Barnard and Maureen Bell, *The Early Seventeenth-Century York Book Trade and John Foster's Inventory of 1616* (Leeds: Leeds Philosophical and Literary Society, 1994), 19, for a comparative portrait of the active book culture among the gentry and clergy in seventeenth-century Yorkshire.

57. The majority of the texts in the divinity section were authored by mainstream clergymen; Jeremiah Burroughs, William Fenner, Henry Hubbard, as well as Presbyterians like John Collinges all merit at least an entire column or more of entries. While works dedicated to groups such as Jews, Jesuits, Anabaptists, and Antinomians strike a balance between vitriolic attacks and detached curiosity, the titles on Quakers are universally negative. The Puritan Richard Baxter's myriad anti-Quaker texts include *Quakers' Catechism* and seventeen other titles in the 1657 *Catalogue*, seven in the 1658 *Supplement*, and fourteen in the *Catalogue of New Books*. Despite London's rhetoric of tolerance (touched upon in n.35, above), none of the most prolific Quaker authors are represented. He does list a *History of the Life of John Naylor* (f. X3), as well as the works by the "Newcastle Ministers" responding to Naylor (first printed by Stephen Bulkley in Gateshead at London's expense), but not Naylor's works themselves. See John Feather, *A History of British Publishing*, 2nd ed. (London: Routledge, 2006), 234.

58. Barnard and Bell, *Cambridge History of the Book*, 4:678.

59. London, "Epistle Dedicatory," ff. B, [A4]*v*, A3. One of the primary meanings of "peculiar" during the period was "special, remarkable; distinctive" (*OED Online*). London's decision not to name a specific individual for his dedication suggests that he was not seeking an

official patron. Perhaps he did not wish to choose one particular prominent man in the Newcastle area at the risk of alienating other customers.

60. Among the learned women mentioned by London in his introduction, Lady Jane Gray was the only near-contemporary figure (ff. E3*v*–[E4]). He lists books stemming from the *querelle des femmes* throughout the catalogue, as well as titles by several female authors (including poems by Margaret Cavendish, Duchess of Newcastle, f. F[f]). Nevertheless, the preponderance of book buyers in the English provinces would have been male. See Levy, "How Information Spread," 32, and Roy, "The Libraries of Edward . . . and others," 35–46; on the *querelle* and women as readers, see Barnard and Bell, *Cambridge History of the Book*, 4:91, 435–51.

61. London, f. [A4]*v*.

62. Steven Shapin, *A Social History of Truth: Civility and Science in Seventeenth-Century England* (Chicago: University of Chicago Press, 1994), 170.

63. Ibid., 63; Braithwait: ff. [F4]*v* and V; Peacham: ff. I and Y*v*.

64. London, f. B*v*. Naudé proposed a similarly public-spirited aim for literary gentry: "render your name illustrious by that of your library," *Advis pour dresser une Bibliothèque: presenté à Monseigneur le président de Mesme*, 2nd ed. (Paris: Rolet le Duc, 1644), 4. See also de Bury, *Philobiblon*, chap. 18, for a discussion of books serving the common benefit of scholars, rather than just the private pleasure of their wealthy owners.

65. London, f. [G4]*v*, also f. C, etc.

66. 1660 supplement, f. A2.

67. H. R. Plomer, and R. A. Peddie, "Stephen Bulkley, Printer," *Library* ser. 2, 8 (1907): 1–112. See Smolenaars, "William London"; Hunt, *Book Trade in Northumberland*, 60; Kiséry, "They are Least Usefull of Any," 19n.38. For a lucid explication of the relationship between William London, Bulkley, and the anti-Quaker Newcastle divines, as well as the connections between Newcastle and London printers (Richard Tomlins, Francis Tyton), see Kiséry, "They are Least Usefull of Any," 13–21.

68. Kiséry, "They are Least Usefull of Any," 32–33.

69. Thomas Tillam, *Banners of Love Displayed over the Church of Christ, Walking in the Order of the Gospel at Hexham: By the out-stretched arm of the King of Saints, against the jesuiticall designe lately attempted by the false Jew; or, An answer to a narrative stuf'd with untruths, by foure Newcastle gent* ([Newcastle?]: Are to be had at the stationers in Newcastle, and also at Will. Hutchinson bookseller in Durham, and Rich. Dobson in Hexham, [1654]), Wing T1164A.

70. London offers both English and Latin editions of John Skene's *Regiam Majestatem* [f. Cc2]; the Latin edition may have been either the Edinburgh *editio princeps* or the 1613 London reprint, whereas the English is more likely to have been the 1641 London edition than that of 1609 from the original Edinburgh printer.

71. f. P*v* lists seven titles by Mourton, who donated much of his substantial library to St. John's College, Cambridge. See http://www.joh.cam.ac.uk/library/special_collections/early_books/pix/provenance/morton/morton.htm.

72. Hobbes's salvo appears in the history section, f. X. See Lisa T. Sarasohn, "Thomas Hobbes and the Duke of Newcastle: A Study in the Mutuality of Patronage before the Establishment of the Royal Society," *Isis* 90, no. 4 (1999): 715–37.

73. London, f. [G4]*v*.

74. London, f. [Cc4], Wing M2563.

75. Robert Gentili, trans., *La Chemin Abregé* (London: Humphrey Moseley, 1654), pp. 48–49 (Wing C3779A [CD-ROM, 1996] accessed via EEBO; listed on f. [X4] as *Le Cheminabridge . . . by Card. Richlew*.

76. London, f. F; William Cornwallis, *Essayes* ([London]: for Edmund Mattes, 1600–1601), STC 5775.

77. London, ff. C3*v*, F. See Fritz Caspari, *Humanism and the Social Order in Tudor England* (Chicago: University of Chicago Press, 1954), for the humanist interpretation of this debate.

78. London, f. D.

79. London, f. B2. On the concept of "knowledge as a collective good," see Shapin, *Social History of Truth,* xxv and chap. 1 passim.

80. London, f. B3*v*.

81. London, ff. [C4]*v*–D, and further ff. A3, B3*v*, E.

82. London, f. D. On "informal instruction" during the period, see Kenneth Charlton, *Education in Renaissance England* (London: Routledge; Toronto: University of Toronto Press, 1965).

83. London, f. [C4].

84. London, f. D*v*. London once again echoed Gentili's sentiments from *La Chemin abregé:* "Finally, men are borne for knowledge, and it is a notable wrong done to them, to take away the means, and make the way thereunto hard and difficult. The Schooles . . . ought to be open to all the world" (Gentili, *La Chemin Abregé,* 48–49).

85. Ken Arnold, *Cabinets for the Curious: Looking Back at Early English Museums* (Aldershot: Ashgate, 2006), 188. Shapin has measured "the influx of gentlemen into the new public schools and the universities in the period from c. 1558–1642" (*Social History of Truth,* 170).

86. See Taylor, *Mathematical Practitioners,* 50: Gresham College (founded 1597) aimed to "bring important branches of learning within reach of the ordinary Londoner" by giving public lectures in English as well as Latin. See also A. J. Turner, "Mathematical Instruments and the Education of Gentlemen," *Annals of Science* 30, no. 1 (1973): 51–88; Frances Willmoth, "'The Genius of All Arts' and the Use of Instruments: Jonas-Moore (1617–79) as a Mathematician, Surveyor, and Astronomer," *Annals of Science* 48, no. 4 (1991): 355–56.

87. In Taylor's list of more than 600 works by "mathematical practitioners," 430 were published between 1600 and 1700. Rupert Hall, *Scientific Literature in Sixteenth and Seventeenth Century England* (Los Angeles: William A. Clark Memorial Library, 1961), 23–24, suggests that "we should need to multiply this figure by ten or twenty to estimate the whole number of the books and pamphlets on scientific matters printed in England during the same period."

88. "Whosoever labour for their livelihood and gain have no share at all in nobility or gentry," in Peacham, *Compleat Gentleman,* 23, cited in Shapin, *Social History of Truth,* 50. See Shapin chap. 8 for further discussion of the "knowledge-skill distinction," where skills are included within the category of manual labor, whereas "knowledge [is] conceived not as work but as thought" (361).

89. Willmoth, "Genius of All Arts," 356.

90. London, ff. [B4]*r–v*.

91. London, ff. C, [B4], E2.

92. William London included rudimentary navigational textbooks such as Henry Phillippes's *The Geometrical Sea-man* (first ed. 1652) alongside John Wallis's *Due correction for Mr. Hobb[e]s* (1656), a theoretical debate that would catch the attention of members of the Royal Society. For Phillippes, see Taylor, *Mathematical Practitioners,* work #204; for Wallis, Wing W575, see Willmoth, "Genius of All Arts," 357.

93. London made occasional errors, omitting asterisks from certain recent titles, or incorrectly assigning a symbol to an older work.

94. Joad Raymond defines pamphlets as shorter works of between eight and ninety-six pages, typically stitched rather than bound, in *Pamphlets and Pamphleteering in Early Modern*

Britain (Cambridge: Cambridge University Press, 2003), 5; John Barnard, "London Publishing, 1640–1660: Crisis, Continuity, and Innovation," *Book History* 4 (2001): 1–16.

95. On the explosion of new vernacular works after 1650, see Barnard and Bell, *Cambridge History of the Book*, 4:514.

96. London, f. C. While both William London and Robert Clavel planned to produce comprehensive Latin catalogues, neither completed them.

97. This language analysis presents approximate figures based on the title transcriptions. Although London's printer provided typographic clues, setting names and Latin terms in italics throughout the catalogue (and reversing the schema in the textbook section, to more easily distinguish English-language books), this reader might have been "cosen'd" by the occasional short title.

98. Feather, *History of British Publishing*, 20.

99. Inferences based on extant editions listed in WorldCat; in cases where several editions are possible, multiple dates are listed.

100. Laurens Banck's *Roma Triumphans* (Franeker, 1640 or 1656); Johann Heinrich Alsted's *Thesaurus Chronologiae* (Herborn, 1627, 1637, or 1650); Philips van Lansbergen, *Tabulae motuum coelestium perpetuae* (Middleburg [Zealand], 1632 or 1653); Giuseppe Biancani's *Sphaera mundi* (Bologna, 1620 or Modena, 1653).

101. Shapin, *Social History of Truth*, 171.

102. Ibid.; London, f. [A4]*v*. One of William London's favorite authorities, the Jacobean physician Richard Burton, had much to say on "idleness as the 'badge of gentry' and the cause of gentle melancholy" in his *Anatomy of Melancholy* (1628). Note that in contemporary usage, "*leisure* (or even *idleness*) did not mean the absence of activity, only the absence of *valued* activity"; see Shapin, 51–52, and cf. Thorstein Veblen, *Theory of the Leisure Class* (New York: Macmillan, 1899), chap. 3. Naturally, London believed reading to be a simple cure for this endemic idleness (f. F2*v*).

103. London, f. F2.

104. Lisa Jardine, *Ingenious Pursuits: Building the Scientific Revolution* (New York: Doubleday, 1999). See also Shapin, *Social History of Truth*.

105. Thomas Sprat's *History of the Royal Society* (London, 1667), quoted in Arnold, *Cabinets for the Curious*, 29.

106. London, f. F3.

Marketing Longitude

Clocks, Kings, Courtiers, and Christiaan Huygens

Nicole Howard

You are, Sir, among the few men for whom this book was made, and who I hope to have as readers; because of this I am obliged to send you this example.
—Huygens to Pierre Bayle, 17 February 1690

Introduction: The *Horologium* of 1685

In 1665 Christiaan Huygens, one of the most famous Dutch mathematicians, made an unusual appearance on the docks in Amsterdam. His purpose was to host a seminar on the use of his newly invented pendulum clock, and his audience consisted of sea pilots and sailors who could use the marine timekeeper on their ships. In a small room along the waterfront Huygens detailed the clock's mechanisms, the proper mounting of the instrument, and the manner in which time could be determined at sea. We can only imagine the scene: the upper-class gentleman with his elegant clock, describing for seasoned sailors how the determination of longitude was now possible; the sailors listening dubiously to the promise of an expensive new instrument that could forever change their navigational techniques. Predictably, the workshop was less than appreciated. The sailors hardly disguised their absence of faith in the instrument, as Huygens explained to his father, the renowned Dutch poet and diplomat Constantijn Huygens: "Being in Amsterdam I conferred with several of our seamen, as well as with . . . those who understand navigation; they cannot deny [the clock's] utility. However, I have noticed how slow and unwilling our seamen are to acknowledge something new which has such obvious utility."[1] Huygens quickly realized that personal appearances alone would not make marine sailors accept his clock. But his meeting with a group clearly outside of his normal community of mathematicians and natural philosophers provides an excellent example of his attempts to reach different audiences with his work.

In what follows, I will explore the way Huygens actively cultivated heterogeneous audiences for his published works by tailoring them to particular readers and distributing them in strategic ways. Analyzing his authorial intentions in this manner not only enhances our reading of these important works in the history of science, it also helps us to understand how mechanics permeated cultural boundaries in early modern Europe. Though Huygens published across the spectrum of scientific disciplines, with works on mathematics, mechanics, natural philosophy, astronomy, and optics, I focus here on his three publications related to the pendulum clock: the *Horologium* of 1658, the *Kort Onderwijs (Brief Instructions)* of 1665, and the *Horologium Oscillatorium* of 1673.[2] The first two were written when Huygens was an independent scholar in the Low Countries, the third while he was a member of the French Académie Royale des Sciences, under the patronage of Louis XIV and Jean-Baptiste Colbert. Thus the intellectual and institutional contexts in which the works were composed varied, but they had a common objective.

Huygens's aim was to produce a pendulum clock that was accurate enough to determine longitude at sea, and he had begun working on the problem in 1656.[3] After developing and testing several prototypes he had a model that he felt would solve the problem, and in 1658 he made his design public in his *Horologium*. By that time Huygens had already shared diagrams of his new clock with a French correspondent, the councillor to the king of France, Jean Chapelain, but upon realizing that he had a marketable instrument, he asked Chapelain to refrain from sharing the design: "Not having at present the time to respond as I would like to your obliging letter, I offer here only a few lines in order to ask you not to communicate to anyone the construction of my clock, which, while vague enough, could be understood by someone."[4] Chapelain promised to keep the information private, agreeing that disclosure might cost Huygens priority. The work was finished in mid-June, and Adriaan Vlacq, a well-known Dutch printer, published it in early September 1658.[5]

The *Horologium* was a simple quarto, only fifteen pages including the dedication. Its purpose was clearly to make the technology and its inventor known. Huygens sought priority not only for himself but for the Low Countries as well, dedicating the book to "The Most Illustrious and Most Powerful Lords of the State of Holland and of the Western Region," the governing body of the Netherlands: "I felt myself strongly impelled to ensure to our country the credit for this and for any future discoveries, and so I have followed the way which alone seems proper to this end—*to make known the whole idea and construction of the new mechanism*, which I, the inventor himself, have undertaken to describe in a few words and to produce to the public in a reasonably brief volume."[6] Huygens goes on to explain that it is not just the book that is being dedicated to the States-General, but the invention itself. By accepting his dedication, they will recognize the public benefit of his instrument, which he compares to the legendary sundial installed in Rome by the censor Quintus Marcius Philippus. The Romans, having relied on a poorly functioning clock for nearly a century "infinitely appreciated this gift," Huygens writes, because it improved their lives and brought glory to Rome.[7] His own clock promised to do the same for the Low Countries. Moreover, he claimed that publishing the *Horologium* would help to forestall other nations that might attempt to steal the idea—a notion that would ultimately prove contentious.[8]

Huygens tailored the *Horologium* for an educated audience. Like other works of mathematics or mechanics of the period, it is in Latin, but careful examination of the text and images reveals his hope to gain a wider readership interested in the technology. The book's detailed explanation of the clock asks readers to merge the visual description of a carefully labeled diagram with the written account of its construction, and Huygens's narrative facilitates this. He describes the weight δ (delta), attached to the pulley F, and a series of gears that turn up through the saw-toothed wheel L (figure 1). L turns the vertical arbor MN, which moves the vertically mounted crown wheel P and the crutch QR, and here Huygens's instrument stands out among others of the day, because the crutch is what keeps the pendulum from swinging wildly. The oscillation impelled by the weight δ is kept in check and consistent. Following the description Huygens writes, "These are indeed the details of my mechanism which require precise explanation because the point of the whole invention turns on them."[9] The account he provides reads like a modern patent request, a "virtual construction" wherein the details are essential for preserving priority.[10] Indeed, Huygens did apply for patents for his clocks in the Low Countries and later in England, but as Mario Biagioli has shown, legal protection of an invention was typically granted when one could show authorities a working model. Written descriptions of instruments and their inner workings were almost never necessary.[11] Why then publish such precise details of his clock? For Huygens, the issue was about earning credit for his invention—not simply in the legal sense, but credit in terms of a reputation as an authority on pendulum clocks and in terms of priority for developing such a clock before anyone else.[12]

We can then surmise that Huygens intended the *Horologium* to be read by mechanicians—at least those versed in Latin—who had some understanding of how clocks work. However, his targeted audience went beyond this narrow group of readers. In Huygens's private workbook, under the heading "Exemplaria Horologij, primum editionis," he listed fifty-nine individuals to whom he planned to send a copy of the book (figure 2 and Table

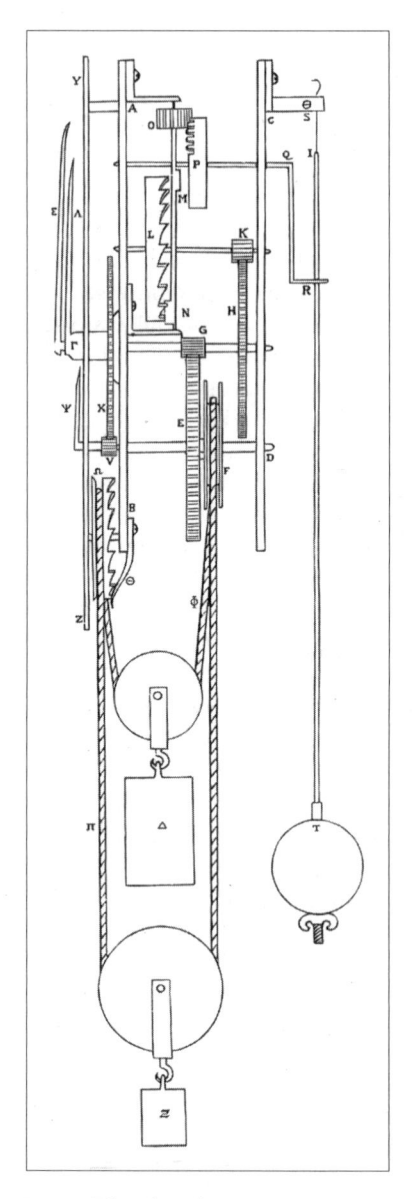

Fig. 1 The plate from Huygens's 1658 *Horologium*.

1).[13] Huygens drew up such a list of designated recipients for each of his major publications. Buried among his notes, these rosters provide insights into his desired audience for a given work. They are all the more valuable because in many cases we have letters from Huygens to his chosen recipients, as well as the recipients' responses to presentation copies. No other natural philosopher or mathematician from the period is known to have left such a clear indication of their intended audiences, especially over the course of a lifetime.[14]

In the case of the *Horologium* of 1658, the names on his recipients list are loosely grouped according to nationality. Topping the list is the States-General, the governing body of the Low Countries that had approved a patent for Huygens's clock on 16 June 1657.[15] As dedicatees of the work, they were also given a pendulum clock by Huygens, which was hung in the chamber where the representatives met. Following the States-General is the name of Johann de Witt, Councillor Pensionary of Holland and former student alongside Huygens at Leiden. De Witt supported Huygens's efforts to obtain patent rights for various clock models.[16] A number of scholars from the Low Countries follow De Witt on the list almost immediately: Andreas Colvius, Robert Paget, Caspar Caltoff, Adrian van der Waal, Nicholas Heinsius, and Isaac Vossius. These men—with the exception of Caltoff, who was a mechanist—were poets, ministers, and savants with little mechanical aptitude or technical background. For them, the gift of the *Horologium* was a symbolic gesture from a fellow countryman—a signal of friendship and respect.[17]

In addition to these men of letters, various astronomers and mathematicians throughout Europe were sent copies, among whom were John Wallis (whose name appears third on the list), Giovanni Battista Hodierna, Ismael Boulliau, Guy Personne de Roberval, and Johannes Hevelius. These men understood the benefits of an accurate timekeeper for taking astronomical observations, and they welcomed Huygens's new model. Hevelius wrote to thank him for sending the description, noting that the clock was "of significant use to all things astronomical."[18] Wallis too praised the "exceptional and noble" work.[19] Additionally, the French Royal Geographer and engineer Pierre Petit was sent a copy of the book. Petit had a great interest in mechanics (particularly clocks and automata), and upon receiving the details of Huygens's design he entered into a lengthy correspondence with him about the construction of various clocks.[20]

Finally, there were members of the nobility and aristocrats to whom Huygens sent the *Horologium*. Princess Elizabeth of Bohemia, René Descartes's former correspondent and patron, received a copy, as did Leopold de' Medici, whose volume was accompanied by an actual clock.[21] Leopold responded reticently to Huygens's gift, leaving no doubt as to his concerns

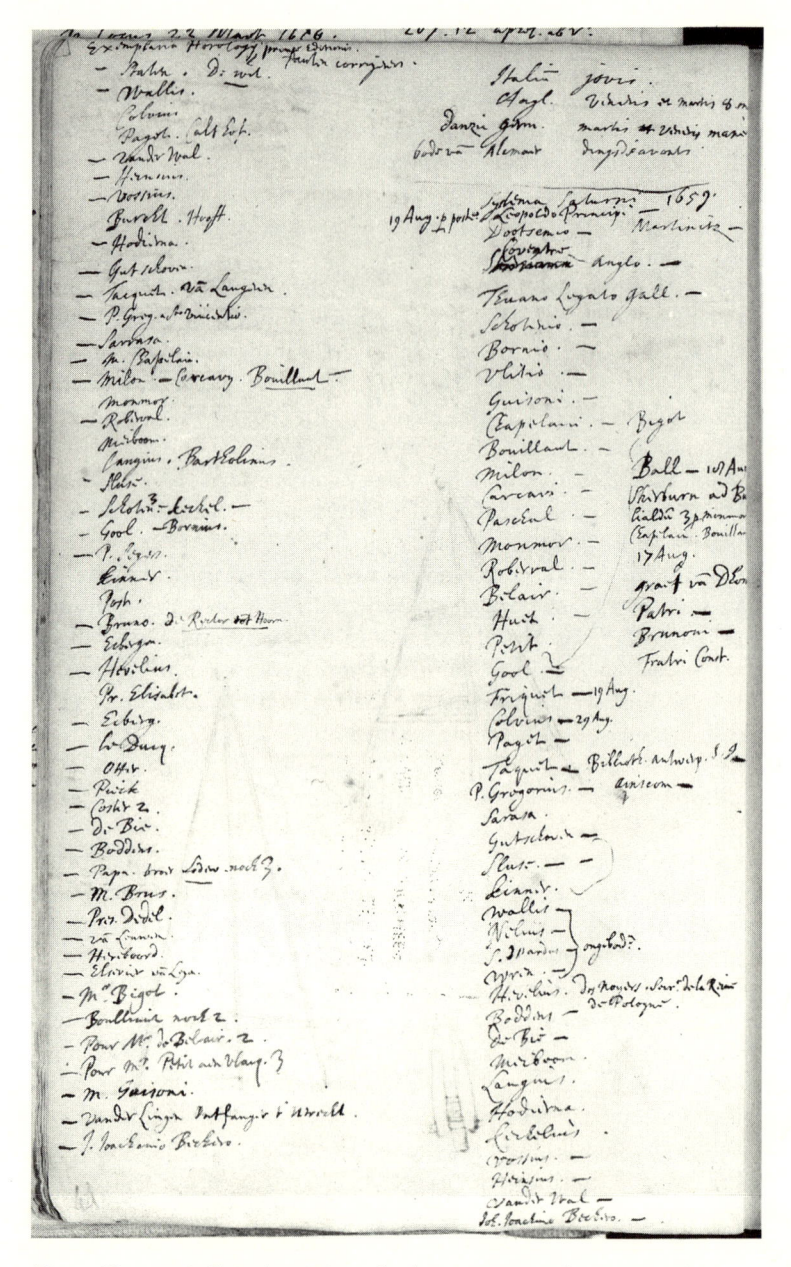

Fig. 2 Huygens's list of recipients for his 1658 *Horologium*. Leiden University Library, ms. HUG 10, fol 22v. Reproduced with permission of the University of Leiden.

Table 1. List of Recipients for the *Horologium* (1658)

Recipient as listed	Full Name	City
Staten	States-General	The Hague
De Wit	Johann De Witt	The Hague
Wallis	John Wallis	Oxford
Colvius	Andreas Colvius	Dordrecht
Paget	Robert Paget	Dordrecht
Calthof	Caspar Calthoff	Dordrecht
Van der Wal	Adriaan van der Walle	The Hague
Heinsuis	Nicholas Heinsius	Amsterdam
Vossius	Isaac Vossius	Leiden
Burcht	Cornelis Pietersz	Amsterdam
Hooft	Pieter Corneliez Hooft	Amsterdam
Hodierna	Giovanni Battista Hodierna	Palermo
Gutschoven	Gerard van Gutschoven	Louvain
Tacquet	Andreas Tacquet	Antwerp
Van Langeren	Michael van Langeren	Brussels
P. Gregorius a St. Vincentio	Gregory of St. Vincento	Ghent
Sarasa	Alfons de Sarasa	Ghent
M. Chapelain	Jean Chapelain	Paris
Milon	Claude Mylon	Paris
Carcavy	Pierre Carcavy	Paris
Bouillaut	Ismael Boulliau	Paris
Montmor	Henri Louis Habert de	Paris
Roberval	Gilles Personne de Roberval	Paris
Meiboom	Marcus Meibomius	Copenhagen
Langius	Wilhelm Lange	Copenhagen
Bartholinus	Erasmus Bartholin	Copenhagen
Sluse	Rene Francoise de Sluse	Liege
Schoten (3 copies)	van Schooten	Leiden
Kechel	Samuel Carolus Kechelius	Leiden
Gool	Jacob Golius	Leiden
Bornius	Henricus Bornius	Leiden
P. Seghers	Daniel Seghers	Antwerp
Kinner	Kinner a Lowenthurn	Prague
Post	Pieter Post	The Hague
Bruno (de Rector tot Hoorn)	Henricus Bruno	Hoorn
Eibergen	Gijsbert Eickbergh	The Hague
Hevelius	Johannes Hevelius	Danzig
Pr. Elisabeth	Elizabeth, Princess of Bohemia	Herford
Eiberg	Hermann van Eiberg	Groningen
Le Ducq	Adriaan Duyck	The Hague
Otter	Christiaan Otter	Nijmegen
Pieck	Willem Pieck	The Hague
Coster (2)	Solomon Coster (2 copies)	The Hague
De Bie	Alexander de Bie	Amsterdam
Boddens	Abraham Boddens	Amsterdam

Table 1. (Continued)

Recipient as listed	Full Name	City
Papa	Constantijn Huygens (father)	The Hague
Lodewijk (3)	Lodewijck Huygens (brother)	The Hague
M. Brus	Alexander Bruce	London
Pres. Dedel	Madamoiselle Dedel	The Hague
Van Leeuwen	Simon van Leeuwen	The Hague
Hereboord	Adriaen Heereboord	Leiden
Elsevier van Leyen	Elsevier publishers	Leiden
M. Bigot	Emery Bigot	Paris
Bouillaut	Ismael Boulliau (2 copies)	Paris
Pour M. de Belair (2)	Charles Bellair	Paris
Pour Mr. Petit aen Vlacq (3)	Pierre Petit and Adriaan Vlacq	Paris
M. Guisoni	Pierre Guisony	Paris
Van der Lingen	van der Lingen	Utrecht
J. Jachimo Bechero	Johan Joachim Becher	Mayen

NOTE: Boulliau is listed twice by Huygens. The first time he is fifteenth on the list (alongside the names of Milon and Carcavy). The second time he appears is toward the end of the list, and next to his name is a note about two copies. Huygens seems to have meant to send one copy to Boulliau himself and others to him for distribution.

over Huygens's claim to priority, which he felt belonged to Galileo.[22] A tension between the Italian prince and Huygens resulted, leaving the latter in a precarious position. Meanwhile, in France Monsieur Du Gast wrote to Huygens to confirm delivery of the *Horologium* to Blaise Pascal and to Louis Charles d'Albert, the Duc de Luynes, both of whom thanked Huygens for the gift. Du Gast characterized the latter as "very intelligent in all things mathematical, and . . . in particular a great amateur of horology, after having read your work with esteem and praise."[23] He was so fascinated with Huygens's technology that he requested four clocks be personally chosen by Huygens (from Huygens's clockmaker's available stock) and delivered to him. Huygens's response, delivered via Du Gast, indicates that he was honored to be asked and would see to it that the Duc de Luynes received his clocks as quickly as possible.[24]

Finally, Huygens sent the *Horologium* to various instrument makers, including two copies to Solomon Coster, his primary clockmaker in The Hague, and one to an instrument maker in Dordrecht. Though it is unlikely that either of these men read Latin, the book served as a signal of Huygens's gratitude and his achievement. Moreover, a modern horologer interested in clocks of this period has been able to reproduce Huygens's 1658 clock from the plate alone, demonstrating its utility without any accompanying explanation.[25] The images in the work, then, could serve as blueprints.

The brief text and its chosen audience make clear that the *Horologium* was fundamentally a description of the instrument and a justification of Huygens's priority for its discovery. A young man known more at the time for his mathematical works than his mechanics, Huygens needed to secure credit for his invention. To stake his claim he circulated more than sixty copies of the book in different intellectual, political, and social arenas. Some recipients were capable of delving into the mechanistic details, others less so, but all would relate the name of Huygens to the clock that could—potentially—solve the longitude problem. With this accomplished, he could work on small but important design changes to make the clock seaworthy.

Practical Interlude: The Instrument Guide for Sailors

As luck would have it, a major breakthrough came for Huygens within months of publishing the *Horologium*—not a mechanical innovation but a mathematical one. In early 1659 he discovered that a curve known as the cycloid is isochronous (literally "equal time"). When applied to clocks, the curve ensured that no matter what height the pendulum fell from, it would always sweep out its path in the same amount of time.[26] Huygens immediately mentioned in correspondence his desire to issue a new edition of the *Horologium* that included newly designed cycloidal "cheeks," as he called them. But before doing so, he wanted to build prototypes of the clock and test them at sea. If the mathematical theory of the isochronous curve was among the most important theoretical findings of the century, using that discovery to solve the longitude problem would be a masterful feat.

Drawn to this goal of uniting the theoretical and practical, Huygens had clockmakers produce numerous models of his timekeeper, which were then sent off with experienced seamen in a series of well-documented voyages.[27] One went with Captain Robert Holmes on what proved to be a fairly successful trip to Lisbon from April to September 1663. Robert Moray, Huygens's collaborator in London and a member of the Royal Society, sent Huygens data from the voyage's logbooks and commented that "the clocks are working as well on the ocean as in your chamber."[28] The following year clocks were put on ships sailing to Guinea and the West Indies, this voyage also led by Holmes. The results from this trip were so positive—the calculated longitude values so accurate—that a report on the instrument's success was enthusiastically read before the Royal Society in 1665. Holmes had recorded the distances the ship had traveled and the reliability of the clock in determining the ship's position. His report also noted that at a crucial point in the trip winds pushed the ships off course by approximately eighty leagues to the east. While other pilots were unaware of the drastic change of position, Holmes had discovered the deviation by using Huygens's clocks, "which shewed that these watches were capable of discovering the currents in the ocean, as well as the longitudes; a thing that was never yet done, and thought impossible to be done."[29] In a letter to Moray, Huygens could hardly conceal his surprise. "I am delighted to learn of the report of Captain Holmes. You could not send me anything more agreeable. . . . I am truly surprised that [the clocks] have been accurate enough to be able, by their operation, to find a small island."[30]

The level of success Holmes had achieved with the instruments was excellent news for Huygens, and—coming on the heels of a privilege granted by the States-General of the Low Countries—affirmed for Huygens the value of his instrument.[31] He moved to market his instruments more aggressively, though he was concerned that the price for a single clock set by the clockmaker, at three hundred florins, might be too high for some sea captains.[32] Nevertheless, the success at sea would earn Huygens recognition and—just as importantly—patents from English and French officials.

In the midst of these voyages Huygens decided that his clocks should be made widely available to seamen, and that operators on the ships would benefit from a clear set of instructions on how to use the instrument. Thus in 1665 he published *Kort Onderwijs*, or *Brief Instructions* [*on the subject of using the pendulum clock for finding the eastern and western longitudes*]. Its purpose was to explain how to properly mount, operate, and maintain his marine clocks.[33] Not only was the work in his native Dutch but it was an entirely different genre from Huygens's other publications, an instructional manual as opposed to a polished exposition of his theories or discoveries. Such practical guides did exist in the seventeenth century, but it is rare to see them coming from someone of Huygens's stature.[34] His move to publish the instructions reflects his conviction that widespread, successful use of his clock was the key to demonstrating its utility and proving the power of his theoretical discovery of the cycloid.

The *Brief Instructions* is a rare work today (only two extant copies in the original Dutch are known), and by all indications the thirty-two page manual was not bound, but rather tied together with a simple string, common for small ephemeral works of the period. The title page contains just text—no images—and there is neither dedication nor preface. Huygens opens the work with several endorsements of his instrument by well-known Dutch navigators, men whose names carried weight with other seamen, like the mathematician and astronomer Dirck Rembrantz van Nierop.[35] Since the founding of the Dutch East India Company in 1602, there was a strong link between commercial and technological interests in the Low Countries, a link that fostered efforts to improve navigation techniques. Van Nierop and others had produced a significant body of literature on navigation, and with the *Brief Instructions* Huygens was placing himself in a long tradition of technicians and instrument makers in Dutch society.[36]

Following van Nierop's endorsement, Huygens advises the user of his instrument to bring at least three or four clocks on board the ship in case one is damaged or malfunctions. Since he was independently wealthy and was not relying on the commercial success of his clocks, this admonition seems to reflect Huygens's genuine desire to see positive results from functioning clocks, rather than a marketing ploy for financial gain. We can take Huygens at his word when he writes to a colleague that "I do not pursue profits, but rather the satisfaction of having found something useful for the public. . . . I will not fail, given the chance . . . to demonstrate that the sciences are not without fruit."[37]

Brief Instructions then recommends that the person attending to the clocks have intimate knowledge of their mechanisms—learned directly from the clockmaker himself, if possible—to avoid misunderstandings. As noted, Huygens himself personally taught sea pilots in Amsterdam about his clock. The details of this meeting were not recorded, but the scene conjures up the image captured by David Vinckboons in his sketch *A Nautical Lesson by Petrus Plancius* (1620), where the famous Dutch cartographer Plancius is depicted teaching a room full of sea pilots about navigation (figure 3). Although Huygens complained about his meeting with the "gens de mer," it nevertheless testifies to his genuine desire to see his clocks properly mounted and operated.[38]

Huygens goes on to provide directions for mounting the clocks to the mast "where they may be freest from moisture or dust, and out of danger of being disorder'd by knocking or touching."[39] He then explains a chart that contains his equation of time, which navigators would need in order to determine the length of the solar day (which varied slightly each day) while at sea. This was a breakthrough for sea pilots: Huygens's clock was user-friendly as well as accurate.[40] Following his discussion of determining longitude with his clocks, Huygens closes the *Brief Instructions* with a practical "trouble-shooting" section. Equivalent to a modern-day FAQ, this part of the pamphlet was, in all likelihood, derived from reports of difficulties by the various sea pilots who had used his clocks.

After preparing the *Brief Instructions* for the publisher, Adriaan Vlacq, Huygens worked to promote it and reach new audiences. First, he made plans to advertise the sale of his clocks in periodicals and scientific journals. To Moray he wrote: "I had already decided to advertise in our gazettes that they [the clocks] be offered for sale, when your letter arrived indicating that further experiments had been conducted, thereby, increasing my confidence

Fig. 3 David Vinckboons, *A Nautical Lesson by Petrus Plancius*, 1620. Courtesy of the Rijksmuseum, Amsterdam.

in my decision."[41] Whether Huygens followed through on these plans is uncertain, but in the *Philosophical Transactions* he was quoted as telling Moray, "I have this week published, that the said watches shall be exposed for sale, together with an information [sic] necessary to use them at sea: and thus I have broken the ice."[42]

Huygens also promoted his clocks by translating his *Brief Instructions* into English and French. From England, Robert Moray wrote to applaud its success: "you explain everything in very intelligible terms for those who need to use it."[43] With some guidance from Moray, Huygens worked on the English translation in the hope of targeting members of the Royal Society as well as English sea captains. Because the instructions would appear as an article in the *Philosophical Transactions,* as opposed to a separate publication, Huygens and Moray dropped the endorsements of Dutch navigators at the beginning of the work, which would have meant little to the English. On Moray's suggestion Huygens also added a brief astronomy lesson, along with an explanation of how that theory connected with the practical use of his instrument. Readers of the journal were likely to be more interested in the theory behind Huygens's equation of time than the Dutch sea pilots for whom Huygens had written the original *Kort Onderwijs*. With Moray's assistance, Huygens made additional minor adjustments such as these throughout the English version.

Despite the fact that the English translation of the instructions was ready for publication in 1665, the "Instructions concerning the use of pendulum-watches for finding the longitude at sea" did not appear in the *Philosophical Transactions* until May 1669. The delay in publishing stemmed from growing doubt on the part of English sea pilots about the integrity of the clocks.[44] When he finally received his copy of the journal from the Royal Society, Huygens wrote to Moray:

> I must thank you again for the copy of your latest *Transactions*, in which I find the translation of my instructions for determining longitude; your mathematicians have done well to omit a certain pretty long demonstration which might confuse pilots, and the example of a log for the clocks, which they have added, fills the space more usefully. I am sorry that in the fifth article a little error has slipped in. . . . It would be a good idea to correct this passage in another edition.[45]

Huygens's French version of the *Brief Instructions* fared little better, though he began the translation process with high hopes of advertising the clocks to interested *savants* and pilots in Paris. He emphasized successful voyages where his clocks had been used, which meant downplaying the less successful voyages. On 31 July Huygens's French colleague and correspondent Jean Chapelain wrote him a letter about the instructions, specifying the kind of language he felt should be used in a French edition. Chapelain understood the marketing required to make Huygens's instrument a public success, as well as the importance of witnesses in creating "matters of fact":

> I would like it more if before publishing the justification of the use of your pendulums at sea, you publish it in the form of an original recounting of what Captain Holmes observed, which was written by him, if this is possible. . . . Because if you present it as coming directly from you, whatever candor you had brought to the composition of the report, you would never avoid the suspicion of those difficult to persuade that you might have accommodated the truth to suit your own interests; and you know how uncharitable the world is. If, however, you are unable to obtain [those reports] it will be necessary to make them yourself and without doubt it will

be better understood than theirs would have been, although it doesn't constitute as strong a proof.[46]

In the end, the translated *Brief Instructions* never appeared in France—even after Huygens took up residence there in 1666. He withheld the book, he said, until additional sea trials could corroborate earlier successes.[47] It would be a long wait.

Although Huygens does not seem to have identified recipients for presentation copies of his *Brief Instructions*, we know from correspondence that he sent the Dutch edition to various men in the Low Countries who had navigational interests. On 24 February 1665 Huygens wrote to René François de Sluse to inform him that "I put forth instructions for sailors on the use of the pendulum clock, which will soon be corroborated with experiment. I will send an example if you understand our language."[48] One month later Sluse wrote to Huygens that he would read it to the best of his ability.[49] Johannes Hudde, the mathematician and Amsterdam burgomaster, also received copies, several of which he was to distribute. He wrote to Huygens on 5 April: "According to your wishes I have delivered almost all the examples of your instructions on longitude to Gietermaker, as well as one or two others to those who know navigation and instruction."[50] A week later he wrote again to Huygens, confirming that he had delivered one copy to Gietermaker and another to Dirk Rembrantz van Nierop.

Thus Huygens marketed *Brief Instructions* not to learned scholars but to lay readers who would employ his technology. If they found the clock to be a significant improvement on what was already in use, Huygens's invention would be a commercial success. But his motivation was not pecuniary. Instead, what was really at stake was the economy of ideas. The technology that emerged from Huygens's mathematical theory needed to be functional if he was going to impress natural philosophers and potential patrons alike, not to mention gain patents. By appropriating a genre with a didactic purpose and writing in the vernacular, Huygens was hoping to use the *Brief Instructions* to coopt a group traditionally outside of scientific or natural philosophical circles to support his development. The mechanics itself did not rely on sailors. Sea pilots could neither understand nor appreciate the mathematics of the cycloid, but they were in a position to evaluate the clock's utility as an instrument at sea if they were familiar with the proper way to use it. Huygens provided them with a step-by-step handbook to ensure that his clocks would yield good results. Those results, in turn, confirmed the usefulness of his invention, demonstrated its utility in finding longitude, and duly impressed the States-General, the Royal Society (of which he was made a member), and the King of France.

Casting a Wider Net: *Horologium Oscillatorium* and Its Readers

In 1666 Huygens's achievements in mechanics and mathematics earned him an invitation to join the newly founded Académie Royale des Sciences. He welcomed the move to Paris, as did his many correspondents there, including Jean Chapelain, who continually urged Huygens to publish a second edition of his 1658 *Horologium*. Back in August 1660 Chapelain told Huygens that the *savants* of Paris anxiously awaited a new and updated edition of his work on the pendulum clock, to which Huygens replied that "my treatise on the clock has been finished for a while, but there has not been an opportunity to have it printed before my trip."[51] Chapelain reiterated his plea in December 1661: "I have great impatience to see your latest thoughts on the clock and in advance I congratulate you on the improvement that this admirable invention will have received due to your fortunate attention."[52] Despite these urgings, the publication was delayed for years while Huygens waited for better results in sea trials.[53] Finally, in February 1673 Huygens sent a draft of the new edition of the *Horologium*, now entitled *Horologium Oscillatorium*, to Chapelain, soliciting his comments. Huygens made the few changes his colleague suggested, and the work was printed by François Muguet in March 1673.[54] Shortly before it was published, Huygens once again drew up a list of people to whom copies would be sent.

To understand Huygens's goals for the *Horologium Oscillatorium*, it is useful to consider the work as three distinct parts, each of which targeted a different subset of readers. At one end of the spectrum there were recipients who could fully understand Huygens's book. They read carefully and analytically with an expertise suited to the mathematics involved. At the other end of the spectrum were readers who lacked either the desire or ability to read the work at all. Their appreciation of the book was purely a matter of prestige: it was an object they could put on display in their library or cabinet as a scientific status symbol. In between there were gradations of readers: those who might only skim the work, those interested in Huygens's propositions but not the underlying proofs, those keen on familiarizing themselves with the language of horology though they lacked the technical training to master the topic. In writing the *Horologium Oscillatorium* Huygens recognized this spectrum, and his book is tailored to such a heterogeneous audience. The dedicatory preface speaks principally to Huygens's patron, the king—although implicitly to Colbert as well. The introduction to the book and part 1—which describes the construction and usefulness of the pendulum—are directed primarily at technically inclined readers: gentlemen interested in mechanical devices, sea captains who needed the clock as an instrument of navigation, and instrument makers. The latter sections of the book (and certainly the bulk of it), parts 2–5, are directed at those readers strong enough in mathematics to follow Huygens's masterful demonstrations. Less proficient mathematicians would find themselves challenged, yet even they would be able to glean something from these sections. At a minimum they could accept—without scrutinizing the proofs—Huygens's propositions about centripetal force and centers of oscillation. Examining the *Horologium Oscillatorium* in light of its multiple audiences renders an enhanced reading of this classic work and illuminates Huygens's abilities and intentions as an author.

Aesthetically, Huygens's 1673 publication is a beautiful object, a seventeenth-century coffee-table book. Many copies—we don't know how many—were printed in folio with gilt edges and bound in calf with the title tooled on the cover in gold. The book is dedicated to Louis XIV, a contrast to his 1658 dedication to the States-General of Holland and all the more striking since the Sun King was, at that very moment, sending French troops into the Low Countries. About his magnum opus Huygens writes:

> I believe I have done my best work when I have dealt with things whose usefulness is connected with some subtlety of thought and difficulty of discovery. . . . I confess that I have pursued this double goal with greater success in the invention of my clock than anything else. For the clock is not only a mechanical invention, but much more importantly it is constructed on geometric principles. . . . It is not necessary to say very much to show you, most powerful King, how useful this is. For since my clocks were deemed worthy to be placed in the private chambers of your palace, you are aware from daily experience how much better they are in displaying equal hours than other such instruments.[55]

The emphasis on utility in the dedicatory comments is noteworthy, since the clocks had not performed consistently at sea, but Huygens glosses over that fact and points out instead how well they work in Louis XIV's private quarters. In fact, he does the same thing throughout the book, citing examples of the clock's reliable performance in places where it is simply not in question: on land. Also of interest in this statement is Huygens's assertion that the clocks are "more importantly constructed on geometric principles." By framing his invention as something tethered to theory, he shores up support for other theoretical pursuits that—on the surface—might not seem to yield something useful. It is a gentle reminder to the king that the applied technologies he seeks through science are often ushered into existence through more abstract channels.

Much of this dedication conforms to the standard rhetoric and style of the period, but the circumstances surrounding it are unique.[56] In 1672 Louis XIV was invading the Low Countries. The fate of the Dutch Republic and the States-General, the dedicatees of Huygens's 1658 work, were seriously threatened by France's offensive. That Huygens could dedicate his work to the "Great King" put him in a precarious situation, particularly since his family had such close connections to the Stadtholder, William III. But Huygens was tethered to the patronage of the academy, and he had longstanding ties to the intellectual and social communities in France. These connections superseded any feelings of loyalty he had to his homeland, and they required him to present the book to the French king.[57]

While Huygens pays tribute to the king, he is simultaneously invoking the king's power and authority as a means of supporting the integrity of his invention in the eyes of those interested in the clocks as technology. To them, it would be meaningful that the Louis XIV found such clocks worthy of his personal use. Thus, the king is treated directly as a patron, and used indirectly as a broker for the technology.[58] "By your order, more than once our clocks have been transported by sea," Huygens proclaims. "Also under your auspices many clocks intended for astronomical uses can be seen in that outstanding observatory which you recently ordered to be built with a remarkable generosity surpassing all other kings."[59] Naturally, there is little discussion here of the problems encountered in those sea trials; Huygens gives the impression that no difficulties arose. He is also careful to mention the use of his clocks at the Royal Observatory, reemphasizing their reliability as astronomical instruments. Again he uses a frame of reference wherein the clocks' capabilities are not questioned, which is to say on land. The trick behind the longitude problem was finding it at sea, with no consistent reference points.

Much has been written about the importance of dedicatory prefaces in this period, and the manner in which they should be read as rhetorical pieces, often invoking classical models. Huygens's dedication does not lie outside this tradition, but the language he employs, and the way in which he frames the subsequent text, makes clear that the preface is targeting an audience beyond Louis XIV. Huygens expected that his dedication would resonate with individuals who employed mechanical devices—especially clocks—in their work, with those who built them as an occupation or hobby, and with those who viewed the king's faith in the clocks as testimony to their reliability. This targeting of multiple audiences is corroborated by an analysis of Huygens's introduction to the book and in part 1. The introduction, which follows the dedication, begins with a brief justification for this "second edition" of the *Horologium:* "Because we have discovered many things since [1658] relating to the improvement of that instrument, we have decided to explain them in detail in this book. These things are so closely related to the perfection of this invention that they can be considered to be its most important part and to be the foundation, previously neglected, of this whole instrument."[60] The key to regular oscillations, Huygens states, lies in the cycloid, to which he devotes several pages of decidedly nontechnical discussion, replete with testimony about the curve's importance: "After applying this line [the cycloid] to the clocks, we have found that their motion is so accurate and constant that, after many experiments on both land and sea, it is now obvious that they are very useful for investigations in astronomy and for the art of navigation."[61] Their efficacy on land was never questioned, but the reference to successful performance at sea is nothing short of salesmanship.

Huygens then explains how the cycloid is generated: "This line is traced out in the air by a nail which is fixed to the circumference of a rotating wheel that revolves continuously."[62] Considering the complex mathematical theory behind the cycloid, it is fair to characterize this description as very unsophisticated. But when he first applied the curve to his clocks in 1659, Huygens told Frans van Schooten that he would "teach the artisans themselves how they may draw the curve with no difficulty,"[63] and the lay terminology offered here does precisely that. Huygens continues: "The geometers of our age have named this line a cycloid and have carefully investigated its many other properties. *Of interest to us is what we have called the power of this line to measure time,* which we found not by expecting this but only by following in the footsteps of geometry."[64] The phrasing is subtle but significant: as he describes the geometers' investigations into the cycloid's properties, he removes himself from that group by explaining what is "of interest to us," as if he were not one of the geometers in question. This casual distinction, creating an "us versus them" dynamic, offers the nonspecialist reader a small token of assurance: don't be afraid of the complex mathematics associated with this curve; what *we* are concerned with is the cycloid's ability to give us accurate time. Of course, one need only look to parts 2–5 of the book to see that Huygens's interest in the curve was mathematical, and deeply technical at that. But the rhetorical approach of the introduction was necessary to reach the audience that he targeted.

Following his prefatory remarks, Huygens begins part 1 of the *Horologium,* where "the mechanical construction of the clock and the application of the pendulum will be presented in a form found to be best adapted to astronomical uses, and all other clocks can easily be related to this sketch by making the required changes."[65] Here he provides exact diagrams of two pendulum clocks from different perspectives.[66] The cogs, gears, crown wheel, and related mechanisms are all labeled for reference (similar to, but not exactly like, figure 1), and the new cycloidal cheeks are clearly shown.

The description Huygens provides for the clock's assembly is quite detailed, closely resembling that of his 1658 edition and making it seem as if Huygens himself is, piece by piece, building his clock.

Huygens elaborates on the unique traits that make the 1673 clock better than earlier models, including a more constant pendular swing and a newly added seconds hand for greater accuracy in measuring time. He then examines the cycloidal cheeks once again, only this time using geometry. This is the only place in either the introduction or part 1 where he employs mathematics, but what is presented is entirely accessible to the layman: geometry for nonmathematicians. There are no rigorous proofs of the isochronous character of the curve and no dense geometric constructions; those would come later. Instead, Huygens offers a physical, rather than mathematical, explanation of how to construct a cycloidal curve, providing a three-dimensional graphic of a cylinder rolling along, and a point on this cylinder tracing the shape of the cycloid as it rotates (figure 4).[67] With everyday objects and markedly simple language, Huygens lets the reader see the generation of the curve. Clockmakers who sought to replicate the cycloidal cheeks, or interested laymen who wanted to understand the basic nature of the curve, would be satisfied. Two additional diagrams demonstrate another way to

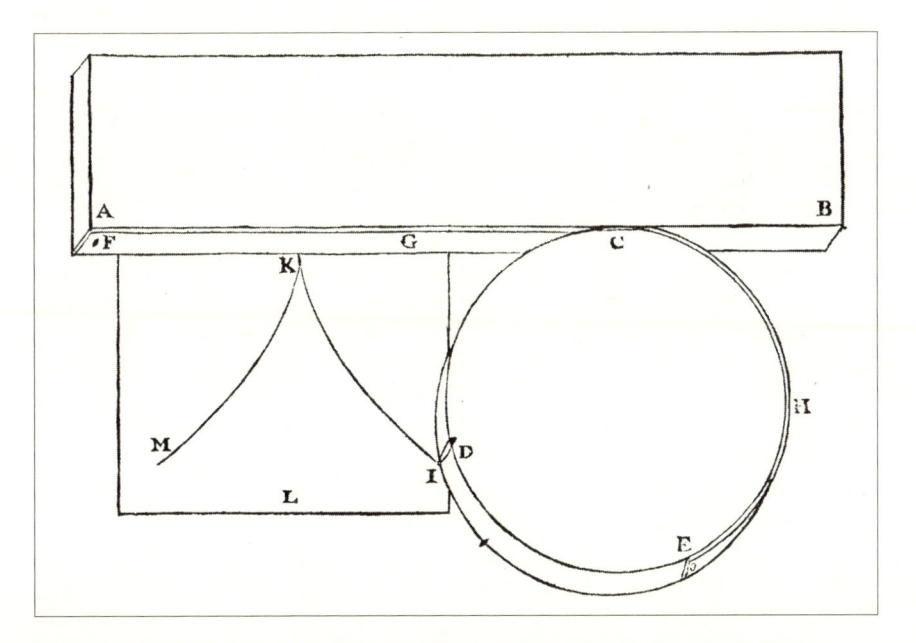

Fig. 4 Graphic on generating the cycloid, from Part I of Huygens' *Horologium Oscillatorium*.

generate the cycloid. The accompanying instructions are straightforward and limited to two paragraphs.

After explaining how the curve is generated, Huygens provides the reader with the same table of the equation of time that he presented in his *Brief Instructions,* a critical aid to help sea pilots reconcile the difference between the solar day and the twenty-four hour day. Just as his layman's discussion of the cycloidal cheeks was written for someone interested in actual technology (rather than pure mathematics), the inclusion of the table of equalization of days was intended for someone interested in utilizing the clock at sea or in an astronomical observatory. Together, these components emphasize hands-on experience, practical knowledge, and the physically tangible aspects of his invention.

At the end of part 1 Huygens emphasizes yet again the success of his marine clocks in sea trials. Given that publication of the *Horologium Oscillatorium* was delayed for years in the hope that such trials would yield more successful results, this is a revealing strategy. Huygens highlights successful voyages of 1664 and 1669 to enhance the legitimacy of his pendulum clock as a sea instrument. He scarcely hints at the difficulties sea captains experienced with his clocks on other voyages, and when he does, he places the blame for difficulties not on the technology, but on those operating it: "After this, these experiments were repeated several times . . . under the order of the Most Serene King. The results varied, but in such a way that frequently the fault could be attributed to the carelessness of those entrusted with the clocks rather than to the clocks themselves."[68] It is this supposed carelessness on the part of seamen that Huygens had hoped to remedy with his *Brief Instructions.* The reader finishes part 1 with a distinct sense that Huygens's clock—adapted to the regulating shape of the cycloid—is the most critical invention in navigational instrumentation of its time.

In contrast to the general accessibility of the dedication, preface, and part 1, parts 2–5 of the *Horologium Oscillatorium* are purely mathematical. Huygens offers numerous demonstrations related to gravitational fall based on the cycloid, a theory of the generation of the curve, a discussion of the geometric properties of the cycloid as they apply to his pendulum clock, and some theorems on centrifugal force—again derived with the help of a pendulum. Few readers without serious training in classical geometry would find these sections of the book—about 80 percent of it—accessible. This analysis is therefore not intended to diminish the mathematics or recast the work as something other than a masterpiece of classical geometry, only to raise awareness of Huygens's efforts to reach multiple audiences—through both his text and his distribution strategy.

When it was printed, the *Horologium Oscillatorium* was sent to editors of learned journals such as the *Philosophical Transactions* in London, the

Journal des Sçavans in France, and *Giornale de Litterati* in Italy. Reviews of the book appeared in all of these.[69] They were of course good publicity, as this anonymous 1673 review from the *Journal des Sçavans* demonstrates:

> The invention of pendulum clocks is one which brings the greatest honor to our century because it is of utmost importance, principally for astronomy and for navigation, to have a reliable means of measuring time exactly. . . . M. Huygens is the first who has found a way of rendering these clocks most accurate by applying a pendulum, and by making all the swings equal by means of the cycloid, which is nothing other than a curved line that a nail, fixed to a wheel, traces in the air, while the wheel turns.[70]

In addition to widespread journal coverage, Huygens (per his custom) had copies of the book distributed to selected individuals, his chosen readership. In one of his workbooks he recorded a list of forty-nine individuals to whom he planned to send a copy of the *Horologium Oscillatorium* (figure 5 and Table 2).[71] The list includes Royal Society members, mathematicians, natural philosophers, and a number of leading French intellectuals. The way Huygens structured the list is also revealing: there are two columns of names, with the left-hand column split into two distinct sections. Names on his other lists were typically arranged according to nationality, but here the groupings reveal an additional level of categorization based on national as well as intellectual status.

Huygens's lists always began with the most important person or group, in this case Louis XIV. After the king's name is Jean-Baptiste Colbert, chief minister of finance and the man responsible for securing Huygens's position in the Académie. Following the major patrons are a number of French academicians listed as a bloc, most of whom had significant mathematical skill: Gilles Personne de Roberval, Bernard Frenicle de Bessy, Jean Gallois, and Edmé Mariotte. Antoine de Niquet and Jacques Buot, both engineers for the king with mathematical backgrounds, are also in that group.

The second cluster of names (still in the left-hand column) consists of Frenchmen who would be considered *savants*, but who lacked serious mathematical skills. Still, the early parts of Huygens's work would have been accessible to them, and the book would likely have been considered worthy of a place in their collections. Among these recipients are Antoine Arnauld, Charles Honoré d'Albert de Luynes (Duc de Chevreuse), Jean Chapelain, Valentin Conrart, Henri Justel, and Melchisédec Thévenot, none of whom were in the Académie des Sciences, though Justel was the editor of the *Journal de Sçavans*. Huygens was promoting his work to men of influence in the scholarly and literary community: writers, secretaries, and humanists.

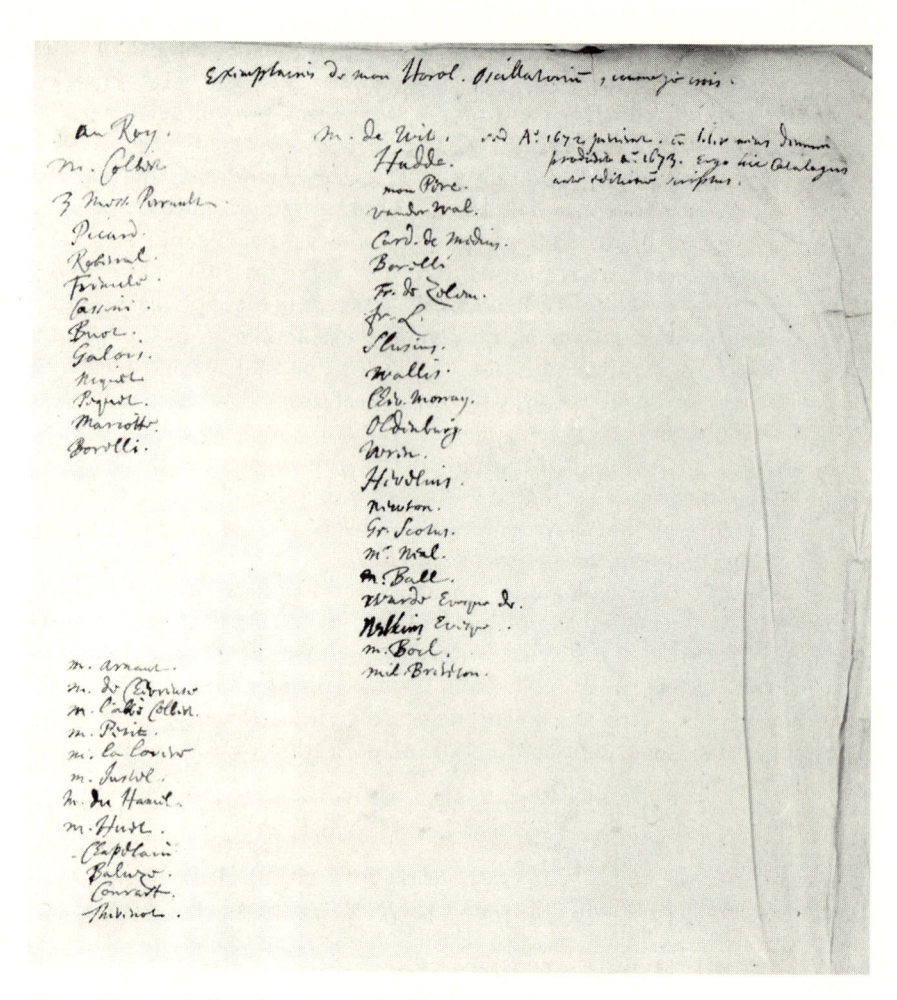

Fig. 5 Huygens's list of recipients for his 1673 *Horologium Oscillatorium*. Leiden, University Library, ms. HUG 2, 437. Reproduced with permission of the University of Leiden.

In the right-hand column of Huygens's list are recipients in the Low Countries, Italy, and England—in roughly that order. Dutch recipients include the mathematicians Rene-François Sluse and Johannes Hudde; the poet Adriaan van der Wall (who authored the poem at the beginning of the work); and Huygens's father, Constantijn, and brothers Constantijn and Lodewijck. The fifth person listed in the right-hand column is Leopold de' Medici, clearly removed from the position of distinction he held at the top of an earlier list of recipients for Huygens's 1659 publication on Saturn.[72]

Table 2. List of Recipients for the *Horologium Oscillatorium* (1673)

Recipient as listed	Full Name	City
Left Column		
First grouping		
Au Roy	Louis XIV	Paris
M. Colbert	Jean-Baptiste Colbert	Paris
3 Mess. Perrault	Pierre, Charles, and Claude	Paris
Picard	Jean Picard	Paris
Robeval	Gilles Personne de Roberval	Paris
Frenicle	Bernard Frenicle de Bessy	Paris
Cassini	Giovanni Domenico Cassini	Paris
Buot	Jacques Buot	Paris
Galois	Jean Gallois	Paris
Niquet	Antoine de Niquet	Paris
Pecquet	Jean Pecquet	Paris
Mariotte	Edmé Mariotte	Paris
Borelli	Jacques Borelly	Paris
Left Column		
Second grouping		
M. Arnaut	Antoine Arnauld	Paris
M. de Chevreuse	Sir Charles Honoré d'Albert	Paris
M. l'Abbe Colbert	Nicholas Colbert	Rouen
M. Petit	Pierre Petit	Paris
M. la Lovere	Antoine de la Loubére	Paris
M. Justel	Henri Justel	Paris
M. du Hamel	Jean Baptiste Du Hamel	Paris
M. Huet	Pierre Daniel	Caen
Chapelain	Jean Chapelain	Paris
Baluze	Etienne Baluze	Paris
Conrart	Valentine Conrart	Paris
Thevenot	Melchisédec Thévenot	Paris
Right Column		
M. de Wit	Johann de Witt	The Hague
Hudde	Johannes Hudde	Amsterdam
Mon Pere	Constantijn	The Hague
vander Wal	Adriann van der Wall	The Hague
Card. de Medicis	Leopold de' Medici	Florence
Borelli	Giovanni Alfonso	Rome
Fr. de Zelem	Constantijn Huygens	The Hague
fr. L.	Lodewijck Huygens	The Hague
Slusius	René François de Sluse	Louvain
Wallis	John Wallis	Oxford
Chev. Morray	Sir Robert Moray	London
Oldenburg	Henry Oldenburg	London
Wren	Christopher Wren	London
Hevelius	Johannes Hevelius	Danzig

Table 2. (Continued)

Recipient as listed	Full Name	City
Newton	Isaac Newton	London
Gr. Scotus	James Gregory	London
M. Neal	Sir Paul Neil	Oxford
M. Ball	William Ball	Oxford
Warde Evesque de.	Seth Ward	Oxford
Wilkins Evesque	John Wilkins	London
M. Boil	Robert Boyle	London
Mil. Brereton	William Brereton	London

Huygens was eager to share his latest advancements with Leopold, especially considering their history of priority disputes about the pendulum clock. Another Italian recipient is Giovanni Alfonso Borelli, the Cimento academician who in the early 1660s had decided a dispute about the shape of Saturn. Below the Italians are the English recipients—Royal Society members like John Wallis, Robert Moray, Christopher Wren, Isaac Newton, and Robert Boyle. In May 1673 Huygens wrote to Henry Oldenburg, the secretary of the society, "It is now already some time ago that I sent you a dozen copies of my book on the clock ... and I ask you kindly to take care of the distribution of all the books according to the inscriptions which I have put in them."[73] Oldenburg confirmed receipt and distribution of the copies, noting that "When these gentlemen whom you have entertained with your book have read and pondered it, and thought good to share their opinions of it with me, you shall not fail, Sir, to be informed."[74] Some recipients responded promptly to Huygens's gift, including Isaac Newton: "I received yr letters with Mons. Hugens kind present, for wch I pray you return him my humble thanks. I have view'd it with great satisfaction, finding it full of very subtile and usefull speculations very worthy of ye author."[75]

Overall, Huygens's list of recipients confirms that he targeted a diverse group of readers, and his own breakdown of recipients into categories, exemplified by the clusters of names, reveals that he imagines his readership as a set of distinct subgroups. Some were members of the mathematical and natural philosophical community, while others can at best be considered gentlemen amateurs. Huygens understood the advantages of targeting such a heterogeneous audience, and realized that he could do so by properly tailoring and distributing his text. As he wrote toward the end of his life, "I could wish indeed that all the world might not be my judges, but that I may choose my readers ... for with such I might promise myself a favorable hearing, and not need to make an apology for daring to vent anything new to the world."[76] Was Huygens was unique in thinking about his readership in this way? How common was his practice of targeting recipients for his work? The answers lie beyond the scope of this article, but Huygens's case does demonstrate a potentially rich area of research for historians of science.

Notes

1. *Oeuvres complètes de Christiaan Huygens,* Publiées par la société hollandaise des sciences (The Hague: Martinus Nijhoff, 1888–1950) (hereafter *OC*), 5:277. Huygens to Constantijn Huygens (father), 26 March 1665. In addition to consulting a 1673 edition of this work at Indiana University's Lilly Library, I used the French translation of the *Horologium Oscillatorium* in *OC* 19:69–368 and the English translation by Richard Blackwell, *Christiaan Huygens' The Pendulum Clock, or, Geometrical Demonstrations Concerning the Motion of Pendula as Applied to Clocks* (Ames: Iowa State University Press, 1986).

2. For information on Huygens's mathematics and mechanics, see A. E. Bell, *Christiaan Huygens and the Development of Science in the Seventeenth Century* (London: E. Arnold, 1947); *Studies on Christiaan Huygens: Invited Papers from the Symposium on the Life and Work of Christiaan Huygens,* ed. H. J. M. Bos et al. (Lisse: Swets & Zeitlinger B. V., 1979); René Taton, *Huygens et la France* (Paris: J. Vrin, 1982); and Cornelis Dirk Andriesse, *Titan kan niet slapen: Een biografie van Christiaan Huygens* (Amsterdam: Contact, 1993), recently edited by Andriesse and translated into English by Sally Miedema as *Huygens: The Man Behind the Principle* (Cambridge: Cambridge University Press, 2005).

3. The literature on Huygens's efforts in solving the longitude problem is vast. For discussions on the problem of determining longitude see *The Quest for Longitude. Proceedings of the Longitude Symposium,* ed. William J. H. Andrewes (Cambridge, Mass.: Collection of Historical Scientific Instruments, Harvard University, 1996). Huygens's efforts to solve the problem are also discussed in Michael Mahoney, "Christiaan Huygens: The Measurement of Time and Longitude at Sea," in *Studies on Christiaan Huygens,* 234–70.

4. *OC,* 2:169. Huygens to Chapelain, 18 April 1658.

5. Though he published an array of books and pamphlets, in the sciences Vlacq is remembered for publishing the logarithms of the first 100,000 numbers to ten decimal places, and of those, he calculated 70,000 on his own. See A. J. Thompson and Karl Pearson, "Henry Briggs and His Work on Logarithms," *American Mathematical Monthly* 32, no. 3 (1925): 129–31. Vlacq had also published work for Constantijn Huygens, Christiaan's father.

6. *OC,* 17:45. In addition to the *Oeuvres complètes de Christiaan Huygens* I have referred to the translation of Huygens's *Horologium* provided by Ernest L. Edwardes in *The Story of the Pendulum Clock* (Altrincham: John Sherratt and Son 1977), 62–97.

7. *OC,* 17:45–47. According to the story Huygens relates, the sundial had originally been taken from Sicily in the Roman Year 477 (approx. 164 B.C.) and set up in Rome, but not being calibrated to the new latitude, it gave inaccurate time for ninety-nine years. The censor Q. Marcius Phillippus put up a new clock to replace it. My thanks to the reviewer who pointed out that Huygens's source for this story is Pliny.

8. *OC,* 17:55. A pendulum clock designed (but not built) by Galileo was said by many in Italy to be the first such clock in existence. It was built by his son Vincenzo after Galileo's death, but Huygens nevertheless maintained that his own, not Galileo's, was the first pendulum clock. This claim led to a priority dispute between Huygens and various Italian mechanicians and patrons, including Leopold de' Medici. See Silvio Bedini, *The Pulse of Time: Galileo Galilei, the Determination of Longitude, and the Pendulum Clock* (Florence: L. S. Olschki, 1991); and Michael R. Matthews, Colin Gauld, and Arthur Stinner, eds., *The Pendulum: Scientific, Historical, Philosophical and Educational Perspectives* (Dordrecht: Springer, 2005).

9. *OC*, 17:61.

10. The notion of virtual construction is derived from Schaffer and Shapin's idea of "virtual witnessing," which "involves the production in a reader's mind of such an image of an experimental scene as obviates the necessity for either its direct witness or replication." See Steven Shapin and Simon Schaffer, "Pump and Circumstance: Robert Boyle's Literary Technology," *Social Studies of Science* 14, no. 4 (1984): 491. A longer discussion is found in idem, *Leviathan and the Air Pump* (Chicago: University of Chicago Press, 1989).

11. Mario Biagioli, *Galileo's Instruments of Credit: Telescopes, Images, Secrecy* (Chicago: University of Chicago Press, 2006), 120–22. Biagioli notes that if authorities believed an instrument warranted legal protection, they could issue a privilege through a "letter patent" that would grant the inventor exclusive rights to develop and use the technology. But as Christine MacLeod has shown, "letters patent" could grant many kinds of special privileges, and the patent system varied widely in different regions. See Christine MacLeod, *Inventing the Industrial Revolution: The English Patent System, 1660–1800* (Cambridge: Cambridge University Press, 1988).

12. I am grateful to the reviewer who suggested I parse the concepts of credit and priority, as well as the legal issues related to patents and privileges. There is a complex relationship between these concepts, as Biagioli and MacLeod have shown. See also Rob Iliffe, "'In the Warehouse': Privacy, Property and Priority in the Early Royal Society," *History of Science* 30 (1992): 29–68. In this essay I focus Huygens's efforts to obtain credit for himself and privileges for his clocks—clocks that were often licensed to one of Huygens's clockmakers. Michael Mahoney has briefly addressed Huygens's desire for fame, fortune, and privileges in "Christiaan Huygens: The Measurement of Time and Longitude at Sea," in *Studies on Christiaan Huygens*, 234–70, esp. nn.4–5.

13. Huygens's manuscripts are housed at the University of Leiden in a collection entitled *Codices Hugeniorum*. The list of his intended 1658 recipients is found in Hug. 10, fol. 22v.

14. John Evelyn, a member of the Royal Society of London, a well-known diarist, and a scholar of horticulture, also kept track of individuals to whom he sent presentation copies of his work. Evelyn discussed this habit with the bookseller Benjamin Tooke, and a letter from Tooke to Evelyn of 11 January 1698 contains a list of 34 recipients of Evelyn's *Numismata*. See Giles Mandelbrote, "John Evelyn and His Books," in *John Evelyn and His Milieu*, eds. Frances Harris and Michael Hunter (London: British Library, 2003), 76–77.

15. *OC*, 2:237–38. States-General to S. Coster, 16 June 1657. Salomon Coster was Huygens's clockmaker, in whose name a patent was granted for twenty years.

16. Herbert H. Rowen, *John de Witt, Grand Pensionary of Holland, 1625–1672* (Princeton: Princeton University Press, 1978), esp. 416–17.

17. On the meaning of gifts and their exchange, see Mary Douglas, "No Free Gifts: Introduction to Mauss' Essay on *The Gift*," in *Risk and Blame: Essays in Cultural Theory*, ed. Mary Douglas (London: Routledge, 1992), 155–66; and Natalie Zemon Davis, *The Gift in Sixteenth Century France* (Madison: University of Wisconsin Press, 2000).

18. *OC*, 2:261. J. Hevelius to Huygens, 26 October 1658.

19. *OC*, 2:304. J. Wallis to Huygens, 1 January 1659.

20. *OC*, 2:253–58. P. Petit to Huygens, 18 October 1658.

21. Edwardes, *The Story of the Pendulum Clock*, 26. The clock was received by Leopold in 1657, and as such would be the model Huygens's clockmaker Coster built prior to publication of *Horologium*. Correspondence reveals that there were recipients whose names did not appear on the list, including some detailed here.

22. *OC*, 2:404. Leopold de' Medici to Ism. Boulliau, April 1659. "Circa le Orivuolo regolato dal pendulo, certo è che l'inventione è bella, mà non si deve defraudare della gloria douutali il nostro Signore per sempre ammirabile Galileo."

23. *OC*, 2:317, Du Gast to Huygens, 16 January 1659. Louis Charles d'Albert, Duc de Luynes (1620–90) was the son of Charles Marquis d'Albert (one of Louis XIII's falconers) and like his father was an influential person in the French aristocracy as well as a competent mathematician. He was responsible for a translation of Descartes's *Geometry* in 1647. Through correspondence with Montmor, he had learned of Huygens's letter describing Saturn's moon and the new pendulum clock, about which he hoped to know more. On 28 February, Montmor wrote Chapelain to request further information about the clocks so that he could inform d'Albert about their mechanism. See *OC*, 2:147–48. H. L. H. de Montmor to J. Chapelain, 28 February 1658.

24. *OC*, 2:342–43, Huygens to Du Gast, 5 February 1659. Louis Charles d'Albert intended to share the clocks with Madame la Duchesse de Chevreuse (his mother) and with three other important (but unnamed) people. The clockmaker building these was Solomon Coster.

25. Edwardes, *Story of the Pendulum Clock*, 39.

26. Details on his discovery of the cycloid's properties can be found in Joella Yoder, *Unrolling Time* (Cambridge: Cambridge University Press, 1988).

27. See J. H. Leopold, "The Longitude Timekeepers of Christiaan Huygens," in *The Quest for Longitude*, 102–14. Successful voyages in 1662 and 1664 were encouraging, but ultimately Huygens's pendulum clocks were not able to solve the longitude problem due to slight changes in the pendulum length (and therefore its swing) caused by the changing gravitational pull at different latitudes. Huygens, like others at the time, was unaware of this physical change in pendular length.

28. *OC*, 4:444. R. Moray to Huygens, 29 November 1663.

29. Thomas Birch, *The History of the Royal Society of London for Improving of Natural Knowledge*, ed. A. R. and M. B. Hall (London: Johnson Reprint, 1986), 2:23.

30. *OC*, 5:224. Huygens to R. Moray, 6 February 1665.

31. Huygens wrote to Moray in January 1665, "Concerning the pendulum clocks, you know I have obtained the privilege of the States-General, along with letters from the United Provinces of Holland. It protects against all use of the pendulum clocks at sea." *OC*, 5:186.

32. In a letter to Henry Oldenburg, the philosopher Spinoza also commented on the cost of the clocks: "I do know, that the workman [Oosterwijck] who alone has the right to make them, is giving up the manufacture altogether, because he cannot sell them; whether because of the interruption in commerce, or because he charges too much for them (for he values each at 300 Caroline florins) I do not know" (*The Correspondence of Henry Oldenburg*, ed. A. R. and M. B. Hall [Madison: University of Wisconsin Press, 1966], [hereafter *CHO*], 2:541).

33. Huygens actually started work on his instructions prior to hearing of Holmes's voyage, though Holmes's account provided even more stimulus for spreading the pamphlet.

34. Theoretical works on mechanics were common (Descartes, Mersenne, and Huygens all offering examples), but Huygens's *Kort Onderwijs* was entirely practical and expressly not theoretical. An example of something similar is Galileo's self-published work *Le operazioni del compasso geometrico e militare* (Padua, 1606). Galileo only printed sixty copies of the guide, which was given to those who purchased his compass.

35. Huygens quotes Van Nierop's endorsement: "In this matter, I would esteem most praiseworthy the new clocks invented by the honorable Christiaen Huygens of Zuylichem, which are regulated by the weight of a pendulum in stead of by a balance and concerning which I have been informed by worthy men of faith that they are capable of measuring the time with great exactitude over weeks and nearly over months; I support the above, I advance with confidence that one would receive a great advantage in employing these clocks; I esteem myself that at even the tossing about of the ship would not be an obstacle and one would arrive practically at the resolution of the problem of finding longitude of the east and west" (*OC*, 17:203).

36. Examples of practical Dutch guides to mathematics, cartography and instrumentation from the period include Adrien Metius, *Manuale arithmetic[a]e & geometri[a]e practic[a]e: in het welcke beneffens de stockrekeninge ofte Rabdologia J. Nepperi, cortelijck en[de] duydelic 't gene den land-meters en[de] ingenieurs* ... (Amsterdam: Henderick Laurentsz., 1634); idem, *Astronomische ende geographische onderwysinghe* (Amsterdam: Hendrick Lauwerensz, 1632); Dirck Rembrantz van Nierop, *Des aertrycks beweging en de sonne stilstant . . . Met noch verscheyden Aenmerckingen, soo van de vindingh der length van Oost en West* . . . (Amsterdam: Gerrit van Goedesbergh, 1661); and Willem Janszoon Blaeu, *Het Licht der Zeevaerdt* (Amsterdam: Willem Janszoon, 1608).

37. *OC*, 5:246. Huygens to J. Chapelain, February 1665.

38. When the Royal Society's Robert Moray heard about Huygens's efforts to personally instruct these men he was hardly surprised by the fact that they found Huygens's clocks difficult and (one must assume) not worth their effort. See *OC*, 5:322. R. Moray to Huygens, 10 April 1665: "Je ne trouve nullement estrange que les gens de mer chez vous sont difficiles a mettre en pratique l'invention des Horologes pour la longitude."

39. *OC*, 17:202–4.

40. According to John Leopold, this is the first such chart to be calculated specifically for use with a clock (J. H. Leopold, "The Longitude Timekeepers of Christiaan Huygens," in *The Quest for Longitude*, 114). For more on this table, see *OC*, 18:50–52; Mahoney, "Measurement of Time and Longitude," 234–70n.33; and John Heilbron, *The Sun in the Church* (Cambridge: Harvard University Press, 1999), 175–279.

41. *OC*, 5:224. Huygens to R. Moray, 6 February 1665: "J'avois desia resolu de faire publier par nos gazettes qu'on les exposoit en vente." It is unclear which particular gazettes Huygens was referring to, and the matter is not raised in correspondence again.

42. *Philosophical Transactions*, 6 March 1664/5, 14.

43. *OC*, 5:268–69. R. Moray to Huygens, 13 March 1665.

44. Henry Oldenburg wrote to Robert Moray in October 1665 about the fact that the pendulum clocks were being doubted even among Dutch navigators. While he doesn't expressly say that the English shared those doubts, it is implicit in his letter. See *CHO*, 2:549–50. Oldenburg to Moray, 7 October 1665.

45. *CHO*, 2:459. Huygens to H. Oldenburg, 26 June 1669.

46. *OC*, 5:425. J. Chapelain to Huygens, 31 July 1665. "Matters of fact" and the way they are established through the proper kind of witnessing are discussed by Steven Shapin and Simon Schaffer in *Leviathan and the Air Pump* (Princeton: Princeton University Press, 1985).

47. *OC*, 6:440. Huygens to H. Oldenburg, 29 May 1669: "I translated [the *Brief Instructions*] into French a long time ago with some slight changes, but I have never thought it necessary to have it printed, which will be done after one is satisfied with the trials. The people we are sending to America for that purpose will not leave for six weeks or two months, so that we are still very far from having news of success."

48. *OC*, 5:241. Huygens to R. F. de Sluse, 24 February 1665.

49. *OC*, 5:315. R. F. Sluse to Huygens, 27 March 1665. On 10 April he wrote to Huygens that he received the book but had had little time to examine it fully.

50. *OC*, 5:309. J. Hudde to Huygens, 5 April 1665. Claas Hendricksz Gietermaker was an instructor of mathematics and navigation for the East India Company. His book *Het Vergulde Licht der Zeevaart* (The Golden Art of Navigation) was the primary sourcebook for seamen in the Low Countries until the eighteenth century. See *OC*, 5:304n.1; and *Adresboek Nederlandse Drukkers en Boekverkopers tot 1700*, ed. J. A. Gruys and Jan Bos (The Hague: Koninklijke Bibliotheek, 1999), 62.

51. *OC*, 3:115. J. Chapelain to Huygens, 26 August 1660; and *OC*, 3:120, Huygens to J. Chapelain, 2 September 1660.

52. *OC*, 3:411. J. Chapelain to Huygens, 20 December 1661.

53. For just a few examples of Chapelain's persistence see *OC*, 4:154. J. Chapelain to Huygens, 15 June 1662; *OC*, 5:111. J. Chapelain to Huygens, 5 September 1664; *OC*, 5:233. J. Chapelain to Huygens, 13 February 1665; *OC*, 5:263. J. Chapelain to Huygens, 10 March 1665.

54. *OC*, 18:29, 34. Muguet, the printer, worked at the sign of the Three Kings in Paris from 1658 to 1702. In 1661 he became printer ordinary to the king and in 1664 printer to the archbishop of Paris. See Henri-Jean Martin, *Print, Power, and People in 17th-Century France*, trans. David Gerard (Metuchen, N.J.: Scarecrow, 1993), 493.

55. Christiaan Huygens, *Horologium Oscillatorium* (Paris: F. Muget, 1673), sig. ij–iij.

56. On dedicatory prefaces, see Robert Westman, "Proofs, Poetics, and Patronage: Copernicus' Preface to *De revolutionibus*," in *Reappraisals of the Scientific Revolution*, ed. David Lindberg and Robert S. Westman (Cambridge: Cambridge University Press, 1990), 167–206; and Gerard Genette, *Paratexts: Thresholds of Interpretation*, trans. Jane E. Lewin (Cambridge: Cambridge University Press, 1997), 117–34.

57. A closer study of Huygens's relationship to both the Crown and the Low Countries during this war would shed light on the cultural and political meaning of patronage in periods of national conflict. Huygens, despite his ties to the king of France, continued to write letters to family in 1672 and 1673 wherein he expressed pleasure at hearing of military successes against French forces. See, for example, *OC*, 7:181, Huygens to Lodwijck, 1 July 1672. See also *OC*, 7:191, from 8 July 1672; *OC*, 7:193–95, from 15 July 1672, where Huygens discusses his safety with Lodewijck; and *OC*, 7:365, from 22 September 1673, when Huygens writes of his happiness to hear that William III's troops have taken the French garrison at Naarden.

58. For the dynamics of the broker-client-patron relationship, see Sharon Kettering, *Patrons, Brokers and Clients in Seventeenth Century France* (New York: Oxford University Press, 1986), chap. 2, as well as Roger Chartier, "Princely Patronage and the Economy of Dedication," in *Forms and Meanings* (Philadelphia: University of Pennsylvania Press, 1995), 25–42.

59. Christiaan Huygens, *Horologium Oscillatorium* (Paris: F. Muget, 1673), sig., ij.

60. Huygens, *Horologium Oscillatorium*, 1.

61. Ibid., 2.

62. Ibid., 2.

63. *OC*, 2:522. Huygens to Fr. van Schooten, 6 December 1659. See also *OC*, 17:100. In addition to a rough description, Huygens gave his clockmakers the formula for determining the length of the pendulum, and then showed them how to use that length to construct the cycloidal cheeks.

64. Huygens, *Horologium Oscillatorium*, 2. Emphasis added.

65. Ibid., 3.

66. The technical drawing was an important part of the communication in a book, intended to accompany the text, but also to stand alone and represent the instrument (a clock in this case) without words. See *Picturing Machines 1400–1700*, ed. Wolfgang Lefèvre (Cambridge: MIT Press, 2004); and Paolo Galluzzi, "Portraits of Machines in Fifteenth-Century Siena," in *Non-Verbal Communication in Science Prior to 1900*, ed. Renato Mazzolini (Florence: Leo S. Olschki, 1993), 53–90. While Galluzzi focuses on Renaissance drawings and the manner in which technical illustrations were emancipated from texts, a similar issue is raised in Shapin and Schaffer's *Leviathan and the Air Pump* where they emphasize the accuracy of the air pump sketches as integral to the process of "virtual witnessing." See especially chapter 7.

67. Compared to other discussions of the cycloid by Huygens's mathematical peers, his explanation of the curve in this part of his work can be characterized as simplistic. His aim in

this section is to give the reader a sense of the basic shape of the curve and how it is generated, not to explain its mathematical properties or its construction based on mathematical principles. For a history of the cycloid in the seventeenth century, see E. A. Whitman, "Some Historical Notes on the Cycloid," *American Mathematical Monthly* 50, no. 5 (1943): 309–15. On the importance of mathematical diagrams for different readers see John Roche, "The Semantics of Graphics," in *Non-Verbal Communication in Science Prior to 1900*, ed. Renato G. Mazzolini (Florence: Olschki, 1993), 233.

68. Huygens, *Horologium Oscillatorium*, 28–29.

69. Huygens does not specifically request reviews by these journals, but he does send copies to individuals affiliated with them, such as Henry Oldenburg, Gottfried Wilhelm Leibniz, and Guiseppe Campani.

70. *Journal des Sçavans* (1664), 157.

71. *Codices Hugeniorum* 2, 437. Because Johann De Witt is on the list, we can ascertain that Huygens wrote it prior to publication, since De Witt died in 1672. This reinforces the notion that these lists were thought out ahead of time, rather than simply a record of what had transpired ex post facto.

72. After dedicating his *Systema Saturnium* (1659) to Leopold, Huygens was left waiting for over a year to hear a response from the prince. In part this was because of Leopold's reticence regarding Huygens's theory of Saturn's ring, but it was also due to lingering concern over Huygens's claims of priority for the pendulum clock. Just before Huygens sent Leopold a copy of the 1673 *Horologium*, the two once again exchanged letters about Galileo's model for such a clock, and whether it was equivalent to what Huygens had developed. See OC, 7:279–80, Huygens to Leopold de' Medici, 22 May 1673, and OC, 7:281–86.

73. OC, 9:674–75. Huygens to H. Oldenburg, 31 May 1673.

74. OC, 7:304. H. Oldenburg to Huygens, 12 June 1673.

75. OC, 7:325–26. Is. Newton to H. Oldenburg, 3 July 1673. Newton's copy, with Huygens's personal dedication, can be found in the library of Trinity College, Cambridge.

76. Huygens, *Cosmotheros* (The Hague: Adrian Moetjens, 1698), preface.

"Patron of Infidelity"

Scottish Readers Respond to David Hume, c. 1750–c. 1820

Mark R. M. Towsey

On 5 February 1762, the Duchess of Atholl wrote to her son about how much she was looking forward to reading the latest volumes of David Hume's *History of England* (1754–62). She admitted being "very well entertained" by what she had "already read of his historical writings," and added that the latest releases had been "very well spoke of" in the critical press.[1] She was not to be disappointed, reporting back to her son on 2 March: "I am just now reading Mr. Hume's History of England, and am more entertained and more instructed (that is to say, I can form more distinct notions, and retain them better in my memory of what were the transactions, laws and customs of the earliest times of this island) than I ever was by any history of England I have read formerly; were you to read it, I'm persuaded you would think your time very well bestowed."[2]

The duchess's comments reveal a great deal about what David Hume could mean to Scottish readers. He was not just to be admired for his "very pretty style and fine language," but he was also regarded as an edifying authority in the Atholl household, held in high enough trust by the matriarch of the family to be recommended to the son that was destined to inherit one of the greatest titles in Scotland.[3] Even so, there was an important note of caution in her commendation of Hume, for though she admired "his style" greatly, she maintained she "should be still fonder of him, did he not show so strong an inclination upon all occasions to have a fling at the clergy, be their profession what it will."[4]

Hume was a ubiquitous presence in libraries throughout eighteenth-cen-

---

I would like to thank David Allan, Warren McDougall, and the anonymous *Book History* reviewer for their comments on an earlier draft of this paper. The Edinburgh Bibliographical Society allowed me to try out some of the arguments in a paper delivered to the society in autumn 2007, and I am grateful for the feedback they provided. I thank the staff of the Glasgow University Library, the National Archives of Scotland, and the National Library of Scotland for allowing me to quote from sources in their custody, and to the owner of NRAS 234 for granting me permission to view the papers in his possession. Finally, I acknowledge the financial assistance provided by a doctoral research award from the Arts and Humanities Research Council.

tury Scotland. His *History of England* was the most widely distributed title of any work by a Scottish author and performed consistently well at every library for which borrowing records survive.[5] Meanwhile, the *Essays and Treatises* (1752) were among the most readily available philosophical books in the country, offering readers a digest of his most significant writing on moral philosophy, literature, politics, and religion—so that despite the notoriously poor performance of the *Treatise of Human Nature*, most Scottish readers who were willing to do so could cast judgment on his controversial views for themselves.[6] However, it is only through surviving evidence of their reading experiences that we can tell whether they really took advantage of this publishing strategy and engaged with Hume's philosophy on their own terms. Commonplace books, marginalia, journals, and personal correspondence demonstrate what Hume meant to readers, how well his ideas were understood, and why his writings were considered a good use of time by many readers less affluent than the Duchess of Atholl.

Of course, the use of such sources in developing an empirical approach to the history of reading is by no means unproblematic.[7] Though they do allow us to glimpse the "hows" and "whys" of individual reading experiences, in Robert Darnton's influential phraseology, they are limited in what they can tell us about the wider world of reading.[8] Innumerably more acts of reading have taken place in the past that were never committed to paper, not to mention the written responses to books that have been lost or that still lie undiscovered in the closed collections of private libraries. We must therefore be wary of reading too much into our limited evidence. The variable sophistication of the dozen readers surveyed here, coupled with the small size of the sample, makes it difficult to draw meaningful generalizations about how Hume was read in eighteenth-century Scotland. Nevertheless, the case studies that follow illuminate the ways in which readers in Scotland could respond to Hume, even though we have no way of knowing if their attitudes to his works—which usually ranged from passive suspicion to outright resistance—were representative of the larger Scottish reading public.

Perhaps the best illustration of Hume's impact on the lives and thoughts of individual readers can be found in the reading notes of the youth of Scotland—such as law student David Boyle of Sherralton (1772–1853), who eventually became Lord President of the Court of Session.[9] Boyle read Hume's *History* when still a teenager over the autumn and winter of 1788–89, with his notes restricted exclusively to the Stuart volumes.[10] It may be that he kept notes on the earlier volumes in separate notebooks, though we have no evidence that he actually read any period before 1603. It is equally conceivable that his focus on the Stuarts was deliberately intended as a personal commemoration of the momentous Revolution of 1688–89, whose centenary coincided so neatly with his reading of Hume and whose Whiggish sentiments he wholeheartedly condoned. We know from the surviving records of a number of book-lending institutions in contemporary Scotland that such selectivity was common among Scottish readers of Hume's *History*. In the early years of the Wigtown Subscription Library, founded in the southwest corner of Scotland in September 1795, Hume's *History* was one of the most regularly borrowed titles of any genre—outstripping the *Monthly Review,* Johnson's *Lives of the British Poets,* a number of popular travel books, and a host of bestselling novels. Very few members borrowed every volume of Hume's *History,* however, and the Stuart volumes clearly emerged as the most popular. Similarly, the tenth volume of Cadell's twelve-volume duodecimo edition of 1793–94, which covered the crucial years of the Civil War up to the trial and execution of Charles I, was borrowed by more individuals than any other at the School Wynd Congregational Library in Dundee in the 1820s, and the Stuart volumes also emerged as the most popular in borrowing data from the Gray Library in Haddington between 1804 and 1816.[11]

David Boyle's commonplace book reveals first and foremost how Hume's *History* functioned as a comprehensive guide to English history for a young man on the make, giving him a directory of basic information that he could later deploy in an eminent career in the Scottish law courts, or simply in polite conversation. Boyle would no doubt have been familiar with the vast literature on reading history, and followed the advice of writers like Thomas Sheridan, who recommended that young readers of history make an "abstract of each reign . . . taking notice only of the most material facts, without entering into the spirit of the parties, politics, or intrigues of the times." This method, Sheridan argued, was best suited to render history "useful . . . to all who are to be legislators, or concerned in the management of public affairs."[12] Accordingly, Boyle only rarely chose to quote his source directly, preferring instead to note in sequential order summaries of Hume's text. From the third chapter of Hume's account of the reign of Charles I, Boyle noted

> Peace with France and Spain . . . Sir Charles [sic] Wentworth, a Puritan, became the King's chief favourite and was created Earl of Strafford. The superstitious ceremonies which Laud Bishop of London wished to introduce approached very near to those of Rome. Violent and illegal exactions of the crown, without the authority of any Parliament. Journey of Charles into Scotland 1633. Pretended affection to him in all his subjects. A Parliament held in Scotland. Ship money levied. Violent prosecutions and sentences of the

star chamber. The Puritans restrained in England emigrated to America."[13]

In this manner, Boyle gave himself a basic though fairly detailed abridgement of Hume's original narrative that he could consult time and again. At particularly critical junctures in Whig historiography (such as the Scottish Covenant, Stafford's trial, and Charles I's notorious raid on the House of Commons), Boyle quoted or summarized Hume at much greater length. Very rarely did he impose his own value judgments on events: he was generally happy to take Hume's interpretations on trust. This compliant treatment of Hume's complex and often controversial text also extended to elements that had little relevance for Boyle's understanding of British politics, including Hume's extended commentaries on developments in literature, agriculture, and industry—confirming that Boyle's objective was basic education. A note on Hume's appendix to the reign of James I explained that there had been "Improvement in the art of Agriculture during this reign—a bad taste in learning prevailed in England, of which James himself was by no means free. Shakespeare died, in 1617 [sic] aged 53 years. He undoubtedly possessed a fine genius, but wanted the polish of the finer arts."[14] Boyle thus used Hume's *History* to understand where modern Britain had come from, entirely in line with contemporary advice that history should be read to inform students' understanding of modern society.[15] This included, alongside modern party politics and the diplomatic and political map of Europe, an understanding of English literature before the Enlightenment.

In the process, Boyle also used Hume's *History* to rationalize momentous events in the modern world. Following a note that Strafford "defends himself with ability innocent of high treason," for instance, Boyle (apparently already considering his prospective legal career) commented in brackets that "the commons proceeded against him in the same way as they are now managing Hastings trial."[16] Boyle also found a teleological explanation for the separation of Britain's North American colonies in the annals of the reign of James I, copying Hume's observation that "doubts arose to some men in those days that these colonies would in future periods shake off the yoke of the mother country and establish their own independency." As Boyle commented, "*although Mr Hume did not live to see that period, yet the event has truly verified the opinions of those men.*"[17] Boyle was too young to remember the political events of the 1760s and 1770s, and may have identified in such seventeenth-century prophesies a neat way of rationalizing what was already a fact of life. Hume, our reader tacitly acknowledged, had been wrong to conclude in the 1750s that "time has shewn, that the views, entertained by those who encouraged such generous undertakings, were more just and solid. A mild government and great naval force have preserved, and may still preserve during some time, the dominion of England over her colonies."[18]

Hume's controversial account of the Stuarts may also have served to consolidate Boyle's nascent Whiggish instincts. Boyle thought that Hume had been "unable altogether to conceal his partiality for the Royal cause, which ... ought to be guarded against by every honest and candid historian." This Whig reading of Hume's political agenda, carefully considered over a six-month period, and reflecting widespread disaffection among Scottish readers generally over Hume's partiality as a historian, was further reflected at critical points in Boyle's note-taking.[19] In response to Hume's account of the "very small" supply to Charles I by Parliament in 1625, he added his own critical gloss: "How far this conduct of Parliament ... considering the necessities of the state was either kind or dutiful to their sovereign I shall not pretend to affirm. But it certainly is owing to their method of proceeding and other circumstances, that we now enjoy this state of civil liberty."[20]

But despite these political differences, Boyle was sufficiently able to detach himself from his Whiggish sensibilities to judge Hume's narrative on its own merits, striving hard to adopt the critical disposition that was so strongly encouraged in eighteenth-century readers.[21] For all his undue partiality for the Royalist cause, Boyle wrote, "Upon the whole ... Mr Hume has maintained all the requisite dignity of an historian," and he refused to let Hume's politics sour his reading experience of the *History*. He felt "Mr Hume gives a very just and striking tho dreadful account" of the Irish rebellion in 1641, for example, and praised Hume's "great character" of Charles I—the mortal enemy of the Whig party.[22] Thus, as a historian of party politics, Hume seems to have succeeded, notwithstanding Boyle's censure of his *History* on party grounds.[23] Boyle acknowledged that Hume's narrative illuminated the "wonderful degree of party spirit displayed on both sides" and condemned "that pretended sanctity under the veil of the deepest hypocrisy" that influenced men of all parties under the Stuarts, further reflecting that it "is most astonishing how easily were the people in those days deluded by the most glaring absurdities." Ultimately, Boyle concluded that "the greatest of men have had their faults": Hume had let his politics get the better of him on occasion, but this was merely a reflection of humanity's imperfection.[24] In this, he reflected the vast weight of fair-minded critical opinion that (in the words of Philip Hicks) rated Hume's *History* "as a literary achievement [and] as a source of national honour for having solved the chronic problem in English historiography."[25] Even in faraway India, James Forbes, an expatriate Scot, highlighted Hume's alleged Toryism but grudgingly admitted that "the work afforded me a very high pleasure and much improvement in the perusal."[26]

* * *

A more mature reader who treated Hume as a source for classical *sententiae* was the anonymous compiler of a commonplace book now held in the Innes of Stowe collection in the National Archives of Scotland. Given its provenance, it is probable that the reader was a relative of the fabulously wealthy banker Gilbert Innes, perhaps even Innes himself, and the notes appear to have been compiled in the 1790s when Innes was in his late forties. The approach is nothing if not conventional: using Bell's 1770 edition of Locke's printed commonplace book, Innes compiled notes from many different books under a wide range of subject headings—including standard topics of eighteenth-century moral philosophy like *virtue, courage, liberty,* and *reason*—and he produced a manuscript index.[27]

Innes's entries were actually highly constrained by the generic elements of commonplacing. Rather than offering a real sense of how he regarded Hume, his notes were driven more by a search for pithy phrases and memorable aphorisms.[28] There are some notes whose significance is entirely irrecoverable: they may simply have been included because they amused or entertained him. This must surely be the context of a note on "the English," which appends an anecdote from Addison's *Freeholder* confirming their fondness for puddings: "David Hume relating the manner in which Henry the 8th gifted the revenues of the convents says, 'he was so profuse in these liberalities that he is said to have given a woman the whole revenue of a convent, as a reward for making a pudding which happened to gratify his palate.'"[29]

Other notes apparently reflect an interest in current affairs, such as this one on the "Irish," probably in the context of the union of 1800: "So great is the ascendance, which, from a long course of success, the English have acquired over the Irish nation that . . . they have never in this own country been able to make any vigorous effort for the defence or recovery of their libertys." Many more notes seem applicable to events in France in the 1790s: Innes compiled maxims on "change" from at least four separate volumes of the *History*. An early note reflected the optimism with which the French Revolution was first received in Britain: "in the beginnings of reformation . . . the benefit resulting from the change is slow effect of time, and is seldom perceived by the bulk of the nation." However, Innes may have been quickly disillusioned, since other notes highlighted the negative effects of revolution: "a violent revolution, however necessary, can never be effected without great discontents"; "'Tis seldom that the people gain anything by revolutions in government; because the new settlement, jealous and insecure, must consequently be supported with more expence and severity than the old."[30] All these were easily memorable phrases which Innes probably noted down so that he could later recycle them in polite conversation as evidence of his own wide reading and sound judgment.

Religion also features prominently throughout the Innes commonplace book. An extensive passage on "saints" in which Hume ridiculed the ignorance of the Scottish reformers may have been included for its entertaining punch line.[31] Another on "women" might have served as a suitably sardonic instance of Hume's notorious disrespect for organized religion: "DH tells us that the fair sex have had the merit of introducing the Christian doctrine into all the most considerable kingdoms of the saxon heptarchy."[32] These occasional notes on the deleterious effects of religious extremism (which more devout readers usually greeted with howls of protest) probably reflected a serious effort by Innes to embrace Enlightenment religious toleration—or at least ensured that his conversation reflected such sentiments with apparent effortlessness.[33] Under the heading "disputes" he noted the glib sound bite that "the more affinity there is between theological parties, the greater commonly is their animosity," while a much longer comment aptly demonstrated the potential impact of such "disputes":

> David Hume discussing the reigns of Philip & Mary says, it is needless to be particular in enumerating all the horrid cruelties practiced in England during the course of three years that these persecution lasted: the savage barbarity on the one hand, & the patient constancy on the other are so similar in all these martyrdoms that the narration, very little agreeable in itself would never be relieved by any variety. Human nature appears not, on any occasion so detestable, and at the same time so absurd, as in these religious persecutions, which sink men below infernal spirits in wickedness, & below the beast in folly. A few instances only may be worth preserving in order if possible to warn zeal bigots forever to avoid such odious & such fruitless barbarity.[34]

In fact, Hume provided Innes with a complete collection of maxims to learn and repeat. One spoke to a problem that had long been a preoccupation of rhetoricians and political theorists: "the spirit of faction when it becomes inveterate is very difficult for any man entirely to shake off." Another note addressed the thorny contemporary problem of pensions and bribes, which, Hume had argued, "are dangerous expedients for government; and cannot be too vehemently decried by everyone who has a regard to the virtue and liberty of a nation." Innes also took down vacuous truisms: "where great evils lie on all sides, it is very difficult to follow the best counsel," and "words are often more offensive than actions."[35] There is little sense that Innes actually subscribed in any depth to such sentiments, and at no time did he introduce his own independent commentary on the notes he extracted.

A far more thoughtful approach to Hume was taken by the Reverend William Cameron. Cameron had studied under Hume's bitter opponent James Beattie at Marischal College, Aberdeen, and continued to correspond with him after his presentation to the parish of Kirknewton, outside Edinburgh, in August 1786.[36] As such, one might expect Cameron to have been a belligerent and unresponsive reader of Hume,[37] but his commonplace book actually represents the most intensive reading experience of Hume's philosophy yet uncovered for eighteenth-century Scotland, in which the Great Infidel was treated with as much decorum and respect as such conventional authorities as Hugh Blair, Samuel Johnson, and Vicessimus Knox.[38] Cameron proceeds sequentially through a posthumous edition of Hume's *Essays and Treatises*, commenting on nearly every essay in volumes 1 and 4 (the essays that originally constituted the *Essay Moral, Political and Literary* [1742] and *Political Discourses*). He summarizes Hume's arguments, fairly in most instances, and occasionally quoting directly. A close comparison of Cameron's notes and the original text makes clear that he reflected seriously and independently on many of the issues raised by Hume in extemporaneous discussion and critical comment—more so than Innes did.

Cameron focused particularly on Hume's discussion of "the Delicacy of Taste and Passion," reflecting both his sensitivity to advice on reading and his special interest in the workings of taste as an aspiring poet in his own right.[39] He first summarized Hume's key terms to establish the parameters of the argument: "Delicacy of Taste is a desirable accomplishment & production of refind and exquisite pleasure. Delicacy of passion is a misfortune & production of more pain than pleasure as the more common incidents of life are too gross & unsatisfactory to yield pure delight." In just a few lines he distilled in his own words Hume's prescription for good taste: "a man of refined taste & improved understanding must lay his account with meeting few persons & few incidents in life that can yield him pleasure without a mixture of base alloy. This will serve to guard him against the pain of disappointment & to blunt his too refin'd delicacy of passions so as to make him more indifferent with regard to such objects."

On the related topic of the "Rise and Progress of the Arts and Sciences," Cameron quoted Hume nearly word for word: "when the arts & sciences arrive at perfection in any state they naturally & necessarily that moment begin to decline & never can again revive in the same nation." He clearly agreed with Hume on this point, following up with his own observation that "the arts & sciences require a fresh soil to revive in. . . . Newton checked the progress of mathematical learning in Britain by his supreme excellence which extinguished emulation."[40]

Hume also provided thought-provoking advice on one of a parish minister's key responsibilities, the delivery of sermons. That much is evident from his comments on the essay "Of Eloquence," which are by far his longest and most detailed notes from Hume. Cameron's own experience no doubt had taught him that "plain sense & logical argument properly expressed... is not suited to a popular audience," and that "good sense, a lively imagination, self-command, an ardent zeal with the natural expression of an expert speaker tho' not the most correct qualify much better for addressing a promiscuous multitude." To Hume's argument that "tho a laboured style of language in oratory is not to be too minutely studied, yet method & order in argument is to be attended to as of essential importance," Cameron added his own reflection that "If the memory cannot command this exactly it may be assisted by a few notes which will relieve fear & anxiety which tend so fatally to damp the spirit of the orator." Indeed, Cameron seemed particularly eager to prove himself a critical reader on this point, adding the further note, based on his own years of experience, that "almost daily practice in his art is necessary to finish the orator & it requires him to speak some considerable time before he can reach the proper pitch & key of true eloquence."[41]

Cameron generally treated Hume with utmost respect. He even avoided censuring directly Hume's treatment of organized religion, perhaps in deference to contemporary standards of politeness.[42] Yet his tacit disapproval of Hume's irreligion is nonetheless evident. On noting Hume's argument that "superstition [will] ... promote the due fear of both civil & rel: authority," for instance, Cameron inserted a snide aside about "the tendency of sceptical philosophy to destroy the power of both." More dramatically, he launched a sustained attack on Hume's account of the violence of the early Church: "Hume says here that the persecution raised against the first Christians was owing to the violence instilled into their followers—but this violence if it was so is not the spirit of true Christianity but the reverse owing to the abuse of it. Christianity neither provokes nor inculcates in the least degree the spirit of persecution. It was the rage of system & disputation borrow'd from phil'y that corrupted Chr'y & raised party-spirit & the violence of faction in the church."[43] Hume had earlier suggested that "as philosophy was widely spread over the world, at the time when Christianity arose, the teachers of the new sect were obliged to form a system of speculative opinions," and in this instance Cameron ingeniously turned the argument around to blame philosophy for the corruption of the early Church—in the process, alluding to the destructive power of Hume's own skepticism.[44]

Cameron's belligerent treatment of Hume provides us with a rare opportunity to connect personal reading experiences with writing and publishing. Soon after these notes were compiled (probably in the mid-1780s, though Cameron did not date them), Cameron published at Edinburgh a collection called *Poetical Dialogues on Religion in the Scots Dialect* (1789). In the last dialogue in the collection, Cameron created a character named Hippolitus who seemed to represent what he saw as the Humean position on religion:

> Religion, I agree with H——,
> Has wrought more bloodshed, fire and fume,
> Than fiercest tyrants e'er atchiev'd
> Than fellest furies e'er conceiv'd.
> A bugbear, clear, I hold her law,
> The stupid vulgar mob to awe.

In response, Cameron has a character called Theophilus replay his attack on Hume's irreligion in still more extreme terms than he had earlier used in the privacy of his own commonplace book. Theophilus does not deny that many crimes have been committed in the name of religion, and acknowledges that it was actually superstition which was Hume's real target. Nevertheless, he insists once more that Hume (the "infidel") has gone far too far, with religion caught in the crossfire by Hume's assault on superstition:

> The abuse you mean, I ne'er pretend
> Or to deny or to defend;
> But 'tis a bold and impious crime,
> To brand Religion's pow'r sublime,
> Because a fiend assumes her name,
> And wastes the world with sword and flame.
> As aim'd at Superstition's heart,
> The infidel directs his dart;
> And while his shafts at random fly,
> He wounds Religion standing nigh,
> Confounds them in his parallel,
> Tho' differing wide as heaven and hell.[45]

This published version of Cameron's attack on Hume is far more developed than his earlier reading notes, reflecting the importance he attached to understanding and refuting Hume's most obnoxious pronouncements. In fact, it is remarkable that Cameron was not more scandalized by Hume's notorious views on organized religion when we examine his notes from the *Essays and Treatises* in their proper context. They were immediately preceded in Cameron's commonplace book by passages on "heresies of the first century" and on "the proofs of the divinity of the Scripture," as well as notes from "Barclay's Apology" and "Neiker's Religious Opinions."[46] Moreover, Cameron interrupted his notes on Hume to record a page of "Scriptural Expressions," perhaps as an antidote to readings like the one quoted above, a vital reminder of the devotional bases of his faith to anchor his progress through the dangerous realm of Hume's skepticism.[47]

In fact Cameron's responses to Hume's *Essays* were probably conditioned, however subconsciously, by critical assessments widely disseminated in the public domain. Hume was generally held in very high esteem by professional reviewers who patrolled standards of taste in eighteenth-century Britain. One of the *Monthly Review*'s most prolific critics, William Rose, was typical in arguing that "if we consider them [the works of Hume] in one view, as sprightly and ingenious compositions, . . . there is a delicacy of sentiment, an original turn of thought, a perspicuity, and often an elegance, of language, that cannot but recommend his writings to every Reader of taste."[48] Such sentiments encouraged readers like Cameron to set aside their concerns about what another reviewer called Hume's "singular . . . notions of religion" to appreciate his wider achievements in polite letters.[49]

Nevertheless, some reviewers became increasingly wary of Hume's treatment of religion, particularly in its impact on his tremendously popular *History*. Roger Flexman, in the *Monthly Review*, went so far as to warn that Hume's "treatment . . . of every denomination of Christians [in the first volume, reviewed in March 1755] . . . is far from being such as becomes a gentleman, and may, we apprehend, prejudice his reputation *even as a historian*, in the opinion of many intelligent and considerate readers."[50] While reviewers of subsequent volumes tended to be "most flattering" in their praise for Hume's *History*,[51] some readers could not see beyond Hume's reputation as the great skeptic of modern British literature and took immediate offence to his apparent lack of respect for their beliefs.

In this regard, the most remarkable reading experiences so far uncovered are the "reflections" on Hume's *History* that pepper a series of commonplace books entitled "Amusements in Solitude."[52] The notes are anonymous, and identification of their compiler has so far proved elusive. However, the compiler was certainly a mature reader, often reporting conversations with younger friends with an air of self-confident condescension, and at one point transcribing her own letter to "My dear young souldiers—To my Beloved Nephews." I write "her," because the tone of this letter, along with the handwriting and a number of textual clues, strongly suggests that the compiler was a woman.[53]

Whoever she was, her strength of religious feeling shines throughout the three commonplace books that have survived. Her pious response to returning to church after a long absence in April 1779 was typical ("we forget that this world is not our Home—that we are only passing thro it to an eternal state") and deeply devotional outbursts litter her reading notes. The reader repeatedly contrasts her own piety with the "pride and vanity" of modern philosophy, especially in her initial reaction to an unnamed book that she "thought a wild goose chase in quest of the origin of evil thro the mazes of philosophic reasoning; where pride and vanity often lurks; and dazzles the mental eye, with a false, flare of light; was but a fruitless pastime at my time of life."[54] And one particularly offensive modern philosopher—David Hume—dominates her commonplace books.

The signs are initially propitious. Our anonymous reader praises the utility of history in terms remarkably reminiscent of Hume's essay "Of the Study of History," "as one of the most usefull Entertainments of a rational Mind." However, her view of history quickly diverges from Hume in fundamental terms:

> It is not a Knowledge of facts merely, that affords me Delight. It's the arrangements of facts in such order, as enables me to Trace out the great Sovereign Lord of the universe ruleing [sic] amongst the Kingdoms of Men; as the Moral Governour [sic] of Rational Creatures: amongst whom he both Established a Decree, that Righteousness Exalteth a Nation, but vice, & wickedness, is the ruin of any people. With this view I read History, and if I don't find my mind improven [sic] in the Knowledge of right & wrong,—my Heart warmed with the Love of Moral Excellence, inspiring Sentiments of rational piety & virtue; the History affords me no Entertainment.[55]

Clearly, Hume's *History* did not meet the mark: "that celebrated author appears to me the most detestable—& contemptible Historian I ever Read.... Thro. two Quarto vol: in which is contain'd His History of the ancient Britons,—the Conquest of them by the Romans—Saxons—Danes—& Normans; there is not one anecdote to give the Mind Delight, or Lead to Rational Reflection." In this early period of English history, our reader found it astonishing that the historian could not find a better explanation for the development of organized religion as sponsored and supported by secular rulers. Her extended commentary on this topic exemplifies her sarcastic tone, as well as her note-taking style, recording her opinions on Hume rather than transcribing material directly from his original text:

> The original Cause he assigns, for a Legal Establishment of Clergy, is so outrage even in him, that it surprised me. I expected the com-

mon place Kinds, finely wrought up—viz. that Religion was a Necessary Tool for governing the vulgar, a Bridle for managing & leading them in Submission to the civil magistrate. But as this would have been a tacit Confession that Religion was useful & necessary to society, and a well regulated state, Hume considers it as not only useless, but dangerous. He observes, . . . the encouragement of Legal establishments to the Clergy is to make their activity needless—its to engage them to sink into indolence & ease, careless inattention in their business; for the less they do the better—is not this a very fine sensible account of the Reasons of state for a Legal Establishment of Clergy?[56]

Hume's account of the Reformation—an event our reader considered "one of the greatest event of History, the most usefull & salutary to mankind, introducing Truth, Liberty, with all the liberal arts & sciences, dispelling all the clouds of ignorance, error, superstition, moral and civil slavery"—proved even more vexing:

Nothing can be more shocking than what he expresses with regard to the Reformation. He owns it to be one of the greatest events in History; yet asserts reason had no share in it—for the philosophy had then made no way in Europe—what was this great Event owing to?—Reason is not allowed to have any share. A Divine interposition never comes within the limits of his plan—Fortune—chance—& nature—venerable names!—oft without meaning, are frequently found with him—But still, this great Event appears an Effect without a Cause; did not the passions, follies, & vices of mankind come to our authors assistance & finish the work.
Can anything be more absurd than this account?—Expressive of the most impious sentiments—devoid of common sense[57]

By all means, our reader frequently acknowledged Hume's reputation for literary excellence: "His extraordinary talents for History, I'm told, has enabled him to collect facts with the greatest accuracies & acuteness; to give them all the Grace of Eligant [sic] Language, adorn'd with the finest Diction—It may be so." But she begs to differ with the literary critics on the true role of Hume's literary skills. She suspects that Hume's elegant style served to hide pernicious lies behind a veneer of "wit and elegance." (Such comments are usually accompanied by sarcastic allusions to his ill-gotten celebrity.) In the example quoted above on the establishment of clergy, for instance, she concludes, "But strong is truth & it will prevail; in spite of such unphilosophic nonsencs, tho' adorn'd with all the Elegance of Mr

Hume's acute wit and Elegant Language. . . . Religion is that Divine Establishment by which we are taught to know & acknowledge our adorable Creator, the invisible God! . . . Clergy are the Established Teachers of piety & virtue." Hume's "Elegance" actually constitutes a horrifying betrayal in her eyes, causing pain akin to the rape of the heart, mind, and soul: "Alas! . . . the mind is not only starved by this Celebrated author; but the Heart is Hurt in all Her delicate feelings. The exercise of all her rational powers perverted."[58]

Many of the reflections on Hume recorded in "Amusements in Solitude" appear to have been precipitated by a dispute with a young friend who had stood up for the great skeptic, pointing out, quite reasonably to the modern reader, that "Mr Hume was not writing Divinity. History was his province." This response gets to the heart of the problem, and provokes an immediate and passionate retort from our anonymous reader:

> But the History of Rational, intelligent, immortal Creatures; the subjects of God—the great, the divine, moral governour [sic] of the universe can never be given with propriety, without a proper attention pay'd to religion. For religion is the distinguishing characteristic of Man; . . . Cut man of[f] from God, the Centre of Souls! What is he more than other Brutes that perish?—more wretched—more contemptible. This makes it Evident to me, that there is no being a Good Historian, without being so far a divine, as to have a Regard for Religion. And the juster his apprehensions of Sacred Truths are, the better he is accomplished for this office.[59]

It is in this crucial regard that "the Celebrated Hume has failed," for without acknowledging "the Divine Governour of the universe Directing this great Event making the wrath and folly of man to praise him; & their stormy passions fulfil his Councils," he reduces the history of mankind to the history of the beasts. "The war of the Cranes—or the Battle of the frogs is more instructive by far. The History of Tigers—Bares [sic]—wolfs & foxes; making wars upon herds of tamer Cattle & flocks of sheep; would make as good a figure & as improving an History in Mr Hume's Hand, as the History of England—indeed I imagine it would be a fitter subject for that author." The result, inevitably, is that his secular historiography has no inherent improving value: "The sentiments he inspires, is a contempt for Human nature—indignation—rancour—& painful feelings of Heart, without one Ray or balancing Hope, or Sublime consolation. . . . His mind is incapable of Distinguishing or relishing the true Sublime."[60]

The contrast with this reader's response to William Robertson's *History of America* (1777) could not have been sharper: "Dr Robertson's History of America has greatly entertained me. He has indeed unfolded a new world to my view—and tho' we cannot discover the place where—the time when—or the manner how, this new world has been peopled; yet we find by certain marks they bare that they are our Brethren." Whereas Hume had consistently caused offence, Robertson immediately engaged her interest and sympathy: "Robertson increases & strengthens my faith in Moses account of creation, & the history he gives of man, before & after the fall—confirms my belief of the necessity of a divine revelation, to restore human nature to purity & happiness; and the excellency of the Christian Religion for accomplishing that Glorious purpose."[61] This was what she expected to get out of history: "In America, we find mankind in that state of nature, into which man sunk & was reduced by his disobedience of the divine law . . . unenlightened by divine revelation, uncultivated & unimproved by human civilization . . . the Dust returns to the Dust." This was not the state of nature argued over by so many of eighteenth-century Europe's greatest minds ("of which we have heard so many fine things said by our philosophic geniuses"), but a state of nature that apparently corroborated the biblical account of man's fall. The prospect thrilled her: "I attended Columbus thro' the whole voyage with ardour. Hope & fear alternate rose—but when I heard the cry, land—Land!—my heart leap'd—tumultuous Joy roused every power—when we struck the shore of that new—that unknown world. . . . My soul took wing to the eternal world—the amazement of the sailors, seem'd to me a lively picture of our own souls."[62]

The "fallen" state of the native population of America may have consolidated this reader's faith in the story contained in the Old Testament, but Robertson's subsequent portrayal of the "depravity" of the Spanish conquest of America also had important implications for the way she saw the modern world. "The highest refinement of philosophic vanity—arts—science—government—wealth—liberty—peace—learning & luxury" may "polish and improve the human mind & manners, smoothing the boars skin," she conceded. "But alas! The seeds of vice springs up amidst the finest culture—this is woefully exemplified in the discoverers—conquerors & late possesours [sic] of this new world." She continued: "The state of the Americas affords a proof in fact of the necessity of a divine revelation; to introduce civilization amongst mankind, and the constant influence of a divine energy is what alone can carry it on to perfection. If we resist this grace, it will fly from us. If we neglect & despise the heavenly call of the father of lights!—he will forsake us, & leave us to ourselves—then woe must be our lot."[63]

Naturally enough, the compiler of "Amusements in Solitude" could not help drawing comparisons between Robertson and Hume: "Ah! Thought I—How amazed would the fine genius of D: H—e be to find all the sublime truths of Christianity; which he doubted of—despised, & neglected, as below the regard of philosophy." But it was not just her positive experience of other historians that made her berate Hume. His literary crimes weighed so heavily that she frequently returned to him, interspersing her comments on other books with further bitter reflections on Hume. The most apposite came in response to her reading of "Dr Owen on the Christian Doctrine," whom she found a great deal more edifying than Hume: "What could induce the virtuous Mr Hume to reflect the Holy Jesus as a Divine Teacher?"[64]

It is probably a good thing that the compiler of "Amusements in Solitude" never forced herself to endure Hume's philosophy more directly—at least as far as we can tell. The case of the minister of Stitchell in Berwickshire, Reverend George Ridpath, shows that Hume's skeptical philosophy could compromise responses to the *History* even for the most enlightened of provincial readers. Ridpath supported the *literati* on many of the key issues of the day, including their opposition to the motion to have Hume excommunicated from the Church of Scotland for his alleged atheism.[65] He had once breakfasted with Hume, and he wrote reverentially in his diary of the occasion when his friend "David" had treated him to a tour of the Advocates' Library, drawing his attention to "the collection of Medals, Ancient and Modern, and the Mummy."[66]

Even so, Ridpath could not condone Hume's views in the privacy of his own journal. He welcomed uncontroversial essays on taste and tragedy ("good philosophical criticism"), but his view of the essay on trade ("in this, as usual, he finds all the world mistaken but himself") was much more consistent with his wider take on Hume. He thought the *Natural History of Religion* was "entertaining and has curious things in it, but its tendency is very bad," while he was scandalized to report that "David Hume has got printed at London a Collection of Atheism which his bookseller Andrew Millar dares not sell." He correctly described the *Enquiry on the Passions* as "an attempt to elucidate and popularize part of the *Treatise of Human Nature*," but he nevertheless considered it "both very useless and still . . . very obscure."[67]

Ridpath's concern for Hume's dangerous association with atheism clearly influenced his subsequent reading of Hume's *History*—as was the case for so many of Hume's published critics.[68] "There are always entertaining things in him but not without a great mixture both of trifling and blundering" was Ridpath's characteristically pithy judgment immediately on borrowing the first two volumes from the Kelso Subscription Library. In a more carefully considered assessment, Ridpath pinpointed exactly what it was about Hume's *History* that so unsettled him, despite its "entertaining" literary style: "His account of James [II]'s reign and of the [Glorious] revolution is, in general, fair and candid, but the detail is often wanting that is sufficient to enable a man to judge for himself."[69] Ridpath's unwillingness to take Hume's *History* at face value anticipated recent historians' assessments of Hume's avowedly "impartial" approach to history, which most now agree was a thoroughgoing attempt to deconstruct the great myths of English political history—among which Whiggish accounts of the Glorious Revolution of 1688–89 loomed large.[70] Moreover, his distrust of Hume spilled over the pages of his diary into sociable encounters with friends, drinking companions, and fellow members of the Kelso Library. On one occasion, when another clergyman mentioned that he had been reading Hume's *History*, it became a topic of "much disputation" over dinner after a meeting at the library. On another, Ridpath reported a discussion of a critical review of Hume in which the ensemble agreed "he is treated severely enough, yet not more than he deserves."[71]

Ridpath's assessment of Hume as an untrustworthy historian was repeated in much more urgent terms by Hanna Hume (no relation), who was desperate to convert a daughter living in London away from her youthful and naïve enthusiasm for the *History*.[72] She first outlined some conventional criticisms: "what is called his history is allowed to be an apology for the family of the Stuarts & written for that purpose only. The great deceit in his book is that he does not distinguish between the constitution & administration & so supposes that whatever is done by the most wicked kings or ministers is constitution." Robertson was again cited to demonstrate in quite detailed terms "the falsity" of this position:

> It is certain that most of the kings before the Stuarts were as tyrannical as they but you who have read Robertson will easily account for their being so. When the king acted contrary to law, the people being little more than vassals were not able to oppose him & the barons supported him for the sake of supporting their own tyranny, but when he quarrelled with any of the powerful barons they pointed out his arbitrary proceedings & opposed him with arms & between them the people were constantly oppressed for the barons no more considered their good than the kings did. Notwithstanding this, the constitution was all the time quite free as appears not only from history & law books, most clearly but from express acts of Parliament then in force & repeatedly renewed in support of liberty & against arbitrary powers: laws could avail little against force. Thus things continued till by the civil wars most of the powerful barons were destroyed or had forfeited their estates[.] Liberty of selling their estates was then given them by using that & by other causes they lost their power which with their property fell into the hands of the people who became considerable enough to oppose

tyranny. How does it follow that because the kings were tyrants before the Stuarts tho in defiance of the most plain & express laws that the Stuarts are justifiable in following their example. It the Stuarts had not been as ill judging as tyrannical they would have found out that they had no powerful barons to support them.[73]

Like Ridpath, Hanna Hume thought that David Hume had been unduly sympathetic to the Stuarts, and she advised her daughter to chase up Robertson's *History of Scotland* for a more impartial account. As she put it, "Mr Hume is charged with want of veracity in not telling the whole truth but only as much as serves his purpose by which an action may be represented quite contrary to what in reality it would appear if the whole truth was told." More intriguingly, she also warned her daughter that the *History* could not be considered independently of Hume's "diabolical" philosophy, assuring her that she would "detest him as a philosopher" for endeavoring "to overturn natural & revealed religion & all morality & to establish atheism": "His favourite doctrine is that we have no knowledge of anything not even from the evidence of our sense. We are mistaken when we fancy that we see, hear, feel etc. He says if you pretend to know or believe anything you are fools & then adds as impudently as absurdly that he knows with the utmost certainty that his own opinions are true. You will doubt whether he is mad or wicked."[74]

It is instructive to unpack the various layers of reading experience here. The recipient of the letter had evidently informed her parents of her admiration for Hume after reading one of the early volumes, so on one level the letter is an attempt to reform her view of Hume—itself apparently formed with the help of the daughter's Tory husband. Hume's scandalous philosophical views were highlighted in order to effect a change in the daughter's initial judgment, her parents attempting to safeguard her piety from the danger his ideas posed. On another level, the letter is clearly the result of a reading experience shared by the recipient's parents. Their response to their daughter's dangerous misreading of Hume was not simply intended to break down the trust she placed in his *History,* it was also a reaffirmation of their own shared response. Moreover, the parents' perception of Hume was itself contingent on the dialogue between Hume and more orthodox members of the Scottish *literati,* namely Robertson and Beattie. Indeed, their belligerent reading of Hume's philosophy was entirely dependent on Beattie's exposition of his ideas in the "essay on truth & immutability" (which, they say, their daughter can borrow "from a circulating library in London"). The mother admitted as much, conceding that "I did not compare the quotations with the original because I could not suppose any man so foolish as to quote the words of a living author & refer you to the page where they are to be found if the quotations were not true. He does not quote the meaning of Mr Hume's words but the words themselves." At no stage is there any suggestion that the correspondents had actually read any of Hume's philosophical works, and indeed the recipient of the letter was expressly forbidden to do so—being allowed instead to read "five or six pages" only of Beattie's safely orthodox account.

Despite the widespread distribution of Hume's *Essays* in contemporary Scottish libraries, Hanna Hume was actually typical of many Scots' approach to Hume's philosophy. Direct readings of his philosophical works were extraordinarily rare in Scottish commonplace books of this period. Cameron's measured engagement aside, no sympathetic accounts of Hume's philosophical works appear to have survived—and even Cameron ignored the two *Enquiries* as they appeared in volumes 2 and 3 of the *Essays and Treatises*.[75] In fact, Hume's philosophy featured far more frequently in contemporary reading notes when mediated through the hostile commentary of his philosophical antagonists, including Joseph Priestley, Thomas Reid, James Oswald, George Campbell, and Beattie.[76] At the same time, Scottish readers thereby reflected with remarkable consistency their enthusiastic reception of another important facet of the Scottish Enlightenment's philosophical legacy, in effect using the Common Sense philosophers' defense of orthodoxy to validate their own deeply held beliefs and values. This much can be inferred from borrowing patterns at Scottish libraries, with Thomas Reid's *Inquiry into the Human Mind* (1764) and *Essays on the Active and Intellectual Powers of Man* (1785 and 1788) in particular becoming increasingly popular in libraries as varied as the Innerpeffray Library, the Selkirk Subscription Library, the Leightonian Library in Dunblane, and especially the School Wynd Congregational Library in Dundee. At the last of these, for which we have borrowing records from the mid-1820s, Reid's works enjoyed astonishing success, with the *Essays* far outstripping the popularity of many more mainstream works, including Robertson's *History of Scotland* and *History of America,* Blair's *Lectures on Rhetoric and Belles Lettres,* and James Thomson's *The Seasons*.[77] Surviving reading notes make it apparent that such enthusiasm for the works of Hume's Common Sense antagonists was inextricably linked to readers' profound distrust of Hume's philosophical views.

The compiler of "Amusements in Solitude" is a case in point. Faced with the effrontery of Hume's "cock and bull" *History,* she turned to authorities who could reinforce her faith in divine revelation. These included well-known divines like John Owen, Walter Marshall, and the Moderate principal of Glasgow University, William Leechman.[78] Hugh Blair also contributed to what was a systematic defense of the mental world she believed

Hume had attempted to subvert: "Its [sic] beautifully observed by Dr Blair—that the manner in which these divine communications are convey'd by God to the Heart, we may be at a loss to explain; but no argument can be thence drawn against the credibility of the fact—the operations which the power of God carries on in the natural world are no less mysterious than those we are taught to believe that the spirit performs in the moral world."[79] In fact, our anonymous reader's use of Moderates like Blair, Robertson, and Leechman to counter Hume suggests that he made them appear mainstream rather than ultraliberal in their religious views. Without Hume, the Moderates might have received much rougher treatment at the hands of their contemporary readers—which may help explain the sheer popularity of Blair's provocatively Moderate *Sermons* throughout Scotland.[80] After all, John Ramsay of Ochtertyre, a fervently devout reader who obstinately ignored the threatening presence of David Hume on Scottish bookshelves, frequently fulminated against the Moderates' laxness in religion, condemning Blair's sentimental preaching as "spiritual blamange [sic] . . . with [which] nothing will go down but the ice cream of *sentiment* heightened by the raspberry flavour of style pushed to extreme."[81]

A more conventional opponent of Hume's skepticism was the Principal of Marischal College, Reverend George Campbell, whose *Dissertation on Miracles* (1762) took deliberate aim at some of Hume's most exceptionable ideas. The Stirlingshire seed merchant William Drummond, for example, eagerly entered an account of Campbell's efforts "to refute Hume and defend our holy religion" into his commonplace book on 30 November 1814.[82] Drummond enthused that Campbell proved "Hume's favourite argument is founded on a false Hypothesis," and added his own somewhat confused gloss that "The plain conclusion from his [Hume's] argument is that no testimony should receive our assent unless supported such an extensive experience as had we not had a previous and independent faith in testimony could never have been acquired—such absurdity!!!" Drummond seems never to have read Hume in the original, and took Hume's antagonist entirely on trust because he had so confidently reaffirmed Drummond's own most deeply held beliefs. Having listed many of Campbell's "collateral arguments" in favor of miracles, Drummond concluded triumphantly that "he completely silences Hume notwithstanding all his arts and ingenuity."[83]

The patriotic amateur antiquary Rev. John Grant of Dundurcas and Elgin also found relief and consolation in Campbell's defence of one of the most dearly held tenets of Christian faith. He noted Hume's intention "to prove that miracles which have not been the immediate object of our senses, can not reasonably be believed on the testimony of others," and accurately quoted Hume's argument that "a miracle is a violation of the laws of nature, and as a firm and unalterable experience has established these laws the proof against a miracle from the very nature of the fact, is as complete as any argument from experience can possibly be imagined."[84] In Grant's case, however, Hume was not mediated through Campbell alone but further filtered through the editorial processes of the *Encyclopaedia Britannica;* his notes are clearly based on an entry that reproduced key extracts from the debate between Hume and Campbell on miracles.[85] Though Grant's notes accurately reflected Hume's arguments against miracles, we can be pretty certain that he had never actually read them in the original. Moreover, while he was willing to reproduce Hume's side of the debate in his commonplace book, he remained convinced that "Dr Campbell successfully shows the fallacy of this argument by another single one" and spent even longer clarifying Campbell's proof—again, exactly as it appeared in the *Encyclopaedia Britannica*.

Seedsman Drummond also demonstrates how another major philosopher of the Scottish Enlightenment could be deployed by contemporary readers as a bulwark for the most basic elements of their mental world. Drummond was evidently horrified by Hume's attempt "to prove by the evidence of reason that there was no evidence in reasoning," this time filtered through the arguments of Hume's most eminent opponent Thomas Reid. "Mr Hume's argument is this; judgement and reasoning resolve themselves into conception, or the mere formation of arbitrary and fanciful ideas. And to make the matter very clear, he tells us in treatise of human nature, that an opinion or belief may most accurately be defined a lively idea related to or associated to a present impression." This Drummond utterly dismissed as "nothing but unintelligible explanations and self contradictory assertions," adding that "scepticism takes its origin from a complete misapprehension of the nature of reasoning; which of necessity must rest upon some foundation something must be taken for granted which is called a first principle or an intuitive truth." Reid's response was instantly comforting:

> Dr Reid establishes the authority of the five senses very successfully[.]
> The means according to Reid by which we may know first principles to be true or false are 1st To shew that a first principle stands upon the same footing of others which we implicitly admit. 2nd The proof ad absurdum by shewing the inconsistencies that would result from rejecting it. 3rd Proving that the principle in question has had the consent of all ages and nations. 4th Shewing that it has had a place in the human mind from the earliest infancy. 5th That it influences our practise.[86]

Andrew Douglas, a paymaster in the Royal Navy, also focused on the issue of human perception in a list of "Propositions contest by Dr Beattie" transcribed into his own voluminous commonplace books. Having already dispatched Descartes, Malebranche, Locke, and Berkeley, Douglas turned in much more detail to Beattie's treatment of Hume. The basic argument that "All our perceptions are from Impressions, and Ideas copied from Impressions" was easily enough dealt with. Having conceded with Beattie that this was "true in general," Douglas eagerly followed "how in the Anatomy of the human mind [it] is a secondary consideration: Previous is the desire which prompts the infant to search for the mothers [sic] breast . . . : there nature has implanted a craving instinct prior to external impressions or ideas." Douglas noted Beattie's demolition of each succeeding proposition with increasing enthusiasm, drawn in by the scathing sarcasm of his arguments. On Hume's proposition "That an idea differs only from its corresponding impression in being weaker, but in other respects is not only similar but the same," Douglas notes in his own words "My Idea of an Ass does not confound my hearing—the near bray of an ass might." In response to Hume's suggestion that "All Ideas of solid objects are equal in magnitude & solidity to the Objects themselves," he gleefully retorted "when he can prove he may pay the national debt with a guinea, . . . he from being a lucky chargees des affair may be beneficially promoted to be first Lord of the Treasury." In riposte to Hume's controversial view of the self, Douglas poses the question "is not this more like the language of a big infant than of a philosopher," and he concludes his account of Beattie's duel with the skeptics with one final proposition of Hume's:

> 6th: The soul is only a bundle of perceptions
> Ans: Pray, where is the percipient? Has Mr Hume mislaid his? It may be so—yet still it may exist—and may God have mercy on it. Prior's three blue beans etc is as learned—& more comic than Hume's Bundle[87]

Thus Douglas was yet another contemporary reader who took delight in belittling Hume's philosophy without apparently reading any of his works. He nevertheless identified thoroughly with Hume's Scottish antagonists and entered the fray with his own extemporaneous criticisms of the pernicious influence of Hume's rhetorical skill: "there may be some art in endeavouring to establish unintelligible maxims, whereon to found sophistical arguments & false conclusions, but it is absurd & awkward for a philosopher to play off axioms which are obviously false or nonsense." Moreover, in a vicious endnote Douglas made plain exactly why it was so important to resist Hume's attempt to undermine the whole edifice of Christian belief, which Beattie had argued posed such a real and present danger to humanity's future prospects: "To endeavour to overturn the plainest principles of human knowledge, to subvert the foundations of morality & religion *is philosophically playing the Devil. If the Devil had given Eve such an insipid Hume apple, she would have spit it in his face.*"[88]

Another prolific commonplacer, Mrs. Elizabeth Rose, would have wholeheartedly agreed, although the lady laird of Kilravock tended to be much more respectful in her reading notes—even in her treatment of authors she so clearly distrusted. Her last commonplace book (begun in 1806) contained a telling section she entitled "Of Mr Hume's Philosophy—from Dr. Beattie's Essay on Truth," in which she transcribed at length a sequence of Beattie's most combustible attacks on Hume's skepticism. In doing so, she relied entirely on Beattie's characterization of Hume (his summary of Hume's belief "that body has no existence, but as a bundle of perceptions whose existence consists in their being perceived," for instance), without apparently consulting Hume's original at any stage—even though the Kilravock Library catalog she commissioned in 1783 listed Hume's *Essays and Treatises* alongside Beattie's *Essay on Truth*.[89] Not only did Elizabeth associate herself entirely with Beattie's ridicule of Hume's skepticism, she even (uncharacteristically) emulated the heat of Beattie's language in indicting "modern sceptics":

> Do they with sacrilegious hands attempt to violate this last refuge of the miserable, & rob them of the only comfort that had survived the ravages of misfortune malice & tyranny! Did it ever happen that the influence of their execrable tenets disturbed the tranquillity of virtuous retirement, deepened the gloom of human distress or aggravated the horrors of the grave? . . . Ye traitors to human kind, ye murderers of the human soul, how can ye answer for it to your own hearts.[90]

This represents the most dramatic extract in Elizabeth Rose's entire life of reading, giving full rein to the bombastic language of a writer whom she had once met in person and who clearly remained an important influence on all her reading experiences.[91] She fervently believed in the power of books to fill her "mind with truth," and was convinced that the key to her family's future solvency was the successful moral education of her young son—"an infant son to truth engage," as she put it in a poem she composed in 1788. She may have adopted the term from Beattie's heated defense of Christian belief, *An Essay on the Nature and Immutability of Truth, in Opposition to Sophistry and Scepticism*. Beattie's final statement of the importance of the task in which he was engaged was transcribed eagerly by Elizabeth: "It is time for Truth to vindicate her rights, & we trust they shall be yet completely vindicated. Such are the hopes & the earnest wishes of one . . . in promoting ... the cause of virtue & true science, & in bringing to contempt that sceptical sophistry which is equally subversive of both."[92]

Predictably, Rev. Cameron also turned to his former mentor Beattie when he came to ruminate on the dangers that sophistry and skepticism posed for the modern world. Though he was happy to treat Hume as a trusted authority on a wide range of issues, the Great Infidel came eventually to cast a long shadow over Cameron's thinking. This much is clear from "Verses written on reading Dr Beattie's 'Essay on Truth,'" which Cameron composed in 1806, when he was already in his late fifties and presumably contemplating his own future prospects. Cameron starts by acknowledging the status of British letters in the modern world, putting his own spin on the "new-created light" of Edinburgh for which "all the nations sound applausive noise."[93] He rhetorically questions Beattie's impolite attack on Hume, asking "Why wakes O Beattie, thy discordant voice, / to damp the general joy, to rouse alarms / of treason, rapine, blood-besprinkled arms?" But Beattie, Cameron believes, will have his day: "Thy voice O Beattie, shall be heard at last, / As wak'd by Truth in energetic strain, / Her injured rights & honours to maintain." He continues, echoing the title of Beattie's major work,

> When wildering Scepticism shall have spread
> Throughout the world her desolation dread,
> Immutable, eternal Truth shall rise,
> & illuminate the earth and skies,
> Like Phaebus, beaming with celestial light,
> Dispel the fen-born meteors of the night;
> Then shall her enemies be fain to hide
> Beneath the crumbled pillars of their pride;
> Thy name, O Beattie, then shall be rever'd,
> To her, to all her faithful friends endear'd,
> Approv'd for warmth & energy of heart,
> Disdaining Sophistry's entangling art,
> With mists of Doubt o'erwhelming all the mind,
> Where Faith and Truth no stable footing find.[94]

Throughout Cameron's eloquent hymn to Beattie, French philosophy is the primary target, with Britain's "new-created light, / From Gallic oracles reflected bright." However, the allusion to Hume would have been unequivocal for Cameron and his contemporaries: accusations of "sophistry," "scepticism," and "pride" were synonymous with Hume after Beattie's sustained and notoriously impolite attack on him.[95] Exactly the same inference was drawn by the founder of the Perth Literary and Antiquarian Society, Reverend James Scott, who warned his fellow members against "the false philosophy . . . which, for above half a century, has prevailed much in France, and which was adopted by some writers in our own country."[96]

At least Cameron had read Hume's *Essays,* and was sophisticated enough to assess them sympathetically and seriously. Most knew of Hume's skepticism by reputation alone, and all the frustration, bafflement, effrontery, and sheer horror that his alleged views evoked were ultimately reflected in direct attacks on his character. The author of "Amusements in Solitude" is a case in point. Coming across Adam Smith's famous letter describing Hume "as approaching as nearly to the idea of a perfectly wise & virtuous man, as perhaps the nature of Human fraility will permit," she was plainly horrified: "He became the patron of infidelity—advocate for, & teacher of the most abominable & Horable vices—vices, shocking to nature; & destructive to every virtue, & rational enjoyment.—Is this the man of wisdom & philosophy—the man of compleat virtue?" This naturally led her into a fully rationalized dismissal of Smith's conclusion along now familiar lines:

> I could hardly agree with M. Smith that his Beloved Friend, had attain'd the summit of Human wisdom & virtue.—He falls infinitely below the wise and virtuous Heathens, who darkly but vigorously felt after Truth.
> But as a power of Believing is implanted in the human soul, as a sister eye to reason; and Mr Hume had within his reach, The Divine Revelation, made to man of the Sublimest Truths, Teaching the Divinist virtues, exciting us by the most exalting Hopes, to go on towards perfection;—surely the proper exercise of this internal eye, is as necessary to compleat the perfect character of a wise and virtious man, as the exercise of reason & experience in the most extenseive learning, & the greatest Depth of Thought, & Elegance of Language.—Blind of an Eye the celibrated author appears—Lame of a Leg, tho' prop'd by Friendship & all the Grace of cheerfull good Humor—and Gayeity to the Last.[97]

Ultimately, Hume's "blindness" to the orthodox objects of Christian faith made him little different than the "Brutes" whose history she thought he was most qualified to write, and she accordingly dismissed him as a force of nonsense:

> This brings to my Rememberance a verse found in Professor Hutchisons Class one morning:
>
>> Three Sages, in three Different nations Born;
>> England & Ireland & Scotland did adorn.

> The first from nature banished Spirit quite;
> The second Kick'd of[f] Mat[t]er, out of Spite.
> The force of Nonsence [sic], could no further go;
> To form a Hume, she join'd the other two.[98]

A much more personal attack on Hume seems to have been circulating in mid-eighteenth-century Scotland posing as an addition to Hume's *Essays and Treatises*. It was clearly modeled on his satirical "Character of Sir Robert Walpole," which first appeared in 1742:[99]

> ESSAY XIII   Character of the author of the Essays
>
> Mr Home [sic] Author of the Essays & Ambassador extra-ordinary from the Republick of Letters to the Common-wealth of Petticoats, a person of great Abilities, but no Genius; of some Judgment, but no Invention; of vast Reading but no Taste. His Stile is smooth, not easy, proper, not elegant, concise not lively. His Reflections are more uncommon than natural; more curious than useful. His writings are larger than his Fame, his Fame less than his Vanity. He would have merited more Praise, had he never been an Author tho' it must be confessed, he would have made a good Schoolmaster. As a Man I love him, as he is a Pedant I pity him; and as he affects to be a Critick & a Man of Mode, I despise & laugh at him. With many Faults and few Excellencies to atone for them, he has incurred the Displeasure of the Ladys, instead of gaining their Favour. I would therefore advise him to retire from their Court to his Brother's House at Ninewells, where he may pass the Remainder of his Days in Solitude and obtruse Speculations.[100]

Versions of this skit survive in at least three archival collections in Scotland, and though their original source has yet to be uncovered, such wide distribution illustrates the popularity of the sentiments it expressed.[101] The Earl of Leven even transcribed an abridged version into the end pages of his own copy of the *Essays*, directly following on from Hume's character assassination on Walpole.[102] In all extant versions, Hume's notorious predilection for female company was ridiculed ruthlessly as a prelude to a thorough debunking of his literary fame. In the process, Hume's *Essays* were tarnished with those very literary qualities he was so keen to condemn, including pedantry, bad taste, and inelegance.

Scotland was still a deeply spiritual nation in the age of Enlightenment, and part of Hume's great notoriety in his own lifetime derived from his scandalous disregard for organized religion.[103] Nevertheless, Hume's works tended to be an important influence on the lives and attitudes of the people who read them—and often people who did not directly read them. No two people in this survey read Hume's works in the same way, though they often seem to have been influenced by well-known critical analyses, and most readers' experiences were carefully variegated—adapting some of his views to consolidate their own opinions, while at the same time censuring his perceived Tory politics or threatening stance on religion. Even those who appear not to have read Hume at all recognized that his arguments had fundamental implications for the way in which they saw the world, and deployed other Scottish Enlightenment philosophers to man the barricades against his secularism and alleged atheism.

Their reading experiences inform recent debates about Scottish culture in the age of Enlightenment. With important caveats, George Elder Davie's suspicion that the ideas of the *literati* "were eagerly overheard and assimilated throughout Scotland, and freely commented on and criticised by persons of the most varied backgrounds" reflects far better the evidence presented here than David Hoeveler's contention that they were "largely irrelevant to the Scottish population."[104] As James Raven, Helen Small, and Naomi Tadmor point out, "the history of reading is also a history of the culture in which it takes place, requiring close attention to what it was possible to think, to perceive and, not least, to feel, in particular situations at particular moments in the past."[105] Though our small sample of contemporary readers may not reflect the nationwide response more generally, the case studies discussed here illuminate what it was possible to think of Hume in Georgian Scotland, and they shed new light on the highly complex relationship that developed between David Hume and his original readers.

Notes

1. National Register of Archives for Scotland (hereafter NRAS) 234, Box 49/I/32; 5 February 1762. On critical responses to Hume's History in print, see Philip S. Hicks, *Neoclassical History and English Culture: Clarendon to Hume* (Basingstoke: Macmillan, 1996), 194–202; James Fieser, "The Eighteenth-Century British Reviews of Hume's Writings," *Journal of the History of Ideas* 57 (1996): 645–57; James Fieser, ed., *Early Responses to Hume,* 10 vols. (Bristol: Thoemmes, 1999–); Stanley Tweyman, ed., *David Hume: Critical Assessments,* 6 vols. (London: Routledge, 1995); and Mark G. Spencer, ed., *Hume's Reception in Early America,* 2 vols. (Bristol: Thoemmes, 2002).

2. NRAS 234/Box 49/I/56; 2 March 1762.

3. NRAS 234/Box 65/II/8; 7 January 1776; *Oxford Dictionary of National Biography* (hereafter *ODNB*).

4. NRAS 234/Box 49/I/32; 5 February, 1762.

5. Hume's *History* appeared in 294 of 450 surviving library catalogues I surveyed in my doctoral research; for 44 subscription library catalogues, see my article "'All Partners

may be Enlightened and Improved by Reading them': The Distribution of Enlightenment Books in Scottish Subscription Library Catalogues, 1750–c.1820," *Journal of Scottish Historical Studies* 28, no. 1 (2008): 20–43. For analyses of library borrowing records in print, see Vivienne S. Dunstan, "Glimpses into a Town's Reading Habits in Enlightenment Scotland: Analysing the Borrowings of Gray Library, Haddington, 1732–1816," *Journal of Scottish Historical Studies* 26 (2006): 42–59; Paul Kaufman, "The Rise of Community Libraries in Scotland," *Papers of the Bibliographical Society of America* 59 (1965): 233–94; Paul Kaufman, "A Unique Record of a People's Reading," *Libri* 14 (1964–65): 227–42. Hume's works were prominent at libraries in England: see, for example, Paul Kaufman, *Borrowings from the Bristol Library 1773–1784: A Unique Record of Reading Vogues* (Charlottesville: Bibliographical Society of the University of Virginia, 1960); and David Allan, *A Nation of Readers: Lending Libraries in Georgian England* (London: British Library, forthcoming [2008]). Hume also led the way in borrowings from Harvard College between 1773 and 1782; Mark Olsen and Louis-Georges Harvey, "Reading in Revolutionary Times: Book Borrowing from the Harvard College Library, 1773–1782," *Harvard Library Bulletin* 4 (1993): 57–72. Mark G. Spencer, *Hume and Eighteenth-Century America* (Rochester: University of Rochester Press, 2005) reproduces a vast amount of material relating to consumers' reception of Hume's works, especially in his appendix A, "Hume's Works in Early American Catalogues," and appendix B, "Subscribers to the First American Edition of Hume's *History of England*," 302–463.

6. The *Essays and Treatises* appeared in 194 Scottish library catalogues; for libraries in England and North America, see the sources cited above. On the publishing strategy underlying Hume's *Essays*, see Richard B. Sher, *The Enlightenment and the Book: Scottish Authors and Their Publishers in Eighteenth-Century Britain, Ireland, and America* (Chicago: University of Chicago Press, 2006), esp. 45–52; Richard B. Sher, "The Book in the Scottish Enlightenment," in *The Culture of the Book in the Scottish Enlightenment: An Exhibition,* ed. Paul Wood (Toronto: Thomas Fisher Rare Book Library, University of Toronto, 2000), 40–60; Spencer, *Hume and Eighteenth-Century America,* esp. 13. Compare with David Lundberg and Henry F. May, "The Enlightened Reader in America," *American Quarterly* 28 (1976): 262–71; Spencer argues that their account of the reception of Hume's philosophy is "downright deceptive" because they fail to recognize that the *Essays and Treatises* included the *Principles of Morals* (1751), *Enquiry on the Human Understanding* (1748), *Political Discourses* (1752), and, from 1757, *Four Dissertations*. On the reception of the *Treatise,* which Hume famously admitted "fell dead born from the press," see John P. Wright, "The *Treatise*: Composition, Reception and Response," in *The Blackwell Guide to Hume's* Treatise, ed. Saul Traiger (Oxford: Blackwell, 2006), 5–25.

7. For critical discussion, see David Allan, "Some Methods and Problems in the History of Reading: Georgian England and the Scottish Enlightenment," *Journal of the Historical Society* 3 (2003): 91–124; David Allan, "A Reader Writes: Negotiating *The Wealth of Nations* in an Eighteenth-Century English Commonplace Book," *Philological Quarterly* 81 (2004): 207–33; David Allan, "Opposing Enlightenment: Revd Charles Peters' Reading of the Natural History of Religion," *Eighteenth-Century Studies* 38 (2005): 301–21; John Brewer, "Reconstructing the Reader: Prescriptions, Texts and Strategies in Anna Larpent's Reading," in *The Practice and Representation of Reading in England,* ed. James Raven, Helen Small, and Naomi Tadmor (Cambridge: Cambridge University Press, 1996), 226–45; Stephen Colclough, "Recovering the Reader: Commonplace Books and Diaries as Sources of Reading Experiences," *Publishing History* 44 (1998): 5–37; Anthony Grafton, "Is the History of Reading a Marginal Exercise?: Guillaume Bude and His Books," *Papers of the Bibliographical Society of America* 91 (1997): 139–57; Anthony Grafton and Lisa Jardine, "'Studied for Action': How Gabriel Harvey Read His Livy," *Past and Present* 129 (1990): 30–78; Norman Holland, "Recovering the 'Purloined Letter': Reading as a Personal Transaction," in *The Reader in the Text,* Susan

R. Suleiman and Inge Crosman (Princeton: Princeton University Press, 1980), 350–70; Jonathan Rose, "How Historians Study Reader Response; or, What Did Jo Think of *Bleak House?*" in *Literature in the Marketplace,* John O. Jordan and Robert L. Patten (Cambridge: Cambridge University, 1995), 195–212; Jonathan Rose, "Rereading the English Common Reader: A Preface to a History of Audiences," *Journal of the History of Ideas* 53 (1992): 47–70.

8. Robert Darnton, "First Steps toward a History of Reading," *Australian Journal of French Studies,* 23:1 (1986): 7–12.

9. ODNB. Boyle was listed in Professor Barron's class at St. Andrews in 1786 (*The Matriculation Roll of the University of St. Andrews 1745–1897,* ed. J. M. Anderson [Edinburgh: Blackwood, 1905]), and matriculated at Glasgow in 1789 (matriculand 5014, *The Matriculation Albums of the University of Glasgow, from 1827 to 1858,* ed. W. Innes Addison [Glasgow: James Maclehose & Sons, 1913]).

10. Glasgow University Library MS Murray 170, Notebook of David Boyle of Sherralton; compare David Hume, *The History of England,* 6 vols. (1754–62; repr., ed. William B. Todd, Indianapolis: Liberty Press, 1983).

11. Library borrowing data is derived from my unpublished Ph.D. thesis, "Reading the Scottish Enlightenment: Libraries, Readers and Intellectual Culture in Provincial Scotland c.1750–c.1820" (University of St. Andrews, 2007). Notably, Hume's *History* was among the most popular titles at six of the seven noncommercial libraries for which borrowing evidence survives. On the Gray Library, see Dunstan, "Glimpses into a Town's Reading Habits."

12. Thomas Sheridan, *A Plan of Education for the Young Nobility and Gentry of Great Britain* (London: E. and C. Dilly, 1769), 98, 122. Joseph Priestley suggested readers compile "a common-place-book of English history" in which, "as everything is classed under its proper head, it is seen, in a moment, what was the state of any article we are enquiring about in any particular reign"; see *An Essay on a Course of Liberal Education for Civil and Active Life* (London: C. Henderson, 1765), 77–78. For the growth in the popularity of history in England before this period, see Daniel R. Woolf, *Reading History in Early Modern England* (Cambridge: Cambridge University Press, 2000).

13. Notebook, 21–22; in this instance, Boyle briefly elaborates on marginal headings in Hume, *History,* 217–41. Note, however, that he mistakenly called Sir Thomas Wentworth "Sir Charles Wentworth."

14. Ibid., 9; summarized from Hume, *History,* 148–51. Boyle was not the only contemporary reader to copy down inaccurately the date of Shakespeare's death, given by Hume correctly as 1616; compare the commonplace book of William Constable, discussed in David Allan, *The Making of British Culture: English Readers and the Scottish Enlightenment* (London: Routledge, forthcoming [2008]).

15. Priestley argued that "it is only a knowledge of how things were actually brought to the state in which they now are, that can enable us to judge how they may be improved"; *Essay on a Course of Liberal Education,* 71. Hume was frequently recommended to students in America in the last decades of the eighteenth century; see Spencer, *Hume and Eighteenth-Century America,* esp. 78–79.

16. Notebook, 17; commenting on Hume, *History,* 314; cf. Geoffrey Carnall and Colin Nicholson, eds., *The Impeachment of Warren Hastings* (Edinburgh: Edinburgh University Press, 1989). Boyle studied law under John Millar at Glasgow, and was called to the Scottish bar on 14 December 1793; ODNB.

17. Ibid., 9; the emphasis is Boyle's own, probably to denote his own phraseology.

18. Hume, *History,* 148. Note that Boyle did not quote this portion of Hume's narrative.

19. For other partisan readings of Hume's *History,* see Allan, "Some Methods and Problems," 13–16; Allan, *Making of British Culture;* Hicks, *Neoclassical History,* 193–94; Spencer, *Hume and Eighteenth-Century America,* 254–55, 275–76.

20. Notebook, 10; compare with Hume, *History,* 156–65. In refusing to endorse the patriotic theme of English liberty, Hume "played upon and subverted reader expectations for a work of this type"; Karen O'Brien, "The History Market in Eighteenth-Century England," in *Books and Their Readers in Eighteenth-Century England: New Essays,* ed. Isabel Rivers (London: Leicester University Press, 2001), 112.

21. Reinhard Wittmann, "Was There a Reading Revolution at the End of the Eighteenth Century?" in *A History of Reading in the West,* ed. Guglielmo Cavallo and Roger Chartier, trans. L. G. Cochrane (Cambridge: Polity, 1999), 284–312; James Engell, *Forming the Critical Mind: Dryden to Coleridge* (Cambridge: Harvard University Press, 1989); Frank Donoghue, *The Fame Machine: Book Reviewing and Eighteenth-Century Literary Careers* (Stanford: Stanford University Press, 1996); Allan, *Making British Culture,* chap. 2. See also my own contributions, "Reading the Scottish Enlightenment" and "The 'Age of Criticism' and the Critical Reader: George Redpath," to Warren McDougall and Stephen W. Brown, eds., *The Edinburgh History of the Book in Scotland,* vol. 2, *1707–1800* (Edinburgh: Edinburgh University Press, forthcoming).

22. Notebook, 18, 13, 19; quoting Hume, *History,* 338–47, 349. Boyle adds his own note that "Mr Hume *vindicates Charles* from any knowledge of concurrence in the Irish insurrections," though it is impossible to tell whether Boyle agreed with Hume here or was simply recording his view.

23. Most now agree that Hume's *History* represented a deliberate attempt to deconstruct the partisan myths of the English past so that modern British politics could be released from the ancient quarrels of Whig and Tory; see Duncan Forbes, *Hume's Philosophical Politics* (Cambridge: Cambridge University Press, 1975); Hicks, *Neoclassical History;* Colin Kidd, *Subverting Scotland's Past: Scottish Whig Historians and the Creation of an Anglo-British Identity, 1689–c.1830* (Cambridge: Cambridge University Press, 1993); Karen O'Brien, *Narratives of Enlightenment: Cosmopolitan History from Voltaire to Gibbon* (Cambridge: Cambridge University Press, 1997); Nicholas Phillipson, *Hume* (London: Weidenfeld & Nicholson, 1989); J. G. A. Pocock, *Barbarism and Religion II: Narratives of Civil Government* (Cambridge: Cambridge University Press, 1999); Victor G. Wexler, *David Hume and the History of England* (Philadelphia: American Philosophical Society, 1979).

24. Notebook, 78

25. Hicks, *Neoclassical History,* 208–9.

26. Beinecke Rare Book and Manuscript Library, Yale University, Osborn Bound MS Fc132, Commonplace Book of James Forbes, 1766–c.1800.

27. The Innes notes on Hume appear in a copy of *Bell's Common Place Book, Form'd generally upon the Principles Recommended and Practiced by Mr. Locke* (London: John Bell, 1770), at NAS GD113/1/475. John Bell's was one of at least ten different editions of Lockean commonplace book templates that were published between 1770 and 1820, on both sides of the Atlantic. For Locke's method and more background, see Earle Havens, *Commonplace Books: A History of Manuscripts and Printed Books from Antiquity to the Twentieth Century* (New Haven: Beinecke Rare Book and Manuscript Library, Yale University, 2001), 57–58; Lucia Dacome, "Noting the Mind: Commonplace Books and the Pursuit of the Self in Eighteenth-Century Britain," *Journal of the History of Ideas* 65 (October 2004), 603–26 . For commonplace books before the eighteenth century, see Ann Moss, *Printed Commonplace-Books and the Structuring of Renaissance Thought* (Oxford: Clarendon Press, 1996); Ann Blair, "Humanist Methods in Natural Philosophy: The Commonplace Book," *Journal of the History of Ideas* 53 (1992): 541–51.

28. There was considerable debate on precisely this point in the eighteenth century, with many insisting on the priority of independent thought and judgment in the compilation of commonplace books. The worry that too many readers would fall into the trap of merely

compiling mindless collections of vacuous truisms was reflected in Swift's notorious quip, "What tho' his *Head* be empty . . . , provided his *Commonplace-Book* be full"; quoted by Robert DeMaria, Jr., *Samuel Johnson and the Life of Reading* (Baltimore: Johns Hopkins University Press, 1997), 89.

29. *Bell's Commonplace Book*, 20; quoting from Hume, *History*, 3:255.

30. Ibid., 176, 83; quoting Hume, *History*, 5:424, 3:369, 4:100, 5:520. On Scottish responses to the French Revolution, see Emma Vincent, "The Responses of Scottish Churchmen to the French Revolution, 1789–1802," *Scottish Historical Review* 73 (1994): 191–215.

31. Innes extracted the passage from Hume's notes to the third volume of the *History of England*, recounting "a great dispute at the university of St Andrews, whether the *pater* should be said to God or the saints": "A simple fellow, who served the sub prior, thinking there was some great matter in hand, that made the doctors hold so many conferences together, asked him one day what the matter was; the sub-prior answering, *Tom*, that was the fellow's name, *we cannot agree to whom the paternoster should be said*. He suddenly replied, *To whom, Sir, should it be said, but unto God?* Then said the sub-prior, *What shall we do with the saints?* He answered, *Give them Aves and Creeds enow in the devil's name; for that may suffice them*. The answer going abroad, many said, *that he had given a wiser decision than all the doctors had done with all their distinctions*"; *Bell's Commonplace Book*, 36, taken from Hume, *History*, 3:479.

32. *Bell's Commonplace Book*, 38; quoting Hume, *History*, 1:40.

33. On the relationship between toleration and established religion in the Enlightenment, see Ole Peter Grell, Jonathan I. Israel, and Nicholas Tyacke, *From Persecution to Toleration: The Glorious Revolution and Religion in England* (Oxford: Clarendon Press, 1991); Ole Peter Grell and Roy Porter, eds., *Toleration and Enlightenment in Europe* (Cambridge: Cambridge University Press, 2000).

34. *Bell's Commonplace Book*, 144, 65; quoting Hume, *History*, 1:93, 3:437.

35. Ibid., 1, 124, 55, 19; quoting Hume, *History*, 2:479, 6:366, 5:276, 2:20.

36. *Fasti Ecclesiae Scoticanae*, 9 vols., ed. Hew Scott (Edinburgh: Saint Andrew Press, 1915); *ODNB*.

37. On the relationship between Hume and Beattie, see James Somerville, *The Enigmatic Parting Shot: What Was Hume's "Compleat Answer to Dr Reid and to That Bigotted Silly Fellow, Beattie"?* (Aldershot: Avebury, 1995).

38. NAS CH1/15/3, commonplace book of William Cameron, minister of Kirknewton.

39. The rest of Cameron's commonplace book is filled with material plundered from Samuel Johnson's *Lives of the Poets* (1781), Thomas Wharton's *History of English Poetry* (1774), Daniel Webb's *Remarks on the Beauties of Poetry* (1762), and James Beattie's *Essays on Poetry and Music* (1776).

40. Commonplace Book of William Cameron, f72v; f75v; summarized from Hume, *Essays*, 3–8, 135–36, esp. 6.

41. Ibid., f75r–75v; summarized and adapted from Hume, *Essays*, 98, 109. On Hume's Essay "Of Eloquence," see Adam Potkay, "David Hume (1711–1776)," in *Eighteenth-Century British and American Rhetorics and Rhetoricians*, Michael G. Moran (Westport, Conn.: Greenwood, 1994), 124–27.

42. This precise point with regard to Hume's reception is made by Sher, *Enlightenment and the Book*, 146.

43. Commonplace book of William Cameron, f73v; f75r; f74v; reflections based on Hume, *Essays*, 73–79, 62.

44. Hume, *Essays*, 62. Notably, Cameron did not transcribe or comment on this passage.

45. William Cameron, *Poetical Dialogues on Religion, in the Scots Dialect, between Two Gentlemen and Two Ploughmen* (Edinburgh: Peter Hill, 1788), 38–39. I gratefully acknowl-

edge the anonymous reviewer for *Book History* for drawing this invaluable source to my attention.

46. Commonplace Book of William Cameron, f65r, f67r, ff71v–72r. His references here relate to Robert Barclay, *An Apology for the True Christian Divinity: Being an Explanation and Vindication of the Principles and Doctrines of the . . . Quakers* (1678; 7th ed., London: W. Richardson and S. Clark, 1765); Jacques Necker, *Of the Importance of Religious Opinions* (London: J. Johnson, 1788).

47. Ibid., f69r. I have not confirmed whether Cameron's collection of "Scriptural Expressions" originated from the Bible directly, or whether they came from some other devotional textual source.

48. Quoted from Rose's review of the *Four Dissertations* by Fieser, "British Reviews of Hume," 648–49.

49. The phrase appears in Roger Flexman's review of Hume's *History* in the *Monthly Review* for March 1755, quoted by John Vladimir Price, introduction to Daniel MacQueen, *Letters on Mr Hume's History of Great Britain* (Edinburgh: Kincaid and Donaldson, 1756; repr., Bristol: Thoemmes, 1990), vi.

50. Quoted by Price, introduction, vii.

51. Fieser, "British Reviews of Hume," 650.

52. NLS MSS 8238–40, Amusements in Solitude.

53. NLS MS 8238, f16v. Most convincingly, the writer had recently endured a period of confinement under "a gentle distress," a term typical of the euphemisms often used for childbirth in this period; see Amanda Vickery, *The Gentleman's Daughter: Women's Lives in Georgian England* (New Haven: Yale University Press, 1998), chap. 3.

54. NLS MS 8238, f3v; f5v.

55. Ibid., f19r; compare with Hume's "Of History," in *Essays,* 563ff. The notion that "history tends to strengthen the sentiments of virtue by the variety of views in which it exhibits the conduct of Divine Providence" was forcefully advanced by Joseph Priestley, among others; *Essay on a Course of Liberal Education,* 41.

56. NLS MS 8238, f19r; ff17r–17v.

57. Ibid., f19v. William Rose in the *Monthly Review* granted that many readers would not be pleased with what Hume "has advanced in regard to Religion, the Genius of the Protestant Faith and the characters of the first Reformers"; quoted by Price, introduction, viii.

58. NLS MS 8238, f19r; f17v; f19v; f17r.

59. Ibid., f17r. The compiler's concern for the young friend with whom she had discussed Hume may be compared to Abigail Adams's comments that his works were corrupting American youth; see Spencer, *Hume and Eighteenth-Century America,* 80.

60. NLS MS 8238, f19r–v.

61. NLS MS 8239, ff16r–16v; for the relevant passage, see William Robertson, *The History of America,* 2 vols. (London: Strahan, Cadell and Balfour, 1777), 264ff.

62. NLS MS 8239, ff16v–17r; compare Robertson, *History of America,* 146, 90.

63. Ibid., ff16v–17r.

64. Ibid., f17r; NLS MS8238, f18v. "Dr Owen was almost certainly John Owen (1616–83), theologian and independent minister; *ODNB*. The specific work cited here may have been Owen's *Christologia; or, A Declaration of the Glorious Mystery of the Person of Christ, God and Man* (1677; Edinburgh: John Gray, 1772), which went through numerous editions in the second half of the eighteenth century at Glasgow, Edinburgh, and Falkirk.

65. See Richard B. Sher, *Church and University in the Scottish Enlightenment: The Moderate Literati of Edinburgh* (Edinburgh: Edinburgh University Press, 1985), 65–68, 73–74.

66. *Diary of George Ridpath, Minister of Stitchel 1755–1761,* ed. Sir J. Balfour Paul (Ed-

inburgh: Publications of the Scottish History Society, 1922), 19, 250, 143. The original manuscript is in the National Archives of Scotland, CH1/5/122–3.

67. Ibid., 131, 319, 73, 118.

68. Price, introduction; the anonymous *Directions for a Proper Choice of Authors to Form a Library* . . . (London: J. Whiston, 1766) advised that Hume's "visible disesteem for religion, and his carelessness in some facts, make [the *History*] not so valuable a work as so capable an author might have rendered" (12). Ridpath was a particularly keen follower of the critical press, as I make clear in "The 'Age of Criticism' and the Critical Reader," in *The Edinburgh History of the Book*.

69. *Diary of George Ridpath*, 262, 264.

70. Phillipson, *Hume,* puts the *History* in the wider context of Hume's intellectual biography. On Hume's treatment of his sources, see Hicks, *Neoclassical History*, 189–91; Mark S. Phillips, *Society and Sentiment: Genres of Historical Writing in Britain 1740–1820* (Princeton: Princeton University Press, 2000), 62–65.

71. *Diary of George Ridpath*, 130, 6.

72. Beinecke Rare Books and Manuscripts Library, Yale University, Osborn MS7733, Letter of Hanna (Frederick) Hume discussing David Hume (no date).

73. Ibid.

74. Ibid.

75. On American readers' responses to Hume's philosophy, see Spencer, *Hume*, 75–79.

76. For this group, see *Scottish Common Sense Philosophy: Sources and Origins*, 5 vols., ed. James Fieser (Bristol: Thoemmes, 2000).

77. I feature a close analysis of borrowing patterns at these libraries in my Ph.D. thesis "Reading the Scottish Enlightenment."

78. On Owen, Marshall, and Leechman, see *ODNB*.

79. NLS MS8240, ff14v, 24v; the compiler seems to splice passages from Hugh Blair, *Sermons* (Edinburgh: William Creech, 1777–1801), 2:138, 51.

80. Blair's *Sermons* appeared in 198 of the 450 Scottish book catalogues sampled, and was one of the most frequently borrowed texts at the Gray Library between 1804 and 1816. On the Moderate party in the Church of Scotland, see Sher, *Church and University;* Richard B. Sher and Alexander Murdoch, "Patronage and Party in the Church of Scotland, 1750–1800," in *Church, Politics and Society: Scotland, 1408–1929*, ed. Norman MacDougall (Edinburgh: Donald, 1983), 197–220; Ian D. L. Clark, "From Protest to Reaction: The Moderate Regime in the Church of Scotland, 1752–1805," in *Scotland in the Age of Improvement: Essays in Scottish History in the Eighteenth Century*, eds. Nicholas Phillipson and Rosalind Mitchison (1970; Edinburgh: Edinburgh University Press, 1996), 200–224. Their Popular Party opponents (who did not consider the Moderate ministers Leechman, Blair, Robertson, et al. the least bit orthodox) are less well understood, but see John R. McIntosh, *Church and Theology in Enlightenment Scotland: The Popular Party, 1740–1800* (East Linton: Tuckwell, 1998).

81. *Letters of John Ramsay of Ochtertyre 1799–1812*, ed. Barbara L. H. Horn (Edinburgh: Scottish History Society, 1966), 74.

82. NLS Acc.5699, Commonplace Book of William Drummond. On Campbell, see Jeffrey M. Suderman, *Orthodoxy and Enlightenment: George Campbell in the Eighteenth Century* (Montreal: McGill-Queen's University Press, 2001); Hume held Campbell's response in such high regard that he defended himself in a letter to Blair—see J. Y. T. Grieg, ed., *The Letters of David Hume* (Oxford: Clarendon Press, 1932), 348–51; Henry Sefton, "David Hume and Principal Campbell," in *Aberdeen and the Enlightenment*, ed. Jennifer J. Carter and Joan H. Pittock (Aberdeen: Aberdeen University Press, 1987), 123–28.

83. Drummond, ff50v–51v. The phrase "the whole is built upon a false hypothesis" ap-

pears in George Campbell, *A Dissertation on Miracles: Containing an Examination of the Principles Advanced by David Hume, Esq; in an Essay on Miracles* (Edinburgh: A. Kincaid and J. Bell, 1762), 14. The subsequent notes appear to be Drummond's own summary of Campbell's case.

84. See NAS GD248/614/1, Notes from reading, miscellaneous notes of John Grant, minister of Dundurcas and Elgin, unpaginated. Grant quoted directly from the article on "Abridgement," in *Encyclopaedia Britannica* (2nd ed., Edinburgh, 1778–83), 1:22. For further analysis of Grant's reading experiences and strategies, see my contributions to the forthcoming *The Edinburgh History of the Book in Scotland*.

85. On the relationship between commonplacing and the new encyclopedias, Richard R. Yeo, "Ephraim Chambers' *Cyclopaedia* (1728) and the Tradition of the Commonplaces," *Journal of the History of Ideas* 57 (1996): 157–75.

86. Drummond, ff15r–17r; here Drummond summarizes Thomas Reid, *Essays on the Active Powers of Man* (Edinburgh: John Bell, 1788), 6; and Thomas Reid, *Essays on the Intellectual Powers of Man* (Edinburgh: John Bell, 1785), 550. Many English readers used their notes from Reid for similar purposes; see Allan, *Making British Culture*.

87. NLS Adv. MS17.1.11, f130v, Commonplace Book of a member of the Douglas of Cavers family. Throughout this section Douglas produces his own colorful interpretation of James Beattie, *An Essay on the Nature and Immutability of Truth, in Opposition to Sophistry and Scepticism* (Edinburgh: A. Kincaid and J. Bell, 1770), 265–67. Douglas's note on the sixth proposition probably alludes to the English poet Matthew Prior (1664–1721), who used the phrase "'Tis Three blue Beans in One blue Bladder'" in satirizing scholarly rivalry between the Universities of Oxford and Cambridge in "Alma, or the Progress of the Mind in Three Cantos," in *Poems on Several Occasions* (London: J. Tonson, 1721), 2:26.

88. NLS Adv. MS17.1.11, f131r; compare with Beattie, *Essay on Truth*, 361 (my italics represent Douglas's addition to Beattie's original).

89. NAS GD1/726/9, Commonplace Book of Elizabeth Rose, 75ff. In this instance, Elizabeth Rose quoted directly from Beattie, *Essay on Truth*, 266. NAS GD125 Box 1, Kilravock Library Catalogue, 1783. I explore Elizabeth Rose's reading in much more depth in "'An Infant Son to Truth Engage': Virtue, Responsibility and Self-Improvement in the Reading of Elizabeth Rose of Kilravock, 1747–1815," *Journal of the Edinburgh Bibliographical Society* 2 (2007): 69–92.

90. Ibid., 76–77, quoting directly from Beattie, *Essay on Truth*, 526ff.

91. Richard Sher points out with regard to the controversy caused by Hume's infidelity that "when harsher language was used, as in Beattie's *Essay on Truth*, there was controversy and concern about whether the bounds of politeness had been overstepped"; see *Enlightenment and the Book*, 146. Elizabeth clearly had no such worries.

92. NAS GD1/726/9, 79; typically, Rose quoted directly and accurately from Beattie, *Essay on Truth*, 530.

93. Cameron's praise of Edinburgh's "capital of the mind" is reminiscent of contemporary comment by Carlo Denina, Tobias Smollett, and others with whom he may have been familiar; Sher, *Enlightenment and the Book*, esp. 68; James Buchan, *Capital of the Mind: How Edinburgh Changed the World* (London: John Murray, 2003).

94. NAS CH1/15/5, Poetic Commonplace Book of William Cameron, ff3r–3v.

95. Ibid., f3v.

96. Quoted by David Allan, "The Scottish Enlightenment and the Politics of Provincial Culture: Perth Library and Antiquarian Society, c.1784–1790," *Eighteenth-Century Life* 27 (2003): 19.

97. NLS MS8239, f22r. The compiler of "Amusements in Solitude" may have attacked Smith's letter on Hume because she had seen James Boswell's comment on it in *The Journal of*

a Tour to the Hebrides (London: Charles Dilly, 1785), 22–23. Smith wrote "One single, and as I thought a very harmless sheet of paper, which I happened to write concerning the death of our late friend Mr Hume, brought upon me ten times more abuse than the very violent attack I had made upon the whole commercial system of Great Britain"; Adam Smith to Andreas Holt, 26 October 1780, *The Correspondence of Adam Smith,* ed. Ernest Campbell Mossner and Ian Simpson Ross (Indianapolis: Liberty Press, 1987), 251; for the offending document, see Adam Smith to William Strahan, 9 November 1776, 217–21.

98. NLS MS8239, f22r; f17v.

99. Its similarity to Hume's essay on the character of Sir Robert Walpole was noted by at least one contemporary; see NAS GD18/5143; Hume, *Essays,* 574–76. It was withdrawn in 1770.

100. NAS GD26/13/279, Essay on the Character of David Hume.

101. For instance, compare NAS GD18/5143 and Edinburgh University Library La.II.451/2.

102. Leven's copy of Hume's *Essays* is now held in a private collection.

103. On religious belief in eighteenth-century Scotland, see Callum Brown, *Religion and Society in Scotland since 1707* (Edinburgh: Edinburgh University Press, 1997); Callum Brown, *The Social History of Religion in Scotland since 1730* (London: Methuen, 1987); T. C. Smout, "Born Again at Cambuslang: New Evidence on Popular Religion and Literacy in Eighteenth-Century Scotland," *Past and Present* 97 (1982): 114–27.

104. George Elder Davie, *A Passion for Ideas: Essays on the Scottish Enlightenment II,* ed. Murdo Macdonald (Edinburgh: Polygon, 1994), 1; Hoeveler is quoted by David Allan, *Virtue, Learning and the Scottish Enlightenment: Ideas of Scholarship in Early Modern History* (Edinburgh: Edinburgh University Press, 1993), 4.

105. James Raven, Helen Small, and Naomi Tadmor, eds., introduction to *The Practice and Representation of Reading in England* (Cambridge: Cambridge University Press, 1996), 21.

Cadell and the Crash

Ross Alloway

> It is as clear as the shining sun that all of us—I mean you, Ballantyne, and we—are wading,—that we have all too much existence by wind-capital,—that such a capital constantly floating is at all times to be deprecated, but in times like the present *must be removed; if it is not*, we will all of us be *removed into the Bankrupt List*.
> —Robert Cadell to Joseph Ogle Robinson, 14 January 1826[1]

On 21 January 1826, Robert Cadell prepared a mandate for sequestrating Archibald Constable and Co. It was a calamitous end to one of the most innovative and distinguished publishing houses of the early nineteenth century. It shocked both the book trade and the wider public, as it threatened to ruin not only the venerated Archibald Constable and the talented printer James Ballantyne, but the world's widest read living poet and novelist, Sir Walter Scott. The tragic effects of the sequestration, or bankruptcy, on Scott are well known, but the events leading up to it are far less evident because Cadell, the central player in the drama, has remained in the background.[2]

Cadell, pictured in figure 1, operated as Constable and Co.'s chief financial officer, making the day-to-day decisions about paying the bills, borrowing money, and negotiating with the trade as well as the firm's authors. Cadell joined the publishing house in 1807 as a nineteen-year-old clerk and became a partner four years later. He established a firm relationship with Scott and, as the firm's head of finance, became regularly frustrated with Constable's lavish spending. In her seminal work, *Scott's Last Edition,* Jane Millgate details how Cadell set out on his own as the publisher of Scott's novels, producing a collected edition of *Waverley* novels from 1829 to

---

This paper could not have been written without the generous assistance of a number of individuals, including Peter Garside and Sam McKinstry, who commented on various drafts. Fraser Elgin helped me navigate accounting ledgers on several occasions, and Scott Wortley helped me make sense of the financial terminology. Paul Barnaby provided assistance with research into the portraits, and archivists at the National Library of Scotland and the Bank of Scotland provided expert research support. The research was undertaken during a British Academy Postdoctoral Fellowship.

Fig. 1 Robert Cadell, from a portrait by Sir John Watson Gordon. The plate is extracted from James L. Caw, *The Scott Gallery: A Series of One Hundred and Forty-Six Photogravures* (Edinburgh: T. C. & E. C. Jack, 1903).

1833, also known as the magnum opus edition.³ Its success led to other editions, which helped to expand Scott's already considerable readership and repay his creditors.

Cultural and economic theorists like Pierre Bourdieu and Martha Woodmansee have shown that authors must negotiate carefully the intersection of literary production and finance. This was certainly the case for Scott. Following the crash, Cadell operated as the unacknowledged facilitator of what Caroline McCracken-Flesher has described as "the intertwined relationship between Scott's finances, his status, and national reputation."⁴ The great profits that resulted from Cadell's privileged position and his unwillingness to invest in less remunerative authors severely diminished any symbolic capital that arose from his association with Scott. A good example of his marginal status is the famous 1849 painting by Thomas Faed of an imaginary gathering, entitled *Sir Walter Scott and His Literary Friends at Abbotsford* (figure 2).[5] Most of the well-known figures in Scott's circle are present, including Ballantyne and Constable. Cadell was not "literary" enough to appear, even though a publisher and printer—enthusiastic capitalists both—were deemed fit to join the grouping. Scott's immense stature meant that Cadell, as Constable before him, could lay claim to both symbolic and financial capital, but he was far too interested in the latter to concern himself with the former. Comparing the two paintings brings this distinction into sharp relief: on the one hand an upright Cadell impatiently sits while holding correspondence (or possibly bills) while Scott's friends are more contemplatively reposed or earnestly engaged in discussion. The cultural politics that omitted Cadell from the painting have also marginalized his role in the crash, limiting our understanding of this pivotal event in British publishing history.[6] Indeed, when Cadell has been mentioned, he is often portrayed as

Fig. 2 Sir Walter Scott and His Literary Friends at Abbotsford, by Thomas Faed (1849). Scottish National Portrait Gallery. The painting was produced from preexisting portraits. Seated from left to right are Thomas Thomson, James Ballantyne, Archibald Constable, Thomas Campbell, Tom Moore, Sir Adam Fergusson, Francis Jeffrey, William Wordsworth, John Gibson Lockhart, George Crabbe, Henry Mackenzie, Scott, and (on footstool) James Hogg. Standing from left to right are Sir Humphrey Davy, Sir David Wilkie, Sir William Allan, and Prof. John Wilson.

a scheming businessman who led a great writer and publisher to their downfall.[7] But Cadell, rather than ruining Scott, Constable, and Ballantyne, single-handedly delayed the sequestration for far longer than would have been possible without his aid. In fact Cadell's business acumen nearly saved Scott.

The financial crisis of 1825–26, popularly known as the "crash," was completely unexpected. It lasted for only several months, from October to January, and was primarily confined to England, though a number of Scottish businesses with financial dealings in the south failed as a result. According to economic historian Stefan Altorfer, the underlying cause of the crash was Britain's "difficult transition to a peacetime economy after the Napoleonic Wars."[8] A governmental policy of economic expansion encouraged low interest rates and an abundance of banknotes. The easy money encouraged reckless speculation in joint stock companies. In April 1825 the Bank of England tried to rein in financial markets by withdrawing notes from circulation, and frightened investors tried to liquidate their holdings, causing a collapse in the stock market and a run on banks. In the panic a large number of English banks failed. Numerous English businesses that had borrowed in order to finance speculation went bankrupt, because lenders were unwilling to renew debts that had come due or to loan more money.

Before and during Cadell's partnership, the firm had accumulated large debts that were regularly renegotiated and rarely discharged, a situation Cadell had previously found alarming.[9] As Peter Garside and Iain Gordon Brown observe, Archibald Constable and Co., Scott, James Ballantyne, and his brother John experienced a cash crisis in 1814 that caused "desperate concern."[10] The low interest rates available at the end of 1824 encouraged Cadell to overlook past experiences: "I may . . . state the general comfort I have had throughout the year, in AC & Cos. [m]atters[.] [T]here has been more comfort, particularly in finance, than I have enjoyed since entering the concern."[11] In 1825 Archibald Constable and Co. took advantage of this situation, and published no fewer than seventy-five book titles, when the year prior they had published only forty-seven. Many of the titles took at least a year to complete from commissioning to distribution, and the decision to publish was made long before any sign of financial problems, but the attendant costs would come due just when cash was increasingly scarce.

Any historian of the business of publishing needs to understand financial instruments, but they have long perplexed literary scholars, including Mary Poovey, who errs in her recent book *The Financial System in Nineteenth-Century Britain*.[12] For early nineteenth-century booksellers, there were three commonly used methods for generating capital: discounting a bond, discounting a bill of exchange, or discounting an accommodation bill. Cadell used all three methods in the ensuing crisis, and it is helpful to define them.

A bond was a written deed by which a person obliged him- or herself to pay a sum to another party. A bill of exchange was a negotiable instrument that was generally drawn and signed by a business that provided goods to another business for a certain price, such as a shipment of books or the transfer of copyright. If the party that received the goods agreed that they owed the amount, they also signed the bill and were obliged to pay the sum by a due date that could range widely. For example, a short-dated bill might be due in one month, while a long-dated bill might be due in forty-five months. The party that provided the goods and drew the bill was known as the drawer, and the party that received the goods and was obliged to pay the bill was known as the drawee or acceptor.[13]

Accommodation bills were visibly indistinguishable from bills of exchange, the crucial difference being that the drawer had not provided the drawee any goods. As they appeared as bills of exchange, accommodation bills were treated as negotiable instruments, and they allowed the drawer to raise cash. In essence they were a form of credit, an "accommodation" granted by the drawee to the drawer, and were immensely useful for businesses like bookselling and publishing that required ready cash to fund future profits.[14]

Similar to a loan based on collateral, banks (and sometimes businesses) offered cash for bills of exchange and accommodation bills. The banks held the bills until the stated due dates, after which time the party who cashed the bill was obliged pay back the amount. This was known as redeeming the bill. For their service, banks charged a small fee between 3 percent and 5 percent of the stated value of the bill, calculated monthly. Thus the longer a business took to redeem the bill the more money they would owe. The transaction was referred to as "discounting," as the bank was discounting the value of the bill. Much like cash, a bill of exchange or accommodation bill could also be exchanged between numerous parties as long as it was endorsed over to the person who held the bill, by way of signature. This is shown in figure 3, where the 1825 bill is endorsed five times. The last endorser was expected to redeem the bill when it came due, but if he failed to do so the holder could call upon any party who had signed it to pay the amount.[15] If the drawer, the drawee, or the endorsers failed to redeem the bill, a suspicion of insolvency fell on all parties and further bills including any of their names would immediately be refused for discount, making it impossible to raise cash. In such circumstances, bankruptcy was a foregone conclusion.

The Bank of England's cash withdrawal in April was immediately noticed by Archibald Constable and Co.'s London agents, Hurst, Robinson and Co. Writing on 18 April, Joseph Ogle Robinson (Cadell's counterpart at Hurst,

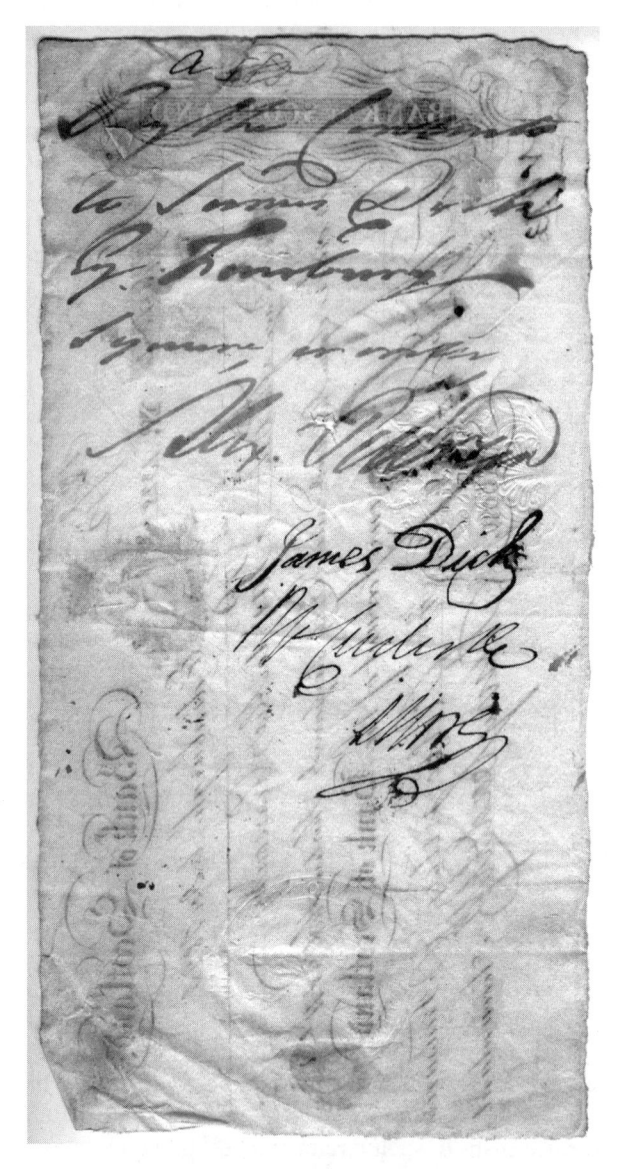

Fig. 3 Bank of Scotland bill of exchange endorsed by multiple parties between 1825 and 1826. Acc. 2003/105, 6 December 1825, v. Bank of Scotland.

Robinson) complained to the Edinburgh firm that "money is by no means plentiful, and the reason assigned is that the Stock-jobbing companies have swallowed much good money."[16] Scottish banks operated with a large degree of autonomy from English banks, and the cash shortage didn't arrive in Edinburgh until 1 October, when Cadell wrote to Robinson: "It is curious this sudden change in cash matters—it is now working here, and one is afraid to go to a Bank from the fear of getting, what is so unusual, a refusal."[17] Nine days later the first bill was refused.[18]

Cadell likely thought of the refusal as an inconvenience, but he knew that if the shortage continued it could lead to Archibald Constable and Co.'s financial ruin. In the course of business with Hurst, Robinson the Edinburgh firm had exchanged numerous bills that had been signed and immediately sent for discount, and a great amount of debt had been accrued by both parties. The majority of the London publisher's business was transacted in England and they dealt primarily in English bills, the payment for which was often delayed because of the cash crisis, putting a strain on Hurst, Robinson's finances. Cadell knew that if Hurst, Robinson failed to pay any bills bearing his signature, Constable and Co. would automatically be refused discount; any threat to Hurst, Robinson's finances was a threat to Constable. Thus it was of paramount importance that Cadell helped to pay Hurst, Robinson's creditors, as well as making sure that Constable and Co. had enough money to pay their own. The third party implicated in Hurst, Robinson's cash crisis was the printing firm Ballantyne and Co., headed by James Ballantyne and partly owned by Scott. Ballantyne and Co. had exchanged around £25,000 of bills with Constable and Co., and if the Edinburgh publisher applied for sequestration after Hurst, Robinson stopped paying their bills, the printing firm would soon follow. Ballantyne and Co. helped to keep the London firm solvent by providing accommodation and sending bills for discount. Indeed, Constable and Co., Hurst, Robinson and Co., and Ballantyne and Co. formed a fragile triumvirate of debt; if any party failed to pay a single bill that came due, all would be ruined. As Cadell wrote to Robinson, "he, and you and us are one."[19] But Constable and Co. was the link in this chain, and it fell largely to Cadell to perform the delicate task of propping up Hurst, Robinson without letting their debts (or Ballantyne and Co.'s) overrun them:

> I hand you sundry bills of Ja[mes] Ballantyne Co. which may turn to some use in your hands—I could have sent you some more . . . but you have spoken of the London Bill market in such away that I considered it unnecessary. . . . [The statement] which you have with this will shew you how A[C and Co.'s] bills come round the same due in November is £4216—I am sorely puzzled how to manage

it—I think it is better to draw for them, which I now do—and at short dates.[20]

Cadell's reference to "short dates" is telling. Previously, many of the bills discounted would have matured in six months. But in the uncertain climate, banks were reluctant to discount unless the bill was redeemed in one to two months. Cadell knew that such relief was only a hasty patch to a groaning dam, and his plan was to postpone bills due with cash from other discounted bills in the hope that the situation would soon change. Furthermore, when banks discounted bills they were taking a stake in the business from which the bill originated. A bill that carried any hint of the stock market—like a broker's bill—was not only likely to be refused, but would also impugn the company applying for discount. This was a problem for Hurst, Robinson, which regularly traded in the stock market. Upon receiving several such bills from Robinson as a cash payment, Cadell wrote back with the refusal, "such is the state of War . . . they looked so like Cotton bills that we thought it prudent not to put them in for disc[ount] here at all—I mean Cotton speculation bills—I do not think money is to get better soon—I do not like the tone of some of my banking friends."[21]

The strategy of paying bills due by further discount was threatened by Robinson's losing speculations in hops, and Constable's incessant borrowing, both of which absorbed much of the money raised. John Gibson Lockhart claims that Hurst, Robinson's total loss from hops was around £100,000 and there is no compelling reason to doubt this.[22] If Lockhart's estimation is anywhere near the actual amount, it was an enormous sum of money to lose, worth around £74,000,000 today.[23] Although there is no clear evidence indicating the exact nature of the speculations, from the correspondence it seems have been a cumulative loss sustained from November to at least mid-January. A drawn-out loss for such a large amount suggests that Robinson, much like a losing gambler attempting to best the house, was trying to recover his losses with larger and larger bets. While commentators have long delighted in vilifying Robinson for his failure, it is worth observing that he experienced some success in hops and that Cadell even encouraged the enterprise. Indeed, just seven days after complaining about Robinson's cotton bills, Cadell not only pronounced the speculations a legitimate strategy for generating capital, he hoped to take part in the future:

> I have your excellent letter of the 7th. I very much rejoice at the success of your adventures—you are acting must judiciously in the way of disposing of the proceeds. . . . You asked me the other day for some of my . . . brass—the truth is, it is at present all locked up in sundry spec[ulation]s . . . I shall not *Hop* out so well as you but

> I think I will get some little to add to the purse. I will most cheerfully join you in any speculation. . . . I wish you had told me of your Hop spec[ulation] . . . I was buying shares here that will not return a percentage of your gains—I shall try to reccollect [sic] next year if there is a good opening.[24]

Clearly, Robinson didn't lose the money in a single throw of the dice, and Cadell's letter no doubt persuaded Robinson to continue in his course. Cadell even defended Robinson when the speculations started going poorly. In one instance, he found himself surprised by an anxious Scott who

> told me plumply and plainly that a friend had waited on him and told him that reports to the discredit of this house (AC & Co.) were current in London that our principle correspondents had been engaged in other Trade besides bookselling—this you will allow was not a little posing . . . with regard to our correspondents I was going to explain the Hop transaction but he said he was obliged to go—in about half an hour not more, he returned . . . I then told him of the Hops matter.[25]

Cadell no doubt endorsed Robinson because, as a part owner of Ballantyne and Co., Scott had the power to stop the crucial trade and accommodation bills to the London firm. Furthermore, it is likely that as a self-fashioned day trader himself, Cadell believed that Robinson would recover from his increasingly rapid fall. Indeed, there is no evidence that Cadell ever censured Robinson for speculating, whereas Constable freely expressed his misgivings, as Cadell reported to Robinson: "When anything was whispered about your men engaged in other speculations—[Constable] would be very apt to say 'I told Mr Robinson of this Sir, I disapprove of it highly. I have advised Mr. Robinson to sell them all off and attend to his own business' and all this from a person who for six years has been building houses—and by every device getting money from his business to assist his operations."[26] One can empathize with Cadell's annoyance. Though Robinson's speculation only provided what Constable called "hopping payments," at least some income was made available.

Constable had long treated his publishing house as a personal bank, spending a considerable amount of the firm's money on property. He owned a tavern, the firm's shop on Princes Street, and a flat in Park Place. What money Constable made from his property was not returned to the firm but quickly absorbed by a lavish lifestyle. As Cadell relates, "he boasted when in London that his property was so much increased in value . . . that he must borrow."[27] But in early January, at the moment the money was most needed to fund Hurst, Robinson's debts, Constable conspired to keep it: "Mr Constable has got £2500 borrowed on a part of his property—he supposes I know nothing of it—but guess my horror to hear that £1000 is for you—it turns out that he has a debt of £1500 in Glasgow which no one ever heard of before . . .—you ought to write red hot shot at him for the whole sum, were I in your station I would not spare him."[28] This was normal behavior for Constable. From the very beginning of the crisis Cadell complained of his senior partner's withdrawals from the firm. However, as he acknowledged in early October, Cadell was reluctant to reprimand him—and might have even encouraged him—because whatever money was taken out of the concern reduced Constable's stake in the business: "How very grievous is imprudence—if Constable had in four years spent only say £4000 or £5000—what a nice thing £6000 or £7000 in hand cash would have been to the concern at this punished time . . . I spend nothing myself which makes it all the worse for him—as it makes the concern more and more mine—it is very odd that he does not see that—but nonsense vanity and vain glory are with him the order of the day—and will be to the end of the chapter."[29]

Cadell soon realized that this was a losing strategy: whatever portion of the business was gained was completely worthless in the event of sequestration. By late November Cadell altered his response to Constable's excesses: "in place of Mr C being of the smallest aid he got £650 on 11 Nov & £130 to day—nearly £800 in such times is infamous. I have written to him to say that I will not pay the allowance to his family on 1 Dec[ember]."[30] Cadell also employed other tactics: for example, when Robinson wrote in mid-November with a positive assessment of finances, Cadell refused to show it to Constable, fearing that it might inspire more expenditure. On the contrary, Cadell suggested that Robinson rewrite the letter in a tone "as gloomy as you please."[31]

Cadell had to be careful that his dash for ready money did not raise suspicion. In early nineteenth-century financial markets, the ability to acquire a discount was based almost exclusively on the reputation of the parties that were named on the bills. Rumors of desperate borrowing by any party could very quickly reduce the list of bankers willing to touch the bills. From 18 November both Constable and Co. and Hurst, Robinson had been named in the book trade as likely to fall, and Cadell endlessly conjectured as to the identity of the whisperers.[32] As long as the rumor stayed within the trade, its impact on their ability to discount would have been negligible, but once it spread to the banks, it had the potential to ruin them. On 22 November, when Cadell relayed to Robinson that Scott had warned him "it was openly stated in [John] Murray[']s shop that you and us had gone—and that our Banker had cast us off," he was no doubt anxious about the mention of his banker.[33]

The bank to which Scott likely referred was Dixon and Co. The Edinburgh firm's account with the London banker was secured by long-dated bills against which they would submit bills for discount.[34] Because of this security Dixon and Co. were more willing than most banks to provide regular discounts and even held a cash account for Constable and Co. from which they paid their London creditors. However, Dixon and Co. would not accept just any bill, as Constable relayed to Cadell: "Mr. D[ixon] was extremely out of humour yesterday about the amount of our drafts, and the *pell-mell* mode of new ones succeeding the old. The amounts, he remarked, carried accommodation on the face of them and might injure the credit of the house."[35] While in a more plentiful time accommodation bills might be quietly accepted, in the anxious days at the close of 1825, they were seen as indications of potential failure.

But banks were secretive organizations. They did not want to divulge information about overextended borrowers, as it would reflect poorly on their own finances. Cadell used this to his advantage, preferring to discount at the smaller private banks first, many of which soon became "as poor as rats."[36] Only as a last resort did he submit bills to major banks including the Bank of England, the Bank of Scotland, and the Royal Bank of Scotland. Cadell scrupulously recorded financial dealings in his diaries, and by totaling the various references to discounted bills it is possible to construct a relatively accurate picture of Constable and Co.'s cash operations during the crash.

As figure 4 shows, October was a relatively light month for discounting, partly because the threat to solvency wasn't fully comprehended, and partly because it was a "moderate" month for due bills.[37] November, which was a relatively "heavy" month, coincided with Cadell's realization of the full threat to the firm, and he stored up extra cash in order to outlast the shortage.[38] In December Cadell would have been even more concerned about stopping payments, but the accumulation of bills had become so great that he was regularly denied funds.

One strategy used to outwit the banks was a form of loan-laundering. Constable and Co. would draw accommodation bills on Hurst, Robinson, get them discounted, and then send the cash to the London publisher. While providing badly needed funds for Hurst, Robinson it helped the Edinburgh firm to appear somewhat more secure than if they had accommodated in the normal fashion, because they appeared to be creditors. But this strategy had limitations, as Cadell explained to a begging Robinson: "your Cos. name is so thickly studded in all directions that our discount a[ccounts] are full, and will not be relieved for some time—during last week we had five

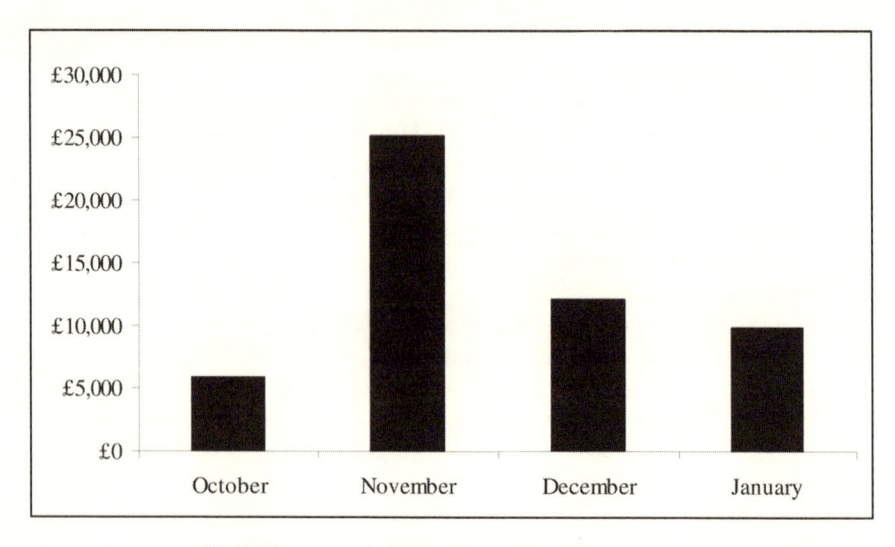

Fig. 4 Amount of bills discounted during the crash (October 1825–January 1826). The amounts are calculated from Cadell's diaries.

refusals of discount."[39] Mindful that bills from both firms were widely disbursed, Cadell and Robinson also sent bills for discount without endorsement.[40] If they were following established procedures it would have been impossible to get a bill discounted that did not bear their signature, so they must have used the services of a trusted acquaintance who presented it for discount and then handed over the funds.

But despite these measures, Constable's incessant borrowing and the losing hops speculations continued to devour available cash, while Robinson persisted in his demands. After Robinson asked Cadell to provide accommodation for the outrageous sum of £20,000 the latter wryly replied:

> Your letter of the 14th recd this morning put me precisely in the situation of the Turk, who was ordered to send the Sultan £20,000 (men) or his head, the one being possible, the other being impossible, he coolly replied that the head was very much at his highnesses service—It is very easy for you living at Constantinople to say, do this, but can it be done? the [sic] fact is, it is impossible.... [I]n fact to do what you say would be to demolish the credit of this concern—utterly demolish it.[41]

James Ballantyne had been regularly sending Cadell trade and accommodation bills for amounts as large as £2,500, but in the face of such pleas it was clear that Constable and Co. needed another source of capital if it was to outlast the panic. The firm found it in Sir Walter Scott. In searching for a villain in the narrative of Scott and Constable's downfall, Cadell has regularly been offered as a sacrifice, partly on the assumption that he took money from Scott when he knew it would be of little aid. John Sutherland, for example, claims that Cadell "lulled" Scott into a bond.[42] However, this elides both Constable's and Ballantyne's roles in the affair—and of course Scott's as well. Cadell relayed to Robinson that the first bond on Scott for £5,000 was proposed by Constable on 22 November: "Mr. Constable cannot command a shilling.... [He] suggests some plan of getting £5000 on a Bond with Sir Walters name and ours—which I think may be managed and perhaps within 2 or 3 weeks from this time."[43] His diary entry on the next day confirms that "Mr C[onstable] came to town . . . sent for Ballantyne—we all went to Sir W[alter] Scotts—and arranged to get £5000 on his name by Bond—& for it he is to discount £5000 of our & Hurst & Cos Bills."[44] This certainly makes more sense than laying the entire episode at Cadell's feet, as Scott was too canny of an operator to co-sign a bond at Cadell's behest alone. Indeed, in his journal Scott records Constable as the director of the meeting, while Cadell and Ballantyne are merely "present."[45] To everyone's relief, Scott signed the bond on 29 November, and on 1 December the resulting cash was made available.

The idea for the next bond that Scott signed did originate with Cadell. On 13 December Cadell wrote to Ballantyne suggesting he press Scott to take out £10,000 on Abbotsford in order to "put himself free from danger."[46] Inasmuch as Cadell's strategy was to pay only the mature bills until more money could be earned, he hoped that £10,000 would enable Scott to do the same. Clearly at this point Cadell expected that the worst was likely, and he wanted to save Scott from sinking along with him. Constable was not so generous in his assessment, according to Cadell's diary entry of 19 December: "Mr C[onstable] returned from Sir Walter & Ballantyne—[I] had along talk with him when he said to my utter astonishment that if a disaster befel [sic] us it would *be brought on by Sir Walter Scott*—and this when I stated that I mourned over the idea of Sir WS being levelled by Booksellers."[47]

Writing on 29 November 1825, a commentator for the *Morning Herald* commented that "the book trade was never known to be in so depressed a state as at the present time. The Bank of England has refused for the last three weeks to discount any bookseller's bill."[48] As what had once been the subject of rumors increasingly became common knowledge, the pressure on Cadell increased, and it had already been far from comfortable. Indeed, one week before the *Herald* report, Cadell revealed in a letter written to Robinson at "1/4 p[ast] 4" in the morning: "Little sleep is my lot just now . . . you should know that for some weeks we have scarcely tried Bank or

Banker *from fear*—now we must try them for we must have cash for our own payments and I tremble for the trial—one does not know till they do try or [how] far reports have had an effect on them."⁴⁹

As the head of the firm's finances, Cadell shouldered almost the entire responsibility for coordinating payments with Robinson and Ballantyne, which by late November had become incredibly complex arrangements in order to preserve the appearance of solvency. In the following letter to Robinson, one can sense the strain that the labyrinthine programs of payment had placed on Cadell:

> We drew on you . . . [for] £1,630 due on 26/29 Decem[ber] now having got Dixon & Co. free to a certain extent, I now enclose on them £1,631. 2/ which will exactly fit said sum on 29th December this I hope may be of use to you, I trust to be able in about a week or Tuesday, to send you some more, perhaps as much as [to] cover the bill [for] £2000 you gave to Mr C[onstable] for Dixon Co.—but to enable me to do this, I hope you will without difficulty to manage the following for me. I enclose [a bill] on Dixon & Co.—nineteenth instant at 2 mos due 19/22 Jany [for] £1589.12—this will reach you on the 21st present the draft [for] £1.631 2/ on receipt but the other it would be better if you could keep till the 24th—on second thoughts the 23rd will do—but I want you to pay to Dixon Co. on the 24th £1000 and on the 25th £560 the 21st would do if the 25th is not so convenient.⁵⁰

As companies in the early nineteenth century operated with unlimited liability, Cadell's personal estate was under threat as well, and in late November he began selling his own stock holdings in order to pay the firm's debts, advising Robinson to do the same.⁵¹ Cadell also began to approach other members of the book trade, friends, and relatives for personal loans. He was able to raise a considerable sum by mid-December: the engravers Lizars discounted two bills totaling £1,000, and "private friends" loaned £2,500.⁵²

By far the most important of Cadell's personal acquaintances were his brother William and his nephew Henry, William's son. William was conveniently placed as the Treasurer of the Bank of Scotland, and Henry as an accountant under his charge. The office of treasurer was the second highest position at the bank, and his main duty was to approve bills for discounting. Each discount Robert applied for would have required the signature of the treasurer or a secretary signing with his authority. If the bank did not pay the discounted bill in bank notes, it would have used bills of exchange, which would have required signatures from William (or his secretary) and the accountant (see figure 5). Thus William would have been able to both accept Robert's bills and to pay him with limited oversight.

Unsurprisingly, Cadell could get bills discounted at the Bank of Scotland that were likely to be refused elsewhere. From October to January, Cadell had submitted thirty-five bills to William and Henry for discount, for a grand total of £13,143 23s.[53] Excluded from this total is a discount on 29 December 1825: Cadell thanks "God the Bank of S[cotland] did all we asked[,] £3300." The meticulously kept ledgers at the Bank of Scotland archives do not show a discount for the firm on this date, nor for this amount. While the omission need not be anything more sinister than a misplaced ledger entry, it is instructive to note that Constable and Co. were never asked to pay the amount when sequestrated, and that the bank's gatekeepers, William and Henry, would have had to sign off on the discount.

Were William and Henry colluding to defraud the bank? Possibly. Sometime after the crash William was investigated by the bank and was accused of having accepted a large number of bad bills and of failing to operate in an open manner. Following his resignation in 1832, procedures were altered.[54] There is evidence to suggest that William—and by extension Henry—was aware of the precariousness of Constable and Co. For example, on 18 December, a day when Cadell feared for several hours that Hurst, Robinson would stop payment, he notes that "William called I was very gloomy with

Fig. 5 Bank of Scotland bill of exchange signed by Henry Cadell, accountant, and Robert Cormley, secretary to William Cadell. The bill is one of only three surviving bills of exchange during issued during Cadell's treasureship from 1824 to 1832. Acc. 2003/105, 6 Dec. 1825, r.

him," implying that Robert had informed him of the probable failure.[55] In early January, when William arranged bills for the firm, Cadell noted "he was very kind."[56] At the very least, William and Henry's loyalty to Robert seems to have overridden their responsibility to make prudent discounts. By January major banks like the Bank of England, the British Linen Co., and the Royal Bank of Scotland had been refusing Constable and Co.'s bills with regularity, but under William's treasurership and Henry's accountancy, the Bank of Scotland continued to discount the questionable bills right up until 13 January 1826, one day before Hurst, Robinson stopped payment.[57]

The deception necessary to gain people's trust weighed heavily on Cadell's conscience. In the conclusion to his 1825 diary he morosely opined:

> If this Journal and this memorandum should at any time after my decease be read by any son that I may have, let him have my pew—the warning that experience gives of the utter want of comfort in trading upon borrow and capital—it is always deceitful & always dangerous, and places one if uncomfortable under such circumstances in the appalling situation of mining many persons ignorant of his situation—and who trusted and aided him on the strength of his character and Knowledge of business.[58]

Aside from William's considerable support, Robert was essentially alone in running the business. When Constable did appear at the bookstore, his advice was a distraction: "Mr C[onstable] does me no good & I never consult him—indeed his advice is of no use—money is what I am in search of."[59] By early January 1826 Cadell was exhausted by his efforts to keep the three firms solvent: "Such a course of anxiety as these times have brought with them, I hope never to see again—it is quite terrible, first you are ill and get well again—then a fresh disease—we have a touch of it next, along with Ballantyne and all of us now have it to such a degree as to make the case one of deep distress—I confess I shudder at the very sight of your [Robinson's] letters."[60]

This was the mindset of an individual who had already given up on the business. Though it is often claimed that he waited to leave Constable until the sequestration began, he had already done so in December. Spurred on by Constable's financial counsel, on 20 December he resigned from the firm, as he detailed in his diary:

> My mind much bent on telling Mr C[onstable] about . . . my resolution to leave AC & Co. when this present danger is over . . . found [Mr. Constable] in the shop . . . [we] came to a fair out & out conversation when I told him peremptorily *that I would no longer*

go on with him—the present danger once over . . . that I was resolved to be off with the creditors . . . paid off & Sir W Scott once free from the danger through us, I was resolved to part company with him & Mr Constable. I told him this calmly—after I got my mind resolved I went and told the whole to [James] Ballantyne—out and out—I agreed to his telling Sir W[alter Scott] about it.[61]

To save Scott, to be free of the guilt of deceiving his friends and family, to be free of Constable and the stresses of arranging payments, Cadell recognized that a bolder strategy than paying off creditors piecemeal was needed. On 2 January 1826 Cadell wrote of the hope of acquiring "a large monied aid," which he estimated was nothing less than £46,000.[62] In a display of creative finance, Constable suggested the scheme of raising £57,000 from London banks, a total comprising Scott copyrights valued at £37,000 and a bond on Scott for £20,000.[63] If they were able to borrow the amount in long dated bills and then recoup it in book sales, the plan was a reasonable solution. Banks would not loan such sums to a junior partner, and the scheme required the full authority of Constable's presence in London. But, thwarting the plan in predictable fashion, Constable declined to travel, claiming ill health. In Scott's view, Constable "dawdled here till in all human probability his going or staying became a matter of mighty little consequence."[64] It was not until a number of bills were refused on 12 January that Cadell demanded that Constable go to London at the risk of losing everything if he declined: "Matters are now on such a pivot, that one day may do or undo all. For God's sake think of this; think of the many that must fall with us, and the ruin that must be spread far and wide. There is one other thing,—any delay, even a few hours, may stop you in a snowstorm, and upset all! Oh that you had been in London now, as at first intended."[65] Constable capitulated and traveled the next day. By the time he arrived on the morning of the 16th, it was already too late.[66] Two days before, on 14 January, Hurst, Robinson refused to redeem a £1,000 bill that had come due. Cadell feared it had been discounted at the Bank of Scotland. It was the threat that Cadell had fought against for nearly four months. In his own words it "settle[d] the business," ruining all three firms.[67]

On 17 January Constable performed the quixotic task of attempting to wring money from bankers who knew his firm was ruined. Along with Robinson, Constable first called on Dixon and Co., who politely declined to loan Constable money, prompting Robinson to frantically ask for a £5,000 to £10,000 advance on bills. Upon being refused, Robinson left, and Dixon informed Constable that "the dealings of Hurst, Robinson, and Co. had become greatly too extensive, and he had been anxious for some to me to have seen our connexion with them lessened."[68] The next banker was a Mr.

Carstairs, who again declined any discount or loan, and after that a Mr. Mills, who, with unwitting irony, recommended he try Scottish banks. One financier, a "Mr. Green of Enfield," offered to loan Hurst, Robinson and Co. £10,000, but only on security of £40,000, and his proposal was rejected outright.[69] Without any hope of finance, Constable tried the Bank of England for a loan of "£100,000 to £200,000" on the security of his copyrights.[70] Unsurprisingly, the bank refused. Upon informing Cadell of the events, Constable condescended to observe that "it is a sad misfortune that either you or myself had not been here a fortnight ago," and indeed it was, as Constable's tardiness ensured that Cadell's remarkably successful discounting of over £53,000 only led to more debt for Robinson, Ballantyne, and Scott.[71] After receiving news of the stoppage, Cadell exclaimed to Constable: "Alas! alas! such is the end of all our hopes and expectations. I have struggled hard. I have fought as for my life . . . but now I see no escape."[72]

Someone had to be held accountable for the failures that led to Scott's downfall. While Scott has not escaped blame entirely, he has often been overlooked as a culprit, possibly because of his status as an eminent author. In John Lockhart's influential Life of Sir Walter Scott (1837–38) and The Ballantyne-Humbug Handled (1839), both of which were originally published by Cadell, the two guilty parties are James Ballantyne and Constable.[73] But Lockhart's portrayals are selective—unsurprisingly so, given Cadell's role as publisher. For example, Lockhart blames Ballantyne for mismanaging funds, but, obviously, Scott entered into the partnership with James of his own volition and had he limited his financial relations with the printer, he would have avoided the crisis. To remove Scott's responsibility is a condescension that ignores his pecuniary skills, recently elaborated by Sam McKinstry and Marie Fletcher.[74] On balance, Lockhart's depiction of Constable is more justly rendered: Constable is shown traveling to London until it is too late and behaving with unjustifiable bombast, only to be deflated by the ensuing refusals.[75] Though Lockhart declines to mention it, Constable also took money out of the firm at a time when a £1,000 bill brought all three houses down. But perhaps he should be afforded more leniency. Ill with gout, it would have been excruciating for him to bounce for days in a carriage along the frozen Great North Road. Furthermore, Constable was of an older school of bookselling where deals were made in taverns and rarely entered into ledgers. For years the firm had survived his frequent withdrawals, and it would have seemed outrageous to suddenly rein in his spending. As a publisher who had been a prime force in the popularization of Scottish writers, one can imagine his incredulity at being told to stop pilfering the cash box by a far lesser partner. No doubt in Constable's view,

Cadell had been taken on in order to provide for his excesses, not to restrict them.

Is Robinson then to blame? Certainly his speculations swallowed up far more money during the crash than Constable did, but as Lockhart observes he was not alone in trading beyond the bookshop: "When it was rumoured that this great bookseller, or printer, had become a principal holder of South American mining shares—that another was the leading director of a railway company—a third of a gas company—while a fourth house had risked about £100,000 in a cast upon the most capricious of all agricultural products—*hops*, it was no wonder that bankers should begin to calculate balances and pause upon discounts."[76] But this singles out the book trade at a time when refusals were endemic in all commercial activity. If Robinson can be blamed at all, it is for his judgment not to cut his losses before they grew too great.

But if neither Ballantyne, Constable, nor Robinson are wholly at fault for the downfall, how then have we come to blame Cadell, who sacrificed his reputation and personal wealth attempting to save Scott and the firm? I would argue that Cadell's conviction is partly a result of Lockhart's overly enthusiastic criticism of Constable, encouraging Constable's son Thomas to largely exculpate his father in the hagiographic *Archibald Constable and his Literary Correspondents*. While not entirely exonerating his father, Thomas Constable attempts to throw Lockhart's version of events into doubt, leaving the door open for future scholars to be far less objective in their assessments.[77] The first major work of this nature was Eric Quayle's *The Ruin of Sir Walter Scott*, which offered a host of insinuation but no direct evidence that Cadell was scheming to defraud Constable and Scott. Most recently, in *Life of Walter Scott*, John Sutherland accuses Cadell of cynically profiting from the sequestration he brought about.[78]

Lacking the motivation of Thomas Constable's familial ties, why do Quayle and Sutherland single out Cadell? If one overlooks the evidence, it is more appealing to criticize him than Ballantyne, Robinson, or Constable. Ballantyne is likely given a pass in part because his financial intimacy with Scott meant any sustained criticism would impugn the renowned author and in part because Lockhart had so thoroughly criticized Ballantyne that further attacks would have been redundant. There is relatively little documentary evidence about Robinson's role, so he is difficult to indict. Constable benefits from a reputation as one of the greatest publishers of the nineteenth century, and his immoderation is held out as proof of his literary prowess.

Against the brilliance of Constable, a mere businessman who engaged in the dirty work of deceptive discounting and balancing accounts has little chance. But without Cadell's work, Robinson, Ballantyne, Constable, and

Scott would have been unable to outlast the crash as long as they did, and his preemptive resignation cast him in a more positive light than has been recently imagined. Had he only been after Scott copyrights, as it is so often claimed, he would never have left the firm; he certainly wouldn't have told Ballantyne of his plan to "part company with [Scott]."[79] Before abandoning Cadell to compete with an idealized Constable, perhaps we should consider Scott's view, which is rarely quoted. Upon hearing that Robinson continued paying his bills on 18 December, when it was thought the opposite was true, Scott recalls how Cadell rushed to Abbotsford, bringing good news that Hurst, Robinson "had stood the storm. . . . I shall always think the better of Cadell for this—not merely because his feet are beautiful on the mountains who brings good tidings but because he shewd feeling—deep feeling, poor fellow—he who I thought had no more than his numeration table. . . . I will not forget this if I get through."[80]

Notes

1. Thomas Constable, *Archibald Constable and His Literary Correspondents* (Edinburgh: Edmonston and Douglas, 1873), 3:403–4.

2. For an account of the Constable sequestration based on new archival research, see Ross Alloway, "The Sequestration of Archibald Constable and Co.," in *Papers of the Bibliographical Society of America* (forthcoming in 2009). Simon Eliot considers the impact of the crash on British book production in "1825–1826: Years of Crisis?" in *The Edinburgh History of the Book in Scotland*, vol. 3, *Industry and Ambition 1800–1880*, ed. Bill Bell (Edinburgh: Edinburgh University Press, 2007), 91–95. Furthermore, I provide a detailed statistical analysis of bankruptcies that is based on legal announcements in "Bankrupt Books? The Aftermath of the 1825–1826 Crash on the British Book Trade," in *Publishing History* (2007): 41–52.

3. Jane Millgate, *Scott's Last Edition* (Edinburgh: University of Edinburgh Press, 1987).

4. Caroline McCracken-Flesher, *Possible Scotlands* (Oxford: Oxford University Press, 2005), 18.

5. The painting was commissioned by the publisher James Keith and was displayed to the public in his shop in 1850. Thomas Faed came from a family of painters for whom idealized literary gatherings were a recognized theme. Following his brother, John Faed painted the well known *Shakespeare and His Contemporaries* (1851), which was composed of famous Tudors. In these paintings, historical accuracy gave way to literary celebrity. For the Walter Scott painting, there is no correspondence that proves Cadell was actively excluded, however Thomas acknowledged that the participants were "suggested to me by several Gentleman" (quoted from Mary McKerrow, *The Faeds: A Biography* [Edinburgh: Cannongate, 1982], 94–95). Though Cadell's association with Scott was well known, he was obviously not deemed a suitable addition by Faed's advisors. Indeed, the inclusion of Constable and Ballantyne pushed the boundaries of acceptability: Faed later claimed that "they had no right" to be there and they were removed in a version for the American market that included Byron (ibid., 95).

6. The major descriptions of the crash are found in biographies of Scott and Constable, where Cadell (who never had his own book-length biography) is given comparatively minor attention. Such biographies include John Gibson Lockhart's *The Life of Sir Walter Scott* (Edinburgh: Robert Cadell, 1837); Thomas Constable's *Archibald Constable and His Literary Cor-*

respondents, vol. 3; Eric Quayle's *The Ruin of Sir Walter Scott* (London: Rupert Hart-Davis, 1968); and John Sutherland's *The Life of Walter Scott* (London: Blackwell, 1995).

7. Both Quayle and Sutherland give Cadell this treatment; the former accusing him of "double crossing" Constable, the latter of scheming to borrow from Scott.

8. Stefan Altorfer, *History of Financial Disasters 1763–1995* (London: Pickering and Chatto, 2006), 1:161.

9. Upon joining the firm as a partner, Cadell wrote to Constable: "At this moment our engagements in Bills entirely exclusive of Bonds &c. are above the sum of £75,000. I know you will be astonished at this as I was . . . and no less so when, during this year, £42,000 and upwards are payable" (Quayle, *Ruin of Sir Walter Scott,* 85).

10. Peter Garside and Iain Gordon Brown, "New Information on the Publication of the Early Editions of *Waverley,*" *Journal of the Edinburgh Bibliographical Society* 2 (2007): 19.

11. MS 21014, 31 December 1824. National Library of Scotland (hereafter NLS).

12. Poovey inaccurately describes the drawer of a bill as "the person who drafts a bill of exchange against his account, generally in a bank or with a merchant" and notes that the acceptor of a bill "receives a bill of exchange as payment." In fact it is the drawer who receives the payment and the acceptor who pays the drawer. See Mary Poovey, *The Financial System in Nineteenth-Century Britain* (Oxford: Oxford University Press, 2003), 357–58.

13. Technically, a bill of exchange is used to transmit money between countries, and there is a third party involved in the process, a payee, whom the drawer instructs the drawee to pay a certain amount (if he desired, the drawer could also instruct the drawee to pay him). In early nineteenth-century Britain, the bills that the book trade used were legally understood to be "inland bills," in that they were restricted to Britain, and were commonly drawn between two parties, the drawer and the drawee. However, over time, inland bills were conflated with bills of exchange, and in deference to this fact, the article will refer to inland bills as bills of exchange. (For example, see George Rae, "Bills of Exchange" [originally published in 1885], in Poovey, *Financial System,* 51–59; see also "bill of exchange" in the *Oxford English Dictionary.*) For a description of bills of exchange and inland bills, see George Joseph Bell, *Principles of the Law of Scotland* (Edinburgh: William Blackwood, 1830). For financial novices, Bell's descriptions have yet to be surpassed for their clarity and concision.

14. Reflecting upon Constable and Co.'s vast debts after the sequestration, Scott commented that "[n]o doubt trading almost entirely on accomodation [*sic*] is dreadfully expensive" (Walter Scott, *The Journal of Sir Walter Scott,* ed. W. E. K. Anderson [Oxford: Clarendon Press, 1972], 71). Over the years, literary historians have used the passage as proof of the financial extravagance of accommodation. For example, David Hewitt recently reflected on the quote in his *Oxford Dictionary of National Biography* entry for Constable: "Trading on accommodation, in other words relying on bank borrowings to finance the business, was expensive, but although it must have reduced the available profit it does not explain the enormous gap between assets and liabilities." But as accommodation is much like a credit it is the most straightforward way to account for the debt Constable and Co. had accumulated: they borrowed beyond their means. Hewitt's contention that accommodation was necessarily expensive is similarly problematic. As accommodation bills appeared as bills of exchange, they were discounted by the banks at the same low rate. Indeed, as the Bank of Scotland's ledger for the "State of Particular Debts 1820–1832" shows, not one of the bills that Cadell sent to the bank for discounting during the crisis was charged above 5 percent, and many of these would have been bills of accommodation. To give an example, one apparent accommodation bill on Constable and Co. for £1,480, which was discounted at the bank for five months at 4.5 percent, would have resulted in a negligible charge of around £27. ("State of Particular Debts 1820–1832," NRAS945 1/166/2, Bank of Scotland Archive.) To take the same bill at 4.5 percent interest but now at one month, the discount charge would be around £5; at forty-five months,

£249. Though such charges were far from usurious, one still had to redeem the bill when it matured. For years Constable and Co. had raised the money for a due bill by getting more bills discounted, and with the banks lending money at low interest rates, the firm opted to defer payment and increase debt.

15. The holder would usually claim on the endorsers in ascending order, from the last endorser up to the drawer.
16. Constable, *Constable and His Literary Correspondents,* 3:346.
17. MS 23620, Robert Cadell to Joseph Ogle Robinson, 1 October 1825, f. 93. NLS.
18. MS 21015, 10 October 1925. NLS.
19. MS 23620, 14 December 1825, f. 136.
20. Ibid. ff. 93.
21. Ibid. ff. 93v–94.
22. Constable, *Constable and His Literary Correspondents,* 3:333.
23. The calculation was made from the Web site Measuring Worth (http://www.measuringworth.com/ukcompare) using average the earnings index for 1830 in comparison to 2005.
24. MS 23620, 11 October 1825, ff. 97–98v.
25. Ibid., 18 November 1825, ff. 103–4.
26. Ibid., 27 November 1825, f. 124.
27. Ibid., 4 January 1826, f. 151v.
28. Ibid., f. 150.
29. Ibid., 1 October 1825, f. 94.
30. Ibid., 25 November 1825, f. 122v.
31. Ibid., 18 November 1825, f. 107.
32. Ibid., 20 November 1825, f. 109.
33. Ibid., 22 November 1825, f. 116. John Murray was a well-known London bookseller.
34. Ibid., 13 January 1826.
35. Constable, *Constable and His Literary Correspondents,* 3:375.
36. Ibid., 3:377.
37. MS 23620, 1 October 1825, f. 93v.
38. Ibid.
39. Ibid., 17 October 1825, f. 102.
40. Constable, *Constable and His Literary Correspondents,* 3:377.
41. MS 23620, 17 October 1825, f. 101.
42. Lockhart, *Life of Walter Scott,* 8:286.
43. MS 23620, 22 November 1825, ff. 115.
44. MS 21015, 23 November 1825.
45. Scott, *Journal of Sir Walter Scott,* 9.
46. MS 21015, 13 December 1825.
47. Ibid., 19 December 1825.
48. Constable, *Constable and His Literary Correspondents,* 3:477.
49. MS 23620, 22 November 1825, f. 115.
50. Ibid., 18 November 1825, ff. 105.
51. Ibid., 21 November 1825, f. 111.
52. MS 21015, 14 December 1825; Constable, *Constable and His Literary Correspondents,* 3:394.
53. "State of Particular Debts 1820–1832."
54. NRAS 945 20/4/6, Bank of Scotland.
55. MS 21015, 18 December 1825.
56. MS 21016, 2 January 1826. NLS.
57. "State of Particular Debts 1820–1832."

58. MS 21015, 31 December 1825.
59. MS 23620, 12 December 1825 f. 133v.
60. Ibid., 4 January 1826, f. 150.
61. MS 21015, 20 December 1825.
62. MS 21016, 1 January 1826; Constable, *Constable and His Literary Correspondents*, 3:399.
63. Constable, *Constable and His Literary Correspondents*, 3:406. The bond clearly contradicted Cadell's professed loyalty to Scott, and though he was willing to go along with the plan, he let Robinson know that it was Constable's design. Cadell only referred to it obliquely in his letter to Robinson: "Mr Constable has some plan which he will submit to you, which should yield soon £20,000."
64. Scott, *Journal of Sir Walter Scott*, 60.
65. Constable, *Constable and His Literary Correspondents*, 3:396–97.
66. Ibid., 3:408.
67. Ibid., 3:418.
68. Ibid., 3:409.
69. Ibid., 3:415.
70. Lockhart, *Life of Sir Walter Scott*, 8:163.
71. Constable, *Constable and His Literary Correspondents*, 3:410–11. Though Thomas Constable derides the notion that Constable's earlier appearance would have saved the firm, all the major figures in the incident agree it would have: Cadell, Constable, Robinson, and even Scott (*Journal of Sir Walter Scott*, 61).
72. Constable, *Constable and His Literary Correspondents*, 3:419.
73. In *The Ballantyne-Humbug Handled* (Edinburgh: Robert Cadell, 1839), John Gibson Lockhart gives specific details of Ballantyne's mismanagement: "We have Scott giving [James] the means to pay a debt of £3000 in 1816, and above £4000 from the same source to expunge debt in 1822—we have James squandering £7000 of Sir Walter's from 1822–1826—here we have, without computing interest, about one third of the £46,000 of bills in 1826 accounted for! and if certain entries in James's cash-jottings tell any thing, I suspect no very difficult investigation would bring out, *that private debts, of which he paid the interest, and bills, which he appears to have negotiated for his own purposes, came all eventually to be paid by Sir Walter*, and formed a part of the above sum of £46,000" (114).
74. Sam McKinstry and Marie Fletcher, "The Personal Account Books of Sir Walter Scott," *Accounting Historian's Journal* 29 (2002): 59–89.
75. Lockhart, *Life of Sir Walter Scott*, 8:160–65.
76. Quoted from *Archibald Constable and His Literary Correspondents*, 3:333.
77. For example, Thomas Constable (*Constable and His Literary Correspondents*, 3:396) argues that Lockhart's and Cadell's criticism of Constable's late arrival in London was misplaced.
78. Quayle, *Ruin of Sir Walter Scott*, chaps. 14–17; Sutherland, *Life of Walter Scott*, passim.
79. MS 21015, 20 December 1825.
80. Scott, *Journal of Sir Walter Scott*, 42.

Authorship, Ownership, and the Case for *Charles Anderson Chester*

David Faflik

In his 1955 bibliography for the Philadelphia writer George Lippard, Roger Butterfield mentions the little-known pamphlet novel *Life and Adventures of Charles Anderson Chester* (1849) as "an imitation by another hand"—which is to say, as the labor of an author other than Lippard, and in effect as lifted from Lippard's more fully realized 1850 novel *The Killers*.[1] Both narratives recount Philadelphia's election-night race riots of October 1849, and both do so in sensational fashion. Moreover, the two texts do indeed share, verbatim, extended passages that make comparisons between them inevitable and the charge of plagiarism compelling. Following the lead of Phil Lapsansky, Research Librarian at the Library Company of Philadelphia,[2] I nevertheless maintain that Lippard did in fact write *Chester*.

I contend further that the case in question is symptomatic of changing standards in literary production, and reception, at America's mid-nineteenth century. For not only do the circumstances informing *Chester*'s printedness help clarify bibliographic matters of its attribution; they also reveal just how flexible were the categories of authorship, and thus ownership, and hence attribution, too, within the framework of an antebellum print culture in which collaborative composition had become the rule, and isolated acts of individual creation figured as exceptions. Quite simply, period literary practices transformed the creative act itself. At a vital, if volatile, time in the American past, "creation" ever more lost certain of its traditional romantic connotations, chief among them lingering ideals of original "inspiration," poetic invention, and the definitive, independent, and independently attributable utterance of a commanding seer-sayer.[3] In their place emerged "creative" acts like those involving *Chester*.

Chester's appearance highlights a different aspect of romanticism. It was and is one that recommends the entire artistic *process*, rather than any fin-

---

I would like to thank the editor and anonymous readers of *Book History* for their help in revising this article.

ished literary product, as a legitimate work of art.[4] Crucially, *Chester* reveals how this process continued all the way to, through, and past publication and, further, how the progress of this *artisanal* process relied foremost on an assembled team of "originators." Lippard, like so many others affiliated with the popular press, functioned within what Robert Darnton has called a "communications circuit." Central to that circuit was the mutual interdependence of an assorted group of writers, publishers, printers, readers, and merchandising middlemen—the virtual simultaneity of whose collective endeavors challenged the very notion of autonomous expression, let alone exclusive print-proprietorship.[5] *Chester*'s back pages epitomize this shift from the romantically singular to the emphatically (and democratically) plural.

They demonstrate as well that the combined forces of *Chester*'s varied participants invite an altered conception of what we mean by "originative." Surrounded from the start by a coterie of able abettors, Lippard did not so much initiate a literary act when he sat down to pen this particular pamphlet novel; he instead drew from a preexisting source of common subject matter that he happened upon after the fact, in more ways than one. A native Pennsylvanian, Lippard had moved to the metropolis in his youth, working when and where he could as an orphaned, often unemployed adolescent. He reached the formative age of fifteen in 1837 just as the country slipped into a severe economic recession, and just as many city laborers had begun to exchange more conventional modes of labor organizing for the kinds of radical street protests that would convert Lippard to the working man's cause. Time spent as a vagabond journalist followed, and it was a brief apprenticeship. Lippard progressed in a few years' time from being an able reporter-observer of municipal affairs with an abiding interest in the labor question, to standing tall as one of the era's leading authors of popular city-fiction—from which heights he deepened, rather than curtailed, his involvement in working-class advocacy.[6]

Chester, predictably, derives from a high-profile contemporary incident involving Philadelphia's disadvantaged classes, an incident that already had been much reported on by area newspapermen and much talked about by pedestrians on city streets for some days prior to the time when Lippard's own involvement in this socio-literary event began. No inimitable personal vision this: *Chester* was but one of several opportunistic accounts of race, class, and politics colliding on a then-recent night in the City of Brotherly Love. Lippard duly added his name to a list of commentators on local urban violence after what seems only a short interval. As we will see, he even was willing to *re*-tell later the tale he himself had already told. Meredith McGill describes related instances of U.S. purveyors of print having reprinted—that is, having "repackaged and redeployed"—the works of European writers for American readers in American print venues, without due concern for copyright.[7] *Chester*'s borrowings by contrast are a domestic concern, and cut to the heart of textual generation. Lippard and others had not merely recycled content from a foreign source. They had perpetrated "creative" acts that, in antebellum defiance of the conventional sense of that term, sacrificed inspired solitary authorship to what bibliographer Butterfield would have deemed an "imitative" undertaking, and what any of Lippard's laboring brethren—whether working manually or with words—might have styled fine "copy."

The Lippardians, in short, made no pretense of having "gotten" the story first. At *Chester*'s core accordingly was a narrative "foreign," extrinsic, in a shared sense. It derived from a source not outside the United States proper, but from scattered sources outside any one deliberating author's consciousness. It inhered not in any individual act of invention, but in opportunistic occasions for *re*-invention. *Chester was* the news of the day, and it was fit to print repeatedly on any number of separate occasions, and in any number of almost indistinguishable forms and formats. *Chester* was also, in its reiterative tellings and reliance on an extended community of co-creators, an extreme example of what was fast becoming in certain northeastern quarters an increasingly familiar story—the plot of which traced the conflation of shopwork with piecework with craftwork.

Chester in actuality collapses three stories into one. First among these is the story within *Chester*'s pages that, convoluted though it may be, warrants attention in its own right. Readers' attention centers on the tale's eponymous protagonist. Charles Anderson Chester is a dissolute student at a New England college, where his embrace of a sporting life has seen him neglect his studies, fall heavily into debt, and lose favor in the eyes of his unloving father, a wealthy Philadelphia merchant whose own dissolution rivals that of his son's. Disinherited, Chester junior seeks an interview with the senior Chester, only to discover that his parents (on the verge of marital collapse, with Mrs. Chester about to run off with an English aristocrat) are out of town on holiday. What follows is a rapid sequence that sees the young Chester forge a check in his father's name, abscond to New York with a sizeable sum of family money, and then flee the United States aboard a steamer bound for Havana. Thus ends part 1.

Part 2 overlaps with *Chester*'s second story, the real-world riot that provides a historically informed climax for the dramatic action to come. The facts are as follows. In October 1849, on the night following a tense municipal election, a riot broke out in one of Philadelphia's predominantly working-class districts in the southern precincts of the city. Hostilities revolved around the California House, a mixed-race tavern and bawdy house owned and operated by a local African American dubbed Hercules—whose wife was white. Already roused by the previous evening's election, and nursing pent-up resentments toward socially assertive blacks, agitators turned rioters when they attacked and set the California House ablaze. Several (white) fire companies arrived on the scene to fight the fire, only to begin fighting both black residents and rival (white) area gangs, including the notorious Killers. Back inside the text, meanwhile, Chester has returned from Havana and settled into young adulthood as the Killers' titular leader. He has been nursing grievances of his own during his time in exile, and father and son will reunite in the novel's denouement at the one and only California House.

Chester's third story, a parallel second story outside the text, provides still more gripping interest. For book historians, at least, attention shifts in this instance from a fictionalized account of *destructive* urban tendencies to an instructive telling of *Chester*'s publication history—itself an object lesson in the multiple sites for creative input and collaboration that both prefigured and resulted from the making of many an antebellum text. Thus unfolds this third story. Like Lippard's best-selling romance *The Quaker City* (1844) earlier,[8] and *The Killers* later, *Chester* reached the public by a roundabout route that Lippard traveled often in his short career. *Chester* appeared anonymously, as did the first edition of *The Quaker City* five years before. *Chester*'s copyright page bears the name of a nonexistent publisher, as would *The Killers* shortly afterward.[9] And the expansion by one third of the thirty-six-page *Chester* to the fifty-page *Killers* matches the 20 percent add-on that Lippard effected for *The Quaker City*'s second and third 1845 editions once he realized he had a hit on his hands.[10]

With *Chester*, in short, Lippard seems to have been up to his old tricks of the publishing trade—writing fast and furious to meet market demand,[11] back-pedaling to fill in the holes of his prose, and then moving to secure personal copyright, and thus greater profits, for a work that some other publishing concern (perhaps his own) then might bring out to Lippard's advantage. He had done as much with *The Quaker City*, buying back both the copyright and stereotype plates from his original publisher, G. B. Zieber, with whom he all the while maintained cordial business relations.[12] He would have had reason enough to do as much and more in the case of *Chester* and its close cousin, *Killers*. For even as *The Killers* began appearing serially on 1 December 1849 in Lippard's *Quaker City Weekly* newspaper, the author was deeply involved in the welter of negotiations so often experienced by participants in the print business of his generation. At stake in those negotiations was whether, why, how, and on whose terms authors would or could control their intellectual property.

To begin, Lippard found himself by decade's end in-between publishers for his fiction. That was for him by no means an anomalous predicament. The timing, however, could not have been worse. At the peak of his popularity, by mid-decade Lippard had become the victim of repeated raids by plagiarists who were all too eager to rework (or not) his plots[13]—precisely the scenario Butterfield proposed with respect to *Chester*. Lippard responded in 1846 by forming his own publishing concern. The idea was to capitalize on *The Quaker City*'s success with a sequel, tentatively titled *The Nazarene*, even as the author took steps to stake a greater claim to his art. But when the follow-up never appeared, Lippard having completed but five of the projected twenty-four installments, George Lippard and Co. went bankrupt.

Enter Joseph Severns and Co. The Philadelphian Severns had been Lippard's acknowledged publisher on the fiction front since 1848. Yet the relationship seemed ripe for conflict, or at least mutual dissatisfaction, since Severns also was co-publishing, with Lippard, the very *Quaker City Weekly* newspaper that had launched installments of *The Killers*. That kind of partnership hardly could have been ideal for Lippard, given his longstanding resentment toward profiteering publishers and salaried editors alike, who he felt exploited literary laborers. The relationship seems in retrospect particularly problematic once we recall that the *Quaker City Weekly* more or less began as a forum for Lippard's "own" work. Indeed, the paper's advertisements all but spell out the irreconcilable interests of the *Quaker City Weekly*'s two ringleaders. No less evident is Severns's having taken the upper hand in an economic way. One suspects, for example, that it was co-publisher Severns, and not editor Lippard, who announced with proprietarial flair on 22 September 1849 that "ALL OF MR. LIPPARD'S FUTURE WORK WILL BE PUBLISHED ONLY IN THIS PAPER." In fact, Lippard was not in any condition to boast (or negotiate otherwise) come 1849. His most prolific year as a writer was also the year in which he bottomed out as a businessman, his increasing involvement as founder and leader of the semisecretive radical labor organization The Brotherhood of the Union having once more placed the author in financial straits. In order to pay Brotherhood debts, Lippard had been forced to sell the plates (to Severns) of the five novels that appeared in the *Quaker City Weekly* under his name in 1849. And so while the paper continued to emblazon, as it had from day one, "Lippard's Newspaper" across the masthead of each issue, the phrase increasingly signified little. Lippard in effect had bartered away his authorship, his ownership, and thus his name to Severns even as he composed *The Killers*—again, a work that Butterfield would accuse a similarly anonymous someone of stealing.[14]

Setting aside the irony of an author like Lippard losing title to a work he never owned, and forgetting for the moment the aforementioned interdependence that existed among artisans involved in industrial print production—an interdependence that by implication argued outright against sole textual proprietorship—it is worth pondering the consequences of Lippard's loss. For starters, the "GEORGE LIPPARD" signature that had once appeared atop the columns of works the author had or soon would serialize in the *Quaker City Weekly* died a sudden death. It gave way to a decidedly nonspecific "Written for the Quaker City." That nominal erasure in turn had a rippling effect: it carried over into book advertisements, in which Lippard's name not so mysteriously disappears from Severns-signed, two-for-one promotions of Lippard's (now unattributed) back catalog; it appears as well in the then-present tense, as, to repeat, "Written for the Quaker City" attached itself to an attributively challenged *Killers* even while that work was making its initial run. But despite Lippard's bind, and for all the dollars at issue, he seems somehow to have avoided another loss, a parallel personal loss, that well might have stemmed from such an impasse. As with Zieber before, Lippard sidestepped a falling out with Severns. The two grew if anything still closer for all the perils of authorship and ownership between them. They were linked politically, both men being credentialed Democrats with close ties to the party.[15] They likewise shared an ideological affinity, Lippard like Severns holding an official position in the Brotherhood of the Union.[16] Each apparently recognized his needing the other in a material way that was itself an argument for sustaining an ambiguous friendship, if on troubled terms. For all the entrepreneurial angling between them, Lippard and Severns continued to cooperate as much from sympathy as necessity.

That brings us back to *Chester*. Butterfield might be right, by half: *Chester almost* qualifies as "an imitation," just as it seems not quite literally to have come from "another hand." *Chester* instead ranks like *Killers* as a Lippardian production, albeit one written under an author's extreme duress and with an entire newspaper office's cooperation. At least three alternatives to Butterfield's theory of textual theft come to mind. The first (and least plausible) has Lippard himself dashing off *Chester* as a decoy for a more polished volume, *Killers*, which he ultimately would publish on more favorable terms. That is to say, rather than wait for Severns and Co. to lay claim to a *Killers*-in-progress—a work to which Severns had legal right—Lippard by stealth worked up a *Killers*-in-miniature, *Chester*, for which he hoped to secure personal copyright and greater pay. Such a move would have called upon the author to reset the *Killers* type elsewhere, in some different printing office. The likelihood of Lippard's being able to do so without drawing unwanted attention is slim. Close in kind is a more plausible second alternative. Rather than act behind Severns's back, Lippard could have had his partner's blessing in writing *Chester*, especially given their close personal relationship. As Lippard remained, moreover, the force behind work "Written for the Quaker City," it would have made perfect sense for Severns to grant Lippard the satisfaction of an extra payday that an anonymous, abbreviated *Killers,* or *Chester,* would provide. Severns in that scenario could lend a helping hand to his writer-friend even as he retained the bigger prize of a lengthier, higher-profile *Killers* proper. Both parties thus could benefit from high public demand to read about Philadelphia's most recent riots. And presumably, given the timeliness of the topic, neither treatment (newspaper serial or self-contained pamphlet) would impinge on the other, saturate the market, or, at least from an interested audience's perspective, prove redundant. Third, and finally, Lippard also could have used *Chester* to circumvent copyright law itself as much as he concocted it to run around the obstacle-accomplice Severns. As at midcentury it remained difficult for authors to secure copyright for *any* work they happened to publish first in the pages of a newspaper, one might hypothesize Lippard wrote a marginally altered (altered from the serialized *Killers,* that is) *Chester* so as to claim copyright to an "imitation" written in his "own" hand. With a close-knit *Quaker City Weekly* office of compositors, publishers, editors, and an entire business department working beside him, "author" Lippard even might have counted upon his co-workers cum co-"authors" to assist in the scam. It was the least they could do for the man behind "Lippard's Newspaper."[17] It was no more than they should do for a fellow wage laborer, whose entire oeuvre Michael Denning would say is inflected by "mechanic accents" sympathetic to workers.[18]

We may never know the exact events that materialized before *Chester*'s appearance in print, and yet material evidence itself begins to put the pieces of the *Chester* puzzle in place. The evidence at stake involves two kinds of print artifacts—one in type, one in illustration—alongside a district clerk's handwritten recording of this particular copyright application. The first of the print items consist of existing deposit title and copyright pages for *Chester*. On 4 December 1849 some unknown party entered a copyright request for that work in the Clerk's Office of the District Court for the Eastern District of Pennsylvania. This was the initial step in a three-part series by which antebellum copyright could be secured; it called on the applicant to literally, and locally, deposit with the designated legal authority where publication was to occur mock-up print pages for the title page and copyright page of the work in question, often before said work was even complete. From the date of entry, the publisher, or author, or "proprietor"—or possibly all three—had two months to formalize the transaction by inserting in at least one U.S. newspaper, for a period of not less than four weeks, the text of the clerk's registration. Finally, to complete the transaction, the responsible party was to submit to the office of the Secretary of State in Washington, D.C., a copy of the completed work within six months of its actual publication. That temporal leeway would explain the lag between *Chester*'s 1849 copyright and 1850 publication dates.

Meanwhile, *Chester*'s title and copyright pages, like the script entry, provide explanations of their own.[19] What they tell us is this. We know from the Philadelphia clerk's entry that Lippard (or someone), claiming to be the "propr," or proprietor, of *Chester*, took out a copyright for that work under the name of the fictitious firm Yates and Smith. That step transpired on 4 December 1849, just three days after *The Killers*'s initial run.[20] We know as well that the copyright application's printed title page (again, the only item required up front in that day for official application) promised a narrative of "Adventures" and election-night street-fighting that not even the most prescient of *Quaker City Weekly* readers (read: plagiarists) could have anticipated from a couple of columns' worth of *Killers* content, which is all readers got on 1 December.[21] It is worth reiterating that the subject, storyline, settings, and characters of the two tales make for a near perfect fit. Then, once we recall that an anonymous *Killers* also listed a nonexistent publisher, in this instance Hankinson and Bartholomew—without mention of *any* official copyright whatsoever—and factor in as well that work's appearing *with* copyright in identical form come 1851 under the alternate title *The Bank Director's Son*,[22] George Lippard now listed as author beside the legitimate publisher E. E. Barclay and A. R. Orton, we reasonably can speculate that Lippard was keen to keep at least a corollary claim to *Killers* by any means necessary. *Chester*, the means I propose, is a publicationally vexed text. But so too are the texts with which it is connected, and in suspiciously familiar ways. To question the provenance of the one is to cast doubt on the "origins" of most Lippardian productions.[23]

Having accounted for motive then—recalling our earlier discussion of Lippard's financial problems and Severns's interest in *Killers* and its spin-offs—and having but begun to use our material evidence to get the timing right, we further can employ *Chester*'s deposit title and copyright pages as objects to strengthen the claim that Lippard was at least one of the "authors" (if not quite the owner) of a once-unattributed text. At issue is the proof-stage state of the pages indicated. For starters, by comparing that 1849 deposit title page with *Chester*'s finished 1850 title page, we find a *near*-perfect match. That suggests several things. On the one hand, the Tuesday, 4 December 1849 deposit title page is finished enough, with respect to the final 1850 title page, to argue against *Chester*'s being a hasty rip-off of a serial *Killers*, which, to repeat yet again, appeared in its first installment on Saturday, 1 December. It would have taken more than a mere three days (one of them a "rest" day) to prepare so admirable a print job. On the other hand, the deposit page is not finished enough to suggest that the text it eventually would front had been written (or printed) by that point in its entirety. Ink smudges, in the shape of ghost rectangles, appear where unmasked space-typing has come through during the printing of both the deposit title and copyright page plates. These spectral bars, used to maintain the integrity of column alignment and page layout amid the blank spaces in between printed characters, in turn would seem to indicate that however much of a *Chester*-to-be was ready to be printed in December 1849, it was not a final-form *Chester* but a *Chester*-as-it-was-then that had gone to press. In other words, a serial *Killers* and a fledgling *Chester* were passing into print *simultaneously*, meaning that some rogue author could not conceivably have been lifting his text from one to the other, since the two texts were being printed at the very same time. Throw in the identical double-columned line-endings for the finished *Chester* and the serialized *Killers,* and a tangled tale of attribution unravels: any supposed "plagiarizing" appears to have been an inside job, with Lippard himself reusing *The Killer's Quaker City Weekly* newspaper galleys (not forgetting a few additions and subtractions) to churn out *Chester* in the very same office. Not only does *Chester* look to have come from Lippard's hand, but it figuratively has his inky fingers on the deposit title and copyright pages as well (figures 1 & 2).[24]

A close reading of *Chester* further undermines any claims of plagiarism. *Chester* should and does read like an aborted *Killers*, but it also, and more importantly, borrows freely from *The Quaker City*, so much so as to suggest that Lippard wrote all three works—which he did. Each novel unrelentingly centers its discussion of race and class conflict on the city itself, inasmuch as Philadelphia's specific residential patterns stand in for much of the author's working-class critique. Lippard rehearsed that formula with *The Quaker City* in 1844 and returned to it with fervor in his "Legends of Every Day," completed for the *Quaker City Weekly* in the run-up to *Chester* during the first half of 1849. Then there are a number of otherwise offhand details that, in the aggregate, suggest a more than coincidental connection between *The Quaker City* and *Chester* in particular. The former boasts a pair of "Herculean negro[es]" as domestic servants. The latter contrives an African American villain by the name of Black Herkles, short for the historical Hercules of California House fame. The one has a former clerk, disguised at intervals as a redheaded post-adolescent, tending a mercantile warehouse full of "cogniac" [*sic*]. The other follows suit—same beverage, same spelling, similar use of disguises—but this time employing an actual redheaded office boy. Moreover, much of *The Quaker City*'s interest turns on an aristocratic seducer by the name of Col. Fitz-Cowles, while the action of *Chester* springs to life through the maneuverings of a wife-abducting English nobleman, one Capt. Fritz-Adam. All of which is to say that if *The Killers* had a copyist, then the unidentified writer had an astonishing knowledge of *The Quaker City*'s intricacies. It seems far more reasonable that the hand that wrote *The Quaker City* and the hand that wrote *Chester* were one and the same.

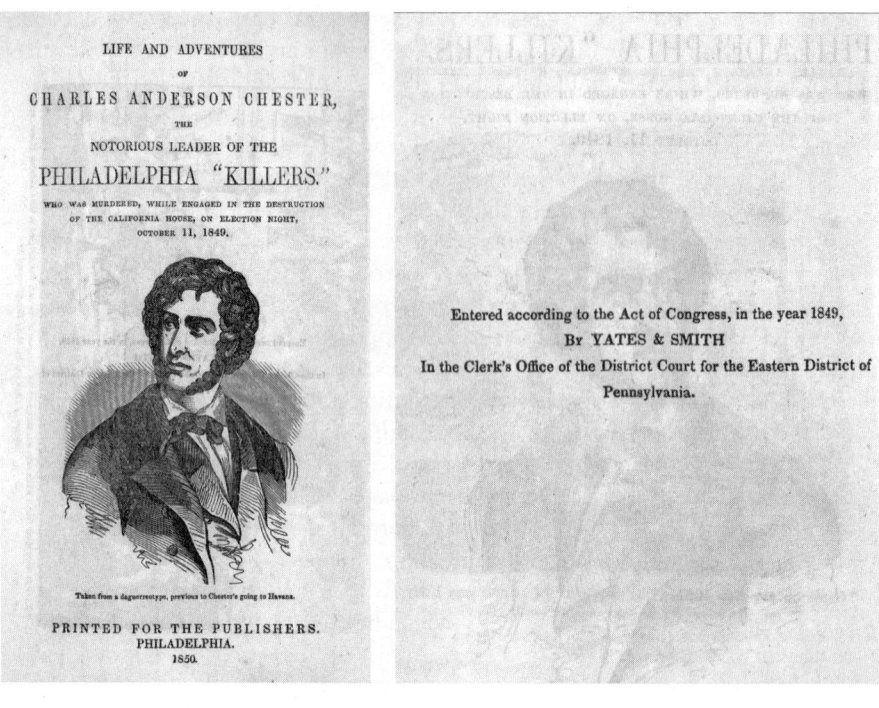

Figs. 1 and 2 The image at left (1) is the title page of the completed novel *Life and Adventure of Charles Anderson Chester*, "author" George Lippard, which appeared for public consumption in 1850. Courtesy of The Library Company of Philadelphia. At right (2) is the final copyright page that greeted readers in that same year. Courtesy of The Library Company of Philadelphia.

That leaves the illustrations. *Chester* might be predictable in plot, but it is anything but when it comes to the images that grace its pages. The most memorable feature of *Chester* well could be the image facing the book's copyright page. A crude woodcut from an original drawing depicts there the aforementioned Black Herkles with dagger in hand as blood runs from the chest wound of his white victim, the protagonist Chester (figure 3). It is, according to Lapsansky, one of the few illustrations of black-white confrontation from the period; as such, it amounts to a rather graphic, racially charged graphic not to be found elsewhere in contemporary publications.[25] Significantly, one finds hidden in the blood trickling from Chester's chest an artist's signature of "Darley" reading from bottom to top (figure 4). Darley was of course F. O. C. Darley, the illustrator of the frontispiece for *The Quaker City*'s follow-up 1845 edition. Darley also illustrated regularly for the publisher G. B. Zieber and Co., the firm responsible for the first run of

CHARLES ANDERSON CHESTER MURDERED BY BLACK HERKLES.

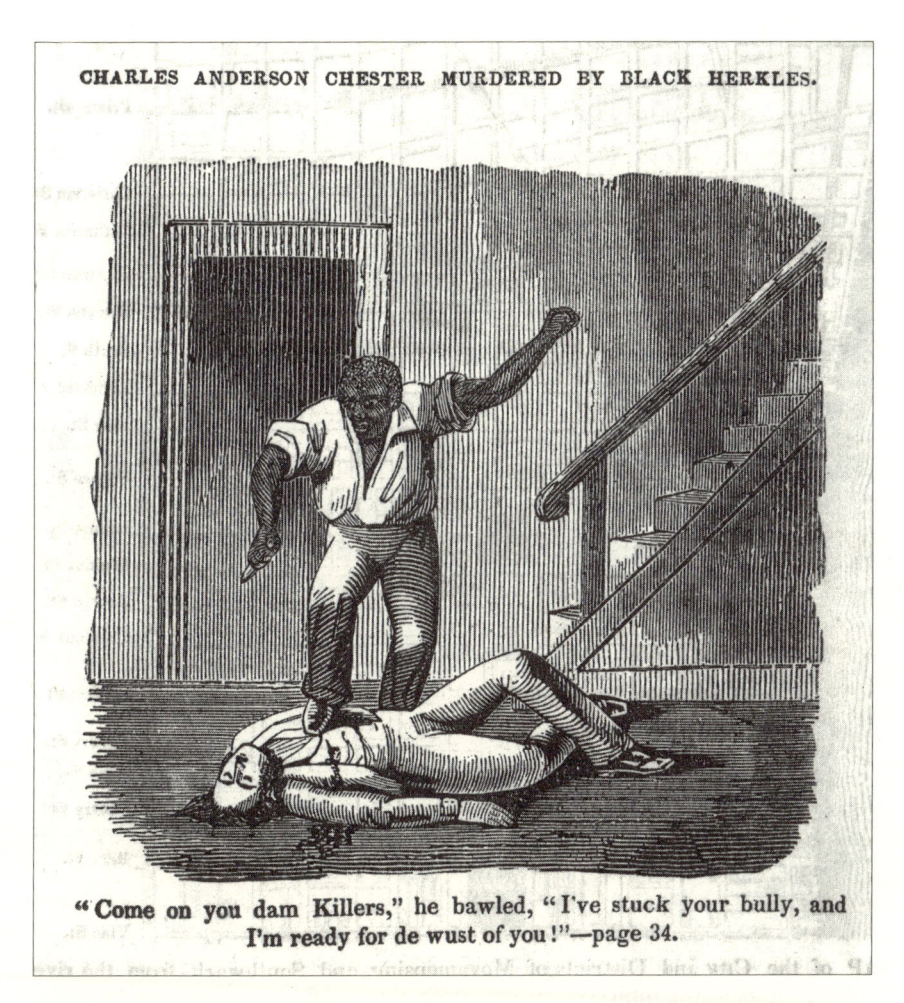

"**Come on you dam Killers,**" he bawled, "I've stuck your bully, and I'm ready for de wust of you!"—page 34.

Fig. 3 Black Herkles, rampant: a singular image from George Lippard's *Chester*. Courtesy of The Library Company of Philadelphia.

The Quaker City. Darley and Lippard in other words had a prior working relationship and kept the same company. So while it is possible that some unscrupulous publisher might have plundered an existing woodcut to enhance *Chester* as a text, both the rarity of the image singled out here, as well as Lippard's close ties to the artist,[26] would indicate that said image was made to order *for* Lippard *for* inclusion in *Chester*.

In the end, then, the author Lippard, born in *Chester* County, Pennsylvania, becomes the leading candidate for *Chester*'s authorship. The publishing ploys surrounding the novel fit. Material evidence sets the timing right. Lip-

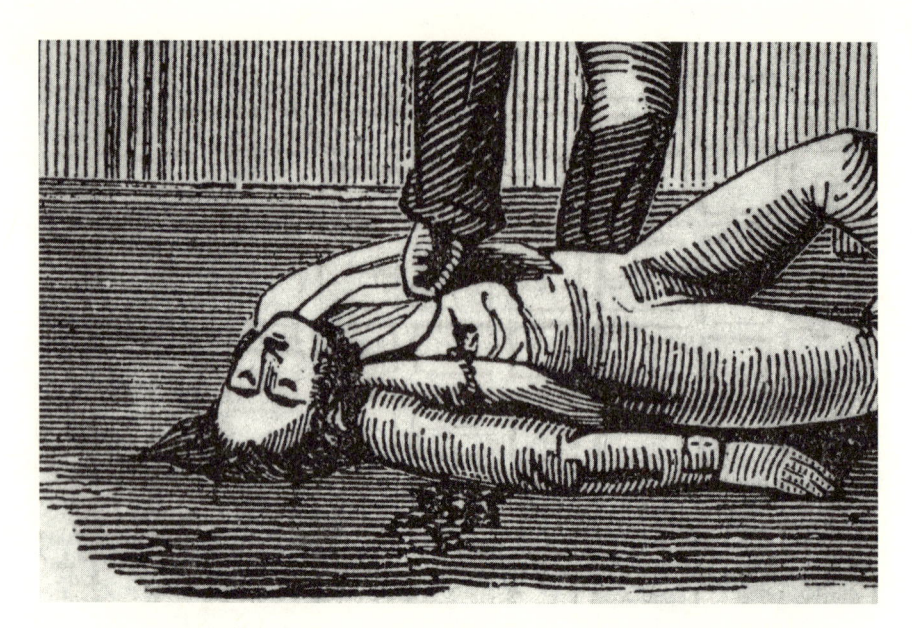

Fig. 4 Detail of Black Herkles's nefarious deed. The cursive signature "Darley" reads vertically at a slight angle. Courtesy of The Library Company of Philadelphia.

pard's *The Quaker City* lurks around every one of *Chester*'s discursive corners. And a visual consideration of *Chester* all but closes the case on an unattributed antebellum artifact. Read with an appreciation for its full context, *Chester* becomes less a literary mystery than a fully reclaimed text.

To return to our opening dilemma, it bears restating that to author a text is not necessarily to own or originate it, as *Chester* makes clear. Lippard was just one of the many individuals who helped make *Chester* happen, and so his rights to the final, yet provisionally unfinished, product must by logic, if not by law, be reduced to partial share. True, the same might be said of any text, considering that modern print culture itself was defined by a "communications circuit" that had long since been in place when Lippard began to write for pay in the early 1840s. It is true, too, that not a few of Lippard's immediate peers within the penny press perhaps were reduced to a similarly circuitous route in bringing their work before the public. The example of Edgar Allan Poe is instructive in this respect, considering the wide range of genres in which he wrote, the number and nature of periodicals within which he initially published, and even his migratory movements up and down the U.S. Atlantic seaboard. Dime novelist George Thompson's peripatetic life and often anonymous writings illustrate much the same straining after publication for pay, if with less lasting literary results. Yet *Chester* seems special. Because of its dizzying copyright history, its rapid passage through the print life cycle, and, again, its calling upon so large a number of collaborators (most of whom the author knew personally, and some of whom well might have composed *Chester*-like texts of their own), it must strike the uninitiated reader as the unlikeliest of publications.

But it was not, by antebellum standards. A joint production, the text of *Chester* makes plain the overlapping processes and peoples that went into the making of American literature at the acceleration stage of its industrial phase. As such it epitomizes not the close "coupling" that Ezra Greenspan associates with an intimately conceived and shared text like poet Walt Whitman's experimental free verse volume *Leaves of Grass* (1855).[27] It instead is testament to a corresponding literary milieu that traded in repeat performances of familiar settings, themes, images, and ideas, not infrequently culled from the very urban environs where the practical mechanics of print production—and consumption—resided. At once unoriginal and communal, then, *Chester* reads on one level as a romantically challenged text. Given, however, the complex logistics of its "creation," the fact of its having been forged against all odds, by so many contributors, and from the most common of journalistic conceits, *Chester* seems creative, indeed. Not every man had a hand in *Chester,* and yet its skilled alignment of such a diverse array of talents and trades seems in itself a feat of almost orchestral dimensions. Like many contemporary texts, *Chester* is extraordinary by virtue of its ordinariness.

What my revised account of *Chester*'s attribution reveals, finally, is but another romantic irony, maybe more. For despite their less than epiphanic origins and more or less mundane outcomes, works like *Chester* provide final proof of a romantic literary practice precisely because their producers vaunted practice for its own sake, rather than any rarefied object-product that we now might associate with high "art." *Coming-into-print* could describe this practice at a time when American Romanticism had begun to merge with the expanding print marketplace. Add to this irony the further one of ownership. Meredith McGill points out that in eighteenth-century England, the celebrated legal cases of *Millar v. Taylor* (1769) and *Donaldson v. Becket* (1774) granted individual authors perpetual ownership, as a natural right, to their copy under a system of common law founded on a respect for the principles of possessive individualism. What held for England, however, by no means held for America. This was especially so some decades later, at the time of *Chester*'s appearance. Many a reader, writer, printer, publisher, or other textual "producer" then would have confronted the difficulty, if not the impossibility, of laying claim to a romantic *process* that lacked handles, as it were, as opposed simply to grasping hold of a tangible end product. More to the point, and as McGill reminds us, a resilient republicanism continued to condition the thinking of not a few Americans up until the end of the nineteenth century, a period inclusive of transatlantic Romanticism.

This residual republican mindset led many to regard print as being less the commodified right of an individual author than the "selfless" extension of citizen-wordsmiths; print from this perspective remained a channel for civic discussion and thus the common good.[28] Of course not all Americans received intermittent news reports of Philadelphia's recurring riots as edifying political spectacle. The well-to-do New York lawyer and diarist George Templeton Strong, for one, would grow so weary of reading of that "Queer" neighboring city to the south of Manhattan as to call it in 1844 "the most anarchical metropolis on this side of the Atlantic."[29] What Strong took exception to as fact, however, many greeted with glee when it arrived in the form of fiction. Earning as he did $3,000–4,000 each year as a writer in the 1840s, Lippard achieved sales figures that are high enough to suggest a ready readership that must have extended beyond his provincial home city. Who his readers were emerges when we return once more to *Chester*. It was the U.S. working classes, says David S. Reynolds, largely, but not exclusively, urban northeastern males, who enthused over exactly the kinds of comic grotesque literary conventions that are on display here—consisting of equal parts stylized violence as sport, and wild verbal play as politically subversive merrymaking.[30] These might seem odd components for an antebellum brand of republicanism. But apparently they were widely enough turned to, in a literary way, to make class identity a common cause across the nation's urban-industrial corridor, notwithstanding important socioeconomic, ethnic, and religious differences that existed between regional cites. From the tropes of urban unrest and antic morbid laughter, then, not only *Chester*, but a whole host of texts emanating from similar professional conditions came to transcend the quest for personal profit—or what we might call romantic self-fulfillment, of a capitalist kind. Writing, by contrast, for and from the masses could become in instances such as *Chester* a pledge made to the reading public for a better *re*-public, regardless of how perverse might seem the means employed to achieve it.

Lofty as it sounds, Lippard was just the man to put republican theory into practice. No doubt the heightened individual interiority and intense emotionalism of his works testify to his heavy investment in literary romanticism. And yet, having based his fame in part on an ongoing series of Revolutionary "Legends," he widely was regarded as being republican to a T. His steady defense of the U.S. working class, in print and in lecture, also made him a willing spokesman for both (and at once) an agrarian ideal and artisanal culture closely associated with republicanism. Nor should we forget that many of Lippard's financial problems, particularly those preceding *Chester,* stemmed from his accepting the debts of a labor organization he himself had founded and led under the title of "Chief Washington." However much the collaborative qualities of *Chester* allow it to qualify as public property, then, and notwithstanding its author's implicit (and perhaps unwitting) commitment to process *as* process, whether "inspired" or otherwise, it is in the end his demonstrated determination to keep the public sphere public that defined his relations with a profit-minded literary marketplace. Written to make money, *Chester* likewise served a cause. It did so even as it converted one (loosely) individual author's paid, and less than ideologically minded, print associates into secondary advocates of something other than ownership.

Notes

1. Roger Butterfield, "A Check List of the Separately Published Works of George Lippard," *Pennsylvania Magazine of History and Biography* 79, no. 3 (1955): 308; George Lippard, *Life and Adventures of Charles Anderson Chester, the Notorious Leader of the Philadelphia "Killers." Who Was Murdered, While Engaged in the Destruction of the California House, On Election Night, October 11, 1849* (Philadelphia: Yates & Smith, 1849) [Library Company Printed Materials]; and Lippard, *The Killers. A Narrative of Real Life in Philadelphia* (Philadelphia: Hankinson and Bartholomew, 1850) [Library Company Printed Materials].

2. A monthlong Mellon Dissertation Fellowship in 2004 at the Library Company of Philadelphia made possible the research for this essay. I particularly would like to thank Phil Lapsansky as well as James N. Green, Associate Librarian, and Connie King, Reference Librarian, for their unfailing assistance.

3. Michael T. Gilmore, *American Romanticism and the Marketplace* (Chicago: University of Chicago Press, 1985); and Steven Fink, *Prophet in the Marketplace: Thoreau's Development as a Professional Writer* (Princeton: Princeton University Press, 1992).

4. For a discussion of this key romantic concept in its American context, see Lawrence Buell's classic study *Literary Transcendentalism: Style and Vision in the American Renaissance* (Ithaca: Cornell University Press, 1973). For an alternate and equally classic view, see Northrop Frye, "Towards Defining an Age of Sensibility," *English Literary History* 23, no. 2 (1956): 144–52.

5. In his seminal work *Literary Publishing in America, 1790–1850* (1959; repr., Amherst: University of Massachusetts Press, 1993), William Charvat describes a shift from independent authorship to the collaborative production of printed material that he traces to the years 1848–1850. Charvat attributes this "new era" of author-publisher relations to the corresponding emergence of authorship as a profession (55–56), by which he has writers abandoning their earlier involvement in book manufacturing, promotion, and publicity to a newly assembled cadre of industry experts. Note that Charvat locates these changes in the exact window of time within which *Chester* appears. In much the same spirit, Robert Darnton has articulated a truism of history of the book scholarship by proposing a dynamic "life cycle" by which books pass from producer to consumer in an overlapping series of social, economic, political, and cultural exchanges (Darnton, "What Is the History of Books?" in *Reading in America,* ed. Cathy Davidson, 27–52 [Baltimore: Johns Hopkins University Press, 1989], 30). Often (wrongly) described as a tripartite sequence of production, distribution, and reception,

with each of the above processes occurring in discrete steps, Darnton's formulation more accurately might be seen as a comprehensive whole—simultaneity and interconnection rather than discontinuity and separation catching the tenor of the "cycle" Darnton describes. See Joan Shelley Rubin, "What Is the History of the History of Books?" *Journal of American History* 90, no. 2 (2003): 557–58.

6. There remains no scholarly consensus on Lippard's working-class credentials. One of the author's earliest commentators, Joseph Jackson, adopted a populist position in his unpublished manuscript biography of Lippard, completed circa 1930: "George Lippard: Poet of the Proletariat," Historical Society of Pennsylvania Manuscripts, Joseph Jackson Collection, box 1, folder 12. Among active scholars, David S. Reynolds likewise describes Lippard's politics and writings as "proletarian." For an overview, see Reynolds's *George Lippard* (Boston: Twayne Publishers, 1982), as editor, *George Lippard: Prophet of Protest: Writings of an American Radical, 1822–1854* (New York: Peter Lang, 1986), and *Beneath the American Renaissance: The Subversive Imagination in the Age of Emerson and Melville* (Cambridge: Harvard University Press, 1988). Heyward Ehrlich provides a complementary view in "The 'Mysteries' of Philadelphia: Lippard's Quaker City and 'Urban' Gothic Fiction," *ESQ: A Journal of the American Renaissance* 18, no. 1 (1972): 50–65. And Leslie Fiedler, in "The Male Novel," *Partisan Review* 37, no. 1 (1970): 74–89, concedes Lippard's having contributed to a new nineteenth-century literature of a "working class" even as he more broadly describes Lippard's fiction as "subpornography" (81), given the author's heavy stylistic reliance on sex and violence.

Others deny the author's supposed radicalism. Larzer Ziff has called Lippard a "traditionalist" inasmuch as Lippard seems to have embraced "eternal social verities" (Ziff, *Literary Democracy: The Declaration of Cultural Independence in America* [New York: Penguin Books, 1982], 87–107, quote on 97). Christopher Looby directly challenges Reynolds's reading when he categorizes Lippard's literary output as domestic-sentimental, rather than egalitarian democratic ("George Thompson's 'Romance of the Real,'" *American Literature* 65, no. 4 [1993]: 651–72). At least one of Lippard's contemporaries, finally, dismissed his work outright because it allegedly "appeals, in structure, plot, incident, and very often language, to the very lowest sympathies and tastes." In a word, Lippard was fit to be "read by the mass," a code word then as now for the working classes. See "New American Writers," *Holden's Dollar Magazine* (July 1848): 423.

7. Meredith L. McGill, *American Literature and the Culture of Reprinting, 1834–1853* (Philadelphia: University of Pennsylvania Press, 2003), 3.

8. Lippard, *The Quaker City; or, The Monks of Monk-Hall. A Romance of Philadelphia Life, Mystery and Crime*, ed. David S. Reynolds (repr., Amherst: University of Massachusetts Press, 1995; originally published Philadelphia: G. B. Zieber and Co., 1844).

9. Butterfield, "Check List of the Separately Published Works," 306.

10. Butterfield explains ("Check List of the Separately Published Works," 303) that the first 314 pages of *The Quaker City* in its first-edition book form appeared originally as separate—and best-selling—serial pamphlets, the first seven parts of a projected ten reaching the public over the winter of 1844–45. Lippard afterwards dispensed with further serialization and made readers wait for an additional 180 pages until mid-April 1845. The bulk of the work thereafter was issued between boards. The resulting 494-page novel would grow an additional 81 pages after Lippard himself obtained, on 5 May, the copyright and stereotype plates from his initial publisher, G. B. Zieber and Co. On the timing involved with the April publication, refer to "Literature Notices," *Philadelphia Home Journal*, 2 April 1845, 3.

11. According to J. M. W. Geist, one of Lippard's contemporary biographers as well as a sometime compositor in the author's newspaper office, Lippard "could rarely be induced to sit down to write until the call for 'copy' became too imperative to be longer resisted." Serial

novels, in particular, found Lippard indulging in a form of literary brinkmanship, "not . . . writing the weekly installment until the morning of the day before the paper had to go to press." See J. M. W. Geist, *Recollections of George Lippard* (Philadelphia: Brotherhood of the Union, 1900), 27–28 (available at the Historical Society of Pennsylvania).

12. Keen to keep Lippard among his in-house authors, Zieber took the unusual step in early 1845 of placing Lippard on his payroll for some three months, during which time the author expanded *The Quaker City*'s emerging first edition. In addition, Zieber also agreed, in consenting to co-ownership of the full-length novel's plates and copyright, to share half of the profits that remained after he himself recovered production costs. Despite all that control, Lippard eventually went his own way—after, and to repeat, buying back *The Quaker City*'s plates and full copyright. The two men did, however, cross paths again. Beginning in 1847, and continuing into the next year, Lippard contributed regularly to the reform periodical *The Nineteenth Century*, published by Zieber up until his firm G. B. Zieber and Co. folded in 1848. See Reynolds, *George Lippard*, 10.

13. Lippard's popular *The Quaker City* was of course his most imitated production. Any number of fellow Philadelphians seized upon that novel's city-mysteries premise as fodder for their own works, while German writer Friedrich Gerstäcker simply changed titles and translated the tale into his native language to "author" a novel of his own. Yet *The Quaker City* was not the sole cause for Lippard's concern. His collected tales *Washington and His Generals* (1847) also were under attack (collaterally, if not critically), prompting the author to single out one particular plagiarist in the 15 May 1847 issue of the *Philadelphia Saturday Courier*. Refer to Reynolds, *George Lippard*, 14–16.

14. Reynolds, *George Lippard*, 17–18; Paul Erickson, "New Books, New Men: Authorship and Antebellum Sensation Fiction," paper delivered at the McNeil Center for Early American Studies Seminar Series, Winterthur Museum, Garden & Library, Winterthur, Delaware, 23 February 2001; and *Quaker City Weekly*, 1 September 1849, 2; 22 September 1849, 4; 1 December 1849, 3. Adding insult to injury, none other than a member of Lippard's Brotherhood accused him of using the *Quaker City Weekly* as a vehicle for personal gain (Reynolds, *George Lippard*, 22).

15. Lippard for his part was a frequent stump speaker for the reform wing of the party before his death in 1854. Severns by 1853 owned the Philadelphia-based Democratic newspaper the *Argus*. Having backed Franklin Pierce in the latter's successful bid to become U.S. President in 1852, Severns held as well the post of naval storekeeper within the administration. See Elwyn Burns Robinson, "*The Pennsylvanian*: Organ of the Democracy," *Pennsylvanian Magazine* 62 (July 1938): 354–55.

16. Lippard, *Journal of the First Annual Convocation of the Supreme Circle* (Philadelphia: n.p., 1850), 9 (available at the Historical Society of Pennsylvania). In Brotherhood parlance, Lippard occupied the top organizational spot of "Chief Washington." Severns, as "Chief Wayne," occupied a lower (yet still prestigious) rung on the Brotherhood ladder.

17. Lippard's sometime compositor Geist suggests a family-like environment at the *Quaker City Weekly*'s headquarters, off Chestnut Street. Co-publishers Lippard and Severns habitually took lunchtime walks together around Center City Philadelphia. Geist himself often supplied and lit Lippard's signature cigars as the author entered writing mode. And the open-door policy at the office meant that workers could and did communicate by shouting to one another between rooms. As the newspaper trade itself proverbially seldom, if ever, slept, one wonders how Lippard could have worked without Severns's knowledge, even under cover of night, had he so desired. See Geist, *Recollections of George Lippard*, 22, 25, 27.

18. Michael Denning, *Mechanic Accents: Dime Novels and Working-Class Culture in America* (London: Verso, 1987).

19. All three items today reside in the Library of Congress's Title Page Deposit for Rare Books.

20. Both the deposit and official title pages declare that *Chester* was "Printed For the Publishers. Philadelphia. 1850." The deposit copyright page (see figure 2) for its part lists the Philadelphia firm of Yates & Smith not as publishers per se but rather as "pro," for proprietor, which designation has been handwritten in by the officiating court clerk. "Pro" becomes "Propr" on the hand-written entry form itself, presumably shorthand spelling of the same. At any rate, no such firm as Yates & Smith appears in city directories from the period. And, technically speaking, Yates & Smith need not be publishers at all, at least according to the letter of the law. The name "Smith" is of course ubiquitous in contemporary directories, whether listed in or outside book-related trades. A handful of Yateses appear, none of them in connection with Darnton's "communications circuit."

Note that the Library of Congress holds Philadelphia copyright requests for only the relevant surrounding years of 1831–38, 1842–46, and 1850–59. Records for the intervening years of 1839–41 and 1847–49 are either no longer extant or else lie moldering in a Philadelphia archive. *Chester*'s initial late December 1849 copyright request, in short, has ensured its inclusion among existing 1850 records rather than among missing 1849 records. See Thomas G. Tanselle, "Copyright Records and the Bibliographer," in *Studies in Bibliography*, Fredson Bowers, ed. (Charlottesville: Bibliographical Society of the University of Virginia, 1969), 22:77–124; and the Library of Congress's Title Page Deposit Records for Rare Books (*Charles Anderson Chester*, No. 466).

21. The tale appeared in its entirety by year's end, 1849. It took five weekly installments, beginning 1 December, to complete the run. Having debuted on 28 December 1848, the *Quaker City Weekly* newspaper shut down in June 1850.

22. George Lippard, *The Bank Director's Son, A Real and Intensely Interesting Revelation of City Life* (Philadelphia: E. E. Barclay and A. R. Orton, 1851).

23. *The Killers* itself was not generally accepted as Lippard's until 1969. Again, "Written for the Quaker City" was the only signature it carried in serial form. "Published by Hankinson and Bartholomew" was its sole identifying tag when it appeared bound in 1850. See Jacob Blanck, comp., "George Lippard," in *Bibliography of American Literature*, ed. Jacob Blanck, Virginia L. Smyers, and Michael Winship (New Haven: Yale University Press, 1969), 5:405–18.

24. Lippard wore many hats during a lifetime in the print business but never that of printer.

25. Lapsansky, private correspondence with David S. Reynolds, 7 March 1994, 2, letter located in the Library Company of Philadelphia. It is worth mentioning that *Chester* reappeared intact as a children's book (extant copies of which rest in the children's collections at the libraries of UCSD and SUNY-Albany) in 1967 under the imprint of Lost Cause Press of Louisville, Kentucky. Whatever their own feelings toward African Americans, *Chester*'s twentieth-century readers, reading against the backdrop of the civil rights struggles of the 1960s, were perhaps not so concerned with Lippard's record on race relations. While the author freely employed racial stereotypes in his writings, he also often invoked slavery as a metaphor for working-class oppression generally and, while on the lecture circuit in the early 1850s, openly denounced the institution—to the discomfiture of his southern audiences.

26. That tie must have been especially close, since Darley relocated from Lippard's Philadelphia to Manhattan in 1848 in order to illustrate late-edition works by two authors Lippard admired—Washington Irving and James Fenimore Cooper. Refer to the entry on Darley from *The New York Historical Society's Dictionary of Artists in America, 1564–1860* (New Haven: Yale University Press, 1957), 165.

27. Ezra Greenspan, *Walt Whitman and the American Reader* (New York: Cambridge University Press, 1990), 13.

28. Meredith L. McGill. "The Matter of the Text: Commerce, Print Culture, and the Authority of the State in American Copyright Law," *American Literary History* 9, no. 1 (1997): 21–25 (see page 24 for the "selfless" quote). See as well Michael Warner, *The Letters of the Republic: Publication and the Public Sphere in Eighteenth-Century America* (Cambridge: Harvard University Press, 1990).

29. Entry for 8 May 1844 from *The Diary of George Templeton Strong, Young Man in New York, 1835–1849*, ed. Allan Nevins and Milton Halsey Thomas (New York: Macmillan, 1952), 1:232.

30. Reynolds, *Beneath the American Renaissance*, 508–12.

From Private Journal to Published Periodical

Gendered Writings and Readings of a Late Victorian Wesleyan's "African Wilderness"

Lize Kriel

In the winter of 1891 a small party of men embarked on an expedition that would stretch the influence of Wesleyan Methodist Christianity far across the northern boundary of the Transvaal into a "Mashonaland" recently occupied by Cecil John Rhodes's chartered company.[1] The leader of the group was Owen Watkins, Chairman of the Transvaal Synod of the Wesleyan Methodist Missionary Society. This would be the last of his many journeys through the interior of southern Africa.[2] He was accompanied by Hugh Shimmin, another British Wesleyan minister stationed in the Transvaal, and by Michael Bowen, an African Wesleyan evangelist, whose name appears in later sources (he was ordained in Johannesburg eight years later) as Michael Boweni.[3] There was also the driver of the wagon, John Peters (described as a "good, reliable native") and the *voorloper*,[4] John Walters ("a Cape half-caste" and "a willing, active man").[5]

In several successive episodes, the preparations for the journey, the expedition itself, and the establishment of a mission station in Mashonaland were reported in *Wesleyan Missionary Notices* (hereafter *WMN)*, the periodical through which the Wesleyan Methodist Missionary Society had been reporting to their supporters in Britain since 1816. Shimmin initiated the missionary society's negotiations with Rhodes,[6] but Watkins, who had been a familiar and popular face with missionary supporters in London, wrote most of the reportage on the journey published in *WMN*. In 1893 one of the editors of *WMN* compiled Watkins's and Shimmin's correspondence up to that date in book form.[7] Since Shimmin had remained behind in Mashonaland to see through the founding of the mission with Bowen, his letters cover the latter part of the book. While Bowen, described by Watkins as a "bright, happy Christian" "who speaks several languages,"[8] was portrayed

The author gratefully acknowledges financial assistance from the National Research Foundation of South Africa.

in pictures in *WMN*, no travel writing by him was included in Wesleyan publications for British readers.

We do not know whether Shimmin and Bowen had written to their wives while on the journey to Mashonaland (we cannot presume that Peters and Walters were married or literate). However, Watkins's collection of private correspondence, which is in the Cory Library at the University of Grahamstown, South Africa, contains not only letters to his wife and fellow Wesleyan ministers, but also a set of letters written by his wife, Mary Watkins. The prize item in this collection is a manuscript on Watkins's Mashonaland journey, in his own handwriting and marked by himself as his "private journal"—"for the use only of my dear ones."[9]

The following excerpts from Watkins's private journal and the report that appeared in *WMN* highlight many significant differences between the two versions (some are alluded to in square brackets). Equally important, however, is the similarity in the basic structure of both compositions:

> Private journal:
> *Tuesday 14th July 1891.* This is a great day in the history of Wesleyan missions in Africa. My dream of years is fulfilled, & we have crossed the Limpopo, & taken possession of the regions beyond in the name of Christ & Methodism.
>
> I got my first sight of the river where it forms the northern boundary of the Transvaal, this morning about 7C. The river is about 150 yards wide, with very high banks covered with great trees & beautiful tropical plants & creepers. The place we cross is Rhode's Drift—& they have cut down great trees 9 & 12 feet round to make a passage through the Bush on both sides, down to the river.
>
> My heart was too full for words as I gazed upon this noble river, with its visions of beauty, as it went on its winding way towards the Indian Ocean, & I thanked God I have lived to see this day. I feel Methodism can never go back, after we have once entered this land.[10]

> Published version in *WMN:*
> *Tuesday, 14th July.* This is a great day in the history of Wesleyan missions in Africa. We have crossed the Limpopo, and have taken possession of the regions beyond in the name of Christ and Methodism.
>
> [The "scientific" recordings of the morning temperature and the width of the river is not present in the published version. The "landscape" in the published version is unspoiled—the "cultivation" of

the wilderness by cutting of a path to the river is only accounted for in the private version.]

My heart was too full for words as I gazed upon this beautiful river, where it forms the northern boundary of the Transvaal, and I thank God I have lived to see this day. I feel that Methodism can never go back, debt or no debt, now we have entered these new lands[11]

We seem to have here two accounts of the same journey, one written for domestic consumption within a colonial family and one published to be read by Wesleyan Christians in Britain. My aim is to draw out the complexities among the private journal and the episodes of this journey to Mashonaland as they appeared in *WMN* during the latter half of 1891. To make sense of the way Owen Watkins differentiated in his reportage between official writing intended for publication and personal correspondence directed at the domestic realm, I find Asa Briggs's explanation useful: "many Victorians in England wanted somehow or other to hold on to the concept of there being an *ought* in life as well as an *is*."[12] I read Watkins's private (more domestic, more confiding, less heroic, less masculine) colonial document as an attempt to affirm (or confess) such an "is." His official (more adventurous, more masculine, more stereotyping, more dismissive, less ambivalent, less open to agency) writings published in *WMN* represent his performance of the "ought" as a prominent figure in public life in colonial southern Africa as well as Wesleyan Methodist circles in London. When we juxtapose these two documents, the differences can further inform our understanding of the making and the consumption of knowledge about Africa, particularly the recurrent trope of the African "wilderness."

More or less at the same time as Mary Louise Pratt's *Imperial Eyes* was setting the trend for the way cultural and literary historians would read published accounts of travelers' tales in the subsequent decade,[13] at least two articles appeared emphasizing the importance of the very process through which accounts were being prepared for publication. In "'Four Years in Asante': One Source or Several?" Adam Jones looked into the various reworked translations and publications of two Basel missionaries' accounts of their experiences and observations during their captivity in what is today the southern part of Ghana.[14] He drew attention to the power of publishers and translators to change, interpret, add on, and remove from what they read in existing manuscripts—and historians' readiness to trust the compromised printed versions.[15] Missionary F. A. Ramseyer's "cautious and matter-of-fact statement[s]" were certainly not the first or the last to have been turned into "confident and value-laden assertion[s]" in printed form.[16] In the article "Exploration/Travel Literature and the Evolution of the Author," I. S. MacLaren also contested the treatment of "the publication as the record of what the traveller experienced."[17] He urged us to consider what he identified as the four stages individual texts had to go through from conception to publication:

1. A field note or log book entry phase.
2. A journal stage.
3. A draft manuscript stage.
4. The printed publication.[18]

Watkins was not just a man of the Book, but also a man of letters. It was part of his long and celebrated career to reach out in writing to fellow British Wesleyans. He needed no ghost writers. We know from Watkins's private manuscript that he was an intelligible author—so much so that, but for minor alterations, substantial sections of the private and the published journal correspond. There was thus ample "common ground" between Watkins's "is" and "ought," which makes the subtlety of the differences so significant.

While MacLaren's four stages imply increasing degrees of finality, the private Watkins journal was not in a more preliminary stage than the draft sent to London or the version eventually printed. It had been produced for a different purpose altogether: for consumption in the domestic sphere. We know from Watkins's instructions to his wife (and this is confirmed by the speed at which the episodes from the travel journal appeared in *Notices* after the actual occurrence of the events) that Watkins prepared the versions of his journey for his family and for the Wesleyan public more or less simultaneously. Both versions of the previous stretch of the journey were time and again handed over to the mail coaches that the traveling party encountered on their way up north to Salisbury, the make-shift "capital" of Rhodes's new territory. The fact that Watkins often concluded the private journal with a hasty note that he had to finish off quickly to be on time for the mail carrier, gives the impression that the private journal may have been a more embroidered exposition produced after the more matter-of-fact (and one could argue, somewhat more urgent) account for *Notices* had been written. Thus, in the case of Watkins, MacLaren's stages two and three may even have been reversed. The careful instructions Watkins gave to his wife about preserving the private account and dispatching the official one to London suggest that he did not keep a duplicate of either with him on the journey.

Just how serious the Wesleyan Methodist Missionary Society was about their publications becomes apparent from the financial accounts in their annual reports. In the 1890s, the society contributed to the printing costs of four regular publications. The total publication expenses for the year 1891 almost equaled the salaries of the "finance assistant, office and warehouse staff."[19] From 1889 until 1893, on average 55,275 copies of *Notices* (and almost as many copies of *At Home and Abroad,* a magazine aimed at juvenile readers) were printed monthly. Roughly a third of the printing costs for *Notices* were normally recovered through sales and advertisements.[20] When a new magazine, *Work and Workers in the Mission Field,* was introduced by a former editor of *Notices* in 1892, a grant of one hundred pounds was provided to help it get off the ground. This new magazine was to address the changing character of Wesleyan work outside of England, as the churches previously founded by missionaries were becoming more established:

> But something more than the *Missionary Notices* is now necessary. Tidings from the field are but a part of missionary literature. Related topics almost innumerable need from time to time to be discussed. Evangelistic and pastoral work, education in its many kinds, the training of native ministers, and the organisation of native churches, the translation and circulation of Christian literature, medical missions, orphanages and industrial homes, social and moral questions in various countries and among different races—these are but a few of the topics that we hope to bring before our readers with the assistance of competent writers abroad and at home.[21]

Watkins reported on a journey undertaken specifically for the purpose of participating in the colonization of Mashonaland, a new project of British expansionism. As the editors of *WMN* commented shortly before Watkins's departure, "To every reader will occur the thought of the manifold opportunities lying at the door of every Christian man, and especially every minister, in a land like British Zambesia, whereby he may aid in the right conduct of affairs, whether private, public, or even national."[22] The schema for this kind of travel reportage was the African journey of discovery as it had been published for consumption by British readers throughout the nineteenth century. Drawing on the research of Elizabeth Elbourne and Brian Stanley, Jennifer Cooper explains:

> Overseas, missionary writings about their converts' Christian experiences both reproduced the evangelical conversion formula and helped to shape a new literary category. While literacy rates increased towards the end of the 18th century, travel accounts and "popular geography" became widely published and circulated. Like

missionary publications, travel literature informed a wide British readership of Britain's operations overseas, and offered descriptions both vivid and scientific of their overseas dominions and the inhabitants of these regions. Both travel and missionary accounts were written for popular consumption, and were held in common by their influence in establishing stereotypes about lands and peoples abroad.[23]

In the 1920s the *History of the Wesleyan Methodist Missionary Society* reminisced on early reportage in *WMN*:

> When those letters [of Missionary Barnabas Shaw of Kamiesberg, South Africa] appeared in the first volume of the WMN [1816] they furnished just the element of romance which was wanting at that time to stir the imagination of the Methodist people, and to fill them with zeal for the conversion of the millions of Africa. The letters describe such prosaic matters as the making of soap or the purchase of timber, yet there is always the feeling of a poet in the expression.[24]

It is clear that the success of these accounts rested less on theology than adventure. Especially since the "river" journeys undertaken by Richard Burton, John Hanning Speke, and David Livingstone in the 1850s and 1860s, African travel diaries had been processed into increasingly popular publications.[25] Seventy thousand copies of Livingstone's *Missionary Travels and Researches in Southern Africa* were printed.[26] The combination of adventure, duty, and valor in the service of science, religion, and civilization all fit snugly under the very masculine blanket of nationalism and imperialism. The publications of the 1860s and 1870s, in the words of James Duncan, "constructed an Africa suitable both to the needs of nineteenth-century imperial interests and to a European readership longing for tales of exotic worlds being mastered by heroic European males."[27] As Mary Louise Pratt comments, "the Victorians opted for a brand of verbal painting whose highest calling was to produce for the home audience the peak moments at which geographical 'discoveries' were 'won' for England."[28] But Pratt overlooks what Adam Jones and Ian MacLaren called attention to: the "evolution" of the traveler into an author through various stages of the production of the text. David Finkelstein's thorough study of the history of John Hanning Speke's book provides a vivid recent example of what Jones and MacLaren were appealing for: clearly differentiating between the travelers' first drafts and the revisions that made their books more sellable.[29]

Watkins the writer was, like his audience, also a reader.[30] He did point out to the intended readers of *WMN* that he and his companions were no longer living up to the challenges faced by "the first travellers [note that he does not restrict it to *missionary* travelers] ever to find their way through this land."[31] But with this very remark he admits that the earlier exploration narratives had become a schema for the representation of later expeditions. By the 1890s verbal paintings had become so much a part of the way he was socialized to see the world that one finds them as much in *Notices* as in the private Watkins manuscript (see the juxtaposed quotations from the two texts above).

It is as if the show was willed to go on, and there is evidence that Watkins was playing his part in response to the demands of an equally willing audience. One of the more exiting moments of the expedition, Shimmin's involvement in a lion hunt, was also "cross-published" in *Work and Workers in the Mission Field*. As we have seen, this new magazine was actually meant to shift the focus in missionary journalism to "evangelistic and pastoral work" instead of *WMN*'s customary "tidings from the field."[32] That this article was selected nevertheless indicates the editors' experience with the ever-popular reception of a certain kind of tiding "from the field": that "which shows that life in that country [Mashonaland] has its elements of hazard and romance." The reading public still had a penchant for unspoiled wildernesses and "estheticized landscapes."[33] The missionary societies (the Wesleyans were not alone in this)[34] were not out of tune when they serialized their travel experiences and "spiritual" territorial conquests in their periodicals, where the thirst for adventure and the duty of evangelization came together. Readers of *WMN* could imagine themselves in Watkins's role, as an adventurous male Christian mastering far-off parts of the globe.[35]

Watkins's private journal, however, was written to a wife, daughters, and sons—an audience of mixed genders and generations, but all within the feminine realm of the Victorian Mother, "the 'women's sphere' of home and hearth."[36] Juxtaposing the written and the published accounts enables one to rethink the masculine adventurism projected in Victorian traveling as performance for an intended British audience rather than the lived experience of a bookish Wesleyan minister.

In the pages of *WMN*, the text related to mission work is ensconced between two outer layers of advertising. An abundance of earthly goods (soap, cocoa, pills, plated cutlery, lace curtains—and books) is offered in the advertisements that sponsored the heavenly work of spreading the Methodist gospel all over the British world.[37] Paratext and text indeed reinforce each other. However, the published accounts of the Mashonaland mission are, in contrast with the private journal, conspicuously silent about consumer items. For example, the continual references to sources of water in the published account could give the reader an impression that the missionaries were in a constant struggle for survival in the wilderness: "Saturday, 4th July. Arrived at Brak River at four o'clock p.m. Our oxen were showing signs of distress, having had no water since ten o'clock yesterday morning. The river is drying up, and the water is only in pools in the river bed."[38] The perils of travel in the interior are, of course, not to be underestimated. However, judging from the private journal's disclosure of the wagonload of gadgets the missionary party had at their disposal to make the journey more comfortable, one does suspect that the compilers of the public version had indulged in some selective omission to exaggerate those perils. On Monday 6 July, in the privacy of his personal journal, Watkins reported to his wife: "Got out our filter and set it going for the water is brackish."[39] The private manuscript is full of references to material amenities for Victorian travelers—pots, tinned foods, medicine, cocoa and myriad other indulgent objects[40]—that never appeared in the published version. The domestic—feminine—comfort of the consumer's world was unmentionable in the adventurous travel narrative about a mission into a supposedly preindustrial realm, the "wilderness."[41] On the other hand, the published episodes were generous with their descriptions of unspoiled nature:

> Tuesday, 7 July. . . . still travelling in a dense bush, which extends to the Limpopo.
>
> Thursday, 9 July. To-day stopped for breakfast at Cream of Tartar Fontein, so called from a number of baobab trees which are found there.
> . . .
> To-night, slept in a forest of turpentine trees.
>
> Friday, 10 July. Still travelling through a seeming endless bush country.[42]

It is as if the comfort that technological advances and commodities enjoyed by late Victorian travelers had become an embarrassment. If mentioned too obviously, it would no longer have been possible for readers to imagine "a primeval and physically equal struggle in which the white man's superiority to the black [and the challenging African landscape] is demonstrated in moral terms."[43] Ironically, the white missionaries' superiority to the black and "coloured" servants trekking with them is illustrated precisely in terms of consumer commodities. Watkins did not bother to keep up appearances either in the inner circle where his passivity as bookish explorer was known, or in the eyes of his wife reading in his personal diary. In July

1891 he wrote to her: "We gave the boys [black helpers] a tin of jam to make merry & they wish I had a birthday every week."[44]

Some passages in Watkins's private diary are directed to specific children in his household: Charley instructed to buy a certain book or to send up the papers, May and Charley congratulated on their birthdays.[45] At other times he seems to be addressing the family as a whole. Although he hardly ever addresses her in the first person, he clearly writes with the assumption that "Mother," Mrs. Watkins, was in charge of the household.[46]

What kind of a listener, or reader, was Mrs. Watkins? When Rev. George Lowe, Watkins's colleague from Potchefstroom, advised him on who should be a suitable acting chairperson during his absence from Pretoria, he remarked: "If Mrs Watkins were eligible, I should put up two hands for her."[47] Mary Saunders had married Owen Watkins in 1868, eight years before they came to South Africa.[48] She must have been a most capable woman, but in a Victorian sense: Lowe added that Mrs. Watkins would be a good acting chair because "she knows better than anybody else *your* own way of working and would be most likely to *satisfy you* when you return."[49] In her letter to her son in England, in which she reported on Watkins's serious illness upon his eventual return from the Mashonaland journey, Mrs. Watkins even afforded herself the customary Victorian "nervous breakdown."[50] In the private journal, instructing his children to behave and not to make life difficult for "Mother,"[51] Watkins conforms to convention by reinforcing the wife's exertion of authority over the household on behalf of the father. And yet he also finds enough of a confidante in Mary Watkins to express to her his frustration regarding Shimmin's irritating habits,[52] and sharing with her his most awkward and embarrassing experiences with a generous scoop of self-effacing humor.[53] It may be that Watkins, during his long absence from home (he got very homesick),[54] depended more on his ability to communicate with her to sustain himself than the other way around.

Did Watkins reach his intended audience? Of course, respectable late Victorian middle-class Methodists read more than religious tracts. They were also patriotic Englishmen and women, and the publication of the journeys of the great African explorers, as well as the "campaign literature" of the Scramble for Africa,[55] would not have passed them by completely unnoticed. Watkins's enthusiasm for British territorial expansion was unconcealed. The following assertion, made in one of his addresses in London in 1893, was still reported with great confidence in the history of the Wesleyan Methodist Missionary Society published three decades later—an indication that hardly anyone seriously questioned it. Watkins affirmed that Cecil Rhodes's company, which colonized Mashonaland, "had done for British influence, for righteousness, and for trade what England ought to have done herself."[56]

When he embarked for Mashonaland, Owen Watkins had already established himself as a popular figure with Wesleyan readers in England. During his visits to London he literally got in touch with actual readers. His lectures were believed to elicit substantial financial support for mission work in the Transvaal.[57] In South Africa too Watkins knew how to drum up enthusiasm among devoted Methodist readers. On the eve of his departure for Mashonaland, he received a request from his colleague George Lowe to write a brief appeal for support in the Potchefstroom *Illustrated Bazaar News*, of which three hundred copies would be printed: "Please do it in a racy style, say something to tickle us all in the right place (pocket)."[58] Watkins also received an encouraging letter from J. F. Rumfitt, who had lately come from England to join the Wesleyan Church in the Transvaal. Rumfitt's enthusiasm for Watkins's travels must have emanated from reading about previous journeys in the *Notices* and more recent announcements of this latest expedition: "I wish I were going to Mashonaland with you for a year or two; I hope you will have a safe & successful visit: is it likely that any of us young fellows will be wanted for M.[ashonaland] at the next G. Mtg [General Meeting]."[59] Visual proof that, on the eve of the Mashonaland journey, Owen Watkins had become the "face" of Wesleyan work in the Transvaal, is found in a request by the London-based compiler of the *Wesleyan Missionary Sheet Almanac* for 1892: "We have decided with your consent to put you in one corner *as representing our work in Africa*. Will you be good enough to send me your photograph for the above purpose? A very succinct history of our work in the Transvaal and Swaziland District might find space in the Almanac *under the picture*."[60] It was anticipated that the picture could later be reproduced in both the *Notices* and in *At Home and Abroad*. If Wesleyan work in Africa (including west as well as southern Africa)[61] were to be essentialized in one image, the portrait of Watkins would suffice. No consideration was given to representing "native work" (which was clearly distinguished from "English work") in the colonies, or to illuminating the careers of successful South African "native" ministers.[62]

Despite the obvious differences between the private and the published messages Watkins addressed to his diverging audiences, they are not wholly contradictory. The following private exclamation merges perfectly with the publicly stated mission of the official journey: "This too is our mission, to go into the regions beyond, & to cry to the thirsty persisting multitudes of dark interior Africa, as we point to the 'fountain of living water,' 'water here, drink & live'" (written upon coming across a signpost marked "water here" left by previous travelers along the same road to Mashonaland).[63] Neither is the private journal devoid of adventure and masculine pursuits.

When Watkins gives instructions to his wife on how to pass on the official version to the missionary society, he clearly states that the private journal should be particularly interesting to his eldest son. The private journal rather aims at filling in what was assumed to be too delicate, too undignified, too derogatory, too personal, too consumerist, too mundane, or too feminine to include in a published travel journal. While the published version resembled the way an audience would experience a performance on stage, the private journal included what was happening "behind the scenes" as well. In its aim to be more complete than the published version, the private journal unmasks the pretence that was inevitable in the published account. It reveals that the genre of imperial travel writing had been propped up with adventure and suspense and unending excitement since (and even before) the days of Shaw and Livingstone—and exposes that melodrama as rather impractical, slightly farcical, quite unrealistic, and already somewhat unconvincing in the 1890s. By this time the "wilderness" was fast giving way to telegraph offices, mail coaches, transport riders, and prospecting settlers and miners encountering "Water here" signposts along the road.[64]

The private correspondence among Wesleyan men opens up a world of women and family that hardly features in published accounts. In addition to his aforementioned assessment of Mrs. Watkins's administrative talents, George Lowe also mentions Elizabeth Bowen, the wife of the "native" evangelist who was earmarked to become the pioneer of "native work" north of the Limpopo. Lowe tries to explain why she would not necessarily have been able to make do with a smaller income in her husband's absence: "He [Michael Bowen] is willing to go & do his utmost *for one year,* if provision could be made for his family. He feels however that the whole of his £48 a year will be needed by them, as his absence would not greatly reduce his expenses in housekeeping, as native women cannot get as much for 2/- as their husbands can get for 1/6."[65] This issue was crucial and was discussed again in a subsequent letter. George Lowe recognized and recorded the compounded jeopardy of being black and female and severed from the security of a communal subsistence economy in the late nineteenth-century Transvaal. The poignancy of this record lies in the concern Mrs. Bowen's predicament has caused her own husband as well as the white Wesleyan men. Yet this remained a private concern, an inevitability to be provided for, but hardly an issue to be raised in public. The case was resolved in the private correspondence between the two white men:

> First, his absence from home will not nearly decrease his wife's expenditure, as much of his time is spent in outside work. A woman is not able to attend market or make such good bargains as a native man.

> Second. He has several small debts, made chiefly in getting his outfit & these he has left in my hands.
>
> Third. I thought he would go with a better heart when fully assured that his wife had a 10/- extra for her expenses.[66]

As much as one is struck by the Wesleyan men's attentiveness to the financial wellbeing of Bowen's wife, one cannot help notice that, in comparison with their reverence for Mrs. Watkins, who was also dependent on her husband's (more substantial) income during his absence, there is nothing in this correspondence that reveals that Elizabeth Bowen was a prominent and influential figure in the African Wesleyan community who would five years later be recognized in the minutes of a meeting as an evangelist in her own right.[67] In fact, neither Mrs. Watkins nor Mrs. Bowen made it into the *Notices*. Households with wives and children were put on hold in Watkins's published diary.

Moreover, the household chores the men had to perform on the journey were likewise screened from the eyes of British readers. This had not always been the case in travel writing. We have seen that the early nineteenth-century letters of missionaries like Barnabas Shaw from Kamiesberg would "describe such prosaic matters as the making of soap or the purchase of timber."[68] In the early decades of the nineteenth century, writes Catherine Hall, domesticity was integral to middle class masculinity: "True manliness encompassed the capacity to establish a home, protect it, provide for it and control it: all these were a part of a man's good standing," and "men had to survive on their own." In his diaries on his Australian experiences published in the first half of the nineteenth century, Edward John Eyre (later in life Governor of Jamaica) shared with his readers how the skills he had learned as a "bachelor farmer—cooking, washing and mending his clothes, dealing with sickness—were quite as essential as those associated with the driving of stock, the keeping of journals and charts, the daily observation of the barometer, the thermometer, the winds and the weather. When times were hard, Eyre, trained in the ways of cleanliness and godliness, retreated to nursery lore and found there was nothing better than 'a good wash to recover himself.'"[69]

By 1891 much had changed. Watkins was not a real explorer or a know-all do-all adventurer: he had succumbed to the growing comforts of urban consumerism as well as the ready availability of colonial labor. His manliness was still vested in his ability to provide for and control his home, but as a man of the Book and a man of books, he made a living through reading, writing, and preaching. These were also the means through which he sustained his manliness in the domestic sphere: "To my great joy we got our letters at Fort Charter. . . . Got Mother's letter of 16th August, enclosing

Spencer's, May's and the Home letter.... Had a good time reading the letters. How my heart longs for a sight of you all. So thankful & glad that you are all so well—but don't like dear Mother being tired so much & so often. Am very interested in reading about the details of the daily lives of my loved ones."[70] Besides *reading* the barometer and the compass (he very meticulously recorded temperature and location throughout the journey), the "skills of the bachelor farmer" did not come naturally to Watkins. Neither did he perform domesticity in a way that could portray it as masculine. Most of the responsibilities of traveling and outdoor living was taken off his hands by his black and colored assistants, so that he could have more time to read and write, to record the journey, and to continue communicating with the "outside world": "Writing all day until my right hand is quite cramped."[71] While he would conceal from his public readers that there were enough dull and leisurely hours on the trip to while away by reading, what he read nourished the construction of a nationalistic account for the *Notices*: "Did not get very far today—the wind was very strong—the sand deep—& two of our oxen very poor. Finished Green's History [of the English people]—& I advise my children to read it, the first chance they get—for they have a grand treat in store."[72] Ironically, in the private "conversation" with his family, Watkins readily confessed to an accusation often leveled against women at the time, that they indulged in so much reading that they neglected their daily responsibilities[73]: "Reading all day—too lazy to do anything else. I forgot to note on Saturday, that John made a good oven out of an Ant heap, & baked us four loaves—& good loaves they are too."[74] Those chores that Watkins had to do himself were performed with such awkwardness that they could not be included in the type of adventure narrative that readers had come to expect from Barnabas Shaw and Edward John Eyre.[75] Watkins's published account of his travels was, to a large extent, a performance and an invention conjured up by selective omission, to please the expectations of generations of readers who had grown up with the stories of the great explorers. Confessions like the following would have undermined this genre and could not leave the realm of the private: "Shimmin out all day shooting, but the Lord is very gracious to the Buck, none of them were hurt or killed. John, the driver, first did the washing. I folded the clothes & did the ironing—by sitting on them. Don't you laugh, it is a first rate way, only it does not answer for white ties & collars, but of course that is because we have no starch."[76]

Besides the private diary, Watkins also sent home photographs Shimmin had taken of him *en route* to Mashonaland. In his personal diary he wrote: "In honour of my Birthday, Shimmin took my picture today standing under the palms."[77] Clearly, Watkins too had succumbed to the aura of an exotic landscape and the temptation of imprinting himself on it. Understandably, this information was also published in the *WMN*: "As I am forty-nine years old to-day, Mr Shimmin took my photo under the palms."[78] The following, however, was only meant for Watkins's wife and children in the private journal: "think it will be well if you could get a special scrap album, as well bound as you can—& get Charley to paste in all the photos I send down.[79]

The illustrations in the *Notices* accompanying the Mashonaland journey conform to the expectations of adventure and travel literature fed by the text. Early in 1891, with the announcement of the intended expedition in the *Notices*, no fewer than five images of white travelers into Mashonaland were reproduced. They were obviously published too early to have been taken by Shimmin, which increases the possibility that they were merely inserted to whet readers' appetites for what was to follow in subsequent months: idyllic camp sites, a member of the "pioneer force" contentedly sipping his pipe against a broad and open horizon, a scene of a crocodile-infested Limpopo River (figure 1), with the caption "admirable fishing here" inscribed on it by hand.[80] The readers of *Missionary Notices* were in for a great treat. Methodism was to be brought to this part of the world, and how exhilarating it would be to pursue this project on paper.

Apart from a map (figure 2) of the first stretch of the journey—through the northern Transvaal, across the Limpopo, and into Rhodes's territory—

Fig. 1 "On the Limpopo River," *Wesleyan Missionary Notices*, March 1891, p. 61.

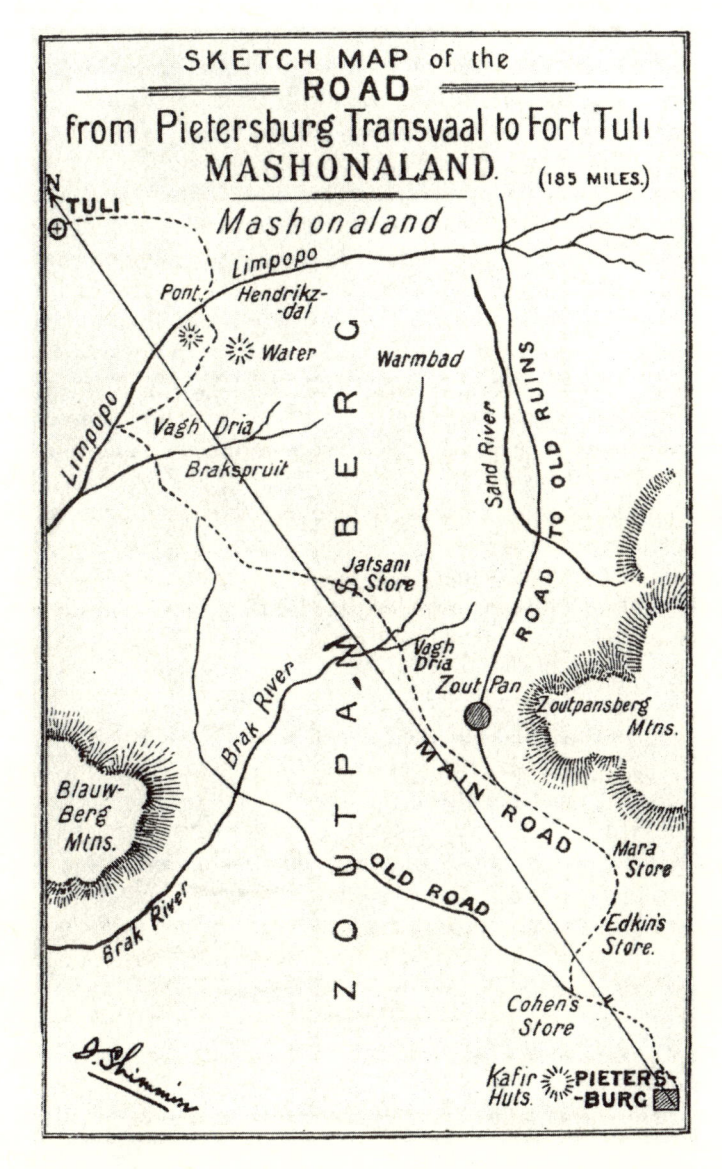

Fig. 2 Sketch Map of the Road from Pietersburg Transvaal to Fort Tuli Mashonaland, *Wesleyan Missionary Notices*, October 1891, p. 230.

only one more image appears in *Notices* to represent Watkins's part in the expedition (figure 3). It shows him and Shimmin wading through the Shashe River to get to Fort Tuli where they would hold a religious service on Sunday 19 July 1891. The line drawing ostensibly proves how much a Wesleyan minister would put up with in the line of duty.

The most typifying African adventure representing the journey, Shimmin's encounter with a lion, only appears after Watkins had already departed from Mashonaland, and of course it had hardly anything to do with mission work. The essay, published in *Notices* somewhat abbreviated from the *Work and Workers* version, still runs almost three pages and boasts its own full-page illustration (figure 4). Shimmin, the brave hunter-missionary, raised his gun, "but before I could fire the lion suddenly swerved and leaped at Stevens [a traveler in the company of the Wesleyans] who instantly fired and then sprang behind a small tree."[81] Predictably, the "natives" in the illustration as well as in Shimmin's verbal painting are made to look silly, and the dead lion majestic. The English readers were given a taste of a supposedly "physically equal struggle" where the white man demonstrated his moral superiority to the black.[82] Yet, in his attempt to be humorous, Shimmin acknowledged the fact that the African hunters had technology far inferior to the whites': "As soon as the natives heard that the lion was shot they came running up with their old flint muskets—very dangerous weapons at the *wrong* end. They were very much excited, and had we allowed them, they would have done wonderful execution with assegai and battle-axe upon their prostrate foe. But the king of beasts looked majestic even in death."[83] The appearance of this nonreligious adventure tale in *Notices* accentuates the discrepancies already shining through the seam between Watkins's published and private recordings of the journey. The Victorians were succumbing to secularization, and their very act of converting Africa to Christianity was promoting this process, not a bulwark against it.

The September 1892 *Notices* brings the readers back to the actual task of the Wesleyans in Africa, the mission among the "natives." This issue contains a line drawing (figure 5) of Shimmin's humble parsonage ("the first Methodist parsonage in Mashonaland"), as well as Michael Bowen, the much applauded and appreciated "native evangelist" sitting in front of his even humbler thatched hut (figure 6). Secular worldliness shines through again as Shimmin remarks: "In fifty years' time, when the great Wesleyan magnates of Mashonaland will have beautiful villas and rich parks, it will do them good to look back to my humble parsonage and trace the beginnings of things."[84]

The images of Mashonaland sketched in the *Notices* do not easily link up with the front cover page of the *Notices* used in the early 1890s (figure 7). It features an "Orientalist" line drawing, complete with architectural

250   JOURNAL OF A JOURNEY TO MASHONALAND, 1891.

assistance of our friends the Bothas; we had thirty-four oxen to pull us through. Outspanned in a grove of palm trees, and are surrounded by (to us) strange forms of beauty. As I am forty-nine years old to-day, Mr. Shimmin took my photo under the palms. I devoutly thank God who has blessed me all my life long until this day, and my heart is singing—

"Lord, in the strength of grace,
With a glad heart and free,
Myself, my residæ of days
I consecrate to thee."

Arrived at Tuli in the dark, but can see the lights of the fort and camp across the river. All wagons of travellers must remain on the north side of the river, and must give their passes and all particulars of the persons and purposes of the journey, and the passes have to be countersigned by the commanding officer of Fort Tuli, before the journey can be continued.

Temperature (in the sun) 12 o'clock noon, 90°, and at 8 o'clock p.m., 60° Fahr.

Saturday, 18th July.—Mr. Shimmin and I went over the river and

Fig. 3 "We walked and waded our passage through," *Wesleyan Missionary Notices*, November 1891, p. 250.

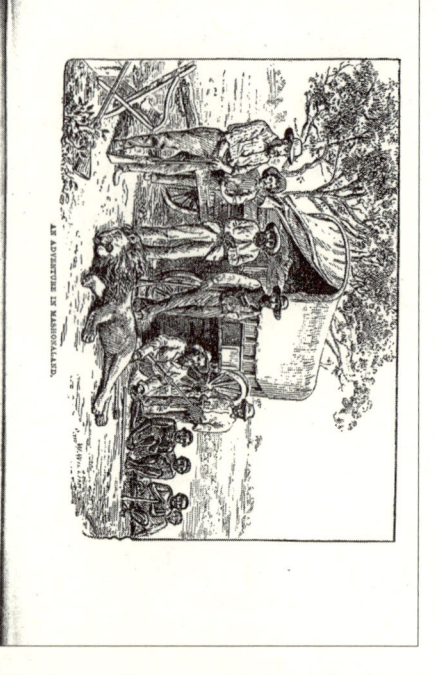

Fig. 4 "An Adventure in Mashonaland," *Wesleyan Missionary Notices*, March 1892, p. 59.

manifestations of "pagan" religions in a picturesque landscape: palm trees and tranquil water in the foreground and snow-covered mountains in the distance. Furthermore, before accessing the missionary content of *Notices*, the reader had to wade through several pages of advertisements—for Cadbury's Cocoa, Pear's Soap, and cures for "female complaints."

These advertisements suggest that the readers of *Notices* were not exclusively male. *WMN* also published a smattering of articles written by women missionaries (not working in the Transvaal, though). For example, Helen W. Gibson proclaimed that "Christian England" could save a France "paralysed by superstition and atheism." Where there were woman writers there were also woman readers. They are found in the lists of financial contributors to missionary work, some explicitly stating that their donation should be directed "per Rev. Watkins" to work in Mashonaland.[85]

Of course, the consumers of the goods advertised in *WMN* were not all women. Watkins knew the comfort of soap, as he reported in his private diary: "Washing day—so did not trek."[86] Watkins also knew the consolation of cocoa, which he used to nurse a fellow traveler who had "been in

Surveyor-General), and he pointed out that, according to the agreement drawn up by Mr. Watkins, the stands granted to our Church could not be sold or transferred without the consent of the Company. This was hardly satisfactory for us, as the constitution of the Company might change to such a degree that a transaction of this sort might be a great difficulty in a few years' time. I wished, therefore, to have it freehold, so that the Wesleyan Church might have full right over the land given. I also saw Dr. Jameson on the subject, and I hope in my next to report that my request has been successful. I shall send you a copy of the new title which will take the place of the provisional certificate. The four stands applied for at Umtali have been granted. (Here follow some particulars with regard to the grants of land, which,

THE FIRST METHODIST PARSONAGE IN MASHONALAND.

at Mr. Shimmin's request, are treated as private, being intended only for the use of the Missionary Committee.)

I have placed this important matter as clearly as I can before you, and it is now for our Church to enter the many doors set wide open before it. The cry for next Exeter Hall Meeting should be: "We want, and must have, fifty native teachers for Mashonaland." The country may go ahead but slowly as far as white men are concerned, but the native work is waiting for us—it has been waiting for many, many years. The harvest is great; send us the labourers.

I wish I had a young man to take my place at Fort Salisbury, as I feel it my duty to travel again as soon as possible, in order to visit the chiefs and secure farms. This grand opportunity has been given us,

Fig. 5 The First Methodist Parsonage in Mashonaland, *Wesleyan Missionary Notices*, September 1893, p. 202.

here between the natives of the country (Mashonas) and the Colony native. I felt it my duty to have several interviews on the subject with Dr. Jameson (Administrator) and Mr. Caldecott (Head of the Legal Department), and requested that the word *native* should apply to every coloured man, no matter from what part of Africa he may have come. They pointed out the difficulty of the case, that as they had taken over the Cape Colony law these "boys" had a right to buy drink, although at the same time they were willing to do all they could to put down drunkenness. I insisted that their own charter had spoken on the point, and if they allowed even a half-caste to buy brandy they were opening the door to a host of evils, and the ruin of the Mashonas would soon follow. I am happy to say that I was successful, the permission

MICHAEL BOWEN, NATIVE EVANGELIST.

being at once revoked. And now in all the Company's territory no native whatever is allowed to buy drink, and any person selling it to him is liable to a heavy penalty. This is a great victory, and we must carefully watch that this good law remains untouched.

STANDS.

As you are aware, we have five stands in Fort Salisbury. On these we pay nothing except the sanitary fees to the Town Board. They are 10s. per month for each stand. I made application to the Sanitary Board for exemption of fees on four out of the five stands, which they kindly granted, and we now pay 10s. per month for the five instead of 50s. Their decision was retrospective (to October last). You will see that this makes a considerable difference, and I shall make this a precedent for stands in the other townships.

Yesterday I had a very important interview with Mr. Duncan (the

Fig. 6 "Michael Bowen, Native Evangelist," *Wesleyan Missionary Notices*, September 1893, p. 201.

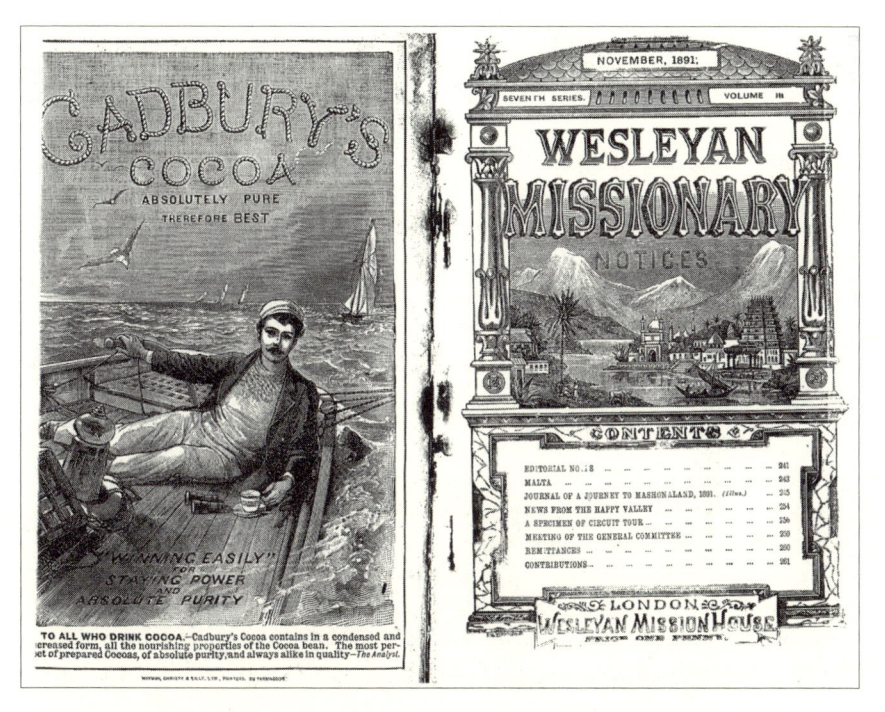

Fig. 7 Cover page of *Wesleyan Missionary Notices* in the early 1890s.

bed for five days. He is a big powerful man, & the fever has laid hold of him properly. He is as weak as a baby. I gave him a tin of cocoa, & he was thankful."[87] The missionary also appreciated the relief of "a dose of chloradine" when he himself was feeling "very seedy all day."[88] Watkins slid perfectly into the role of the Victorian "Mother" when his driver got ill: "He has no fever, but is in a lot of pain. I have been doctoring him, & I think he will be all right tomorrow."[89]

However, women reading the "journey through Mashonaland" in the *WMN* were not told about baking, washing, ironing, and doctoring. For the reading public in England, capitalist consumption was separated from travel accounts of faraway Africa. Does this help us understand how British Christians could have been made accomplices in conquest without realizing its effect? In their reading experience they were transferred into another reality, one of adventure in the wilderness. In Watkins's private journal the slippage between indulgence in a capitalist, technological, consumerist world and the longing for an imaginary lost pastoral tranquility is more apparent. On the day they crossed the Limpopo, Watkins admired the landscape in both the published and his private journal,[90] but only in the private version did he describe some little monkeys, expressing his disappointment that he could not "bring a couple home" for his daughter Nelli—almost as if they were manufactured toys in a catalog or shop window.

"Let nothing escape your lips out of this journal of a private nature, or anything about Mr Shimmin, unless the thing recorded be to his praise or credit. I want everything good to be told of him, but not a word of the other kind."[91] Thus Watkins wrote to his wife after sharing with her his frustrations with his travel companion. For him, acting as chairman of the Wesleyan Society in South Africa was a performance that could be contemplated in private, rehearsed in public life, and perfected in published periodicals. On Sunday 19 July 1891 Watkins and Shimmin donned "full clerical rig out" for the occasion of a parade service for Rhodes's troops at Fort Tuli. The public report supported the illustration of them courageously wading through the river on their way to the fort: "In honour of the day and the service, we put on black suits. It would have done anybody good to see us. . . . We took off some portions of our dress, and rolled up portions of others, and we walked and waded our passage through."[92] In the private journal, however, Watkins confessed to his wife and children: "It was a scene sublime to see the Methodist Bishop and his Curate passing through the waters. On our return, one of our Boer friends, young Botha, would not let me wade through the water, so he carried me through on his back, which took away greatly from my dignity but added to my comfort."[93]

When juxtaposed, his published and private writings reveal the extent to which Watkins prized outward appearance. This in itself was not exceptional at all among Victorian gentlemen. What was exceptional was that Watkins articulated his awareness that the public display was a performance that had a very specific meaning and significance. As the performer, he was conscious of the image he intended to portray—and admitted that it could hardly be upheld permanently. In writing to his wife and family about the Wesleyan party's arrival in Fort Salisbury, Watkins pulled out all stops to eternalize this momentous episode in his life. What could have made his boasting endearing to his wife was that he diminished himself into the role of a little boy, dressed up to be adored by his Victorian "Mother": "We outspanned for breakfast & to have a general wash & brush up. We actually had our boots cleaned & I put on a waistcoat & a paper collar. I felt as grand as a little boy in a new suit of clothes, who thinks everybody is admiring his new 'rig out.' Three miles journey brought us to Salisbury, & I walked into town with all the dignity suitable to a Methodist Bishop."[94] Watkins's change of apparel before entering Salisbury signified the transition from one social space to another: the travelers were entering "civilization" again after weeks in the "wilderness." However, the next day he realized that the binary opposition he had tried to maintain between public and private, between formal and familiar, would need to be redesigned in a makeshift town where people of all races, religions, and social classes were thrown together:

> To have a clean white collar on, is a sign that you have just arrived & have kept your last clean collar to make an impression upon the town. We have Lords & sons of Lords–Barristers & Doctors—Swells from Oxford & Cambridge—Merchants & Traders—Prospectors & Miners—Jews & Gentiles—Roman Catholic—Ch. of Eng & Wes. Parsons—a former member of the Perkins Opera Company, has the Zambesi Hair Cutting Saloon, (in a hut) where he trims your beard or gives you a feeling shave for one shilling. The mild Hindoo is also here & though he has not yet got beyond carrying a bundle of goods on his back to sell or take in washing, & in his spare moments, run a market garden, the produce of which will appear next year. There is no piano for the land as yet, but one has been ordered for the canteen.[95]

WMN would not want to portray their Wesleyan stalwart fraternizing with men of so many different convictions and denominations. This private peep into street life in a newly established mining town also gave Mrs. Watkins and her children insight into an altogether different male space: a lawless wildness rather than an adventurous "wilderness." Watkins himself used the word "wildness" in his diary to refer to undesirable behavior by young Englishmen in the metropole.[96]

In publication, Owen Watkins may have been creating the impression of an untiring champion of the Christian faith traversing the unforgiving wilderness, eventually to appear in godforsaken Fort Salisbury in (as his white audience expected) a speckless spider-white collar under a black suit[97] to stake a claim for his denomination—forever using the "is" of domesticity as the backstage to prepare for the "ought" of public life. Privately, however, he reported tongue-in-cheek on his washday blues, unashamedly admitted his dependence on cocoa and patent medicines, and scoffed at his colleague's attempt at hunting when they could have survived perfectly well on tinned food and spent the time more fruitfully recording the journey in writing. Ironically, his own feverish writing was made possible because the indispensable work of traveling (driving the wagon, baking bread) was attended to by darker-skinned servants and evangelists.

The launch of a new missionary magazine, in the same year that Owen Watkins returned from his last journey through the African interior, also marked the end of an era of reportage on heroic missionary expeditions. As the author of the section on "Rhodesia" in the *History of the Wesleyan Methodist Missionary Society* admitted:

> This mission field is the latest of the many fields in which the seed of the Wesleyan revival has been cast, and as such we shall find that the story we have to tell lacks certain features with which we have become familiar in surveying the work of the Church in Africa. . . . The work was begun at a time when the resources of civilized life were more immediately available to British folk in Africa, and there were alleviations in the toil of the missionary which were unknown to Barnabas Shaw at Kamiesberg or to William Shaw in Kaffraria.[98]

That *Work and Workers* nevertheless pounced upon Shimmin's lion hunt episode (though according to the aims with this new publication, they should have been shifting their focus to the more ecumenical issues of daily Christian activities in a well-established church) indicated a compromise with anticipated readers' responses. Though there was no wilderness any more (if there had ever been), readers were still looking for it. As Mary Louis Pratt has illustrated, we still do.[99] In fact, we now read and reread the "wilderness" into Africa, whether as consumers or producers, tourists or conservationists and entrepreneurs, and we act out these roles of reading the landscape both as Europeans and Africans.

If juxtaposing Watkins's private diary to *WMN* can accomplish one thing, it should be to contribute to a greater recognition of the longstanding and significant, but not altogether wholesome, role of Africa in the way Europeans constructed their concepts of consumerism, nationalism, Christianity, domesticity, masculinity, and femininity. The "African voice" that Africanist scholars encourage us to seek in historical investigation is intended to be heard not just by Africans themselves, but also by the greater audience in the global arena. One way for Africans to address global ignorance about the long European involvement in their part of the world may be to inculcate within this global audience an awareness of their shared experience of modernization during what came to be known as the colonial era. As Ryan Dunch reminds us, in a sense "we have all been colonised."[100] Simultaneous with the missionary endeavor to modernize Africans, Europeans were urbanized, disciplined into clock-time, initiated into consumer culture, and converted to monogamous core-familial relations—something very much like the missionary project in "remote" Africa. Constructions of European modernity should no longer be afforded the misleading compartmentalization that had held out for so long in publications like *WMN*.

The (granted, unequally) incomplete ways in which the modernization of Europeans and Africans were accomplished left scope on both sides of the Atlantic for performances of what the "ought" in life was imagined to be. Already by the 1890s consumer amenities were making it possible to imagine a "softer" masculinity, while an increasing number of women began to convert the masculine roles appropriated through reading into new tensions between the "is" and the "ought" of their lives. One only needs to think of the many women who took up "wilderness" traveling themselves.[101]

This brings us to African readers. We may not have evidence of the way Michael Bowen developed his performative faculties through reading or projected it in writing, but the writings of many other Africans who became acquainted with European writings and readings in the "contact zone" did survive. Exquisite examples of these are discussed in the recently published *Africa's Hidden Histories: Everyday Literacy and Making the Self*, edited by Karen Barber (2006). While *Africa's Hidden Histories* recognizes the influence of missionary writing and publishing practices on African writers and performers in the colonial era, it perhaps makes slightly too much of the newness of the emergent African "kinds of self-representation and personhood."[102] If we make the assumption that the writing of letters and keeping of diaries by Africans in the colonial era was a response to and an appropriation of white missionary writing practices, we should at least open the possibility that there was not just rupture, but also continuity in the ways Africans employed these forms of written expression. In Stephan Miescher's fascinating readings of Ghanaian Presbyterian schoolmaster-chatechist Akasease Kofi Boakye Yiadom we can recognize the various forms of self-representation employed by Owen Watkins:

> Miescher shows that rather than functioning as an aid to spiritual introspection, the diary projected and orchestrated a shifting multiple self and was at least as much a script for the performance of a persona as it was an exploration of interiority. His writings "reflect the multitude of Boyake Yiadom selves and alliances" as the diarist, over the course of his life, "moved in and out of various social contexts with competing expectations of him as an adult man." In the diary, he prepared behind the scenes for a public performance of his self. The diary provided him with a launchpad for "readings" of his life-narrative to his family, readings which involved the oral performance, in Twi, of what he had written in English. He told Mieschner: "I do loudly read my old diaries to my wife, children, grandchildren and the households to their amusement, laughter and sorrow, knowing and studying my progress, backwardness or retrogression in life; so that they too may be aware of themselves in their living."[103]

We should also heed Isabel Hofmeyr's reminder that neither orality nor the interplay between orality and literacy is a "uniquely African" cultural phenomenon.[104] It is not hard to imagine that Mrs. Watkins would have read parts of her husband's reports out loud to her children. Watkins's reading of the barometer and the thermometer, and his photographic project intended to accompany the written record of his journey, was not utterly different from Akasease Kofi Boakye Yiadom's "My Own Life" project. Watkins's personal documents may not contain, like Boyake Yiadom's, the exact result of an eye test or the numbers of all his lottery tickets, but they do include lists of books bought, notes on cash spent on refreshments or the mending of a pair of boots, and schedules related to his responsibilities in the church. As little as African colonial literacy can be understood without reference to European ways of reading and writing, can it be understood without a more thorough investigation also into European colonial reading and writing practices? We have indeed all been colonized, and sort of modernized.

This is not an argument to reduce African literacy to plain mimicry of European versions of modernity. Of course, the restriction and limitation—oppression—of literate Africans in the colonizing project would result in forms of commentary one should not expect to find in the self-representations of white men standing so close to colonial officialdom as Owen Watkins. But in light of the highly original insights of *Africa's Hidden Histories,* one should perhaps guard against overemphasizing the "uniqueness" of African appropriation of forms of reading and writing, which could reify the "otherness" of Africans and imply that they cannot embrace literacy to the same extent as Europeans. This presumption may inadvertently shift the blame for Africa's marginalized position in the global knowledge production industry to something "inherently African," thereby (as in the neatly compartmentalized *WMN*) ignoring the international market forces that worked against the African continent and its inhabitants throughout the colonial era, and still do.[105]

Notes

1. For a brief discussion of Rhodes's activities north of the Limpopo in the context of British Imperialism in southern Africa, see Christopher Saunders and Iain R. Smith, "Southern Africa," in *The Oxford History of the British Empire: The Nineteenth Century,* ed. Andrew Porter (Oxford: Oxford University Press, 1999), 610–12.

2. W. A. Venter, "Owen Watkins," *Suid-Afrikaanse Biografiese Woordeboek,* ed. Willem J. de Kock (Kaapstad: Tafelberg, 1968), 1:907.

3. Joan Millard, "Nineteenth and Early Twentieth Century Missionary Wives in South Africa: Equal Partners or Historical Non-entities?" *Missionalia* 31, no. 1 (2003): 69–70.

4. A person who walks in front of a wagon to lead the oxen.

5. Owen Watkins, "On the Way to Mashonaland," *Wesleyan Missionary Notices,* October 1891, 229.

6. George G. Findlay, *The History of the Wesleyan Methodist Missionary Society IV: Women's Auxiliary; West Africa; South Africa; Europe* (London: Epworth, 1924), 380.

7. Frederick W. Macdonald, ed., *The Story of Mashonaland and the Missionary Pioneer: With Map Specially Drawn and Illustrations from Original Photographs* (London: Wesleyan Mission House, C. H. Kelly, and Wesleyan Sunday School Union, 1893).

8. Watkins, "On the Way to Mashonaland," 229.

9. Archives of the Wesleyan Methodist Missionary Society, South Africa, Cory Library, Rhodes University, Grahamstown: Owen Watkins, "Private Journal of Journey to Mashonaland" (hereafter Watkins, Private Journal), 3 July 1891, 13.

10. Watkins, Private Journal, 14 July 1891, 38–39.

11. Owen Watkins, "Journal of a Journey to Mashonaland, Part II," *Wesleyan Missionary Notices*, November 1891, 248.

12. Interview with Asa Briggs, in *The New History: Confessions and Conversations*, ed. Maria L. G. Pallares-Burke (Cambridge: Polity, 2002), 37.

13. Mary Louise Pratt, *Imperial Eyes: Travel Writing and Transculturation* (London: Routledge, 1992).

14. Adam Jones, "'Four Years in Asante': One Source or Several?" *History in Africa* 18 (1991): 173–203.

15. Also see Lize Kriel, "Colin Rae's 'Maloboch': The Power of the Book in the (Mis)Representation of Kgalusi Sekete Mmaleboho," *South African Historical Journal* 64 (May 2002): 25–41.

16. Jones, "Four Years in Asante," 185.

17. Ian S. MacLaren, "Exploration/Travel Literature and the Evolution of the Author," *International Journal of Canadian Studies* 5 (Spring 1992): 39–68.

18. Ibid., 40–43.

19. Publication expenses were £1,622 14s 4d, while the salaries were £1,629 2s 8d.

20. School of Oriental and African Studies Library, Annual Reports, Wesleyan Methodist Missionary Society, London, 1890–94.

21. Frederick W. Macdonald, "Introductory—To the Reader," *Work and Workers in the Mission Field*, April 1892, 4.

22. Anon., "British South Africa. The Chartered Company and the Missionary Society," *Wesleyan Missionary Notices*, March 1891, 62.

23. Jennifer Cooper, "The Invasion of Personal Religious Experiences: London Missionary Society Missionaries, Imperialism, and the Written Word in Early 19th-Century Southern Africa," *Kleio* 34 (2002): 59. Cooper refers to Elizabeth Elbourne's *Blood Ground: Colonialism, Missions, and the Contest for Christianity in the Cape Colony and Britain, 1799–1853* (Montreal: McGill-Queen's University Press, 2002), and Brian Stanley's *The Bible and the Flag: Protestant Missions and British Imperialism in the Nineteenth and Twentieth Centuries* (Leicester: Apollos, 1990).

24. Findlay, *Wesleyan Methodist Missionary Society IV*, 244–45.

25. Burton's *Lake Regions of Central Africa* was published in 1860; Speke's *Journal of the Discovery of the Source of the Nile* in 1863. Pratt, *Imperial Eyes*, 201, 206.

26. A. N. Wilson, *The Victorians* (London: Arrow, 2002), 493. Livingstone's book was first published by David Murray in 1857 and reprinted until as late as 1912.

27. Duncan points out that, simultaneously, these mid-Victorian representations were themselves "built upon the bedrock of older representations"—the abolitionist literature of the early nineteenth century portrayed the Europeans as the saviors of Africa, the continent itself as a degraded site and the Africans in need of European overseers. See James Duncan, "Sites of Representation. Place, Time and the Discourse of the Other," in *Place/Culture/Representation*, ed. James Duncan and David Ley (London: Routledge, 1993), 49–50. Also see Patrick Brantlinger, "Victorians and Africans: the Genealogy of the Myth of the Dark Continent," in

"Race," *Writing and Difference,* ed. Henry Louis Gates Jr. (Chicago: University of Chicago Press, 1986), 185–222.

28. Pratt, *Imperial Eyes,* 202.

29. David Finkelstein, "Africa Rewritten: The Case of John Hanning Speke," in *The House of Blackwood: Author-Publisher Relations in the Victorian Era* (University Park: Pennsylvania State University Press, 2002), 57–58.

30. See, in this regard, Lize Kriel, "Reverend Watkins's Books," *Innovation: Journal of Appropriate Librarianship and Information Work in Southern Africa* 35 (December 2007): 56–80.

31. Watkins, Private Journal, 29 July 1891, 59.

32. Macdonald, "Introductory," 4.

33. Pratt, *Imperial Eyes,* 202–4.

34. The *Berliner Missionsberichte* (1889), 332, carried accounts of Erdman Schwellnus and Carl Knothe's journey from June to September 1888.

35. "[A]ll periodical space was gendered." Laurel Brake, *Print in Transition, 1850–1910: Studies in Media and Book History* (London: Palgrave, 2001), xiv.

36. Michelle Adler, " 'Skirting the Edges of Civilization': Two Victorian Women Travellers and 'Colonial Spaces' in South Africa," in *Text, Theory, Space: Land, Literature and History in South Africa and Australia,* ed. Kate Darian-Smith, Liz Gunner, and Sarah Nuttall (London: Routledge, 1996), 83.

37. *Wesleyan Missionary Notices,* 1888–93.

38. Watkins, "Journal of a Journey to Mashonaland, Part II," 245.

39. Watkins, Private Journal, 6 July 1891, 18.

40. Pots: ibid., 26 July 1891, 57; tinned foods: ibid., 17 July 1891, 48, and 26 September 1891, 112; medicine: ibid., 19 September 1891, 109; cocoa: ibid., 17 September 1891, 107; other objects: ibid., 1 July 1891, 3 and 3 July 1891, 17. Mrs. Watkins had made curtains for the wagon and cut a hole in a rug in order to make a poncho for her husband to sleep in. He also used the tea cozy to keep his feet warm during the cold nights.

41. For abundant use of the word "wilderness," see Watkins's published diary inscriptions for the first half of July 1891 in *Wesleyan Missionary Notices,* 1891, 246–47.

42. Ibid.

43. Wilson, *Victorians,* 493.

44. Watkins, Private Journal, 17 July 1891, 49. The infantilization of Africans was a missionary tradition already firmly established by the last decades of the nineteenth century: "Adult black males were the 'boys whom the civilizing mission hoped one day to usher into 'moral manhood.' " See John and Jean Comaroff, *Of Revelation and Revolution,* vol. 1, *Christianity, Colonialism and Consciousness in Southern Africa* (Chicago: University of Chicago Press, 1991), 117.

45. Watkins, Private Journal, 1 July 1891, 4.

46. See, for example, ibid., 27 September 1891, 114: "Best love of all for dear Mother. Trusting you are all well & happy."

47. George Lowe, letter to Owen Watkins, 25 May 1891, Archives of the Wesleyan Methodist Missionary Society, South Africa, Cory Library, Rhodes University, Grahamstown (hereafter WMMS).

48. Venter, "Owen Watkins," 907.

49. George Lowe, letter to Owen Watkins, 25 May 1891, WMMS. My emphasis.

50. Mary Watkins, letter to Spencer Watkins, 19 December 1891, WMMS.

51. Watkins, Private Journal, 16 September 1891, 107.

52. Ibid., 3 July 1891, 14; 12 July 1891, 30–31.

53. Ibid., 19 July 1891; 12 September 1891, 104.

54. Ibid., 27 September 1891, 114.

55. For several examples, see Patrick Brantlinger, "Victorians and Africans: The Genealogy of the Myth of the Dark Continent," *Critical Inquiry* (1985): 166–203. The campaign literature on the subjugation of the people of Mashonaland followed only a few years later. See, among others, Lieut. Col. E. A. H. Anderson's *With the Mounted Infantry and the Mashonaland Field Force* (London: Methuen, 1898). In his foreword, Anderson wrote: "This idea assumed definite form when Colonel R. S. Baden-Powell's book *The Campaign in Matabeleland, 1896* and Lieut.-Colonel Plumer's *An Irregular Corps in Matabeleland*, appeared, and the thought, 'why not Mashonaland too?' cropped up." Not all the publications were positive about Rhodes's influence. Olive Schreiner's *Trooper Peter Halket of Mashonaland*, published in 1897, is a "fictional diatribe against Cecil Rhodes" (Brantlinger, "Victorians and Africans," 170).

56. Findlay, *Wesleyan Methodist Missionary Society IV*, 383.

57. Venter, "Owen Watkins," 907.

58. George Lowe, letter to Owen Watkins, 15 June 1891, WMMS.

59. WMMS: J. F. Rumfitt, letter to Owen Watkins, 15 June 1891, WMMS. News about Watkins's "next journey" was traveling fast through the vast Transvaal Synod. On 1 May 1894 Thomas Wainman wrote from Good Hope to enquire: "I hear you are going to Mashonaland. Is it true? . . . shall be delighted if I can render you any service to you on your way."

60. F. Fairbridge, letter to Owen Watkins, 1 May 1891, WMMS.

61. Wesleyan Methodists from Yorubaland (Nigeria) and the Congo contributed to *Wesleyan Missionary Notices*, January 1891.

62. Line drawings of these "civilised" Africans did indeed appear in the *Wesleyan Missionary Notices* of January 1891, 84–85 ("Brief Biographical Sketches"). Ironically, their depictions as perfect gentlemen stood in sharp contrast to the often unspoiled, exotic African landscapes portrayed in the same periodical.

63. Watkins, Private Journal, 3 July 1891, 13.

64. On telegraph offices, see ibid., 25 July 1891, 54; on mail coaches, see ibid., 12 July 1891, 33.

65. George Lowe, letter to Owen Watkins, 4 May 1891, WMMS.

66. George Lowe, letter to Owen Watkins, 25 May 1891.

67. Joan Millard, "Nineteenth and Early Twentieth Century Missionary Wives in South Africa: Equal Partners or Historical Non-entities?" *Missionalia* 31, no. 1 (2003): 69–70.

68. Findlay, *Wesleyan Methodist Missionary Society IV*, 245.

69. Catherine Hall, *Civilising Subjects: Metropole and Colony in the English Imagination 1830–1867* (Chicago: University of Chicago Press, 2002), 38.

70. Watkins, Private Journal, 16 September 1891, 106–7.

71. Ibid., 8 September 1891, 103.

72. Ibid., 15 September 1891, 105.

73. Kate Flint, *The Woman Reader, 1837–1901* (Oxford: Clarendon Press, 1993), 11: "From one point of view, reading was a form of consumption associated with the possession of leisure time, and thus contributed to the ideology, if not always the practices, which supported the ideal of the middle-class home. Yet it could also be regarded as dangerously useless, a thief of time which might be spent on housewifely duties."

74. Watkins, Private Journal, 14 September 1891, 105.

75. Henry Kingsley was responsible for rendering Eyre's experiences presentable in print. See Hall, *Civilising Subjects*, 39.

76. Watkins, Private Journal, 12 September 1891, 104.

77. Ibid., 17 July 1891, 48.

78. Watkins, "Journal of a Journey to Mashonaland, Part II," 250.

79. Watkins, Private Journal, 17 July 1891, 48.
80. "British South Africa: The Chartered Company and the Missionary Society," *Wesleyan Missionary Notices*, March 1891, 58–63.
81. Isaac Shimmin, "An Adventure with a Lion in Mashonaland," *Wesleyan Missionary Notices*, March 1892, 60.
82. Wilson, *Victorians*, 493.
83. "British South Africa," 61.
84. Isaac Shimmin, "The Mashonaland Mission," *Wesleyan Missionary Notices*, September 1892, 203.
85. "Contributions," *Wesleyan Missionary Notices*, October 1893, 215.
86. Watkins, Private Journal, 6 July 1891, 18.
87. Ibid., 17 September 1891, 107.
88. Ibid., 19 September 1891, 109.
89. Ibid., 22 September 1891, 110.
90. Watkins, "Journal of a Journey to Mashonaland, Part II," 248; Watkins, Private Journal, 14 July 1891, 45.
91. Watkins, Private Journal, 3 July 1891, 14.
92. Watkins, "Journal of a Journey to Mashonaland, Part II," 250.
93. Watkins, Private Journal, 19 July 1891, 50.
94. Ibid., 29 September 1891, 115.
95. Ibid., 30 September 1891, 118.
96. Ibid., 4 July 1891, 4.
97. Ibid., 29 September 1891, 115.
98. Findlay, *Wesleyan Methodist Missionary Society IV*, 379.
99. Pratt, *Imperial Eyes*, 201–28.
100. Ryan Dunch, "Beyond Cultural Imperialism: Cultural Theory, Christian Missions, and Global Modernity," *History and Theory* 41, no. 3 (2002): 313.
101. In 1893 Macmillan's Colonial Library published *Adventure in Mashonaland by Two Hospital Nurses*, Rose Blennerhassell and Lucy Sleeman. Also see Michelle Adler's analysis of the published travel dairies written by Sarah Heckford and Florence Dixie, "'Skirting the Edges of Civilization': Two Victorian Women Travellers and 'Colonial Spades' in South Africa," in *Text, Theory, Space*, ed. Darian-Smith, Gunner, and Nuttall, 84.
102. Karin Barber, "Introduction: Hidden Innovators in Africa," in *Africa's Hidden Histories, Everyday Literacy and Making the Self*, ed. Karen Barber (Bloomington: Indiana University Press, 2006), 7.
103. Ibid., 10–11. For Stephan Miescher's chapter, see "'My Own Life': A. K. Boyake Yiadom's Autobiography—The Writing and Subjectivity of a Ghanaian Teacher-Chatechist," in *Africa's Hidden Histories*, ed. Karen Barber, 27–51.
104. Isabel Hofmeyr, "John Bunyan, his Chair and a Few Other Relics," in *African Words, African Voices: Critical Practices in Oral History*, ed. Luise White, Stephan E. Miescher, and David William Cohen (Bloomington: Indiana University Press, 2001), 86–88.
105. See John Lonsdale, "Ethnicity and Democracy: A View from the 'Hopeless Continent,'" in *Globalisation in World History*, ed. Anthony. G. Hopkins (London: Pimlico, 2002), 194–219.

IN THE MARGINS

Regimental History and a Veteran's Narrative
of the First World War

Janice Cavell

"Reading," according to Roger Chartier, "by definition, is rebellious and vagabond. Readers use infinite numbers of subterfuges to procure prohibited books, to read between the lines, and to subvert the lessons imposed on them." The book "always aims at installing an order," but it is never "all-powerful"; instead, "liberty knows how to distort and reformulate the significations that were supposed to defeat it." Reading may seem to be a "passive and submissive" act, but in fact it is "in its own way, inventive and creative." This inventive process can play itself out in an almost infinite variety of ways: Chartier writes that "The dialectic between imposition and appropriation, between constraints transgressed and freedoms bridled, is not the same in all places or all times or for all people. Recognizing its diverse modalities and multiple variations is the first aim of a history of reading."[1]

Chartier's observations have been upheld by many other historians of print culture. Janice Radway, for example, found that the readers of romance novels in the early 1980s were anything but "passive, purely receptive individuals who [could] only consume the meanings embodied within cultural texts." Instead of accepting patriarchal values, these women were often inspired by the adventures of the heroines they read about to be less submissive in their own lives.[2] Jonathan Rose concluded from his study of nineteenth-century British working class readers that even the most propagandistic literature often failed to have its intended effect, and that conservative works could in fact quite readily inspire a radical response even among their admirers. As Rose discovered, the works of Tories like John Ruskin and Sir Walter Scott were favorites among Labour members of par-

---

An earlier version of this paper was presented at the Making Books, Shaping Readers conference, University College Cork, in April 2007. I would like to thank those who offered encouraging and stimulating comments. Thanks are also due to Dr. Jeff Noakes of the Canadian War Museum, who kindly checked the manuscript for accuracy on military matters, and to the two anonymous readers.

liament. Rose therefore cautions against the "receptive fallacy"—that is, the assumption that "whatever the author put into a text . . . is the message that the common reader receives."[3]

There can be no doubt that these conclusions and others like them are valid. However, it is far from certain that books written to forestall dissent never achieved their aims. Few scholars of print culture have actively sought out evidence that some authors did indeed successfully impose their vision on readers, and the lack of attention to such cases may be contributing to blind spots and imbalances in the developing field of book history. One example of a working class reader who willingly accepted the message of a conservative text is provided by Dick McQuade, a Canadian railway worker and veteran of the First World War. At some time after the publication of his regiment's official history in 1926, McQuade read the book with great care, adding pencil notes on his own war experiences in the margins.[4]

Like most regimental histories of the time, Captain S. G. Bennett's *The 4th Canadian Mounted Rifles, 1914-1919* did not deny the often terrifying nature of the war experience. But Bennett, in common with the other authors of such books, insisted that courageous endurance, not insubordination or despair, was the typical response among soldiers. McQuade's marginal writings seem to confirm that this was indeed the case: they often refer to the "tough" conditions in the trenches, but, like Bennett, McQuade emphasized that he and his comrades had successfully overcome such obstacles. The front was "One awful Place. Just lived like Rats[.] Wet and cold for days," he complained, but courage and perseverance were a constant theme. "I used Bayonet to good advantage here," McQuade wrote of the Somme, adding, "We sure gave it to Jerry here lots of fun." The battle to take Vimy Ridge was "pretty Tough[.] But we made it . . . we cleaned Jerry up." Sometimes McQuade wrote that he had been "Glad to get out of this place," but elsewhere he proudly recounted that he and his comrades "gave them Hell here." In a final note, written on the concluding page of the book, McQuade recorded his return to his wife and family in Ottawa with a combination of pride and relief: "I arrived home March 8th 1919 after 3 hard years in France. Glad to get home in one piece[.] Out of 900 men [in the regiment] leaving Canada [in 1915] = 37 came back alive[.] I was one of the 37."[5]

These notes, with their erratic capitalization and occasional lapses in spelling and grammar ("I got a few mouthfulls of Gas"; "1st Time We seen a Tank")[6] at first seem to be entirely direct and authentic records by what Rose calls "the actual ordinary reader in history."[7] The personal story told by McQuade in the margins can be summed up as follows: he arrived in France with his regiment late in 1915, saw the trenches for the first time in November, and was wounded and buried alive by a shell explosion near

Ypres on 20 April 1916. He recuperated in England, then returned to the front in August, going "right into the Somme battle." A close friend was killed on 16 September; McQuade himself came through unscathed. He then took part in the battles of Vimy Ridge, Passchendaele, and the last hundred days of the war, again without coming to any harm. After the armistice, he and his surviving comrades enjoyed a "big time at Mons" with a "Good dinner and lots of fun." Almost miraculously, McQuade was one of the tiny handful of the regiment's original volunteers to survive the years in France and Flanders.[8]

All of this seems reasonably straightforward, if disappointing for present-day scholars in search of evidence that working class veterans with personal experience of the trenches could easily resist propagandistic depictions of the war as a heroic endeavor. However, the evidence of McQuade's service record proves that his account was a complex blend of truth and fantasy.[9] McQuade did indeed serve from 1915 until March 1919, but he did not reach the front until January 1916, and he did not fight at the Somme, Vimy Ridge, Passchendaele, or indeed any other major battle. He was, as he stated, wounded in April 1916, but the wound itself must have been trifling in nature, since there is no mention of it in his medical record. However, the experience of being buried was intensely traumatic. McQuade's hospitalization was caused by shell shock, and while he was in the hospital, many of the original members of his unit were slaughtered at Sanctuary Wood. According to the regimental history, on 2 June 1916, 626 of 702 officers and men were either killed, wounded or captured. During the fighting on the Somme, McQuade was again hospitalized, this time recovering from an appendectomy. After his recovery he never again served in the front lines—not from cowardice, but because as a skilled railway worker, he was transferred from his unit to the newly formed Canadian Railway Troops. Instead of going into battle, he worked at running troop, supply, and hospital trains to and from the front.[10] This was hardly a risk-free occupation, since railway lines were an obvious target for enemy air attacks, but it was far less dangerous than combat.

McQuade's survival, then, was not a near-miraculous preservation through three years in the trenches. Instead, it was due to a combination of fortuitous circumstances beyond his control and what many in his day would have regarded as malingering. McQuade was evidently haunted by a sense of lost opportunity: however useful his railway work may have been, he had never been given the chance to redeem his initial breakdown, and so, in his own mind, he had not really proved himself as a soldier and a man. It seems reasonable to conclude that he was exceptionally vulnerable to and oppressed by feelings of inadequacy, which drove him to formulate an imaginary, idealized war experience.

Bennett's book must have been an unusual item in McQuade's life. His jottings give the impression that he was not an avid reader, since there are no echoes of literary phrasing. For someone little accustomed to reading, this must have been an unusually intense encounter with print. The book spoke directly and compellingly to some of his most painful personal memories, and evoked emotions that McQuade would have preferred to forget—confusion, fear, shame that he had been in the hospital "malingering" when so many of his comrades died fighting at Sanctuary Wood.

But at the same time, the history offered a powerful template for the creation of an alternate and more acceptable narrative, merging authentic details of McQuade's own experience with actual events in which he had not in fact participated, and burying anomalous, inconvenient facts in oblivion.[11] While McQuade presumably did not delude himself into believing his own creation, there was another major consideration: the book held an honored place in his home and was available to others in the family. His name has been underlined in the list of the regiment's members at the end of Bennett's book, and the word "Daddy" is written beside it, showing that he had a child or children.[12] He knew, then, that whatever he wrote in the margins of this particular volume could be read, reread, and pondered by his children, and that, in conjunction with the book itself, the notes would shape their image of him.

This article will begin by examining the avowed purposes and general characteristics of regimental histories from the First World War. It will next reconstruct McQuade's war experience as far as is possible from the laconic service record, and then examine the relationship of Bennett's text and McQuade's notes in order to elucidate how the interplay between official history and personal memory shaped McQuade's marginal narrative.

The shaping and ordering of personal memory was explicitly named by many regimental historians as one of the key purposes of their work. From the best-known book in the genre, Rudyard Kipling's *The Irish Guards in the Great War,* to works by obscure amateur writers like Bennett, regimental histories had a common aim: that of providing a coherent framework for what might otherwise have been random and confusing memories of combat. As historian Eric Leed observed decades later, the confusing maze of trenches and the formless, featureless mud of no-man's-land were physically and psychologically disorienting, "shattering . . . distinctions that were central to orderly thought [and] communicable experience."[13] The fear that ex-soldiers' memories might be overly, even dangerously, incoherent and narrow began in the immediate postwar period. In 1919 the Canadian government published a pamphlet on the events of the last year of the war. Major-General A. C. Macdonell explained in his introduction to the pamphlet that this had been done because he and other senior officers were "anxious that the man in the ranks shall not feel that our fighting is a 'blur' to him. As a great tapestry is woven of many threads, so a great battle is built up by the fight of the individual—by his section or his platoon. In the desire that each might trace his own work through the larger pattern designed by brigade or division or corps, arose the idea of publishing the following ... account."[14]

The first of the Canadian regimental histories was published in 1918, with the majority appearing in the 1920s. They undoubtedly reached thousands of working-class veterans who had never read, and who would likely have scorned, the type of war literature described by Paul Fussell in his *The Great War and Modern Memory*.[15] The regimental histories were almost all privately printed; usually the funds were provided by contributions from the surviving members of the unit and bereaved families. In some cases the books could not have been written without the patronage of wealthy senior officers. The authors were mostly officers of the regiments in question, but a few were professional writers.[16] Whether soldiers or civilians, they, too, all sought to help each veteran to "trace his own work through the larger pattern," thus creating a coherent and satisfying personal narrative. One Canadian writer, Kim Beattie, who had interviewed many veterans while writing his book, observed that "Battalions in attack knew little of what went on beyond their own boundaries and the limit of the individual's vision was often but a few yards. Now and then there were stark impressions—little things burned deep where all else was welter. A comrade twisting, shattered and broken, to the shell-spouting earth, was often the one indelible and clear memory of a battle that changed history."[17] Another, Karl Weatherbe, pointed out that most soldiers "were content to defer consideration of events outside their own experience for [the] anticipated leisure of peace-time firesides," and he noted that his account took into consideration many aspects of the war that might "either have escaped [the soldier's] observation altogether or, through improper focussing in the first instance, have failed to make an impression on his attention." The record provided by the regimental history could therefore play an invaluable role, restoring "sharpness and sequence to the readers' own recollections of those days,"[18] while at the same time adding an awareness of the wider picture.

Regimental historians detailed events as far as possible in strict chronological order. Their books combined a narrative of the overall war effort with the minutiae of the regiment's contribution, including as many soldiers' names and as many individual deeds of gallantry as they could. Veterans were thus offered a framework within which their personal memories could be ordered, preserved, and understood in relation to the history of the war as a whole. The historians took particular pains to write narratives in which each man could discover and follow his particular thread in the tapestry of war. "At the end of each engagement outstanding incidents are given of distinguished conduct and conspicuous bravery. Some 320 of these are mentioned. The fact that many men did the same or similar things does not detract from individual acts and I have deemed them all worth recording,"[19] wrote Lieutenant-Colonel Joseph Hayes in the preface to his history of the Nova Scotia Highlanders. Other details which would be of comparatively little interest to non-soldiers were recounted for the same reason. L. McLeod Gould described his strict adherence to the chronological order of events and his inclusion of many apparently trivial incidents as a means of providing "by-paths of reminiscence down which each man, according to his length of service, can wander at his will."[20]

These Canadian authors had much in common with British regimental historians, including Rudyard Kipling, whose two-volume *The Irish Guards in the Great War* (intended as a memorial to his dead son, an officer in the Guards) was the best known and most commercially successful example of the genre. Kipling was far less concerned than many others to transform the welter of confused and possibly inaccurate personal memories into what he called a "balanced," "neatly groomed" history, but like them he sought to keep memory alive by recording and celebrating the small incidents that demonstrated the common soldier's courageous, persevering spirit. "Recollection fades from men's minds as common life closes over them," Kipling wrote. "It is for the sake of [the] initiated that the compiler has loaded his records with detail and seeming triviality, since in a life where Death ruled every hour, nothing was trivial, and bald references to villages, billets, camps, fatigues and sports, as well as hints of tales that can never now fully be told, carry each their separate significance to each survivor."[21] However, since many British and Canadian regimental histories were published before Kipling's book, which appeared in 1923, they were not imitating his successful formula; rather, he was simply the author who took the formula to its highest development, making the details of regimental life interesting to the general reader as well as to the veteran.

Bennett's history of the 4th Canadian Mounted Rifles was published in 1926. Unlike Kipling (whose book he had read),[22] Bennett did not expect to reach a commercial audience. "Primarily," he noted, "the book was written for the men and for the satisfaction of the next of kin. . . . Despite the necessity of condensation, no time has been omitted or glossed over without some reference to it, so that no man, no matter how short his association with the Regiment, will find a void where his interest centred."[23] However, Bennett's volume had more literary flair than most, thanks to the excellent regimental war diary on which it was largely based. One of the officers had contributed to the diary was Captain Gregory Clark, M.C., later among

Canada's most successful journalists and popular writers. Clark assisted Bennett during the writing of the book.[24]

Because of the audience to which they were addressed, regimental histories could not give descriptions of the war that would be at variance with their readers' no doubt vivid memories of trench life. There is little attempt in these books to gloss over the appalling conditions the men endured. "The very name of the [Ypres] Salient was a nightmare to every man who knew it.... Everyone lived a rodent life,"[25] wrote Bennett, and it was beside this passage that McQuade agreed, "One awful Place." However, once an author had gained his readers' trust through a frank acknowledgment of the negative aspects of the war, he could make suggestions about the meaning of the war experience as a whole that were likely to be accepted by veterans.

The regimental historians were unanimous in asserting that despite the horrors they had seen and suffered, the great majority of men in the Canadian Corps had never given way to despair. "Life in flooded dugouts and in trenches deep with mud was far from agreeable, but the men faced the situation courageously and endured,"[26] wrote R. C. Fetherstonhaugh in his history of the Victoria Rifles. In describing the experiences of the Royal Highlanders of Canada at the Somme, Fetherstonhaugh noted sadly that "trenches were captured, recaptured and captured again, while the whole face of the earth for miles was so torn by concentrated artillery fire as to render familiar scenes utterly unrecognizable.... Men died in this bitter fighting by tens of thousands, but others were found to take their places and the great struggle went relentlessly on.... No unit came out of the Somme unscathed; few came out unshattered."[27] The Royal Highlanders were among the shattered units. After the attack on Regina Trench, where "scores of the Highland dead were seen hanging limply over the wire that had proved their undoing," there were so few survivors that "practically the whole Battalion rode back from Pozières on the limbers, which the Transport Officer had thoughtfully sent forward.... Surely the Battalion bore the mark of having been through that place of evil which was the Somme." Yet Fetherstonhaugh passionately insisted that "[t]he Somme had shattered the 13th Canadian Battalion, but had failed to subdue the Regiment's fighting spirit."[28]

No death was too horrible to be seen in a heroic light: Kim Beattie, describing the April 1915 gas attack at St. Julien in his history of the 48th Highlanders, assured his readers that "in that choking chaos the Highland officers and their men died as splendidly as any soldier ever did on the field of battle." According to Beattie, the "appalling viciousness of the Great War" had called forth "a new and greater endurance, an amazing fortitude, and a courage past belief in the heart of the soldier."[29] Joseph Hayes claimed that even when to advance was "like deliberately walking into a seething cauldron of fire," the Nova Scotia Highlanders had "nobly and unflinchingly . . . marched on with their proud heads erect, truly they were 'Siol Na Fear Fearail'—the breed of manly men."[30]

If any veteran reading the history of his regiment had ever experienced overwhelming terror or utter despair, these were memories for which he would find little if any validation in the text before him. Such emotions were also the least likely to be openly spoken of. It would have been one thing for a veteran to admit to fear, but quite another for him to confess that he had experienced terror too strong to control. Cowardice, desertion, and shell shock were aspects of the war experience that struck at the very roots of masculine identity. This must have been particularly the case for enlisted men, who were denied the expensive and often lengthy psychotherapeutic treatment reserved for officers.[31] The working class ex-soldier struggling to come to terms with disturbing memories might readily conclude that the great majority of his comrades had not shared his more extreme emotions. In the regimental histories the widespread psychological disturbances resulting from combat on the Western Front were either ignored or only obliquely hinted at.[32] Instead, the authors typically claimed that all members of a regiment had done their duty without hesitation; in Beattie's words, "they did not allow panic to creep into their ranks, their actions or their hearts."[33] While some fear and nervous strain were held to be understandable in such hellish conditions, these were presented as temporary responses that Canada's soldiers had gallantly overcome. The idealized Canadian veteran, then, was a man who had faced the worst conditions of modern mechanized warfare and emerged triumphant. He was no victim of either the enemy or the horrors of the western front, but a courageous, resourceful individual who could surmount the most terrifying and formidable of obstacles. Or, as McQuade laconically (and, when seen in the knowledge of his actual war experiences, poignantly) put it in his comments on the attack at Vimy Ridge, "This was pretty Tough[.] But we made it."

So compelling was this image of quiet, determined heroism in the ranks that McQuade felt the need to experience vicariously the perils of a battlefield he had never seen. There is nothing in the admittedly limited evidence of his service record to indicate that he was a habitual liar, who shirked the dangers of the battlefield only to later boast that he had fought courageously. Instead, the small details preserved in the official files, when taken together and considered in the light of his marginal notes, suggest that in all likelihood he saw his shell shock as a disgraceful failure of nerve, and yearned as passionately as Conrad's Lord Jim for the opportunity to regain his lost honor.

* * *

William Henry Ritchie (Dick) McQuade was born in the eastern Ontario village of Osgoode, near Ottawa, in 1883. His attestation papers record a tattoo on his left forearm saying "Chapleau Ontario." This indicates that in his teens or twenties McQuade likely spent some time in the mines or lumber camps of northern Ontario, then a booming resource frontier. When he enlisted in July 1915 he was thirty-two years old, married, and living in Renfrew, a small town not far from his birthplace. He gave his occupation as railway switchman and his religion as Presbyterian. He would certainly have seemed like an ideal recruit. A later note on his medical record describes him as a "[w]ell built healthy looking man." According to the attestation papers, he was 5 feet 10 3/4 inches tall, with a 39-inch chest, gray eyes, and brown hair. He must have been a good rider, since he joined a cavalry unit, the 8th Canadian Mounted Rifles. (The 8th CMR was one of the many new regiments created in 1914 and 1915 by a young nation going to war for the first time. Most of its recruits came, like McQuade, from the Ottawa area. Though many were recent immigrants from the United Kingdom who had served in the British regular army, others may well have been men he had known since boyhood.)

On the surface, then, McQuade was an exemplar of self-confident, respectable working-class masculinity, and he fitted well into the popular stereotype of the Canadian soldier as a brawny outdoorsman, toughened by frontier conditions. He arrived in England with his regiment in October 1915, and reached the front at the end of January 1916. By this time a reorganization of Canadian forces had transformed the various Mounted Rifle regiments into infantry battalions (which nevertheless retained the designation "Canadian Mounted Rifles"). The 4th (Toronto) and 8th CMR regiments were combined to form the new 4th Canadian Mounted Rifle battalion. The former 8th Mounted Rifles therefore joined their new comrades, the members of the original 4th CMR, in the trenches of the Ypres Salient near the Wulverghem-Messines Road. The 4th CMR had been in the field since the previous autumn.

In the Salient, the Allied trenches were surrounded by German-held territory on all sides but one, so that the troops were even more exposed than usual to enemy fire. Only three weeks after his arrival, McQuade reported sick, and on 2 March he was admitted to the hospital in Boulogne with sinusitis. By his own account, as later given to various doctors taking his medical history, he spent some time in a convalescent camp, but there is no mention of this in the records. By April he was back at the front near Zillebeke. The trenches in this area were especially unpleasant and dangerous. The weather was cold, the trenches often knee-deep in water, and, as Bennett wrote, "Machine guns raked the roads, shells of all descriptions enfiladed this strategic death-trap, high explosives crashed on the pavé or fell in the town of Ypres. The night was made more unreal by the flares of the Verey [sic] lights.... During the days in the front line, the men's lives were menaced by bombs and grenades. Dodging minnenwerfers and repairing their damage occupied many hours on duty."[34]

On 20 April McQuade was wounded and buried by one of these explosions.[35] The nature of the wound is not specified either in the official record or in McQuade's marginal notes, but the physical damage must have been minimal. The service record is vague on this point, but it seems that he was away from the front line for only a week or two—long enough for bruises and superficial lacerations to heal. His medical examination on discharge found scars on his right knee and left thigh, and these may have been the only visible results of the shell explosion. The emotional damage, on the other hand, was evidently immense. On 5 May, McQuade went absent without leave and was docked one day's pay. On 7 May the 4th CMR went into new trenches near Sanctuary Wood and the infamous Menin Road. On the 11th they suffered an intense bombardment. Five days later they left the front line, passing through the "hollow, haunted town of Ypres" for two weeks in divisional reserve.[36] At this time, McQuade again reported sick with what was recorded as sinusitis. A medical board found him unfit for active service, and he was sent to the Endell Street Military Hospital in London.

There he complained of "tenderness over frontal sinuses and behind right ear" and numbness in his right hand. He claimed to have eye problems and to be unable to read. He had a "constant desire to avoid noise & to be alone" and was described as "[v]ery depressed, sleepless." He stated that he did not recollect any illness at the time these symptoms began. He had hurt his head in a fall from a horse six months previously, but his problems did not begin until two months after that incident—that is, when he reached the front. An x-ray did not reveal any physical cause for his symptoms. Spectacles were prescribed, and according to the record, these relieved the pain.

The men of the 4th CMR, meanwhile, had returned to Sanctuary Wood from their two-week reprieve. On the morning of 2 June, an exceptionally beautiful summer day, "from a heavenly, peaceful sky broke a deafening detonation and cloud of steel which had no precedent for weight and violence.... The most extravagant imagination cannot picture such a downpour of destruction. Even those who had tasted the bitterest in modern warfare were staggered by the violence of this onslaught. Nothing like it had been experienced heretofore and it is doubtful if its fierceness was exceeded by any later bombardment." The bombardment continued for over four hours. "Trenches were soon demolished, shelters caved in, the ground over which tall weeds and long grass had grown was ploughed, beaten and pock-marked by shells." The "verdant" trees of Sanctuary Wood were "transformed into charred, jagged stumps." For the 4th CMR, "it was a day of obliteration." On 3 June, only 3 of 22 officers and 73 of 680 men remained.[37] Even if McQuade in London was unable to read the newspaper accounts of this tragic day, he cannot have failed to hear of it, and to reflect that by reporting sick when he did, he had saved his life by deserting his comrades. Given that he had spent most of the past year in the company of these men, and that they must have formed strong bonds during training and the long journey from Canada to Flanders, it is hardly surprising that McQuade was sleepless and depressed.[38]

In late June, with his problems supposedly solved by the spectacles, McQuade was sent to the Canadian Convalescent Hospital in Bromley. He now claimed that although the pains in his forehead had been alleviated by the glasses, he still suffered from severe headaches at the back of his head. He told the attending doctor that the headaches had begun after his fall from a horse in December 1915. Then he went to France, where "following an intense bombardment a severe headache, frontal & basal began. This continued until he was forced to report sick on account of it about the latter part of February." McQuade stated that he had been in the hospital in Boulogne for about six weeks, and then was at a rest camp until being sent to Endell Street after a recurrence of the headaches. He said nothing about his return to the trenches and his wound. The doctor noted that McQuade gave "[n]o trouble except some nervousness especially if there is any noise or excitement."

After a short stay in Bromley, McQuade was passed along to the West Cliff Canadian Eye and Ear Hospital. There he reported "severe headaches at back of head and at front as well." As no eye problems were found (the discharge exam later confirmed that he had 20/20 vision in both eyes), McQuade was transferred to the Granville Canadian Specialist Hospital in Ramsgate. The attending doctor at the Granville Hospital, Captain A. B. Wilkes, finally made a diagnosis of neurasthenia. (Considering the classic symptoms he displayed, it seems remarkable how long it took for McQuade's case to be recognized as one of shell shock. This suggests that he appeared genuinely distressed at being away from the front, and so did not fit the prevailing stereotype of the "shirker.") Dr. Wilkes elicited a much fuller, though still not entirely accurate, case history: "Began to have headache as soon as he encountered shell fire for the first time in France. Was in firing zone for about two weeks. Felt pains over both frontal & occipital regions. The pain was sharp over frontal region as tho piercing through temples & dull pain in occipital region. Pain was worse at night keeping patient awake. Felt better after 7 wks in hospital & was sent to Convalescent Camp. Old symptoms of pains in head returned & was boarded & sent to England." Again, McQuade had said nothing about his wound. He clearly could not put into words how the experience of being buried alive had affected him, even to this perceptive, and probably not entirely unsympathetic, doctor.

McQuade now stated that the glasses "gave little if any relief," leaving him with "a constant headache in back of head and occasionally pains across the forehead." The pain was "worse at night when he is restless & does not sleep well." McQuade was given electrical treatment daily for two weeks, and he was presumably also lectured on the contrast between his failure of nerve and his comrades' steadfast willingness to sacrifice themselves (the use of shaming in the treatment of enlisted men with shell shock was standard practice).[39] The result was a "[m]arked improvement." There is no reason to doubt that when McQuade reported sick, he had firmly believed his symptoms to be of physical origin. Now he had to face the unwelcome news that he—no inexperienced eighteen-year-old subaltern but a strong, healthy, practical man in the prime of life—had broken down mentally after only a short time at the front, and that many of his comrades had paid for their greater self-control with their lives. In response, he quickly abandoned his symptoms and stated that he was ready to return to the trenches. He was declared fit for active service at the beginning of August 1916.

However, McQuade was soon back in the hospital, this time with an indisputable physical complaint. He was admitted to the Moore Barracks Hospital at Shorncliffe Camp on 17 August with acute appendicitis. Following the operation to remove his badly swollen and inflamed appendix, he recuperated at the Bevan Military Hospital, Kent, and the Canadian Convalescent Hospital, Hastings, until late October. In September the 4th CMR, brought back up to strength by new recruits, left the Ypres Salient only to endure heavy casualties on the Somme. One of McQuade's close friends was killed in action on 16 September.[40]

McQuade never again reported sick during the entire course of his military service. He was at Shorncliffe throughout November and December 1916 and January 1917. He evidently made strenuous efforts to be a good soldier, and was promoted to lance corporal on 30 November. However, in mid-January he reverted to the ranks after being absent without leave. Late in February 1917 he was transferred from the Mounted Rifles to the newly formed 3rd Canadian Railway Troops, made up of experienced railway workers from all units of the Canadian Corps. He went back to France with his new unit in March, shortly before his old battalion took part in the successful attack on Vimy Ridge.

In October 1917 the 4th CMR left the Vimy sector and returned to the "horrible charnel house" (as Bennett described it) of the Ypres Salient.[41] On

26–27 October they participated in an attack near Passenchendaele, once again sustaining heavy casualties, but also creating a remarkable record of courage. In just two days, the battalion earned a total of twenty-three decorations, including one Victoria Cross, two Military Crosses, six Military Medals, and ten Distinguished Conduct Medals. A few weeks later, McQuade committed his first serious offence against military regulations. He received twenty-eight days of the notorious Field Punishment Number 1 for drunkenness and "breaking out of barracks when under open arrest." Field Punishment Number 1 consisted of hard labor, with the added humiliation of spending several hours each day tied to a post or other stationary object, exposed to the view of all passers-by. The causes of this incident must of course be a matter for speculation, but it does not seem improbable that McQuade's highly uncharacteristic behavior was connected to feelings of guilt over the difference between his conduct and that of the men of his old battalion, with a resulting desire for punishment.

There were no other infringements of the rules until after the armistice, when, following a leave in Paris, McQuade was absent without permission for twenty-seven hours. He forfeited a day's pay and received seven days of the far less draconian Field Punishment Number 2. McQuade left France for England in January 1919 and returned to Canada in February. He was demobilized in Ottawa on 8 March. "The man is in good condition and feels as well as on enlistment," was the comment of the doctor who performed the discharge medical exam.

McQuade and his wife, Margaret, then settled in Ottawa, where McQuade found work first with the Grand Trunk Railway and then with the Canadian National Railway.[42] By 1926, when Bennett's book was published, it is unlikely that the war had faded appreciably from McQuade's memory. Commemoration was an active and ongoing process in Canada, with veterans' groups as well as the government intent on perpetuating an image of heroism.[43] For the veterans, this was essential to their pride as individuals and also for the more pragmatic purpose of ensuring adequate pensions and medical care for those with disabilities. In 1925 the various groups joined together to form the Canadian Legion. Ottawa, as the nation's capital, was naturally the scene of the most impressive commemorative ceremonies.

Wherever veterans of the Great War gathered, the war was endlessly discussed. George Orwell, who served in the Indian Imperial Police during the 1920s, remembered that "As the war fell back into the past, my particular generation, those who had been 'just too young,' became conscious of the vastness of the experience they had missed. You felt yourself a little less than a man, because you had missed it. I spent the years 1922–27 mostly among men a little older than myself who had been through the war. They talked about it unceasingly, with horror, of course, but also with a steadily growing nostalgia."[44] Many veterans must, like McQuade, have missed the hardest fighting for one reason or another, and they, too, would have found themselves feeling a little less than men as they listened to those who had passed the test of battle. McQuade had served in the army for three and a half years, but he had spent only a few months in the front lines, without ever fighting in a major engagement. It seems unlikely that he cut himself off from the comradeship offered by other veterans, but he must have been in an awkward spot whenever the conversation turned to the past. His children, too, would have become increasingly inquisitive as they grew older. With few "originals" of either the 8th or the 4th CMR surviving, there may well have been no one in his circle of acquaintances to contradict him if he lied to his family and friends. Unless he had begun to lie in 1916, Margaret McQuade must have known from his letters that her husband had not been in the trenches for long, but she would hardly have wished to humiliate him by revealing the truth. When Bennett's book was published, McQuade did not shun it as an unwelcome reminder of his failure; instead, he eagerly and carefully read it, perhaps in search of convincing details. If so, what he found far surpassed his expectations.

Bennett's expressed intention was to write a history in which each veteran, however long or short his service, could easily find his own thread in the larger narrative, but in fact the implied reader of the book was a soldier who had joined the original 4th CMR in 1914 or 1915 and served with the unit either until he was wounded or until the end of the war. The date when the men of the former 8th CMR arrived in Flanders was, for example, not even mentioned in the text. Of the soldiers who left the battalion before 1919, only those wounded in heroic circumstances or senior officers transferred to another command were named. When a wounded hero was one of the regiment's original volunteers, the fact was given special prominence. The very structure of the book, then, idealized the surviving "originals," inevitably at some cost to the self-esteem of those whose war service had been shorter or in some way less honorable.[45]

Because of his long service, McQuade could fit himself, though uneasily, into this paradigm. The basic fact emphasized by his marginal narrative—that he had volunteered early and survived to the end—was true. In order to present himself as an "original" as defined by Bennett's book, McQuade wrote as if the 4th CMR had been his first and only unit. He made marginal notes on the change from cavalry to infantry, the arrival in England, the journey to the front, the first time in the trenches, and the first encounter with the enemy under the dates when the men of the 4th CMR, not he himself and his comrades from the 8th CMR, experienced these things. A similar pattern was followed at the end of the book, when he described his last sight of France and Belgium ("on our way home Every Step getting closer")[46] and the return to Canada.

McQuade wrote that his wound had kept him in the hospital in England until August 1916, when he returned to France and went "right into the Somme battle."[47] Appendicitis was hardly a dishonorable reason for having missed the Somme, yet McQuade concealed it just as he concealed his shell shock. This surely reflects the intense desire he had felt at the time to go back to the front and to prove himself: in another note, he claimed that he had "Returned to France from Blighty August 2/16"—the date when he was discharged from the hospital as fit for active service after his treatment for shell shock.[48] As he read, it would have been easy for McQuade to picture himself rejoining his battalion and accompanying his new comrades on their journey to the Somme. Bennett graphically described the scene that met the Canadian troops when they arrived on the battlefield, where fighting had begun on 1 July. The men of the 4th CMR were among the "high-spirited" new arrivals, sobered as they marched down the road to the trenches by the sight of the "unshaven, tired and worn companies silently coming out." "Not a tree was standing," while villages had been reduced to heaps of rubble. Desolation was everywhere: "Shell cases were strewn along the roadside or marked old battery positions. Tangled wire and mutilated trenches covered the barren waste as far as one could see."[49]

When writing about his supposed experiences on the Somme, McQuade sometimes simply echoed whatever was in Bennett's text or illustrations, for example noting "1st Time We seen a Tank" beside a passage describing tanks, with a photograph on the opposite page.[50] More often, he seems to have wished to associate himself with acts of courage. For example, he claimed to have been present at a bombardment with gas shells, during which one officer, Captain A. S. Hamilton, "finding his men overcome in a gas-saturated trench jumped into it, with utter disregard for his own life, and dragged them to safety. Although so badly gassed that his health was permanently injured, he refused to leave the line and it was not known until later that he carried on throughout this and a subsequent action in great personal distress." "I got a few mouthfulls of Gas," McQuade wrote next to this description, in what may have been intended as a hint that he had done something to assist Captain Hamilton.[51] McQuade also claimed to have participated in an attack on the Fabeck Graben trench, where the Germans "at first put up a stubborn resistance which soon wilted under the determined assault" of the Canadians. "I used Bayonet to good advantage here. . . . We sure gave it to Jerry here lots of fun," McQuade added.[52] Bennett noted that the 4th CMR had shown "coolness and steadiness" under fire, accomplishing "in soldierly fashion their difficult task. . . . Even after their objective had been reached they carried on the work of consolidating under heavy rifle and machine gun fire and were not checked by the trench-mortar bombardment which assailed them." "We done a Good Job in this place," McQuade commented in the margin.[53]

In contrast to the Somme, the attack on Vimy Ridge succeeded in the space of a few days, and though victory did not come easily, the battle was far less of an ordeal. Here McQuade's comments were slightly less frequent. The victories of the last hundred days in 1918 received even fewer marginal notes. Clearly, McQuade's focus as he read through Bennett's book was on the prolonged battles fought in a muddy, featureless no-man's-land which, remembering his early experiences in the Ypres Salient, he must have seen as the ultimate test of manhood. The Somme and Passchendaele, where his old unit had achieved glory on one of the most terrible battlefields of all, evoked the strongest responses from him. McQuade's copy of Bennett's book is generally clean and in excellent condition, but the pages that describe these two battles show signs of heavy use. So intense was McQuade's yearning to have been at Passchendaele that he even identified one of the men in a photograph of the muddy trenches as himself. "This is me,"[54] he wrote, with an arrow pointing to a soldier whose features can barely be discerned, and who must have borne a general resemblance to McQuade.

For Bennett, Passchendaele was one of the most significant battles of the war. In the Ypres Salient many of the 4th CMR's original volunteers had been killed or mutilated; to the Ypres Salient their successors returned, and there they proved their determination and their fighting spirit. Bennett carefully described the battalion's journey back to the Salient, passing again through the "eerie" ruins of Ypres and along the road to the trenches, which was "jammed with all kinds of vehicles, from bicycles to gigantic caterpillar-drawn howitzers. The steady stream of men and animals never ceased: field-kitchens, limbers, G. S. waggons and pack-ponies nose-to-tail made an endless chain." Then the men made a night march in heavy rain through a "trackless swamp" of mud to the front line.[55]

Once in the trenches, they were ordered to attack almost immediately. There were few landmarks in any case, and "as the officers and men had been in the line only one day they had very little opportunity to orient themselves and to determine their objectives." It was again raining when they went over the top. The men advanced "slowly across the slime around the brimming craters" in the face of "a heavy barrage and machine-gun fire." The Germans, instead of awaiting the attack in their trenches, were protected by strong concrete pillboxes. Despite all obstacles, the 4th CMR advanced much more quickly than the troops on either side of them, and they successfully held their isolated position. Among many other instances of bravery, Private T. W. Holmes, described by Bennett as "a frail, delicate youth with a contagious smile," single-handedly destroyed a machine-gun nest with an accurately thrown bomb. He then braved heavy rifle fire to hurl another bomb through the entrance to a pillbox, forcing the Germans inside to surrender. For these feats he was awarded the Victoria Cross. Bennett admitted that the heavy casualties sustained by the battalion were "an enormous sacrifice for such little ground gained," but he preferred to emphasize that "The newer blood had retaliated for the older, Passchendaele was a rebuke for Sanctuary Wood."[56]

Again, McQuade was obviously enthralled by Bennett's vivid descriptive writing, and readily pictured himself as one of the attackers. He vicariously experienced both their terror and their success in overcoming it. "I thought it was all off here—This was a tough Job. And took some slugging,"[57] he wrote. Had McQuade's experience indeed been as he recounted it in the margins, the feelings of guilt he had incurred when he evaded death at Sanctuary Wood could have been purged. As it was, reading offered him at least a glimpse of the redemption he longed for. It seems unlikely that McQuade deluded himself into accepting his fabricated version as the actual truth; however, when he wrote his imaginary account in the margins, placing it in such a close physical relation to Bennett's compelling, officially sanctioned narrative, it may have achieved a status in his mind well beyond that of mere fantasy. Bennett's book gave McQuade the opportunity to imagine himself overcoming his fears with a vividness and concreteness he had never before experienced. What the other soldiers of the 4th CMR had done at Passchendaele was, after all, something he too might have done had he been given the chance, and it was not his fault that he had not been given that chance. When he mentally followed the men of his old unit step by step across the featureless no-man's-land of the Ypres Salient, McQuade may well have felt this conviction with a new and reassuring strength.

As scholars in the burgeoning field of memory studies emphasize, both collective and individual memories are shaped around convincing narratives.[58] Bennett's narrative, with its focus on the two contrasting poles of annihilation at Sanctuary Wood and courageous perseverance at Passchendaele, gave a profound meaning to even the limited and dearly bought military victory achieved by the 4th CMR in October 1917. This narrative framework was perfectly, indeed almost uncannily, suited to McQuade's individual emotional and psychological needs. As a result, he readily followed it rather than attempt the more complex and painful task of shaping his actual wartime experiences into a coherent story.

The remarkable success of official literature in molding the personal narrative of this particular reader raises the question of how typical McQuade's response to and use of the book were. Some working-class ex-soldiers may, of course, have rejected official accounts like Bennett's without hesitation, but it seems unlikely that McQuade was altogether unique in his willingness to accept the regimental history as authoritative. While other veterans' needs may not have dovetailed quite so neatly with the regimental historians' purposes, many survivors of the First World War must have shared McQuade's combination of psychological trauma and lingering shame. For McQuade and other shell-shocked veterans to understand and present themselves as victims would have been to reject the compelling image of the ordinary soldier as an active, determined, and resourceful individual. The regimental histories unquestionably offered veterans a strong sense of both collective identity and individual agency. As they read, ex-soldiers could create persuasive personal narratives in the margins—literal or figurative—of these books, gaining a stronger sense of achievement and pride in the process. It is probable that many of them, like McQuade, could do so only by suppressing their actual experiences. Though such reading was hardly "rebellious and vagabond," neither was it passive or entirely submissive. It therefore stands at one extreme of the shifting "dialectic between imposition and appropriation" described by Chartier. It was perhaps only because regimental histories deliberately created a space for active and creative reading that, unlike so many other forms of literature, they could have such a profoundly conservative impact on at least some members of their intended audience.

Notes

1. Roger Chartier, *The Order of Books: Readers, Authors and Libraries in Europe between the Fourteenth and Eighteenth Centuries* (Stanford: Stanford University Press, 1994), viii, and "Popular Appropriations: The Readers and Their Books," in his *Forms and Meanings: Texts, Performances, and Audiences from Codex to Computer* (Philadelphia: University of Pennsylvania Press, 1995), 90.

2. Janice A. Radway, *Reading the Romance: Women, Patriarchy, and Popular Literature* (Chapel Hill: University of North Carolina Press, 1984), 6.

3. Jonathan Rose, "Rereading the English Common Reader: A Preface to a History of Audiences," *Journal of the History of Ideas* 53 (1992): 49. See also Rose, *The Intellectual Life of the British Working Classes* (New Haven: Yale University Press, 2001).

4. The subject of marginalia has been dealt with in H. J. Jackson's excellent *Marginalia: Readers Writing in Books* (New Haven: Yale University Press, 2001). However, the chapter "Motives for Marginalia" gives only limited consideration to marginal writings by readers with personal experience of the events described in a book.

5. W. H. R. McQuade, marginal notes in S. G. Bennett, *The 4th Canadian Mounted Rifles, 1914–1919* (Toronto: Murray Printing Company, 1926), 13, 32, 33, 53, 61, 88, 86, 156. Copy in the MacOdrum Library, Carleton University, Ottawa. For some reason, McQuade later changed the date of his return to 28 March. The correct date is in fact 8 March, as confirmed by his service record.

6. McQuade, in Bennett, *4th Canadian Mounted Rifles*, 31.

7. Jonathan Rose, "How Historians Study Reader Response: Or, What Did Jo Think of

Bleak House?" in *Literature in the Marketplace*, ed. John O. Jordan and Robert L. Patten (Cambridge: Cambridge University Press, 1995), 195.

8. McQuade, in Bennett, *4th Canadian Mounted Rifles*, 10, 14, 26, 33, 148, 152.

9. Library and Archives Canada (hereafter LAC), RG 150, Vol. 7189, file 53.

10. On Canadian railway work in the First World War, see Osborne Scott, *Canada's National Railways: Their Part in the War* (Toronto: Canadian National Railways, 1921).

11. Despite the inaccuracies, the notes are unquestionably by McQuade himself, since the handwriting matches the signature on his attestation papers.

12. In Bennett, *4th Canadian Mounted Rifles*, 271. Another source confirms that McQuade had at least one child, a son named Ritchie. The Ottawa city directories record that Ritchie McQuade continued to live with his parents as a young man during the 1930s. The directories list only adults, so McQuade may well have had younger children who are not listed. Ritchie was evidently an ambitious and upwardly mobile young man. During the '30s he worked as a service station attendant, but he must have been going to night school as well. By 1940 he was an engineer at Trans Canada Airlines. In 1941 Ritchie joined the Royal Canadian Air Force; after a period of active service, he returned to Ottawa and married, establishing a household of his own for the first time. In 1944 he went overseas again. By 1947 Ritchie had found work with Colonial Air Lines, and his parents had moved in with him. This history of shared households seems to indicate a good relationship between father and son.

13. Eric J. Leed, *No Man's Land: Combat and Identity in World War I* (Cambridge: Cambridge University Press, 1979), 21.

14. Foreword to J. D. Craig, *The 1st Canadian Battalion in the Battles of 1918* (London: Barrs and Co., 1919).

15. On the appeal of other conservative, traditional forms of commemoration in the postwar period, see Jay Winter, *Sites of Memory, Sites of Mourning: The Great War in European Cultural History* (Oxford: Oxford University Press, 1994).

16. On the production and writing of the histories, and the historians' relationship with the government, see Tim Cook, "'Literary Memorials': The Great War Regimental Histories, 1919–1939," *Journal of the Canadian Historical Association* n.s. 13 (2002): 167–90, and *Clio's Warriors: Canadian Historians and the Writing of the World Wars* (Vancouver: University of British Columbia Press, 2006), 62–70.

17. Kim Beattie, preface to *The 48th Highlanders of Canada* (Toronto: 48th Highlanders of Canada, 1932).

18. K. Weatherbe, preface to *From the Rideau to the Rhine and Back: The 6th Field Company and Battalion Canadian Engineers in the Great War* (Toronto: Hunter-Rose, 1928).

19. Joseph Hayes, author's preface to *The Eighty-Fifth in France and Flanders* (Halifax, N.S.: Royal Print and Litho, 1920).

20. L. McLeod Gould, *From B.C. to Baisieux: Being the Narrative History of the 102nd Canadian Infantry Battalion* (Victoria, B.C.: Thomas R. Cusack, 1919), 5.

21. Rudyard Kipling, *The Irish Guards in the Great War: Edited and Compiled from their Diaries and Papers by Rudyard Kipling* (London: Macmillan, 1923), 1:vi–vii, xiii–xiv.

22. Bennett, *4th Canadian Mounted Rifles*, quotes Kipling on p. 23.

23. Bennett, *4th Canadian Mounted Rifles*, xi.

24. Ibid., xi–xii. Clark (1892–1977) had a long career as a journalist for the *Toronto Star*, but was perhaps best known and loved for his stories and humorous sketches in the *Star Weekly* and *Weekend Magazine*.

25. Bennett, *4th Canadian Mounted Rifles*, 13.

26. R. C. Fetherstonhaugh, *The 24th Battalion, C. E. F., Victoria Rifles of Canada, 1914–1919* (Montreal: Gazette Printing Company, 1930), 28.

27. R. C. Fetherstonhaugh, *The 13th Battalion Royal Highlanders of Canada, 1914–1919* (N.p.: 13th Battalion, Royal Highlanders of Canada, 1925), 122.

28. Ibid., 140–42.

29. Beattie, *The 48th Highlanders*, 70, 83.

30. Hayes, *The Eighty-Fifth in France and Flanders*, 58.

31. On the threat to masculinity and the treatment of officers by psychotherapy, see Elaine Showalter, *The Female Malady: Women, Madness, and English Culture* (New York: Pantheon, 1985), chap. 7, and "Rivers and Sassoon: The Inscription of Male Gender Anxieties," in *Behind the Lines*, ed. M. Higgonet et al. (New Haven: Yale University Press, 1987), 61–69.

32. On the deliberate avoidance of controversial topics in the regimental histories, see Cook, "'Literary Memorials,'" 180–84.

33. Beattie, *The 48th Highlanders*, 60.

34. Bennett, *4th Canadian Mounted Rifles*, 13–14.

35. 20 April is the date given in both McQuade's service record and his marginal notes, but it appears that the incident actually occurred in the early morning hours of 21 April, when the battalion diary records several direct hits on a trench nicknamed "Dawson Street." See LAC, RG 9, Vol. 4947, file 467 part 1.

36. Bennett, *4th Canadian Mounted Rifles*, 15.

37. Ibid., 18–20. Recent research by an amateur historian suggests that the number of casualties may in fact have been considerably lower. See Ian Forsdike, "The Missing Lost: A 4CMR Myth?" http://www.4cmr.com/myth.htm (accessed 28 June 2007).

38. On the close emotional ties that could develop between soldiers of the same regiment, see Joanna Bourke, *Dismembering the Male: Men's Bodies, Britain and the Great War* (Chicago: University of Chicago Press, 1996), chap. 3.

39. On the treatment of shell shock by painful electric shocks and shaming, see Leed, *No Man's Land*, 170–76. Recent research by Canadian historian Mark Humphries indicates that the type of treatment described by Leed was used only in a minority of cases. Many enlisted men received spa-type treatments similar to those administered to wealthy neurasthenic patients before the war. They involved the use of electric current, but were not painful. Such treatments were used at the Granville Hospital. See Humphries, "Rest, Relax, and Get Well: A Comparison of Canadian and British Shell Shock Treatment in the Great War," *War and Society* (Australia), 27, 2 (forthcoming 2008).

40. McQuade, in Bennett, 33. The name in the marginal note appears to be "Ed McDonald," but it has been erased and rewritten, and the writing is difficult to decipher. The only Canadian soldier with the last name McDonald or MacDonald killed on 16 September 1916 was Private Daniel McDonald, who belonged to a Nova Scotia regiment. (Information from a search on the Canadian Virtual War Memorial, http://www.vac-acc.gc.ca/remembers.)

41. Bennett, *4th Canadian Mounted Rifles*, 25.

42. Information from Ottawa city directories, 1919–47. McQuade did not use his first name, William. Instead, he went by the name Ritchie, or Dick for short (he refers to himself as Dick in some of the notes). He is listed in the various editions under the names Ritchie McQuade, H. Richd. McQuade, Richd. H. McQuade, and H. R. McQuade. The directories indicate that McQuade returned to a close-knit and supportive extended family. His wife had moved from Renfrew to Ottawa during the war. In Ottawa, Margaret shared a house with Clarabel McQuade, a nurse, and Joseph McQuade, who, like Dick, was a railway worker. Clarabel and Joseph were presumably Dick's siblings or cousins. Joseph died in 1920 or 1921; his widow, Jane, lived with Dick and Margaret for several years. Until 1923 the directory also lists another McQuade, Robert, who worked as a train dispatcher for the Grand Trunk Railway. Since Dick McQuade's first job after the war was with the GTR, Robert may have been a brother or cousin who helped him to find work. Dick McQuade worked for the CNR from

1923 until 1937. He was then apparently unemployed for four or five years, until the Second World War brought better economic times. After 1947 Dick and Margaret McQuade are not listed, nor is their son Ritchie (see n.12). It therefore seems that Ritchie junior moved away from Ottawa, perhaps to take a better job, and that his parents moved with him. By this time, McQuade had reached retirement age. Another possibility, of course, is that he had died.

43. See Jonathan Vance, *Death So Noble: Memory, Meaning and the First World War* (Vancouver: University of British Columbia Press, 1997).

44. George Orwell, *Collected Essays, Journalism and Letters,* ed. Sonia Orwell and Ian Angus (Harmondsworth: Penguin, 1970), 1:589.

45. Karl Weatherbe (see n.18) even created a fictional "original" as the author of his book. He combined passages derived from a number of diaries and other sources into a journal-style account that gave the impression of having been written by an observant junior officer with a knack for vivid and often humorous writing, who survived the entire war without so much as a wound.

46. McQuade, in Bennett, *4th Canadian Mounted Rifles,* 153.

47. McQuade, in Bennett, *4th Canadian Mounted Rifles,* 26.

48. McQuade, note inside front cover of Bennett, *4th Canadian Mounted Rifles.*

49. Bennett, *4th Canadian Mounted Rifles,* 30.

50. McQuade, in Bennett, *4th Canadian Mounted Rifles,* 31.

51. Bennett, *4th Canadian Mounted Rifles,* 31, and note by McQuade.

52. Bennett, *4th Canadian Mounted Rifles,* 33, and notes by McQuade on 32 and 33.

53. Bennett, *4th Canadian Mounted Rifles,* 35, and note by McQuade.

54. McQuade, in Bennett, *4th Canadian Mounted Rifles,* facing p. 79.

55. Bennett, *4th Canadian Mounted Rifles,* 73–75.

56. Ibid, 77–89.

57. McQuade, in Bennett, *4th Canadian Mounted Rifles,* 79.

58. The classic work on collective memory is Maurice Halbwachs, *The Collective Memory* (1950; repr., New York: Harper Colophon, 1980). See also James Fentress and Chris Wickham, *Social Memory* (Oxford: Blackwell, 1992). On the application of the concept to historical studies, see John R. Gillis, "Memory and Identity: The History of a Relationship," in *Commemorations: The Politics of National Identity,* ed. John R. Gillis (Princeton: Princeton University Press, 1994), 3–24, and Jay Winter and Emmanuel Sivan, "Setting the Framework," in *War and Remembrance in the Twentieth Century,* ed. Jay Winter and Emmanuel Sivan (Cambridge: Cambridge University Press, 1999), 6–39. On individual memory, see Ulric Neisser and Robyn Fivush, eds., *The Remembering Self: Construction and Accuracy in the Self-Narrative* (Cambridge: Cambridge University Press, 1994).

IN SEARCH OF THE COLLECTIVE AUTHOR

Fact and Fiction from the Soviet 1930s

Mary A. Nicholas and Cynthia A. Ruder

Collectively authored projects were a staple of creative life in the 1930s, part of the literary and historical landscape in this decade of broad strokes and communal gestures. Jointly authored projects captured the imagination of writers and historians in the United States, England, and the European continent, but nowhere was the concept more compelling than in Stalinist Russia. The creation of collective works in the Soviet Union was a complex process, full of such conflicting and contradictory developments that scholars still debate the most fundamental questions surrounding the topic. The end of the Soviet era has made it easier to draw conclusions about this chapter of cultural history, of course, but issues of chronology, authorial motivation, the exact role of coercion in Stalinist literary and historical production, and even questions of terminology remain unresolved. Much of this ongoing debate revolves around the transitional period from the end of the 1920s to the middle of the 1930s, overlapping the first and second Five-Year Plans. This phase in the history of Russian book culture deserves much closer critical attention for what it can tell us about the origins of Stalinism and the role of Soviet writers in creating it.[1]

The years of prewar Stalinism witnessed an explosion of large-scale government-sponsored construction projects, including canals, railroads, public transit systems, even entire cities. From the beginning, those plans went hand-in-hand with schemes of collective authorship. Early Soviet construction projects were rushed, wasteful, and often coercive endeavors, but the regime nevertheless took pride in its efforts to industrialize peasant Russia, and numerous cultural campaigns were organized on the literary front to publicize this push toward modernization. Writers were newly conceptual-

---

Two versions of this jointly authored article were delivered as individual presentations at the SHARP conference in Halifax, Nova Scotia, July 2005. All translations from the original Russian are the authors' own. The authors wish to thank the editors of *Book History* and the anonymous reviewers for numerous cogent and helpful comments.

ized as literary laborers, some even provided with official status and marching orders from local factories.[2] Groups organized into official writer "brigades" were assigned specific tasks, usually to herald a particular construction project or Soviet accomplishment, and there were great hopes that such activities would produce that still elusive but much desired phenomenon: genuine Soviet literature.

Well-known writers in such brigades were valued for their literary and pedagogical expertise and were naturally expected to produce significant individual contributions to Soviet literature. Just as important, however, was the training they were intended to provide for worker-colleagues, who then would be able to give authentic voice to the aspirations of the laboring class. Authors were expected to play the role of both teacher and chronicler, as they set out to document heroic exploits of workers who would ostensibly soon replace them at the writer's desk. The inherent contradictions of such expectations make the Soviet experience with collective authorship particularly interesting to book historians. This article closely examines two of the best-known projects of Soviet collective authorship, surrounding the construction of the Belomor Canal and the Moscow subway, both of which were carried out under the auspices of the publishing house "The History of Factories and Foundries." Together they cast new light on the special role, successes, and failures of collective authorship in the formation of Stalinist literary culture.

Modern readers are understandably skeptical of claims regarding contemporary enthusiasm for the Soviet project, but numerous responses at the time demonstrate a seemingly genuine conviction in the possibilities for collective projects in literature, art, and history. Recent work on long-hidden Soviet diaries makes it clear that even many who doubted the value of the collective nevertheless fervently wanted to believe in it.[3] Historian Sergei Zhuravlev has pointed out that one of the many crimes of Stalin's regime was, in fact, its "parasitic use of the sincere enthusiasm" that people felt during this period.[4] In the literary world, the "utopia of collective creative work" beckoned true believers and fellow travelers alike.[5] Many of these fellow travelers—nonparty writers sympathetic to societal reform—were particularly eager to demonstrate their affinity with the evolving Soviet project, and a number of them specifically requested inclusion in organized trips to actual building sites.

Work on the most prestigious collectively authored volumes was orchestrated by the regime from the beginning, of course, with the ironic result that some reluctant authors were tapped to participate while more enthusiastic writers were often excluded from projects with the highest profile. Novelist and playwright Mikhail Bulgakov, for example, refused all requests to join the Belomor Canal writers' brigade, while writer Mikhail

Prishvin, who asked repeatedly to participate, was denied permission—despite his deep familiarity with Northern Karelia, where the canal was being constructed. That rejection did not deter him from writing about the canal: he produced a novel, *The Tsar's Road,* about the physical and topographical changes the canal project wrought on the region.[6]

Similarly, the staunchly proletarian but idiosyncratic writer Andrei Platonov asked three times to be included in writers' brigades. Platonov was an engineer by training, and his desire to participate in such authorial excursions to the construction site reflected both professional pride and practical self-interest. According to a previously secret police report, or *svodka,* Platonov even hoped to offer technical advice to the builders of the Belomor Canal. He was profoundly frustrated by his exclusion from the canal and from Soviet literature in general, though he was eventually included in a less prestigious trip to Central Asia.[7]

Former Symbolist poet Marietta Shaginian went to the construction site of her own volition. Information about her visit to a hydroelectric plant site in Armenia in 1926 and 1927 can be found in her notebooks, as well as in her production novel *Hydrocentral* and the journalistic account *How I Worked on "Hydrocentral."*[8] The experiences of Shaginian and others like her helped make the notion of collective authorship newly attractive. Shaginian's early mentor, the Symbolist poet and novelist Andrei Belyi, was also planning a production novel shortly before his death in 1933. Eccentric, individualistic, and high strung, Belyi seems an unlikely candidate for work on the Soviet construction site. Nevertheless, he too expressed a desire to participate in such outreach efforts.[9] Clearly, the drive to document construction sites attracted a variety of writers, the majority of whom traveled to these projects in brigades.

The groups were expected to produce works that were topical and widely accessible to the largely untutored and unsophisticated working public, works that would revolutionize Soviet literature and society. What better way to build collective spirit and enthusiasm than through organized writers' brigades to narrate collective labor projects? Maxim Gorky officially sanctioned a "history of factories and foundries" in September 1931, and a publishing house of the same name was founded soon thereafter to produce such books. Gorky's venture reflected a new national fascination with "building socialism." The journal *The USSR under Construction* (*SSSR na stroike*) was created as part of the same campaign to document and publicize all manner of Soviet building projects.[10] The political, cultural, and social atmosphere of the Five-Year Plans was filled with industrial metaphors that appeared in propaganda banners, literature, mass media, and official mandates. "Reforging," "tempering," "constructing," and "rebuilding" permeated official rhetoric and equated the development of the USSR with industrial progress and prowess. The great industrial boom was to be accomplished by collective labor, of course. Even literary production was to be a shared enterprise.

Gorky's series chronicled the creation of this new society, which was to remake human beings into Soviet citizens. As Gorky often argued, a new country demanded a new literature and an "encyclopedia of our construction in motion."[11] His reliance on a dynamic, perpetually evolving model is telling: such dynamism would become essential to later definitions of Socialist Realism. In a compression of present and future that was typical of the time, both Gorky's project and Socialist Realism itself called for literature that reflected the world as it would be rather than as it actually was.[12] Well-known authors were to contribute their professional expertise to the endeavor and to work with specially identified workers. The benefits were intended to be mutual: established writers would impart essential trade secrets to their worker counterparts and would reciprocally gain valuable insights into the working class, the significance of construction, the process of "reforging," and the essence of Soviet power.

Two kinds of "collective authorship" developed as a result. One, best illustrated by the Belomor Canal volume, offered the possibility of actually melding the narratives of individual authors into a hypothetically seamless whole. Here, a collective of writers worked as a single body to design, compose, and edit the work. Credit for authorship was noted only in an alphabetical list after chapter titles in the table of contents. A slightly different approach is illustrated in the volumes dedicated to the construction of the Moscow Metro. There, professional writers and workers joined forces to construct a text that highlighted the collaborative nature of the enterprise while maintaining and applauding individual participation. Such an approach purported to afford fledgling worker-writers the golden opportunity of standing shoulder to shoulder with the most popular authors of the day, while advertising their own "literary" efforts. If one approach to joint authorship mirrored a model collective farm in which all members worked toward a common goal for the common good without individual glory, then the latter mirrored a typical Soviet industrial plan in which all the cogs in the machine cooperated so as to produce a single product that succeeded only by combining collective labor with individual skills.

The 1934 volume on the Belomor Canal, entitled *The History of the Construction of the Stalin White Sea–Baltic Canal* (*Istoriia stroitelistva Belomorosko-Baltiiskii kanali imeni Stalina;* hereafter *The History of Construction*), is perhaps the only work of Soviet literature that truly was written collectively. The elaborately produced volume was eagerly awaited even before publication, but its enduring reputation has been as one of the most suspect texts in Soviet literature. This is particularly the case since

Alexander Solzhenitsyn subjected its creators to scathing criticism for their glorification of a project involving prison camp labor. Solzhenitsyn's understandable ire on the subject has colored critical appraisal of the volume (both in and outside of Russia) for decades, but the issue deserves renewed attention precisely because of the unanswered questions it raises about readership, publication, and authorship.[13] A unique text, even by the unusual standards of prewar Stalinist Russia, *The History of Construction* was the collective effort of thirty-six Soviet writers under the direction of contributor and editor Maxim Gorky. Largely thanks to Gorky's participation, *The History of Construction* was afforded a modicum of legitimacy that it otherwise would not have enjoyed.

In twenty months (November 1931–July 1933) Belomor prisoners produced a canal 227 kilometers (155 miles) in length (37 kilometers are manmade waterways), with six single- and thirteen double-chamber locks, fifteen dams, and forty-nine dikes, all constructed by hand without heavy equipment. The construction brigades were mandated to use only local resources (rock, peat, dirt, timber); an endless supply of slave labor; and primitive tools (pickaxes, wheelbarrows, shovels, horses, and wooden pulleys). As one commentator noted, the approach of the Narodnyi komissariat vnutrennykh del (NKVD; People's Commissariat of Internal Affairs) to the building project was best summed up as, "Quickly, Sturdily, Cheaply. Less metal, less cement, not a single kopeck of foreign currency, more lumber."[14] The NKVD availed itself of every means to ensure that the project was completed on time, and the resulting human cost was immense. There are still no precise data on the number of inmates who died while building the canal, though the total runs into tens of thousands out of the more than a hundred thousand inmates who, at one time or another, worked on it. The death rate is not surprising, considering the harsh geographic and climatic conditions in which prisoners worked. The regimen of a forced labor camp contributed to their misery: inmates were expected to produce maximal results with minimal food, clothing, and sleep.

Here, as throughout the Gulag camp system,[15] inmates provided cheap forced labor for large-scale Soviet construction projects in the early 1930s. Of course, therein lies the problem not only with the Belomor episode itself, but also with its companion volume: political prisoners (kulak farmers, "wayward" intellectuals, purported wreckers and saboteurs) composed the bulk of the work force. In many cases their only crime was to have been born into the wrong social class. The trumped-up charges that proved to be the undoing of every political prisoner nonetheless found credence within the Soviet criminal code; in the view of officialdom, such political offenders were far more treacherous than common criminals. Further damning the project was its supervision by the OGPU/NKVD, the notorious forerunner of the KGB.[16] The direct participation of the secret police in the writing of its own "history" was unheard of in the annals of Soviet literature.

Political prisoners, so-called "state enemies," and common criminals alike were slated to be "reforged," a handy rhetorical strategy, redolent of the industrial metaphors of the time, that overtly strove to remake presumed enemies into productive, skilled Soviet citizens.[17] This reforging, or *perekovka*, would be achieved through hard labor at construction sites. Former enemies, the theory went, would become newly sovietized friends as they labored to build the canals, railroads, mines, and factories needed to spur the economic growth of the Soviet Union. Ostensibly, the writers who produced the Belomor volume would themselves be reforged into certifiable Soviet writers through the unique exercise of collective authorship. Theoreticians of this practice believed that Soviet ideology could be instilled in anti-Soviet individuals through the acquisition of a practical skill honed on a forced labor project. Indeed, letters from workers in the archive for *The History of Construction* relate the new meaning that former thieves and prostitutes found in their lives, thanks to the acquisition of a practical skill such as plastering, carpentry, or a similar trade. Former Belomor Camp inmate Aleksandra Ivanovna Ivanova, for example, writes passionately to the head of the Belomor project, Matvei Berman, "Comrade Supervisor! I am hurrying to thank you for helping me find the right path for my life.... I am reading and am so much happier being a working member of society and of use to the State.... I give you my word that I will work honestly.... I advise all the rest of my former camp mates to find the right path and live by dint of their honest labor. Our working society doesn't need wreckers; we need only honest people who want to live honestly." Insofar as we can believe inmate accounts in the archives, Ivanova's letter seems sincere.[18]

Stalin's oft-repeated admonition that Soviet writers should be "engineers of the human soul" must have been on the minds of those who made up the writers' brigade organized to experience and document the "successes" of the Belomor Canal. On 17 August 1933, 120 writers set out to view firsthand the achievement of the "canal-armyists," as they were dubbed. The brigade included many of the most popular writers of the time: Mikhail Zoshchenko, Valentin Kataev, Viktor Shklovsky, Alexei Tolstoy, Vera Inber, and others. The six-day trip offered them the opportunity to view the canal and meet with inmates still on site. As sources attest, such meetings were well-orchestrated Potemkin-village affairs, designed to impress visitors while ignoring the deprivation, loss of life, and terror that inmates endured. Reportedly, many writers were duped by the artificiality of the trip, while others understood perfectly what the authorities were hiding and why.[19] Out of the 120 brigade writers, only 36 coauthored *The History of Construction*.

The final product was a richly illustrated volume with an embossed portrait of Stalin on its cover. A first run of 4,000 copies was specially designated for delegates to the Seventeenth Communist Party Congress in January 1934. Titled the Congress of Victors in honor of the achievements of the first Five-Year Plan, it provided the original impetus to produce *The History of Construction* so quickly: the volume was written and published in five months. According to contemporary newspaper accounts, a second printing of 45,000 copies was supposed to appear six weeks later, with a final print run of 150,000 copies released still later, albeit sans the embossed Stalin. Indeed this third printing was intended to "move forward into the masses, carrying the story of the wonders on the lakes of bleak Karelia."[20] Yet very few of the masses likely read or even saw copies of the book. Libraries had copies, as did its authors and participants in the Seventeenth Party Congress, and probably some members of the intelligentsia, but it is impossible to document fully ownership and readership patterns for *The History of Construction* since so many copies were destroyed. Successive editions of the book state that the second and third print runs of *The History of Construction* were 80,000 in 1934 and 30,000 in 1935, significantly smaller than originally projected.

Wider distribution of *The History of Construction* was further complicated by the purges of 1937, which claimed among its victims NKVD head Genrikh Yagoda, the entire upper echelon of the Belomor construction project leadership, and some of the volume's authors (including Dmitry Mirsky and Bruno Yasensky), as well as two of its editors (NKVD officer Semyon Firin and literary critic Leopold Averbakh).[21] Consequently, most copies of the volume were pulled from library shelves to be destroyed or placed under a secret classification that was lifted only after the onset of glasnost in 1986. Anyone who possessed a personal copy of the volume either hid it from view or disposed of it. It is unclear how many copies have survived to this day. Oddly, the work was reprinted in Russia in 1998, but without any information as to who reissued it or why, thereby intensifying the aura of mystery surrounding the text.[22] Possibly this reissue was designed to reacquaint readers with a dark and largely forgotten moment in Soviet history. No new editions of the *History of Construction* have appeared since then, and scholars are still puzzling over the origins of the 1998 edition.

An English translation, intended to extend the Stalinist message of the volume beyond Soviet boundaries, was published in 1935. It does not exactly coincide with the Russian original, yet it oddly emphasizes collective authorship more strongly.[23] The Russian version, for example, alphabetically lists each author after chapter titles, while the English translation omits direct authorial references, apparently reinforcing the collaborative structure of *The History of Construction*. The Russian version has subtitled sections that are woven into the larger chapter structure, but the English translation eliminates these individually titled sections and removes several subsections from the text entirely. While mistranslations pepper the English version, the most egregious deviation from the original remains the destruction of its narrative logic, the consequence of illogical editing by the translators.[24]

Only a few concrete details regarding the publication of the English version have emerged. May O'Callaghan, whom the publishers thank for her help "in the work of collating the translation with the Russian edition, and checking and reading the proofs," remains a mystery woman.[25] The editor of the English version and the author of its introduction, however, was the notable Lady Mary Annabel Nassau Strachey Williams-Ellis, or Amabel Williams-Ellis, the sister of British socialist John Strachey and the wife of architect Clough Williams-Ellis. According to G. S. Smith, Amabel visited Russia with her brother early in 1928 and served as the only British delegate to the First Congress of Soviet Writers, held in August 1934.[26] While Williams-Ellis alludes to her interactions with the translators, perhaps the most telling evidence of her role in the project stems from her statements in the introduction enthusiastically endorsing the volume as a work of originality and innovation. She describes the construction of the Belomor Canal as "a ticklish engineering job" performed by enemies of the state, making for "one of the most exciting stories that has ever appeared in print." She claims "for the first time we are here told the story of what goes on in a Russian labour camp."[27] Williams-Ellis neither criticizes the use of punitive work regimes nor questions the Soviet government's motives in building the canal with slave labor.

Slightly more information exists about the publishing house Harrison Smith & Robert Haas, which brought *The History of Construction* to an English-speaking audience. Harrison Smith formerly worked for Harcourt Press, which he left after their refusal to publish William Faulkner's *The Sound and the Fury*. Smith briefly worked with the British publisher Jonathan Cape but left in 1931 to open his own house, to which he brought several authors, among them Faulkner. His list included Isak Dinesen, Antoine de Saint-Exupéry, André Malraux, and "Babar the Elephant." In 1932 Robert Haas joined the company, which remained independent until 1936, when Random House acquired it.

In the late 1920s Harrison Smith spent six months in the USSR and the Far East as a freelance magazine writer, an experience that likely piqued his interest in the Belomor volume. He also served as the editor for the Foreign Press Service. During his brief stint as Jonathan Cape's partner, Smith supervised the publication of works by Maurice Hindus, an early commentator on life in Soviet Russia, and the very same Maxim Gorky who co-edited and co-authored *The History of Construction*. While it has been impossible to trace any personal connection between Smith and Gorky, this tantalizing link cannot be overlooked in any examination of the work.

The Russian edition of *The History of Construction* opens with the names of its three editors: Maxim Gorky, Semyon Firin (NKVD officer and head of the Belomor construction project), and Leopold Averbakh (literary critic and activist). Subsequent pages list the names of the collective authors, as well as one Belomor camp inmate, the incarcerated writer Sergei Alymov. Of the fifteen chapters in the volume, only three were not written collectively. The introduction and conclusion were penned by Gorky (who did not travel to the canal with the writers' brigade), and chapter 12, "The Story of One Reforging," was written by famed Soviet Russian humorist Mikhail Zoshchenko. The remaining twelve chapters were each produced by four to ten writers, whose names are listed after the chapter titles at the conclusion of the work. Archival documents demonstrate that the writers and editors used principles of montage to construct *The History of Construction*.[28] Passages were woven together such that a section authored by Sergei Budantsev, for example, was blended into a section penned by Viktor Shklovsky, whose contribution then flowed into Sergei Alymov's section. While the verbal connections between sections frequently seemed choppy, the overall theme of each chapter—canal workers, NKVD officers, the struggle with nature—served to unite its constituent parts just enough to make it coherent.

Reviews of the volume appeared in all major Soviet publications, including the Communist Party newspapers *Pravda* and *Komsomol'skaya Pravda*, as well as the "thick" journals *Nashi dostizheniia* (Our Achievements), *Znamia* (The Banner), and *Krasnaia nov'* (Red Virgin Soil). Not unexpectedly, the critical response was generally positive.[29] As one critic put it, the Belomor volume exemplified the work of Soviet writers to document "socialist restructuring of the economy and people's psychology."[30] Several reviews predictably praised the writers' efforts to produce a collectively authored work. But in spite of growing limitations on individual expression, the collaborative nature of the volume also attracted some criticism. Certain reviewers, in their otherwise positive assessments, cited a "certain chaotic quality in the distribution of the material, an insurmountable scrappiness, the insufficiently high artistic level of a number of chapters, their 'newspaper article like' quality."[31] One critic cited Mikhail Zoshchenko's contribution in particular as too stylized and, therefore, excessive.[32] Other reviewers lamented the lack of technical information or ideological stringency; they went as far as to insist that the authors should have included a chapter that underscored the ability of the Soviet system to achieve what no capitalist system could—the construction of the Belomor Canal.[33] The publication of such comments illustrates that at this moment in 1934, prior to the First Congress of Soviet Writers in late summer of that year, it was still possible to criticize, albeit formally and mildly, a work that enjoyed enormous official approbation and support. Shortly thereafter, these criticisms, as well as the Belomor volume itself, would disappear.

As the Stalinist era wore on, compliance with official opinion became mandatory, and public figures were expected to demonstrate their loyalty to the shared cause with increasing alacrity. Writers who failed to add their voices to the Stalinist choir could be construed as opposition figures. Even failure to sign a jointly written letter was enough to cast suspicion on an author, and writers who chose to refrain from visible expressions of enthusiasm often did so at considerable personal risk. Thus, Ia. S. Lur'e argues vociferously that famed Soviet humorists Il'ia Il'f and Evgenii Petrov "refused" to work on the Belomor volume out of principled objections to participation in such morally questionable projects. The evidence for this point of view is relatively scant, however, particularly since those two writers were part of the official delegation that visited the canal, which they mentioned explicitly in a subsequent publication. Whatever their motivation regarding the canal volume, Il'f and Petrov were willing to participate in other collective ventures, including the subway volume discussed below. They, like most writers of their era, found that issues of collective authorship were unavoidable.[34]

For other authors, the Belomor event apparently testified to the success and the legitimacy of the Soviet regime; participation in either the trip or the volume would have been an honor. This is the testimony of Alexandr Avdeenko, a working-class writer pulled from relative obscurity to join his more illustrious colleagues on the journey. Writing years later, Avdeenko described the events in question through the eyes of his younger self, who believed then "that the Belomor Canal and the future Moscow-Volga canal were a marvel of creation." In retrospect, Avdeenko explained his feelings at the time as a complicated mix of "self-deception, self-blinding and, along with that, legitimate pride in what had already really been accomplished by your nation and yourself." Describing a "rally of shock-worker canal soldiers" that he and other writers were asked to attend shortly after the official trip to the Belomor canal, Avdeenko noted that "every building site seemed to be the center of the world." Gorky himself was moved to tears by the sight, Avdeenko reported, noting that "what is most interesting, life-affirming is being created right now on countless of our construction sites, full of conflict, courage, heroism."[35]

Other writers were considerably more skeptical. Foremost among them was the formalist critic Viktor Shklovsky, who unequivocally viewed participation in the Belomor volume as the price he needed to pay to extract a much-desired result from the authorities: the release of his brother from the Belomor camp, a wish that subsequently was granted. Still other writers participated in the trip or the volume in the apparent hope that it would serve as a hedge against future requests that might be made of them by the literary or political establishments. Even clearly established writers were under enormous psychological pressure, occasionally self-imposed, to demonstrate their conformity to a continually evolving shared cause. Tamara Ivanova, who accompanied her husband Vsevolod Ivanov on the trip, later wrote that the supposed rehabilitation of criminals on the construction site was an obvious sham, but argued that even such established writers as Ivanov and Mikhail Zoshchenko "wanted to believe!"[36]

Such ambivalent participation in the Belomor volume draws into even sharper relief the contributions writers made to publicize another Soviet construction site: the first lines of the Moscow subway system. The initiative to chronicle this project dates primarily from early 1934 to the middle of 1935. Initial hopes were for multiple volumes devoted to the history of subway construction, and the plan was to capture the authentic perspective of workers as they built what would eventually become one of the most important showcases for Soviet accomplishment and one of the world's largest public transportation systems.[37] Like the Belomor volume, the subway project was originally intended to unite experienced and beginning writers and to give voice to authentic worker sentiments.

Despite the optimism of those early plans, only two collections devoted to the Moscow Metro eventually appeared in the series "History of Factories and Foundaries": *Tales of the Metro Builders* (*Rasskazy stroitelei metro*) and *How We Built the Metro* (*Kak my stroili metro*). Both appeared in 1935 under the general editorship of Aleksandr V. Kosarev. Of the two, *Tales of the Metro Builders* was clearly the most significant to Gorky's original project, and consequently it was the first to appear, in an impressive press run of 100,000. *How We Built the Metro* was also an important publishing event: a prominent review in the newspaper *Komsomol'skaia Pravda* gave it an "A+."[38] But its focus on the engineers, architects, and party workers involved in subway construction made this second volume less of a propaganda tool than the ostensibly authentic worker narratives of *Tales of the Metro Builders*. The prestigious paper *Literaturnaia gazeta* called *Tales of the Metro Builders* an "affecting, joyful book" written by the "entire collective of the subway." Reviewer A. Cherniavskaia emphasized that on the subway project, as on the Belomor Canal, even reluctant individuals could be remade into exemplary Soviet workers. Her glowing review points out how "sincere and convincing" such accounts of conversion were expected to be.[39]

The importance the volume held for the regime is clearly indicated by its lavish production values. A large number of photographs grace the final collection, including formal portraits of the featured authors, as well as on-site shots of ongoing construction. Well-executed "lubok" (woodblock-style) illustrations are used throughout, along with maps, fine paper, and an extravagant page layout. This kind of luxury in an era of continuing paper shortages lent special metaphorical and literal weight to both *Tales of the Metro Builders* and *How We Built the Metro*. A planned third volume, to which popular Soviet writers like Il'f and Petrov contributed essays, never saw the light of day, for reasons that reveal much about early Soviet authorship, readers, and publishing.[40]

Hindsight gives present-day researchers a certain cynicism about Soviet historiography, particularly about shared projects between intellectuals and workers. Although we may find it hard to recapture their sense of purpose, many contemporary observers apparently found experiments in collective authorship and shared history genuinely compelling. This was particularly the case with the fellow travelers, whose ostensibly bourgeois past made them objects of suspicion in the new Soviet world. Both coercion and economic rewards undoubtedly impelled writers to participate in the subway project, but it is equally clear that some authors were genuinely hopeful that trips to the construction site would put them in touch with newly empowered workers and with the profound social changes they saw around them. They may also have welcomed the opportunity to work with optimistic young volunteers instead of suspect political conscripts.

In contrast to the collective prison camp labor at the Belomor canal, activist "shock-workers" (*udarniki*) were recruited for the Moscow subway. Chosen for their political fervor or outstanding labor, they were obvious candidates for any volume dedicated to the wonders of the Soviet workplace. Although some workers shied away from the attention such high-profile projects involved, particularly later in the decade when the risks of participation became more obvious, others were clearly flattered and saw an opportunity for advancement in the written histories they were mobilized to help create. Even the most self-interested participants would have had recourse to the rhetoric of a shared cause; studies of Soviet diaries document how fervently those who did not believe in the collective project wished to do so.[41] Much recent research on Stalinist Russia and Nazi Germany makes it clear that a binary approach to these regimes, in which participants are assigned to one of two categories (supporter/dissenter) is too simple and may underestimate the scope for agency and accommodation under totalitarian regimes.[42]

Initially at least, the success of a jointly constructed history of the subway seemed to depend primarily on enthusiasm and hard work, qualities that optimistic Communist Party organizers, workers, and even authors apparently thought they had in abundance. The writers were to provide literary guidance; the workers would offer diary accounts of life in the tunnels; and party organizers, with a large staff of literary consultants, editors, secretaries, and other help, would guide the project to completion. A 1934 meeting of the State Publishing House for "The History of Factories and Foundries" details the goals that group leaders of these working-class literary circles were supposed to meet. "In order to deploy the literary-mass movement," the archival record of the gathering stipulates, leaders were to organize weekly meetings and encourage participation in the "wall newspapers" and the reading of literature in workers' "barracks, dormitories, and clubs" (GARF, f. 7952, op. 7, d. 224, l. 1). Leaders were encouraged to display portraits of classic and contemporary authors, and they were charged with engaging workers in discussions of the works of famous writers. Workers were to be treated to edifying excursions to the theater and museums, and the leadership was tasked with organizing "creative evenings, debates, lectures, consultations" and with arranging meetings with "Soviet writers and literary members of the Writers' Union." Such events, it was hoped, would create a "permanent connection" with the best published authors and provide subway laborers with "help in creative work." Promising workers were to be "freed from other duties." Tellingly, the most talented could look forward to a trip along the Belomor Canal (GARF, f. 7952, op. 7, d. 224, l. 1, 2).

Fairly quickly, however, it became clear that enthusiasm would not suffice in constructing a collective history of the subway. Not all workers were interested in participating: the crushing physical burden and danger of their work kept most on the edge of permanent exhaustion. Housing shortages, overcrowding, and difficulties with supplies made life off site an additional challenge that absorbed most workers' scarce free time. Even those eyewitness accounts that made it past the censor to appear in the two published volumes make it clear that work in the tunnels was grueling, as laborers struggled with poor equipment, nightmarish conditions, and enormous psychological and physical pressures. Those in low-level leadership positions were often too busy to submit to interviews, while others were wary of public attention. One of those in charge on site, Ia. F. Tiagnibeda, whose portrait was eventually included in *Tales of the Metro Builders,* was originally so reluctant to "advertise himself" that the author assigned to get Tiagnibeda's narrative into print was forced to cancel his contract: his subject was refusing to meet with him (GARF, f. 7952, op. 7, d. 370, l. 64).

Other individuals were willing to cooperate but found the demands of literary life to be beyond their talents. Typical comments from an editor of the workers' manuscripts suggest how difficult it was for these largely unskilled laborers to construct cogent written accounts of their contribution to the building process. On occasion, workers submitted manuscripts that were notable for their "literacy" (GARF, f. 7952, op. 7, d. 225, l. 11), skilled use of "literary language" (op. 7, d. 225, l. 14), and such "sincerity and authenticity" that the diaries became "valuable material" (d. 225, l. 20). Other manuscripts submitted by the worker-authors, however, elicited damningly frank evaluations: "needs fundamental reworking," "material very raw," (op. 7, d. 223, l. 2), or even "could be taken as an example of how not to write" (op. 7, d. 225, l. 11).

Nor were the inexperienced authors the only ones to blame. To expedite the desired communication between published authors and their worker colleagues, series editors were assigned to work with particular writers and to provide them with a steady flow of worker manuscripts from the construction "front line." But the role of interlocutor proved difficult as well. One editorial assistant faithfully quoted A. N. Garri's comments that he had "received the material" and was "starting to write" before adding his own skeptical note that Garri "wasn't working" (GARF, op. 7, d. 370, l. 64).[43] The same source complains that B. Kushner had been given "copious material" by his literary collaborator, I. Gruzinov, but was "dragging" his part of the project and "hadn't been anywhere" (op. 7, d. 370, l. 64).

This last point was a particularly sore spot for workers who were skeptical of authors who wrote about manual labor from the safety of their comfortable studies. Party activists undoubtedly helped exploit such natural working-class skepticism with pointed questions to the authors. Even Valentin Kataev, who based his famous novel *Time, Forward!* on a prolonged personal visit to the new city of Magnitogorsk, was challenged about his credentials. At an organized rally of workers and writers in March 1934 Kataev was pointedly asked what inadequacies he could identify in his novel. "Don't you feel the superficiality" of your work? the questioner wondered. After all, "it isn't possible to find out what is going on in Magnitogorsk in 3 months" (GARF, op. 7, d. 239, l. 75). Kataev self-defensively explained that the "main theme now is construction. That is the mastery of technology. . . . But mastery of technology is successful only when man is made richer, smarter. It's necessary to organize a new human being. The old human didn't master technology. Now there is a battle for a [new] human" (op. 7, d. 239, l. 77). Kataev's explication of official hopes left the workers partially unconvinced. "Which do you think is a better and more accurate way to gather material," asked another provocative voice from the floor toward the end of their March discussion, "standing at the cement mixer for an entire month or standing nearby as an observer?" (op. 7, d. 239, l. 90)

Similar questions had arisen at a meeting of authors and subway workers in January 1934. "The writer should be in the tunnel," archival documents quote S. Persov as saying. "I don't agree with writers studying the technology of this business from books." To work effectively, shoulder to shoulder with subway workers, "the writer needs to be not in the courtyard, not in the office, but there—under the ground" (GARF, op. 7, d. 240, l. 3). For some, however, the notion of professional intimacy between writers and workers made the subway project particularly compelling. Sergei Budantsev noted that he, along with the other authors of the Belomor volume, had only "worked from transcripts, from history, from paper materials" on that project. Acquaintance with the people actually involved in the construction of the canal was, in Budantsev's words, "extremely limited." In contrast, at the metro construction site he saw endless possibilities for a brave new attempt at collaborative history. Here, he proclaimed enthusiastically, "for the first time a mass effort in a book will be guaranteed" (op. 7, d. 240, l. 3). "The thing is," Budantsev concluded exaltedly, "not just that we are building industry. The thing is that people are growing on the job" (op. 7, d. 240, l. 3).

Where were the professional historians in this massive effort to collect oral histories at one of Stalin's most visible public projects? For the most part, they were absent. Extant archival materials document the historical training of several individuals involved in the project. But the metro venture valued ideological correctness over ostensible objectivity, as did similar projects of that era.[44] The multivolume *History of the Civil War in the USSR,* the *Great Soviet Encyclopedia,* and of course the Belomor volume itself all sacrificed authenticity in the name of conformity.[45] Gorky himself complained as early as March 1932 about professional historians who consider the "recollections of workers an unreliable source." He branded that approach "heresy."[46]

Gorky's secret hope, shared with many other writers of the time, was that such literary-historical projects would serve to invigorate and renew Russian literature. Since the early days of the revolution, critics had hounded writers for works impressive enough for their "heroic" times. This perceived crisis of genre left the literary establishment and even many writers suspicious of the short story, lyric poetry, and other supposedly bourgeois forms of literature. The reception of "literary" works like the subway project volume was significantly colored, then, by the sense that such collective projects were the only ones appropriate to this era. Typical of this new sense of what was needed is a comment by author and fellow traveler Iurii Olesha, who claimed to foresee "the demise of *belles lettres.* The demise of the invented novel." Salon literature was antithetical to a Soviet way of life, claimed Olesha, and its replacement was obvious both to Gorky and to his followers: "Gorky, for example, doesn't tell those who listen so carefully to him and consider him a great literary authority, doesn't tell them: write novels, stories. Gorky calls those gripped by literary obsession to write the history of the civil war or the history of the factories."[47]

It was a particular history that was needed, of course. The publishers at "The History of Factories and Foundries" warned series editors of the dangers of "objectivism." This damning label, like that of "creeping empiricism," was commonly applied to those too concerned with facts that contradicted the dominant historical narrative.[48] Details of that narrative were constantly evolving, but the ideological role of history in the project had been firmly established. Thus, at the January 1934 meeting of writers and subway workers, P. I. Anatoliev noted that he was the only professional historian present at the meeting and reminded the audience that the past has active lessons to teach. "We frequently turn to the past," he commented pointedly, "and we mobilize the material of the past in order to understand the present day better" (GARF, d. 240, l. 5). At the March rally, author Kataev cautioned workers to avoid a simple chronology of events, which he called "naked empiricism" (op. 7, d. 239, l. 70) and rejected out of hand.

A certain "Comrade Medyntsev" followed Kataev's caution with one of his own: workers should realize that the metro project was "fundamentally new" precisely because "we are simultaneously both building the subway and writing the history of the subway." That comment underlines the extraordinary approach to recorded history that characterized the metro volumes in particular. Time collapses on this construction site, telescoping thought, word, and deed in such a way that historical narrative can predict and even replace the actual events it attempts to "chronicle." Kataev's famous 1931 production novel announces just such an approach in its very title: *Time, Forward!* reflects the Stalinist conviction that time itself can be mastered by the words we use to describe events.[49]

Such an approach also ostensibly resolved the "contradiction" that had plagued the capitalist system—the division of physical from mental labor. As Comrade Medyntsev proudly noted, "we are both creating the subway . . . and realizing that construction" (*my i sozdaem metro . . . i soznaem eto stroitel'stvo;* GARF, d. 239, l. 132). Soviet functionary Leopold Averbakh was perhaps drawing on his Belomor experiences when he commented in January 1934 that the work of every author should be "directly merged with the masses, so that every writer is an organizer of a group of literary activists" (d. 240, l. 13).

Averbakh's vision of engaged Soviet writers marching in step with the workers they both documented and taught was an ideal from which reality departed rather quickly. One of the problems that had plagued collective literary endeavors in Stalin's Russia from the start was the scarcity of authors who were both politically trustworthy and experienced. As a result, writers considered unreliable, even some of those already publicly accused of duplicity or anti-party sentiments, were nevertheless assigned responsible positions as authors on the subway project. This was the case with Boris Pil'niak and Isaac Babel, both of whom had been laboring under a growing cloud of suspicion for years. Each writer was paired with a group of worker-authors and given a set of manuscripts to prepare for an orthodox collective Soviet history (GARF, op. 7, d. 348, ll. 21, 27–29, 60–61, 79, 80, 84). Although both Pil'niak and Babel would die in obscurity at the hands of state executioners almost before the ink on these volumes was dry, many of the essays with which they had been entrusted nevertheless appeared in the finished volume *Tales of the Metro Builders*.[50]

This fact, like so many others in this still poorly understood period of Soviet literary history, indicates how fluid the supposedly rigid categories of collaborator and dissenter really were during this era. As art historian Ekaterina Degot has remarked in another context, the "understanding of society as split between communists and their victims" is overly "simple, if not to say naïve."[51] A more complex history of the period recognizes that authors' reasons for participation in and avoidance of party projects varied. Some were undoubtedly willing and convinced participants. Those who were more reluctant found that avoiding Soviet experiments in collective authorship did not necessarily carry an immediate punishment, and participation was no guarantee of survival.

Party orthodoxy made it nearly inevitable that even mildly eccentric voices would be replaced with a single, central narrative. On the subway project, too, initial trust in authentic worker responses devolved rather quickly into efforts to shape, control, and finally suppress the spontaneous and naïve reactions of real laborers on the job. As Frederick Corney puts it in his study of another Stalinist historical project, "the objective needs of the revolution in the present" were quickly seen to outweigh "the subjective vanities of the individuals who recalled it."[52] Those in charge of organizing the history of the subway were willing to sacrifice narratives that contradicted the historical "truth" they were crafting, although they continued to insist that anything they published was authentically working class. An introductory note to *Tales of the Metro Builders* claims that the entire book "was written by the shock-worker builders of the metro themselves." In this "first of a series of books about the history of the Moscow metro," their "hands" seem to "make cement penetrable, illuminating it, restoring the panorama of construction," and recreating their own historic efforts in prose. Any historian who arrives on site after the fact will find that the work of interpretation has already been done for him. "Late, late is the chronicler!"[53]

It should come as little surprise, then, that the written history of the construction of Moscow's subway ended somewhat before the official opening of the first line on 15 May 1935. According to archival documents quoted by Sergei Zhuravlev, an atmosphere of secrecy had overwhelmed the construction site by early February 1935, and an order that month forbade the publication of materials "relating to the use of the Metro, the cost of a ride, and so on." By this time the country was entering one of its darkest periods. The continued collective history of subway construction would be only one of the casualties of Stalin's purges, which began in earnest in the late 1930s: a planned third volume on the construction of the subway was shelved, never to be completed. Like the rest of the contents of the archives, the collective history of the metro was now taboo.[54]

The brigade system, in literature and in construction, was intended to organize its participants to complete a monumental task. Yet just as many of the most "heroic" physical structures of Stalinist Russia remained incomplete, many works of literature similarly failed to achieve their vaunted goals. The collective histories of the Belomor canal and the Moscow subway system were meant to capture earthshaking events in the making, but they distorted many of the activities they proposed to cover, in some cases even "documenting" events that had yet to occur.

Yet writers agreed to participate in this process of compiling Soviet "history" despite their lack of professional qualifications for the task. Even some of the most eccentric and talented sought out participation in this kind of collective endeavor precisely because it offered a way to respond to monumental events and because it afforded a kind of anonymity that a single-authored work would not. A writer could operate "below the radar" with the protection that a collective offered. If one need not ascribe one's name to a particular text, then one could not be held singly responsible if that text was less than satisfactory. In addition, collective literary enterprises offered an opportunity for nonconformists to participate in the grand documentation of Soviet state building, a space where skeptical authors could retain suspect views while bending just enough to avoid any appearance of deviation from the cause. Work in a collective also helped writers bridge the widening gulf between the intelligentsia and a newly literate working class still rooted in lowbrow culture. Writers accused of bourgeois tendencies and elite sensibilities could demonstrate their populist sympathies by rubbing elbows with workers in collaborative literary projects.

Indeed, who better to relate tales of grandiose building feats and construction achievements than modernist writers well versed in the art of relativistic storytelling? In their quest to find a role for themselves in an unfamiliar world, Soviet authors from this era demonstrated not "how life writes the book," but "how the book should write life."[55] The collectively authored volumes they created not only conveyed a sense of history in the making, but also served as a road map of sorts, by which both common folk and sophisticated authors could navigate the path to becoming "new" men and women. A strange yet compelling logic piloted these endeavors: the lessons of history that these volumes documented were focused not so much on actual events themselves, but on the models of behavior that they described.

As with many Soviet initiatives, of course, rhetoric promised more than reality produced. But these experiments in collective writing had contemporaneous counterparts in Western Europe and the United States. "Mass Observation" in Britain had loosely organized volunteers taking to the streets in droves in order to create "mass science." The resulting slice-of-life historical picture was expected to reveal hidden patterns of meaning in the ordinary daily activities of a nation.[56] American plans for collective history in the 1930s were equally ambitious, as the Works Progress Administration (WPA) set out to collect thousands of individual stories of the common man as part of the Federal Writers' Project. Over ten thousand interviews were conducted with a diverse group of American men and women whose stories would otherwise have gone untold.[57] We need to explore further the connections between Soviet literature and such projects of collective history elsewhere. Recent discussions concerning the reliability and objectivity of collectively authored material on Wikipedia only serve to remind us that such questions are not confined to one culture or a single time period. The idea that greater authenticity and truth will be the result of jointly constructed history continues to beguile us.

Notes

1. Following Sheila Fitzpatrick's lead in the late 1970s, historians have used the label "cultural revolution" to refer to the period from 1928 to 1931, which was marked by radical experiments in agricultural collectivization, industrialization, and the rise of a new Soviet intelligentsia. While convenient as shorthand, the term "cultural revolution" (and the restrictive time frame associated with it) tends to obscure developments that predate or postdate the period. This is particularly the case with literary history. The utility of the term was called into question in a discussion between Michael David-Fox and Fitzpatrick that appeared in the *Russian Review* 58, no. 2 (1999): 181–211. The institution of a planned economy under Stalin commenced with the first Five-Year Plan that ran from 1928 to 1932. The goals of the first plan were purportedly achieved in four years; hence the second Five-Year Plan lasted from 1932 to 1937. Among the goals included in both plans were targets for construction, agriculture, and heavy and light manufacturing. For specific investigations of early Soviet industrialization, see, for example, Stephen Kotkin, *Magnetic Mountain: Stalinism as a Civilization* (Berkeley: University of California Press, 1995), and Anne D. Rassweiler, *The Generation of Power: The History of Dneprostroi* (New York: Oxford University Press, 1988). Kotkin's book in particular has been influential in its discussion of the ways in which Soviet citizens learned to work within and manipulate the evolving Bolshevik system.

2. For example, the paper *Literaturnaia gazeta* reported plans by the workers of the "Red Proletariat" factory to "adopt certain authors," including Valentin Kataev, to bring their creative endeavors closer to the process of production (*Literaturnaia gazeta*, 5 November 1930, quoted in L. [I.] Skorino, *Pisatel' i ego vremia: Zhizn' i tvorchestvo V. P. Kataev* [The Writer and His Times: The Life and Work of V. P. Kataev] (Moscow: Sovetskii pisatel', 1965), 214–15. Kataev's connection to the factory soon bore fruit: his visit to the Siberian boomtown Magnitogorsk resulted in the publication of *Time, Forward!*, one of the best-known Soviet production novels. This uniquely Soviet genre, which dealt with the process of constructing both industry and the new citizens needed to run it, is discussed in detail in Mary A. Nicholas, "Building a Better Metaphor: Architecture and Russian Production Novels," *Mosaic* 35, no. 4 (2002): 51–68.

3. Fascinating diary accounts can be found in Veronique Garros, Natalia Korenevskaya, and Thomas Lahusen, eds., *Intimacy and Terror: Soviet Diaries of the 1930s*, trans. Carol A. Flath (New York: New Press, 1995), and Joachim Hellbeck, *Revolution on My Mind: Writing a Diary under Stalin* (Cambridge: Harvard University Press, 2006). Hellbeck provides a sophisticated interpretation of the psychological processes by which individuals explained their enduring desire to believe.

4. See S. V. Zhuravlev, *Fenomen "Istorii fabrik i zavodov": Gor'kovskoe nachinanie v kontekste epokhi 1930-x godov* [The Phenomenon of the "History of Factories and Foundaries": Gorky's initiative in the context of the era of the 1930s] (Moscow: Russian Academy of Sciences Institute of Russian History, 1997), 5.

5. See Evgeny Dobrenko, *The Making of the State Writer: Social and Aesthetic Origins of Soviet Literary Culture*, trans. Jesse M. Savage (Stanford: Stanford University Press, 2001), 372.

6. For details on Bulgakov and Prishvin, see Cynthia A. Ruder, *Making History for Stalin: The Story of the Belomor Canal* (Gainesville: University of Florida Press, 1998), 52–53, 188–92, 202–3.

7. N[atal'ia] Kornienko, "'Proletarskaia Moskva zhdet svoego khudozhnika' (K tvorcheskoi istorii romana)" ["Proletarian Moscow awaits its artist" (Toward a Creative History of the Novel)], in *"Strana filosofov" Andreia Platonova: Problemy tvorchestva* ["Country of Philosophers" by Andrei Platanov: Problems of Creation] ed. N. V. Kornienko (Moscow: Nasledie, 1999), 3:367. See also Vladimir Goncharov and Vladimir Nekhotin, "Andrei Platonov v dokumentakh OGPU-NKVD-NKGB, 1930–1945" [Andrei Platonov in OGPU-NKVD-NKGB documents, 1930–45], in *"Strana filosofov" Andreia Platonova,* ed. Kornienko (Moscow: Nasledie, 2000), 4:853. Naturally, the veracity of information in secret denunciations is suspect. According to Kornienko, a volume on the history of the canal's construction resided in Platonov's personal library: see Andrei Platonov, *Vzyskanie pogibshikh: Povesti, rasskazy, p'esa, stat'i* [Exaction of the Dead: Tales, Stories, Drama, Articles], ed. M. A. Platonova (Moscow: Shkola-Press, 1995), 639. Platonov presents a remarkably unorthodox picture of a female subway worker in his novel *Schastlivaia Moskva (Happy Moscow),* which he worked on from 1933 to 1936. The work was only published long after his 1951 death.

8. See Marietta Shaginian, *Kak ia rabotala nad "Gidrotsentral'iu"* [How I Worked on "Hydrocentral"] (Moscow: Profizdat, 1933).

9. For further insight into Andrei Belyi's complicated motivations, see A. V. Lavrov, "*Proizvodstvennyi roman*—poslednii zamysel Andreia Belogo" [Production Novel—Andrei Belyi's final project], *Novoe literaturnoe obozrenie* 56 (2002): 114–34.

10. Jeffrey Brooks, *Thank You, Comrade Stalin! Soviet Public Culture from Revolution to Cold War* (Princeton: Princeton University Press, 2000), 23–27, 38, 48–49, 54–59, notes the importance of metaphors in shaping social perceptions in the Soviet Union. The metaphor of construction was important from the early Soviet years, but the "schema of socialist building

gained sway" particularly after 1927. Rolf Hellebust explores the industrial metaphor in early Soviet society in *Flesh to Metal: Soviet Literature and the Alchemy of Revolution* (Ithaca: Cornell University Press, 2003). According to Zhuravlev, *Fenomen*, 5, the idea for the publishing house arose almost spontaneously. Zhuravlev provides an outstanding overall history of the publishing venture. One clear indication of the significance of "Factories and Foundries" is the number of prestigious publications it put out: see Josette Bouvard, *Le Metro de Moscou: La construction d'un mythe sovietique* (Paris: Editions du Sextant, 2005), 119.

11. Zhuravlev, *Fenomen*, 5.

12. Stephen E. Hanson, *Time and Revolution: Marxism and the Design of Soviet Institutions* (Chapel Hill: University of North Carolina, 1997), suggests that such an approach was distinctly Soviet. Hanson sees the Soviet concept of time as a combined "charismatic-rational" approach borrowed from Marx that attempted to use "rational time discipline to master time itself" (ix). Echoes of this attempt to constrict or control time can be heard particularly in the project to document construction of the Moscow subway.

13. *Istoriia stroitel'stva Belomorosko-Baltiiskogo kanala imeni Stalina*, ed. Maksim Gorky, Semyon Firin, and Leopold Averbakh (Moscow: Istoriia fabrik i zavodov, 1934). All references are to this first edition. The only English translation of this volume was Maxim Gorky, Leopold Averbakh, and Semyon Firin, eds., *Belomor: An Account of the Construction of the Great Canal between the White Sea and the Baltic Sea*, intro. Annabel Williams-Ellis (New York: Harrison Smith & Robert Haas, 1935). For comments on the text and the writers who participated, see Aleksandr I. Solzhenitsyn, *The Gulag Archipelago 1918–1956: An Experiment in Literary Investigation*, trans. Thomas P. Whitney (New York: Harper & Row Publishers, parts 1–2, 1973; parts 3–4, 1974). In parts 1–2, see xii, 42, 157. In parts 3–4, see 78, 86–104.

14. A. S. Insarov (no first name or patronymic given), *Baltiisko-Belomorskii Vodnyi Put'* [The Baltic–White Sea Waterway] (Moscow: Ogiz Gostransizdat, 1934), 55.

15. The word Gulag is an acronym for the Glavnoe Upravlenie Ispravitel'no-trudovykh Lagerei, or the Main Administration for Corrective Labor Camps.

16. Initially the OGPU (Obedinennoe gosudarstvennoe politicheskow upravlenie [United State Political Administration]) and the NKVD were separate entities. They were merged in 1934 under the single heading NKVD.

17. The concept of reforging, or *perekovka*, enjoyed its greatest currency in the first half of the 1930s. The camp newspapers for the Belomor Canal and for the subsequent construction of the Moscow-Volga Canal (1933–37) were both named *Perekovka*. For a more complete discussion of reforging, see Ruder, *Making History for Stalin*, 142–53.

18. Her letter can be found in the Russian State Archive, Gosudarstvennyi Arkhiv Rossiiskoi Federatsii, or GARF. GARF materials, like those in other Russian archives, are catalogued in descending order of size and category, according to *fond* (fund), *opis'* (inventory), *delo* (file), *edinnoe khranenie* (individual file), and *list* (page). Thus, references to materials from GARF are classified in terms of f., op., d., ed. kh., and l. For Ivanova's letter, see GARF, f. 7952, op. 7, ed. khr. 28, l. 20.

19. For a more detailed discussion of the complex response see Ruder, *Making History for Stalin*, 47–85.

20. S. Fin (no first name given), "Kniga o 'chude' na Karel'skikh ozerakh" [A Book about the 'Miracle' on the Karelian Lakes], *Komsomol'skaia pravda*, 24 January 1934, 4.

21. In addition, contributors Boris Lapin and Zakhar Khatsrevin perished in the early days of World War II while serving as Soviet war correspondents.

22. This mysterious volume opens with a letter to the readers of *The History of Construction* "from the publisher." Neither the publisher's identity nor any publishing information appears anywhere in the volume. The only bibliographic data is provided on the title page,

which reads in translation as follows: "*The Stalin White Sea-Baltic Canal. The History of Construction, 1931-1934.* Editors M. Gorky, L. Averbakh, S. Firin, 1998."

23. For a more complete discussion of the English translation see Ruder, *Making History for Stalin,* 192-202.

24. Precisely who translated the volume from Russian to English remains a mystery, given that the translators' names (they consistently are referred to in the plural) never appear in the English version. A publisher's note provides the single clue to their identity when it states that "the English translation used in this edition was prepared in Moscow from the Russian edition" (Gorky, Averbakh, and Firin, *Belomor,* ii), thereby hinting that the translators were Russian.

25. Gorky, Averbakh, and Firin, *Belomor,* ii.

26. G. S. Smith, *D. S. Mirsky: A Russian-English Life, 1890-1939* (Oxford: Oxford University Press, 2000), 248-49. Smith relates the story of Williams-Ellis as part of his study of the literary critic Dmitry Sviatopolk-Mirsky, an aristocratic Russian émigré who lived in England for a number of years after the 1917 Revolution before finally returning to Soviet Russia in 1933. Mirsky was included in the official Belomor writers' brigade, and he reports similar official visits to Central Asia, the Urals, and even the subway construction site (ibid., 220, 244). He perished in the purges of 1939.

27. Gorky, Averbakh, and Firin, *Belomor,* vi, vii.

28. Illustrations of montage in the draft manuscript can be found in Ruder, *Making History for Stalin,* 221-23. For a fuller discussion of the montage process vis-à-vis the Belomor volume, see ibid., 114-40.

29. For a more detailed discussion of critical response to *The History of Construction,* see Ruder, *Making History for Stalin,* 142-43.

30. I. Eventov (no first name given), "Komandiru o sovetskoi khudozhestvennoi literature. (Obzor)" [To the Commander About Soviet Literature. (A Review)], *Krasnaia nov'* 6 (1934): 150-58.

31. Iogann Al'tman, "Kniga o bol'shoi pobede" [A Book about the Great Victory], *Literaturnyi kritik* 6 (1934): 253-62. Al'tman's complaints should be taken with a grain of salt; he apparently regretted not being included in the canal project himself. A copy of the canal volume that once belonged to him contains the following handwritten dedication, dated 31 January 1934 and signed "Iogann": "With great joy for our life, with great regret that I didn't participate in this book, with great hope for participation in future books."

32. Lage (no first name given), "Chelovek i priroda" [Man and Nature], *Kommunisticheskaia molodezh'* 7 (1934): 60-62.

33. See A. Bolotnikov (no first name given), "Kniga dostoinaia svoei temy" [The Book Is Worthy of Its Theme], *Literaturnaia gazeta,* 26 January 1934, 2.

34. Lur'e voices his convictions in Ia. S. Lur'e, *V kraiu nepuganykh idiotov: Kniga ob Il'fe i Petrove* [In the Land of Unafraid Idiots] (St. Petersburg: Evropeiskii universitet, 2005), 142, 159-61. The fact that Il'f and Petrov produced several pieces dedicated to the construction of the subway suggests the authors' continued commitment to the notion of collective authorship and the Soviet project. Documents in the State Archives of the Russian Federation indicate that Fedor Gladkov, Ilya Ehrenburg, Demian Bednyi, Il'ia Sel'vinskii, Lev Nikulin, N. Ognev, Viktor Shklovsky, Boris Lapin, and numerous other well-known authors were initially expected to join Il'f and Petrov in the subway venture (GARF, f. 7952, op. 7, d. 370, ll. 8, 38). Shklovsky's experience editing the Belomor canal volume apparently qualified him for continued service here. On a document dated 15 October 1934 he, Gladkov, and Mikhail Koltsov were listed as "literary editors," apparently in charge of "montage of the book" (ibid., l. 88).

35. Aleksandr Avdeenko, "Otluchenie [Excommunication]," parts 1 & 2, *Znamia* 3 (1989): 5-73, 80-133.

36. Tamara Ivanova, "Eshche o 'nasledstve,' o 'dolge,' i 'prave.' Byl li Vsevolod Ivanov 'zhdanovtsem'?" [More about "legacy," "duty," and "right." Was Vsevolod Ivanov a "Zhdanovite"?], *Knizhnoe obozrenie*, 34 (25 August 1989): 6.

37. More recent histories of the subway construction include Dietmar Neutatz, *Die Moskauer Metro: Von den erten Planen bis zur Grossbaustelle des Stalinismus (1897–1935)* (Cologne: Bohlau Verlag, 2001), and Bouvard, *Le Metro de Moscou*.

38. The unsigned review is entitled "Kniga, sdelannaia na 'Otlichno'" [An A+ Book], *Komsomol'skaia Pravda*, 149/3144 (1935): 4. The review recommends the volume to "all libraries." Thanks go to Mary Aquila and the Slavic Reference Service at the University of Illinois at Urbana-Champaign for bibliographic assistance with this and the following two references.

39. Cherniavskaia's review "Rasskazy stroitelei metro" [Tales of the Metro Builders] is followed by a short selection of poetry from subway workers, as though underscoring the transformation these laborers have made to reach the pages of a preeminent literary periodical. See A. Cherniavskaia (no first name given), *Literaturnaia gazeta*, 30 April 1935, 5.

40. The traditional "lubok," or woodblock-style illustration, had been revived by poet and artist Vladimir Mayakovsky and others for use in revolutionary pamphlets and advertising campaigns. The appearance of such woodblock drawings in the subway volumes, perhaps intended to help bridge gaps between high and low artistic registers, was mildly criticized as "not up to standard" in a review published by N. Nikitin (no first name given), "Rasskazy stroitelei moskovskogo metro" [Tales of the Builders of the Moscow Metro], *Kniga i proletarskaia revoliutsiia* 7 (1935): 57–71. The otherwise luxurious production values of these volumes suggest the significance assigned to this series.

41. See, for example, Joachim Hellbeck, "Working, Struggling, Becoming: Stalin-Era Autobiographical Texts," *Russian Review* 60, no. 3 (2001): 340–59. Hellbeck's *Revolution on My Mind* provides additional insight into the psychological processes at work during this period and clear evidence of the overwhelming interest in the "slice-of-life" diary genre.

42. See, for example, Anna Krylova, "The Tenacious Liberal Subject in Soviet Studies," *Kritika* 1, no. 1 (2000): 119–46; and Steven Harris, "In Search of 'Ordinary' Russia: Everyday Life in the NEP, the Thaw, and the Communal Apartment," *Kritika* 6, no. 3 (2005): 583–614. Harris's review article includes a brief discussion of the importance of *Alltagsgeschichte* in current scholarship on the Nazi period and its relevance to Soviet studies, including work by Sheila Fitzpatrick and Catriona Kelly.

43. Garri was apparently working more diligently than it seemed, since he is listed as a literary editor for the final volume.

44. Zhuravlev notes, for example, that certain minimal standards for work with "general historical literature" were introduced as part of the training for workers compiling the histories of Soviet factories, but he also points out that political concerns consistently trumped historical and literary approaches to the material (Zhuravlev, *Fenomen*, 61, 65). Applications from some of the individuals interested in participating in the project indicated historical training. See, for example, the file (*anketa*) of Konstantin Iakovlevich Vinogradov in GARF, op. 7, d. 232, where Vinogradov describes himself as a "historian (Russian history)" with published "scholarly works."

45. For a general discussion of issues involved in collective authorship in the Soviet Union, see the forum on "monumental Stalinist publications" in the journal *Kritika* 6, no. 1 (2005): 5–106. The forum includes Elaine MacKinnon's study of the creation of Civil War history and an article by Brian Kassof on the first edition of the Soviet encyclopedia. Frederick Corney offers one of several reevaluations of Soviet efforts to (re)write history in his volume *Telling October: Memory and the Making of the Bolshevik Revolution* (Ithaca: Cornell University

Press, 2004). See also the discussion of the role of literature in cultural mobilization projects of the Stalinist 1930s in *Novoe literaturnoe obozrenie* 71, no. 1 (2005): 229–89.

46. Zhuravlev, *Fenomen,* 32–33.

47. Olesha's comments can be found in his diaries from 1930, which were published only long after his death in Iurii Olesha, *Kniga proshchaniia* [Book of Farewell] (Moscow: Vagrius, 1999), 99. Olesha himself would clearly be included in the list of those "gripped by literary obsession" ("oderzhimykh literaturnym zudom"). The tortured response that Olesha has to such collective endeavors—by turns, enthusiastic and disdainful, hopeful and despairing—is typical of writers of the time, especially those who were skeptical of their own ability to participate. See Andreas Guski, *Literatur und Arbeit: Produktionsskizze und Produktionsroman im Russland des 1. Funfjahrplans (1928–1932)* (Wiesbaden: Harrassowitz, 1995), 3–41, for a discussion of the generic implications of the production novel.

48. Zhuravlev, *Fenomen,* 34. Georgii Vasilievich, Valentin Kataev's authorial stand-in from *Time, Forward!,* criticizes his own work for its "creeping empiricism" and destroys the page on which he is working because of it. Valentin Kataev, *Time, Forward!* trans. Charles Malamuth (New York: Farrar & Rinehart, 1933), 104.

49. According to Stephen Hanson, characters in Kataev's novel personify the particular tragedy of the First Five-Year Plan in their conflict over the wisdom of sacrificing the present for the future. The engineer Margulis agrees to do just that by pushing his cement-mixing equipment beyond its specifications, even though that will result in their early amortization. History proved Margulis wrong, Hanson argues, but the system could not admit that since to do so would be to "call into question the theoretical synthesis of charismatic and rational time [that is] at the core of Marxism itself" (Hanson, *Time and Revolution,* 160–61).

50. Most of Babel's manuscripts apparently were reassigned later, and his name was crossed out on several of the handwritten lists of contributors that remain in the archives, making it difficult to ascertain his actual contribution to the novel.

51. Ekaterina Degot, "The Collectivization of Modernism," *Dream Factory Communism: The Visual Culture of the Stalin Era* (Frankfurt: Schirn Kunsthalle Frankfurt, 2003), 86.

52. See Corney, *Telling October,* 153.

53. See *Rasskazy stroitelei metro*, frontispiece, 7–8.

54. Zhuravlev, *Fenomen,* 203n.179.

55. For a full discussion of "how life writes the book," see Thomas Lahusen, *How Life Writes the Book: Real Socialism and Socialist Realism in Stalin's Russia* (Ithaca: Cornell University Press, 1997).

56. See Nick Hubble, *Mass-Observation and Everyday Life: Culture, History, Theory* (London: Palgrave Macmillan, 2006). A more solitary project, but one that nevertheless shared the goal of capturing the shared reality of "Everyman" in prewar England, was George Orwell's *The Road to Wigan Pier* (London: Victor Gollancz, 1937).

57. Numerous authors who later achieved fame on their own began their illustrious writing careers gathering oral histories of everyday Americans for these WPA archives, including Ralph Ellison, John Cheever, Saul Bellow, Zora Neale Hurston, Richard Wright, and Studs Terkel.

Designing John Hersey's *The Wall*

W. A. Dwiggins, George Salter, and the Challenges of American Holocaust Memory

Robert Franciosi

Widely admired in 1950 for a list of authors including Willa Cather, Thomas Mann, and Albert Camus, the House of Knopf was even more esteemed within the book trade for the quality and design of its volumes. Founder Alfred A. Knopf brought to his company a devotion to the bookmaking craft that had been largely absent from American publishing since the advent of machine presses in the mid-nineteenth century, a commitment founded on the premise that excellent texts warranted equally impressive design and production. "I believe that good books should be well made," he wrote in a 1957 publisher's credo, "and I try to give every book I publish a format that is distinctive and attractive."[1] To achieve that publishing ideal, which many would come to associate with Knopf's famous Borzoi insignia, he engaged some of the best designers of his day, artists who infused the firm's list with a sensibility that envisioned trade books as both commercial and aesthetic objects.

As early as 1930 Knopf had stated that books "better-looking-than-necessary" were manufactured when publishers were driven "by an inner compulsion stronger than the arguments of bankers." Although keenly aware of financial imperatives, Knopf was committed to the long-term benefits that producing handsome volumes would bring to his company. He felt that "over a period of time a publisher can win a certain following for what we

---

This article could not have been written without the resources of the following archives and their ever-helpful staffs: Beinecke Library, Yale University (John Hersey Collection); Harry Ransom Humanities Research Center, University of Texas at Austin (Alfred A. Knopf, Inc. Collection); Newberry Library (George Salter Collection); and Boston Public Library (W. A. Dwiggins Collection). Thanks also to the Special Collections library staff at Grand Valley State University, Robert Beasecker and Bob Schoofs, and to the readers from *Book History* who offered valuable suggestions. Research for this article was completed with the help of fellowships and travel grants from the following institutions: Harry Ransom Humanities Research Center, Beinecke Library, and Grand Valley State University.

might call the style of his books," perhaps finally increasing sales and profits. "But he still has periodically to face the unpleasant fact," Knopf lamented, "that he is competing for authors—and for sales—with publishers who have no feeling at all for the book except as a piece of merchandise."[2]

John Hersey, whose mass-market appeal had been early established with the award-winning *A Bell for Adano* (1944), remained loyal to Knopf in no small measure because the publisher had "done more for the appearance of books in the United States than anyone else."[3] A noted correspondent for *Time* and *Life,* Hersey by 1947 had not only won a Pulitzer Prize for this first novel, but had published a long essay on the atomic bombing of Hiroshima that had quickly become a multifaceted media sensation. Based on interviews with six survivors of the blast, "Hiroshima" first appeared in 1946 as an entire issue of *The New Yorker* and was widely excerpted, broadcast on radio, discussed on editorial pages, and even distributed at no charge to Book-of-the-Month Club subscribers.

After Hersey's conversations with A-bomb victims in Hiroshima, he felt compelled to begin research for a novel on another horrific chapter in the annals of the twentieth century, one he had encountered as a reporter during the war's final year: the destruction of Europe's Jews. He had seen the ruins of the Warsaw Ghetto and had interviewed survivors of the Lodz Ghetto. But it was his encounter with the concentration camp system—"where, in the last hours before the Russians came in, the Nazis tried to destroy every human being in their hands"—that had the most profound impact on this American "traveling naïve in the totalitarian jungle."[4] Five years before Anne Frank's diary would captivate American readers, and more than a decade before the Adolf Eichmann trial would at last force many Jewish American writers to address the subject, *Time/Life* journalist John Hersey had somehow arrived at the *terminus a quo* of literary engagement with the Holocaust, what Alvin Rosenfeld astutely identifies as the fundamental challenge posed by the "post-Auschwitz imagination." When "fact itself surpasses fiction, what is there left for the novel and the short story to do?"[5]

Perhaps only a journalist would have attempted as early as 1947 to write fiction about the recent murder of six million Jews. The subject, however, ultimately pulled Hersey away from the reportage that had served him on the Russian front and in Hiroshima's ruins and pushed him toward a new type of historical fiction that he later termed "the novel of contemporary history." Published in 1950, and modeled in part on Emanuel Ringelblum's ghetto archives, Oneg Shabbat, Hersey's *The Wall* is not only an epic account of the Warsaw Ghetto's life and death, but is arguably the first American novel centered on the Holocaust.[6]

Early in 1947, after finishing "A Short Wait," a story about a Lodz

Ghetto survivor that would be published in the 14 June issue of *The New Yorker,* Hersey embarked on what must have seemed a logical course to a writer hoping to understand the extermination of Europe's Jews.[7] He spent several days interviewing an Auschwitz survivor. Not until his 1962 collection *Here to Stay,* though, would the piece he drafted from these conversations, "Prisoner 107,907," be published. Whereas his reporter's notes on the Lodz Ghetto had led to a *New Yorker* story, Hersey's discussions with the Auschwitz survivor dissuaded him from attempting to write fiction about concentration camps. In a 1952 essay on composing *The Wall,* "The Mechanics of a Novel," Hersey explains that he felt the world of the camps had so dehumanized prisoners that it would be impossible to turn their experiences into fiction.

Yet if prisoners in the camps had "been degraded by their experiences to a subhuman, animal level," those in the ghettos, Hersey concludes, "had lived on as families to the very end, and had maintained at least vestiges and symbols of those things we consider civilization—theaters, concerts, readings of poetry, and the rituals of everyday human intercourse."[8] For this American journalist, then, a book on the Warsaw Ghetto would exemplify the novel of contemporary history's ability to illuminate the lives of ordinary people caught in history's snares. His choice to write about Warsaw rather than Lodz, which had been the subject of "A Short Wait" and which would subsequently inspire Leslie Epstein and others, seems based on two factors: the wealth of documentary materials available on the Warsaw Ghetto, and, more importantly, the fictional and inspirational possibilities of the April 1943 uprising.

Using the Warsaw Ghetto as his focus, Hersey also faced two disparate challenges: conveying the tragic sweep of events of the Hitler era and at the same time illuminating the human dimension often buried by traumatic history and mass death. He accomplished the first by resorting to a device as old as the novel itself—the fictional archive. *The Wall* is built upon a series of dated entries from the "Levinson Archive." Recovered after the war by a handful of ghetto survivors, the enormous collection, Hersey's fictional editor explains, "has scant precedent": "it is not so formidable as history; it is more than notes for a history; it is not fiction—[archivist] Levinson was too scrupulous to imagine *anything;* it is not merely a diary; it is neither journalism nor a journal in the accepted modes."[9] Hersey's imagined archive includes hundreds of dated entries from November 1939 to May 1943, every detail based on facts from the ghetto's history. And it incorporates actual *Judenrat* (the Jewish councils appointed by the Germans) and Nazi documents, voicing the full range of Jewish political and cultural life. Indeed, his entries are so convincing that many readers wrote Hersey either asking where they could access the Levinson Archive or attacking him for so "deceiving" his audience.

Hersey understood the sheer unwieldiness of those many excerpts from the Levinson Archive—his unnamed "Editor" tells us they represent only one-twentieth of its four million words. He needed another device to control the narrative, which he found in what he termed "The Family." A small group of ghetto residents whose lives have been thrust together, "The Family" enacts the dramatic moments prompting the commentary of archivist and choric figure Noach Levinson. As a minor official in the *Judenrat*, though also a member of "The Family," Levinson provided Hersey a way to retain a sense of intimacy with his characters while telling the larger story of the Warsaw Ghetto, from the city's fall in 1939 to the spring uprising of 1943. For example, Hersey bases Rachel Apt on the famous underground leader Zivia Lubetkin and uses her both to illustrate clandestine educational efforts in the ghetto and to place us squarely within the world of the Jewish Fighting Organization. Other characters bring to life various institutions and groups that made up ghetto life—the *Judenrat*, the Bund, the Jewish Police, even the Jewish labor crews who built the ghetto wall itself. And, through Levinson, Hersey maintains a steady focus on Dolek Berson, a fictional "drifter" who has contact with the entire range of ghetto life and who depicts the evolution among some Warsaw Jews from passivity to active resistance.

A work of great size and ambition, *The Wall* posed a formidable and unprecedented challenge to Hersey's publisher—how to present and market a novel whose very subject, despite acts of heroic resistance, is ultimately a story of mass death, a story American audiences were particularly ill-prepared to face, not just in 1950 but over the ensuing decades. "How much darkness must we acknowledge," Lawrence Langer would ask his American readers in 1995, "before we will be able to confess that the Holocaust story cannot be told in terms of heroic dignity, moral courage, and the triumph of the human spirit in adversity?"[10] Reflecting a first stirring of American Holocaust consciousness, John Hersey's *The Wall* at least engaged this question. If Hersey perhaps overemphasized the theme of human tenacity in the face of unprecedented mass murder, he mostly resisted sentimentality and a need to view the Holocaust's "lessons" as universal, a mindset that would dominate American responses for several decades. The American desire "to parlay hope, sacrifice, justice, and the future into a victory that will mitigate despair," Langer notes, would be most prominently expressed in the 1955 Broadway production of *The Diary of Anne Frank*. Published five years earlier, *The Wall* largely resists this mitigating impulse—at least within its text. But among those responsible for bringing the physical book to American readers the lure of Holocaust "optimism" would prove almost irresistible.

Hersey delivered a three-hundred-thousand-word draft to Alfred Knopf in June of 1949. It was the kind of massively ambitious work toward which the American publisher of Thomas Mann was especially sympathetic, but the publishing challenges of this story of the Warsaw Ghetto were multiple and formidable. When issuing a book like *The Wall,* one likely to sell many thousands of copies, the temptation would have been to use lesser materials and thereby generate greater profits. In Knopf's system, however, this potential best seller was exactly the kind of book he believed ought to have a pleasing design. A "book sure to have a very large sale . . . carries the publisher's name to thousands of readers who might not ordinarily see it."[11]

What a reader saw in a typical Knopf book, though, was not determined by a particular house style or the singular aesthetic vision of its publisher; rather, the Borzoi imprint represented "an editorial system," one that gave significant latitude and responsibility to individual American book designers and that attracted some of the best talent in the field: William Addison Dwiggins, Warren Chappell, George Salter, Elmer Adler, Ernest Reichel, and Bruce Rogers. As an explicit mark of respect, each Borzoi book ended with a colophon detailing the typeface's history and crediting both designer and manufacturer. "So far as I know," George Salter wrote as late as 1965, "Alfred Knopf is the only book publisher in the United States who consistently gives credit to his designers, in promotion and in advertising." For such notice, the chosen designers were "expected to do their best for the greater glory of the book."[12]

Because of the importance of John Hersey to Alfred A. Knopf, Inc., and because of the firm's hopes for good sales of *The Wall,* there were in 1949 two obvious choices for the designer of the novel: W. A. Dwiggins or George Salter. Both men were among the most respected designers in the American book trade, at the height of their creative powers, and both had long-standing ties to the publisher. Each would bring to Hersey's novel a distinctive approach to bookmaking, yet the two men shared a fundamental principle: a book's design should begin from the inside and move outward.

While Dwiggins felt the text itself should determine such elements as typeface, page layout, illustration, and binding, he assigned little consequence to book jackets. He agreed with Alfred Knopf that such "wrappers" were overvalued by publishers, usually at the expense of what he considered the book's core features. George Salter, a founder in 1947 of the Book Jacket Designers Guild, which sponsored an annual exhibition of jacket art, naturally saw things differently. He believed book jackets posed unusual opportunities for commercial artists, opportunities even more challenging than the selection of type and binding design, ones with far greater impact on books' financial fates. "A good jacket can help sales," he argued; "a poor one can harm them."[13]

Knopf split design duties between these talents and philosophies, delegating the page and cover design to Dwiggins, the book jacket to Salter. Knopf proved his devotion to the author and, more importantly, to his belief that *The Wall* would be a work of great significance by bringing the talents of both men to bear on Hersey's novel. But in the hands of two such strong artists, the cohesive effect that the publisher desired would inevitably prove elusive. As if conflicting design emphases were not problem enough, the novel's subject—not yet known in 1949 as the "Holocaust"—posed its own serious challenges to an American reading public with little understanding of the Warsaw Ghetto and its significance.

An examination of the respective visions of Dwiggins and Salter for *The Wall*, then, will not only illustrate some of the best work in mid-twentieth-century American book design, but offer insight into how one major American publisher, barely five years after the camps had been liberated, was no more prepared than his anticipated readers to engage fully the aesthetic challenges of a novel purporting to address the slaughter of European Jewry.

Sidney R. Jacobs, longtime production supervisor for Knopf, recalled in 1965 how the firm's founder had been involved in all aspects of a book's production. "Every layout and design," he recalled, "every jacket design, every binding layout and setup and sample cover had to be submitted to Alfred for approval."[14] Knopf's desire, however, to oversee all phases of a book's development did not alter a fundamental house principle: the best results would be achieved by hiring the best people and then trusting them to do their best work. Knopf generally served less as a critic of the designs that passed across his desk than as a supporter, an enthusiast whose confidence in the talents of the people he employed seldom wavered. Nowhere was this kind of productive relationship more evident than in the three-decade association between Knopf and W. A. Dwiggins, which has been claimed "among the most influential in modern American tradebook design."[15]

William Addison Dwiggins began his career as a commercial artist in Chicago and worked there until 1904, primarily in advertising and lettering. In 1928 he published *Lay-Out in Advertising*, a text long held as standard in the field. After moving to Boston, he began to create some of the typefaces for which he would become best known, particularly Electra and Caledonia, but by the early 1920s had moved toward full-time book design. He had also begun his association with Alfred Knopf, first working on a limited edition of Stephen Crane's works and in 1926 creating the design for Willa

Cather's *My Mortal Enemy*. Of all the authors on his list, Cather was Knopf's favorite. He was so satisfied with Dwiggins's work on *My Mortal Enemy* that he commissioned him to design all of her subsequent books. Eventually, Knopf would retain Dwiggins as one of his firm's principal book designers.

Their relationship yielded some three hundred volumes, many among the most beautiful published in the United States between the wars. Dwiggins's memorable 1931 edition of H. G. Wells's *The Time Machine* warrants particular notice. Yet he refused to join the movement by many first-rate book designers toward private presses. "He had no patience with those who insisted on retaining hand processes in printing and publishing in the belief that they were inherently superior to machine processes," book historian Paul Shaw explains. Dwiggins's "principle concern ultimately centered on readers and their reading needs, esthetic as well as financial. [His] goal was to make books that were beautiful, functional, and inexpensive."[16] To that end, Dwiggins and Knopf shared a fundamental principle of design: the reader was central and deserved a page that was readable with, in Knopf's words, "a typeface that doesn't trouble the eye."[17] But for Dwiggins, readability was only one factor in the creation of an effective design. He stressed a "unity and harmony" engaging "all of the elements that comprise a book: paper, type, ornament, illustration, binding and endpapers, stamping, and, if possible, the jacket."[18] In all matters of book design, however, Dwiggins was governed by a single credo: "the text of the book is the thing for which everything else exists. In it are involved all the questions of paper, type, and page design. The design of the book begins here and works outward to the cover."[19]

The forbidding nature of *The Wall*'s subject, as well as its unusual archival format, especially tested the designer's talents. Correspondence during the summer of 1949 from the Knopf production head suggests another pressure—Sidney Jacobs wanted Dwiggins to work quickly: "In view of the importance of THE WALL, I am surprised that I haven't heard from you in answer to my letter of last week in which I asked whether you had any notations of the special problems involved so that we could go ahead with sample pages. Do let me hear from you immediately for it is imperative that all the details of the internal typography at least of this volume be established as quickly as possible."[20] The urgency of Jacobs's communication was due at least in part to the sense at Knopf that Hersey's book was not only important, but likely a best seller. That it was also a novel of some three hundred thousand words needing unusual formatting for its archival "entries" only added to the production manager's anxiety. Finally neither Jacobs nor Knopf was willing "to experiment on a book of such importance as THE WALL."[21] The result on the page was inevitably conservative. Because "legibility and readability" were main concerns, Dwiggins was encouraged to use one of his proven fonts, either Caledonia or Electra; he settled on the latter (figure 1).

Dwiggins once claimed that the inspiration for Electra came to him in a dream, in which a "Japanese scribe Kobodaishi instructed him to avoid the re-creation of classic faces and, instead, to design a face that reflected the twentieth century, a face that was full of electricity."[22] Despite the tongue-in-cheek nature of this story from 1935, when the font was first introduced, it does reveal Dwiggins's desire to infuse the spirit of the modern with human warmth. "If you don't get your type *warm*," he replied to his Japanese specter, "it will be just a smooth, commonplace, third-rate piece of good machine technique—no use at all for setting down warm human ideas—just a box full of rivets."[23]

The colophon for *The Wall*, however, eschews wit for a more straightforward declaration of Electra's qualities: "The Electra face is a simple and readable type suitable for printing books by present day processes. It is not

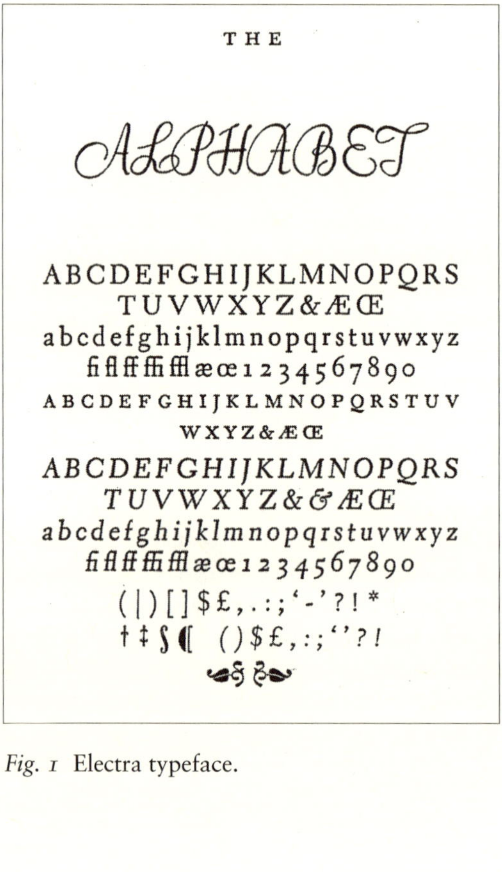

Fig. 1 Electra typeface.

based on any historical model, and hence does not echo any particular time or fashion. It is without eccentricities to catch the eye and interfere with reading—in general, its aim is to perform the function of a good book printing-type: to be read, and not seen."[24] A more technically illuminating account of Electra was offered in 1948 to readers of Willa Cather's *The Old Beauty and Others:* by avoiding "the extreme contrast between 'thick' and 'thin' elements that mark most modern faces," Electra does not stop the reader's eye; instead, this readable typeface strives for "a feeling of fluidity, power, and speed."[25]

Noted book designer Warren Chappell wrote that Dwiggins "understood better than most how to get a meaningful touch of the human spirit past the machines," which a typeface such as Electra demonstrated most clearly.[26] That Hersey's novel recounted the plight of humanity ensnared by inhuman forces must have made the type choice seem all the more apt. Electra seemed the font best suited to provide a human face in the midst of mechanized destruction.

For Dwiggins, selecting a suitable typeface was only the first challenge. His next problem was posed by the design oddities of Hersey's narrative approach, which, as Sidney Jacobs noted even before sending on the first part of the manuscript, consisted of a series of chapters broken into "entries." Styling these would require careful consideration: "I think everything depends on the handling of the opening pages of each section and the Entry headings." Jacobs added to his plea for thoughtfulness another prompt for speed, asking that Dwiggins send along his instructions *"immediately."*[27]

Although Dwiggins's layout choices pleased both Jacobs and Knopf, his design for *The Wall* seems austere, even uninspired. Commenting in 1935 on his work for *Lucy Gayheart,* Dwiggins noted that Cather volumes necessarily restricted what he could do on the page. His explanation of the cause provides a concise view of his general stylistic approach: "The nature of [Cather's] text required that any *variety* that might be expected to give (typographic) sparkle to the pages needed to be contrived with extreme simplicity—out of bits of brass rule, say; and by placing the 'service' elements—page numbers, titles, etc.—with care to make pleasant patterns."[28] Among other "pattern-making devices," he listed such examples as the amount of white space separating text and service elements and the relative thickness of a given brass rule, features he believed the "typography-fancier" at least would appreciate.

Still, for those who favor innovative typographic design, the pages of *The Wall* will largely disappoint (figure 2). The intricate ornamentation for which Dwiggins was much esteemed is entirely absent, nor are there printing devices such as rules or borders to separate the many entries and chapters. Instead, the book's design depends on a subtle use of white space and nu-

> THE WALL
>
> house. The S.S. police had surrounded the house, and had eventually forced an entrance through a rear cellar door, using tear gas and machine pistols. Yitzhok said he had posted Pavel at a second-storey front window, to observe and snipe if possible. When the Germans broke into the house, Yitzhok had yelled to Menkes and the other lookouts to join the core of the group on the third floor. Menkes had been shot from behind while running upstairs.
> Rachel: —— Not exactly a hero's death.
> Yitzhok: —— He did what he could.
> Rachel: —— Did he seem to be afraid?
> Yitzhok: —— He was rather afraid. He seemed rattled—not thinking very clearly. I believe that if he had started up immediately when I called. . . . They tell me that the idea of surrendering to the column before opening fire was his. . . . He was confused in the house; quite muddled. I don't know what his trouble was. . . .
> Rachel: —— Poor Pavel! He wanted so much to be brave.
>
> ## 6
>
> EVENTS JANUARY 18, 1943. ENTRY FEBRUARY 12, 1943. FROM DOLEK BERSON. As Berson picked up the telephone in the hotel lobby to make his morning report on the eighteenth, he says he thought: In ten days I will have been on the Aryan side exactly three months. That is nearly enough. I will ask to be allowed to return to the "village." [NOTE. N.L. Couriers' slang for the ghetto.] Three months is enough time to be in an alien town on this kind of work.
> The operator asked for the number.
> Berson: —— One one—four seven—three two. . . . Correct.
> One becomes nervous and careless, Berson says he thought. And very soon, he thought, his chemical experiment, his student's game, would be completed and either successful or a failure. On the other end, the phone rang and rang, and Berson waited for the familiar, high-pitched, fussy voice of Gribbenes. He pursed his lips and listened to the ringing.
> No! Something queer! On the other end, a harsh, deep voice:
>
> 458

> PART FIVE
>
> —— Na! Hallo! . . . Wer spricht? . . . Hallo! Hallo!
> A German. Gribbenes not answering. Something wrong. Berson hung up without speaking. A man waiting to use the phone looked at him oddly.
> Berson, in Polish, with a disgusted expression: —— This damned service. Nothing but wrong number, wrong number every time.
> Later, Berson and Rutka were talking together in the "false room," behind the double wall in the girls' apartment. Rutka was lying on a mattress on the floor. She was obviously pregnant now. She complained of pains in her back, and she said that when she walked her pelvic bones seemed to grind together; her skin was extremely dry, and she kept scratching herself.
> Berson: —— It might have been a wrong number, but I doubt it. The operator had repeated the number back to me correctly. I certainly wasn't going to take the chance of calling back again. I hate to miss a talk with Gribbenes. It happened once before, another Jew answered and said Gribbenes was sick. . . . But this time: the phone rang so long, and then to have a German answer! I'm sure it was a German. No Jew would have sounded like that.
> Rutka: —— Marysia got a rumor in town today that one could hear shooting in the village this morning.
> —— Where did she hear that?
> —— She didn't say.
> Berson, speaking like a hurt boy: —— How *could* they start without letting us know?
> Rutka: —— Our dear little pistols!
> Berson, questioning himself as much as Rutka: —— What do you suppose it's like?
> Rutka: —— It's better here behind a double wall. Even with a sore back.
> Rutka had been wonderful, Berson says. She had been outside now about nine weeks. She had acquired nearly thirty weapons. She had worked steadily, and seemed to have just as much energy as Berson, if not more. She had helped Berson with the "experiments," and had, in fact, solved the chemical problem: she had made a contact with a worker in a fertilizer plant who had agreed to supply her with potassium chloride smuggled from his factory; this could be reduced by electrolysis to the potassium chlorate that Berson hoped to be able to use in his instrument.
>
> 459

Fig. 2 The Wall (1950): Page design by W. A. Dwiggins.

merals to produce a format reflecting the austerity and regimentation of life in the Warsaw Ghetto. Much like the wall itself, the two-page layout with centered titles (top) and page numbers (bottom) frames or encloses the text's action, the events upon which the Levinson Archive is built. And by delineating each dated "event" with a combination of space and small caps, Dwiggins creates a visual effect that makes the entries seem like notebook or diary pages, a decision very much in tune with Hersey's original conception of the Levinson entries as fragments "from the archivist's notebook."

Perhaps the most fortuitous decision Dwiggins made in arriving at his page design for *The Wall* was to use oversized numerals to indicate new chapters. "Hersey has no strong feelings about the use of the word 'chapter,'" Jacobs reported in response to initial sample pages, "and says that it can be eliminated if you would prefer to do so."[29] Dwiggins could also decide whether to employ Arabic figures instead of spelling out the numbers. The book designer underlined both comments in the letter from Jacobs. Whether or not bold numerals present the kind of typographic "sparkle" that Dwiggins sought, they do a great deal to further the illusion that *The Wall*'s sections are the rough archival materials for a history, rather than chapters formalized in a novel.

Another problem Dwiggins faced in bringing the Levinson archive to life on the page was Hersey's decision to indicate dialogue with dashes rather than quotation marks. Although Jacobs called the practice "somewhat in the French fashion," he advised the book designer to precede each piece of dialogue with a long 2-em dash followed by a space. Jacobs's advice produced the most distinctive typographic feature in the novel (figure 2). Those dashes, twice the usual width, add an air of further historical veracity to the book, as if one were reading the transcript of a legal deposition rather than conversation among fictional characters.

When *The Wall*'s page design was finally settled, Jacobs communicated one last typesetting complication: some twenty or thirty times in the book Hersey had his "editor" use a Star of David as "an identifying symbol," a cross-referencing device to indicate which sections had been supplemented with information from interviews conducted after their entry dates. Levinson undertook the later interviews on 8–9 May 1943, and they shape the last section of the novel in which he and a small group of ghetto survivors wait in a sewer for a truck to take them to the Lomianki Forest. Jacobs told Dwiggins that he could not find any samples of the star in standard specimen books, learning after "a devil of a time" that "only once in the last fifty years was a Star cut, and then only in the 8 point size."[30] Fortunately, this single type form worked well with the book's 10-point Electra.

For a graphic artist like Dwiggins who had dedicated his life to bringing human warmth to the mechanical processes of modern typesetting, printing, and binding, the story of this solitary type form must itself have seemed like the recovered archive of Hersey's novel. The Star of David certainly remained in his mind as he turned his attention from page to cover.

As noted, Alfred Knopf and W. A. Dwiggins shared a vision of the mass-produced book and how it should attend to its readers' aesthetic and economic needs. Initially, their views on book covers seem at odds with those general principles. Most readers (and publishers, for that matter) considered the less-expensive jacket as the crucial piece of external packaging and gave little thought to cloth bindings. Yet both men saw the cloth cover as *the* lasting face the book would carry to future generations of readers. Knopf, in fact, did not even consider the jacket part of the book itself. "It's a label," he said, "a silent salesman, a protection for the too often unlovely object around which it is wrapped."[31] The publisher well knew that his was a voice in the wilderness, that most of his peers spent little time or money on the design and production of their bindings. "Most publishers who bind their books handsomely must do it simply because they want to, because it gives them pleasure" and they want "in making the physical book" to match the pride an "author takes in perfecting his text."[32] Knopf concluded that "a good-looking and well-made book will never do its author any harm anywhere at any time. And it may do him some good."[33]

Of course Dwiggins, the graphic technician, was most concerned with *how* to achieve bookbinding ideals. Like Knopf, he noted that typical book covers were inferior products, but he saw this situation less as a bow by publishers to economic pressures than as an absence of vision. "The jacket has dragged all interest away from the cloth cover," he declared, "because all effort had to be fed into getting the book sold—but there is a duty to the householder, too, who has the book kicking about his/her living room after he/she buys it." Even if books were becoming "ephemera," much like magazines, he wanted "to make them pretty while they live."[34]

Dwiggins believed the main impediment to producing attractive cloth covers was the mechanical process itself. While the modern book was well printed and well made, when it came time to "putting the title on it, and what decoration you want—*with ink*—the process falls down with a roar." Ink stamping "discounts all the good work that has gone before—turns the good sewing and backing and cloth into a bundle of junk—because it is a technique on a level far below the other techniques that precede it."[35]

For Dwiggins, the challenge of stamping designs on book covers was a tactile one, a matter of making them pleasing to the hand as well as to the eye. Surfaces stamped in ink, he felt, had a "negative tactile quality," as if the paint would come off on one's fingers. The only technique "that *adds* quality to the values achieved in the process before stamping is stamping in metal or blind. This added value comes from the light reflected from the edges of the depressed areas, in metal stamping; and from the enriched, changed surface in blind."[36] He would employ both techniques in creating a cover for *The Wall*.

Dwiggins also had distinctive ideas about which colors and combinations worked best in book design, ideas not always well received by Knopf's staff. "I like Far East color combinations," he wrote in a letter to Alfred Knopf, "a chutney-sauce effect with lots of pepper and mustard and spices, odd harmonies that make you sit up." Such effects could best be produced by combining flat cloth colors with precise metal foil stamping, rather than in making multiple passes with different inks. This process avoided the "shiny, painty effect that is inevitable when you try to get a light ink on a dark cloth."[37] Despite his occasional advocacy of paste-on labels as a possible way to create attractive covers ("I have been beating my brains to devise some new approach to ink-stamping that would have style"), Dwiggins resigned himself to relying on die-cut stamps. "The beauty of metal stamping," he wrote, "is sharp finish and the glitter of sharp-stamped edges."[38] But producing such dies depended upon "the die-cutter and the designer working together," as the designer's visual idea had to be translated into an actual tool that would imprint the cloth. "I have never wanted a *facsimile* result," he told Knopf, "but of course all that means that the die-cutter needs to know as much about the fine points of his craft as the designer does."

But, as his page design for *The Wall* had been conservative, so would be the cover's. "Chutney-sauce colors" found no place in Dwiggins's approach to the book's cloth binding. Hersey's novel would likely sell many thousands of copies, so Dwiggins could not push too far beyond the known limits of available techniques, and he relied on a combination of familiar metal and blind stamps. Working within the practical limitations, though, Dwiggins's final cover design was both subtle and memorable.

Because Dwiggins derived his ideas from only the opening sections of the novel, its first page may have had particular resonance. The "Editor's Introduction" recounts the postwar return to the ghetto's ruins by a group of survivors intent on retrieving the Levinson Archive. All that remains of the ghetto, besides the Genisia Street Jail, is the eight-foot wall that had sealed in Warsaw's Jews, its top encrusted with "bits of prohibitive glass."[39] The novel's editor reports Rachel Apt's description: "the walltop sparkled that day in the summer sun, with glints of amber and blue and green." This image of sparkling glass seems to have spoken to the designer and found its way into the Dwiggins color scheme—a bluish-green, with gold stamping on the spine. The muted shade of the green cloth causes a curious effect: the lettering, when viewed face-on, shines from the spine, but fades when seen from an angle. This interplay of blue, green, and gold/amber echoes the wall image from the novel's opening scene and would also find its way into George Salter's jacket design.

As effective as he was with color, Dwiggins's greatest talent as a designer of book covers had been in his stamping of unusual geometric ornaments on a book's spine. For *The Wall,* however, he chose a representational approach, one visually striking though incongruent with the book's subject. Stamped in gold beneath the title and author's name is a figure of three castle-like towers with arched windows and battlements, the crenellated style associated with old European cities (figure 3). Indeed, the ornament gives no accurate impression of the novel or its moment. Viewing the book on a shelf, a browser might assume *The Wall* to be historical romance, complete with knights and ladies, battles and sieges.

The front cover presents more nuanced and suggestive graphic imagery (figure 4). Using a rather shallow blind stamp, Dwiggins echoes the spine's castle towers more abstractly. Instead of using figures, he depicts battlement

Fig. 3 The Wall: Spine design by W. A. Dwiggins.

walls of varying dimensions, each with distinct styles, and creates a multilayered effect, its perspective reminiscent of landscape painting or theater scenery. The isolated castle imagery of the spine translates into overlapping rooftops of an old European city viewed from below.

The predominant element in this cover design, though, and the figure most easily distinguished from the squarish wall images, is a large Star of David in the foreground. That only a single 8-point-sized figure had been cut for the Linotype machine in half a century may have impelled Dwiggins the graphic artist to create one of his own. Much of the cover's attractiveness derives from the star's presence, particularly its size and the way it seems to float, as if beginning to rise above the city wall. The apex of Dwiggins's star draws attention to the unusual battlement above which it seems to rise. Unlike the other rooftop imagery on the cover, this nearest wall is capped by a series of closely spaced posts or spikes that evoke confinement rather than protection. It becomes a striking visual analogue to the actual wall that entrapped Warsaw's Jews and gave Hersey's novel its title.

Fig. 4 The Wall: Front cover design by W. A. Dwiggins.

Reading Dwiggins's cover guided by the novel and its historical context can be especially rewarding. As the symbol of the Jewish people, the Star of David (or Maggen David) is not only a powerful visual representation in itself, but one that had a topical and rich meaning in 1949. When adopted for the flag of the new state of Israel a year earlier, it had been transformed into a sign of renewal from the recent symbol of brutal Nazi occupation and murder. One of the first decrees imposed upon the Jews of Warsaw, after all, had been the mandatory wearing of armbands with the Star of David in the center.[40] Nearly all surviving photographs of the ghetto's residents show them wearing these brassards. Some images even portray people trying to earn a meager living by selling armbands. Whether by design or coincidence, the star Dwiggins created for his cover is roughly the same size as the ones Warsaw Jews had been forced to wear.

The lasting achievement of Dwiggins's cover results from his use of the shallow blind stamping to evoke the Warsaw Ghetto's story. On even the finest extant copies of *The Wall* the cover design is faint, requiring deliberate attention to recognize its pattern. Worn volumes, however, display what Dwiggins no doubt anticipated in choosing to stamp so shallowly. The faded images, like the destroyed city of Warsaw, like its once-thriving Jewish population, leave only the barest of traces.

In some of his best work for Knopf, such as his editions of Cather or of Mencken's *The American Language,* Dwiggins had designed all elements of the books, including the jackets. He acknowledged the importance of these "wrappers" for promotions and sales, but was only satisfied aesthetically when creating jackets that allowed him to employ his "arsenal of strange 'geometric' ornaments" and "unusual color, savage color, strong lines put together in unexpected combinations."[41] By the late 1940s Dwiggins had largely given up on the jacket as part of his designs. "About jackets in general," he wrote to Alfred Knopf, "they don't give me any joy. I'd be glad if you could manage to do all the jacketing in N.Y. and let me spend my efforts on the books inside."[42] For *The Wall,* then, Knopf turned to an artist in New York who at the time was considered not only the strongest and most influential advocate for jacket design, but one of its finest practitioners—George Salter.

Where both Knopf and Dwiggins regarded jackets as distinct from a book's physical make-up, a form of advertising that even interfered with the designer's primary task, George Salter regularly asserted the jacket's exciting possibilities. He had initially worked on set designs in Germany during the Weimar years, producing his first jacket in 1927 and devoting himself thereafter to book graphics and to teaching at the renowned Graphic Arts Academy in Berlin. In March 1933, however, he was banned by the Nazis from further work as a commercial artist and declared a person "incapable of being a trustworthy and responsible member of the profession." The son of assimilated Jews who had converted to Lutheranism, he stopped teaching after a student pulled a knife on him and challenged his "racial" qualifications for the position. Nineteen months later, in November 1934, Salter arrived in the United States and, despite knowing no more than ten English words, quickly resumed his career as a designer, eventually teaching for thirty years at the Cooper Union.[43] Already by 1952 one history of American bookmaking declared that in "the jacket field, no one person has done more, by example, as a patient teacher, both of his students and his printers, and by stubborn refusal to cut corners, than George Salter."[44]

Despite book jackets' modest beginnings in the nineteenth century as temporary protections for book covers, publishers soon recognized and exploited their advertising possibilities. Even so, most serious book designers well into the mid-twentieth century continued to resist their aesthetic possibilities. In one history of American book jackets between 1920 and 1950 Steven Heller and Seymour Chwast note that as late as 1947 the prestigious "Fifty Books Show," sponsored by the American Institute of Graphic Arts, "adamantly refused to exhibit jackets," causing artists such as Salter to form the Book Jacket Designer's Guild.[45] Heller and Chwast admit that much jacket work before 1940, especially on "tawdry" paperbacks, was second rate; but the growing influence of Salter and other European-inspired designers resulted in a move from illustration to design, from the sentimental to the analytical.[46] And as Charles Rosner notes in *The Growth of the Book Jacket,* such work demanded graphic sophistication: "For in a space that on the average is little more than six inches by eight inches it has been necessary to convey visually, by word or design, the feeling and character of a book which often may run into four or five hundred pages."[47]

Salter believed the book jacket played a unique role in the world of commercial art. Unlike other "industrial products which utilize graphic communication, it represents a world of abstract images in contrast to concrete goods."[48] A book, at least a good one, "goes inside your mind, educates, widens your spiritual contentment," he argued; yet he also understood how high were the stakes for publishers and authors: a book's jacket, Salter believed, was indeed its "most potent selling factor," one that put "great responsibility" on the artist.[49]

Throughout his career as a designer and teacher, Salter both espoused the book jacket's possibilities and offered a practical methodology for fulfilling them. Like Dwiggins in his philosophy of page design, Salter put the needs of potential readers at the forefront of all design decisions. "An analysis of the book in decorative or plain form doesn't matter," he said in a lecture at the Cooper Union, "but it should show contents. Through honest jacket interpretation, the reading public should know the kind of books it is examining."[50] Unlike Dwiggins, however, who was content to design after having perused only part of a manuscript, Salter argued that a designer must reject summaries or "blurbs" provided by others and "be in direct contact with the book." He had to read all of it, either from manuscript or galley pages. He described the jacket designer as "a reader with a talent to express graphically what he reads for the use of others," one who had to "subject himself to the book, and not superimpose himself" on it. And despite economic temptations to reproduce a signature style, the designer should treat each project as a singular problem. "No designer can supersede the manuscript and make it a tool for his own notions."[51]

The task Salter faced in creating a jacket for *The Wall* was complicated by several factors. First, his design was created in isolation. There was no consultation between him and Dwiggins. Indeed, the two men disagreed on the fundamental importance of their respective roles. Where Dwiggins saw the jacket as mere advertising, Salter saw the binding as only decorative in nature. He declared that the cover "should take its influence from the book jacket" and, in a memorable analogy, claimed a book's cover as a dermis underlying the jacket, its epidermal surface greeting readers.[52] Second, the novel's subject matter created a strong temptation to produce a "lurid" design—the kind of imagery condemned by Hersey when his *Life* magazine article on the liberated Klooga camp used drawings of Nazi victims that could have been illustrations from the world of pulp fiction.[53] Most formidably, Salter was faced with an enormous book, one filled with dozens of characters ensnared by the traumas of contemporary history.

The design finally rendered by Salter in fact did result in the kind of tonal clash he felt was inevitable when jacket and binding were done by two different artists. Nevertheless, Salter's was the work of an artist who had internalized the spirit of Hersey's epic novel. Unlike his memorable 1937 jacket for Franz Kafka's *The Trial*—an image of Joseph K in a courtroom surrounded by a group of faceless, shadowy jurors and litigants—Salter chose to avoid approaches illustrating scenes from *The Wall*. Instead, he created a complex image employing both realistic and metaphoric elements, a category of design that "elicits the atmosphere of the book" by using "symbolic or psychological imagery."[54] To evoke the rich thematic layers of Hersey's "novel of contemporary history," Salter focused on contrasting, even conflicting, color schemes.[55]

Salter's overall design is disquieting (figure 5). A square, red-brick enclosure is thrust from the streets of a European city we only glimpse. Two sides of the walls are brightly colored, but the most predominant, the one facing the viewer, is darkened, the white mortar between its bricks dulled, even smudged out. The sharp angularity of this dominating rectangle contrasts

Fig. 5 The Wall: Book jacket design by George Salter.

with the detailed pen-and-ink sketched buildings of the surrounding city. The brick edifice's intense reds and dark browns draw the eye away from the pastels of the marginalized cityscape and the bright blue of its sky. Enclosed within the three sides of the brick structure, but flowing off the page and toward an unseen fourth wall, is a mélange of yellows, golds, tans, and browns. Were the bricks of the walls not clearly evident, the yellowish mass might seem the contents of a treasure box.

Spanning the upper part of the longest section of wall—and across three-quarters of the entire jacket design—is a chain of outlined human figures. Although men and women, children and old people can be discerned among the greenish outlines, they are ultimately transparent, ghostlike. At the bottom right of the jacket, drawn in clear white outline, is a figure in a chair, wearing eyeglasses, hunched over and writing on a notepad—Noach Levinson.

However visually arresting the jacket's design might be, what Salter termed its "selling factor" depended upon it working "in *conjunction with* the copy on the flap." If "a bookstore customer is struck by the mood or atmosphere suggested in the jacket design, he will want to turn to the flap copy to find out more."[56] Here is what a curious browser in the spring of 1950 would have read about *The Wall*, "A Novel by John Hersey, author of *A Bell for Adano* and *Hiroshima*": "On the surface THE WALL is the story of the systematic piecemeal extermination of the Jews of the Warsaw Ghetto, and the heroic resistance of defenseless men and women against the full brute force of the Germans. But the real story is the growth in spirit of a group of friends, so that they emerge undismayed and triumphant in the face of physical annihilation" (figure 6). Of course, this commentary by Knopf draws the potential reader's attention back to the jacket, to the line of people chalked on the wall. Many represent the group of friends central to the novel, "The Family." The drifter, Dolek Berson, holding his concertina, stands on the right slightly separated from the group; Rachel Apt, the fighting group leader, wears bandoleers and grasps the hand of a man holding a rifle; then a host of major and minor characters populate the lineup: an older woman wearing a shawl; a husband-wife-son-group, the parents engaging in serious conversation; other family groups; two religious Jews with beards; a weak child being helped up from the ground. (figure 7). These figures outlined in a tarnished copper color appear etched into the dark wall, as if part of a bas relief commemorating the Jews of the Warsaw Ghetto. In fact, a male figure with his right arm crooked (just left of center and near the weak child) is strikingly reminiscent of the Mordechai Anielewicz sculpture central to Nathan Rapoport's noteworthy monument that had been erected in Warsaw a year and a half earlier in 1948 (figure 8).

After evaluating early jacket proofs, Salter instructed that the group he termed ghost figures should "have somewhat the color of tarnished copper" and that this "decidedly greenish" color should be in marked contrast to the "clear white" of the Levinson image at the bottom (figure 9). He further advised the printer that this latter "key character of the book should have almost solid black around him so that he would come out very clear."[57] Throughout his career Salter used a "visual vocabulary" of outlined figures "for rendering imagined or recalled characters, such as the dead."[58] By outlining his Levinson figure in white, then, Salter distinguishes him from the posed group in green, seeming emanations from the archivist's memory or his notebook; at the same time he indicates that the archivist shares their state as ghostly figures. Levinson, we are told in the "Editor's Introduction," did not live to see the recovery of his precious trove of documents.

Salter's design invites further attention to its memorial nature. His earliest instructions to the printer concerned the slice of blue sky in the upper right, which contrasts sharply with the "blood red" of the bricks. The color tension between the peaceful cityscape and the ominous wall collapses timeframes by alluding to the earlier state of the entrapped Jews, who had endured misery in the midst of a Warsaw where life continued almost normally. Their situation is memorably described in Czeslaw Milosz's "Campo di Fiori," a poem Hersey has Levinson recite at one point in *The Wall*.[59] The great Polish poet recounts children riding a carousel and adults

To reveal the full stature of man in the face of catastrophe, John Hersey has used a classical literary device—the rediscovery of lost records. For even though THE WALL is ostensibly culled from "the Levinson Archive," it is a novel. Its substance is history, but its details are invented. It transmutes the record of vast tragic events into a great work of the imagination.

On the surface THE WALL is the story of the systematic piecemeal extermination of the Jews of the Warsaw ghetto, and of the heroic resistance of defenseless men and women against the full brute force of the Germans. But the real story is the growth in spirit of a group of friends, so that they emerge undismayed and triumphant in the face of physical annihilation

What makes this novel so exciting is its universality. The author is interested primarily in separate individuals—Jewish, Polish, German—in people. And so his novel is built out of separate revelations of motive and impulse and actual deed. It probes events in terms of individual responsibility, human values, and personal decisions. It presents characters weak as well as strong, shameful as well as heroic, craven as well as pitiable, sordid as well as sublime, but in the end it becomes a mirror of the preponderant nobility and durability of man.

THE WALL transcends all John Hersey's other work. It is without doubt one of the truly great novels of our generation.

JACKET DESIGN BY GEORGE SALTER
TYPOGRAPHY AND BINDING BY W. A. DWIGGINS

Fig. 6 The Wall: Front flap of book jacket.

Fig. 7 The Wall: George Salter's "Ghost Figures."

Fig. 8 Nathan Rapoport's "Warsaw Ghetto Monument" (1948).

strolling in their Easter Sunday best outside the wall of the burning ghetto. By the war's end, however, nearly all of Warsaw had been decimated. Salter's frame image of an idyllic European city signifies a past that had been overwhelmed by modern barbarity, by the smoke-stained wall raised from its heart.

A bright counter to the looming wall is the puzzling yellow mass that it

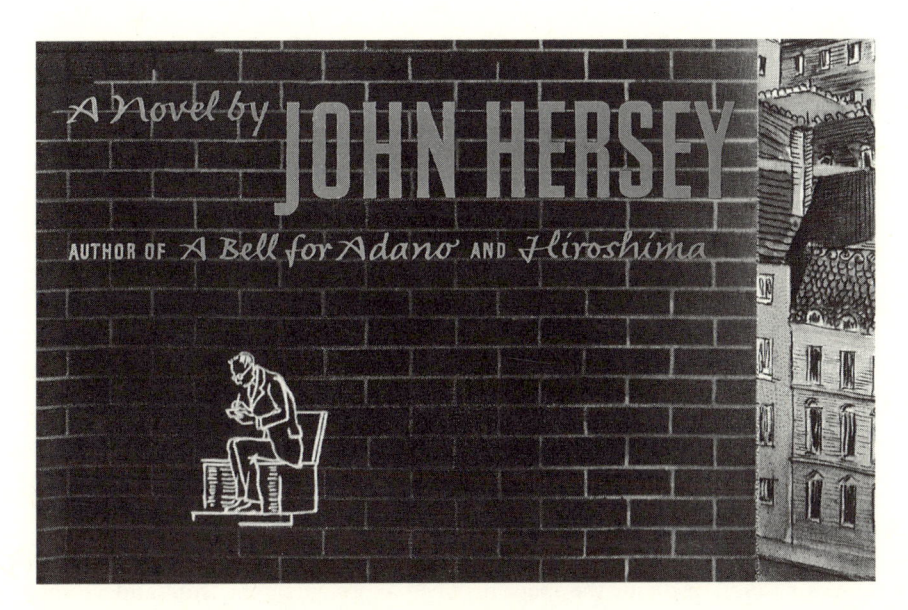

Fig. 9 The Wall: Close-up of Noach Levinson figure.

encloses, a seeming hoard of treasure in a scarred strongbox. According to Salter's notes, it is intended to represent the ghetto ruins. This "rubble area," he told the printer, needed strengthening. "The overall effects of that area should be sulfur + mustard and should be aggressively unfriendly," he said. "It is now too soft." He also hoped that the black plate could be adjusted to "model heights and depths, especially in the rubble area."[60] Salter's stated desire, that this section of the jacket convey the unfriendliness of the ruins, remained unfulfilled, the least realized part of his design. Nevertheless, the bright rubble field echoes the opening pages of the novel, however inadvertently. The "Editor's Introduction" recounts the unearthing of the Levinson Archive from Warsaw's rubble and suggests that viewing the ruins as a precious site is perhaps appropriate. "Two days' digging," we are told, "brought up the whole treasure."[61] However much Salter's printers gave the rubble field too much sparkle, the Levinson Archive is certainly a buried treasure.

Hersey was especially pleased with Salter's design, saying in a letter of 10 October 1949 that it was "a superb conception," one he was certain would help sales of the book.[62] He was less comfortable, though, with the inevitable advertising material that filled the jacket's flaps. Writing a few weeks later to Harold Strauss, he asked whether an author's biography would be necessary. "I feel very strongly that the kind of cereal an author eats for breakfast, together with a photo showing him clamped grimly to a pipe—all that is quite irrelevant. All that matters is what the man has written."[63] Hersey clearly wanted readers to encounter his fiction on their own terms. Strauss persuaded him, however, that his experience as a war correspondent in Poland was certainly information relevant to readers: "any statement you may care to make about your first encounters with survivors of the Warsaw Ghetto all have an important bearing on THE WALL."[64] What Hersey provided for the back flap was a statement that simply outlined the novel's origins: "While based in Russia, Hersey went with other correspondents into Poland and Estonia after those countries had been liberated by the Russians. At that time he saw the ruined Warsaw ghetto, the Lodz ghetto, and a number of concentration camps, and these drew his attention to the circumstances that became the background for *The Wall*." Resistant to writing "blurbs" for other authors, Hersey was even more adamantly opposed to their use on his own books. Over the next four decades, designs for virtually all of his subsequent book jackets either utilize the entire front and back, as with *The Wall* and the memorable 1987 Wendell Minor composition for *Blues,* or divide the space between an image on the front and a large author portrait on the back. Any promotional prose was forced onto the inside flaps. For *The Wall* Strauss convinced Hersey that a major statement over the signature of Alfred A. Knopf was in order (figure 6).

Just five years after the war's end, the Knopf staff knew that the American reading public could easily be put off by a long novel on a "grim" subject, even one written by a celebrated author. Yet Alfred Knopf was an astute enough businessman to recognize that Hersey's renown would dispel many fears that *The Wall* would prove depressing. "*The Wall* transcends all John Hersey's other work," his statement concluded. "It is without doubt one of the truly great novels of our generation." Hersey was comfortable with the first sentence, believing indeed that the novel had been his best work so far, certainly in the area of fiction. Knopf's concluding sentence, however, made him uneasy. "I'd like to ask you and Alfred to reconsider with care that last sentence," he wrote to Strauss. "Much as I would like to believe it, I think it is open to debate in more than one respect, and while it is clearly a 'publisher's claim,' I wonder whether these jacket blurbs do not gain force from understatement and from leaving to the reader the opportunity of deciding for himself."[65] But Knopf chose not to revise the last sentence. It appeared just above his signature, ready copy for newspaper and magazine advertisements.

Of more consequence than the concluding "publisher's claim," however, is the summary written by Strauss and Knopf (with significant advice from Hersey). Hoping to entice prospective readers, they also strived to present with dignity what they viewed as a major novel of the era. Beginning in bright red type with a tag line that would be quoted in subsequent publicity (figure 6)—"To reveal the full stature of man in the face of catastrophe"—the description first notes that Hersey uses a "classical literary device," the "rediscovery of lost records," and then points out to readers that while the book's "substance is history," its "details are invented." As if to assuage any qualms readers in 1950 might have about a novel of human catastrophe—for that matter, one dealing with the "piecemeal extermination of the Jews of the Warsaw ghetto"—the opening paragraph concludes that the author "transmutes the record of vast tragic events into a great work of the imagination."

A need to focus on the "endurance" or "full stature" of men and women in the face of disaster was, of course, at the heart of Hersey's responses to ghetto and camp survivors, but the Knopf statement so emphasizes the triumph of human resiliency that even the heroic resistance of the Warsaw uprising becomes secondary to the "growth in spirit of a group of friends" who "emerge undismayed and triumphant in the face of physical annihilation." However much one might dispute this view of the novel's conclusion, clearly Knopf, his staff, and perhaps even Hersey, felt a need to soften the book's darker aspects. The jacket description only hints at them in a paragraph about the work's "universality," in which its characters are said to be "weak as well as strong, shameful as well as heroic, craven as well as pitiable, sordid as well as sublime." Nevertheless, the publisher's statement—signed by a man who had always downplayed his own Jewishness in favor of cultural elitism—reiterates that the book is most importantly about the "preponderant nobility and durability of man."

This type of idealistic, even naïve, interpretation of the ghetto's life and death must have affected W. A. Dwiggins. There is no evidence that he read beyond the novel's first 150 pages, so he would not have encountered the harrowing central section detailing the great deportation of July–August 1942, when nearly three hundred thousand of Warsaw's Jews were murdered at Treblinka. Thus Dwiggins's cover design, with its shallowly stamped Jewish star and the spine's glittering gold towers, remains a sign of hope, consonant with the publisher's view of the book and anticipating a line that would reverberate in the ears of Broadway audiences five years later at the conclusion of *The Diary of Anne Frank*, when Anne's voice intones, "In spite of everything, I still believe people are really good at heart."

Unlike Dwiggins, George Salter had read all of Hersey's novel with great care. He even caught a host of errors. But Salter had also endured Nazi oppression firsthand, and his jacket design seems implicitly to reject Knopf's words on the front flap, or at least to counter them. Rather than emerging "undismayed and triumphant," the book's characters in his visual conception endure, like their archivist/chronicler, only as ghosts. As chalk-scrawled images on a smoke-stained wall.[66]

"How has the Holocaust been interpreted through an American ideological framework?" This question was posed by Hilene Flanzbaum in her introduction to an important 1999 collection of essays on a range of Americanized Holocaust responses, from the poems of Sylvia Plath to the plays of Arthur Miller, from Art Spiegelman's *Maus* to Steven Spielberg's *Schindler's List*. "Have artifacts of American culture," she wonders, "approached the true horror of the event?"[67] More than a decade before, in 1983, John Hersey had engaged similar questions as he considered his motives for writing *The Wall* thirty-five years earlier. "I had no thought," he recalls, "but to try to break through the appalling ignorance of the fate of the Jews in Europe which I found all around me in America." *The Wall*, he said, by "being very early in opening up to the American consciousness what had happened during the Holocaust," had been something of a "revelation" to American readers, helping them "to understand things they hadn't understood before."[68] Between the trade and Book-of-the-Month-Club editions, a half million copies of *The Wall* had been sold, the novel was short-listed for the Pulitzer Prize and the National Book Award, and nearly six decades after its first publication, remains in print. Even so, Hersey admitted that "much more authentic works" had subsequently been produced by Holocaust survivors like Elie Wiesel and Primo Levi, giving American readers a deeper, more lasting understanding of the destruction.[69]

The group of Americans who worked together in 1949–50 to bring *The Wall* to a postwar reading public was, finally, not very different from that public itself. Alfred Knopf, W. A. Dwiggins, Harold Strauss, John Hersey himself, were all influenced by a tendency to Americanize depictions of the Holocaust and its implications. Such a perspective, Alvin Rosenfeld argues, considers the destruction of Europe's Jews as "a terrible event, yes, but ultimately not tragic or depressing; an experience shadowed by the specter of cruel death, but at the same time not without the ability to inspire, console, uplift."[70] Only George Salter, the refugee who had escaped the very real prospect of "cruel death" under Hitler's rule, seemed to understand the ultimate inadequacy of this American faith. His ghostly figures, which hover over the blackened bricks, serve as tokens of resistance but also of memory. Set against the looming smoke-stained wall, however, they are ephemeral, the barest traces of a Europe Salter had actually known.[71]

Notes

1. Alfred A. Knopf, "The Borzoi Credo," in *Portrait of a Publisher 1915/1965*, vol. 1, *Reminiscences and Reflections by Alfred A. Knopf* (New York: The Typophiles, 1965), 28.

2. Alfred A. Knopf, "The Economics of Book Design," in *Portrait of a Publisher*, 1:82–83.

3. John Hersey, "A Full-Length Man," in *Portrait of a Publisher 1915/1965*, vol. 2, *Alfred A. Knopf and the Borzoi Imprint: Recollections and Appreciations* (New York: The Typophiles, 1965), 214.

4. John Hersey, "The Mechanics of a Novel," *Yale University Library Gazette* 27 (July 1952): 4.

5. Alvin H. Rosenfeld, *A Double Dying: Reflections on Holocaust Literature* (Bloomington: Indiana University Press, 1980), 66.

6. Oneg Shabbat (Sabbath delight) was a clandestine archive guided by historian Emanuel Ringelblum that collected notes, diaries, and documents detailing the Warsaw Ghetto's life and death, evidence that would outlive nearly all its assemblers. Before the destruction of the ghetto in 1943 the archive was stored in metal containers and milk cans, then buried in three disparate sites. On 18 September 1946 survivors of the ghetto dug through its ruins and unearthed one cache. Four years later, on 1 December 1950, the second part of the buried archive was recovered. Despite many searches, the third has never been found. During his research and writing of *The Wall* Hersey had heard "only the vaguest rumoring" about Ringelblum and Oneg Shabbat. "I had learned that there had been such a man," he recounted in 1983, "and that an archive had been buried, and that was all." Nevertheless, it was this sketchy awareness of Ringelblum, the novelist said, that inspired him "to use the device of the archive, and to give my story to Levinson to tell" (*To Invent a Memory: John Hersey's* The Wall [Baltimore: Baltimore Hebrew University, 1983], 16–17). The facts of that story were all based on "a tremendous amount of material about Warsaw and the other ghettos written in Polish and Yiddish, diaries, records of organizations, letters, statistical data, medical histories, poems, plays, songs—all sorts of testimony" ("Mechanics of a Novel," 5). Knowing neither Polish nor Yiddish, Hersey called upon two knowledgeable translators and was especially fortunate in this respect, employing as his Yiddish expert the young Lucy Dawidowicz, who would become a foremost Holocaust scholar, publishing among many works her acclaimed *The War against the Jews 1933–45* (New York: Holt, Rinehart and Winston, 1975).

7. "A Short Wait" was written late in 1946 and published in *The New Yorker* on 14 June 1947. The story fictionalizes the arrival in America of Luba Steiner, a survivor of the Lodz ghetto whose experiences were based on those of Ilsa Hoffman Stern, a Czech woman Hersey had interviewed in Lodz after the Germans had fled. Yet his first literary attempt to engage the Holocaust seems overly reticent, distant from its traumatic sources. Not as graphic or sardonic as some of his articles for *Life*, "A Short Wait" offers only a few details regarding conditions in the ghetto; instead, the narrative focuses on Luba's conflicted feelings toward her American relatives.

8. Hersey, "Mechanics of a Novel," 5.

9. John Hersey, *The Wall* (New York: Alfred A. Knopf, 1950), 6.

10. Lawrence Langer, *Admitting the Holocaust* (New York: Oxford University Press, 1995), 158.

11. Alfred A. Knopf, "A Publisher Looks at Book Design," in *Portrait of a Publisher*, 1:86.

12. George Salter, "There Is a Borzoi Style," in *Portrait of a Publisher*, 2:281–82.

13. George Salter, "Book Jacket Lecture Notes" (1951), George Salter Collection, TS, series 2, box 2, folder 10, The John M. Wing Foundation, The Newberry Library, Chicago.

14. Sidney Jacobs, "Alfred and Designers," in *Portrait of a Publisher*, 2:284.

15. James M. Wells, "Book Typography in the United States," in *Book Typography 1815–1965 in Europe and the United States of America*, ed. Kenneth Day (Chicago: University of Chicago Press, 1966), 361.

16. Paul Shaw, "Tradition and Innovation: The Design and Work of William Addison Dwiggins," in *Design History: An Anthology,* ed. Dennis P. Doordan (Cambridge: MIT Press, 1995), 34, 35.

17. Knopf, "A Publisher Looks at Book Design," 1:85.

18. Shaw, "Tradition and Innovation," 33.

19. Quoted in Shaw, "Tradition and Innovation," 33.

20. Sidney Jacobs, letter to W. A. Dwiggins, 21 July 1949, W. A. Dwiggins Collection, Boston Public Library.

21. Sidney Jacobs, letter to W. A. Dwiggins, 15 July 1949, W. A. Dwiggins Collection, Boston Public Library.

22. Shaw, "Tradition and Innovation," 40.

23. Quoted in Sebastian Carter, *Twentieth Century Type Designers* (New York: W. W. Norton, 1995), 68–69.

24. Hersey, *The Wall,* 634.

25. Willa Cather, *The Old Beauty and Others* (New York: Alfred A. Knopf, 1948), 168.

26. Warren Chappell, "WAD: 1880–1980," in *A Tribute to W. A. Dwiggins on the Hundredth Anniversary of His Birth* (New York: Inkwell Press, 1983), 23.

27. Sidney Jacobs, letter to W. A. Dwiggins, 29 July 1949, W. A. Dwiggins Collection, Boston Public Library.

28. W. A. Dwiggins, "Designer's Note" in Willa Cather, *Lucy Gayheart* (New York: Alfred A. Knopf, 1935), p. 234.

29. Sidney Jacobs, letter to W. A. Dwiggins, 25 August 1949, W. A. Dwiggins Collection, Boston Public Library.

30. Sidney Jacobs, letter to W. A. Dwiggins, 1 September 1949, W. A. Dwiggins Collection, Boston Public Library.

31. Knopf, "A Publisher Looks at Book Design," 1:87.

32. Ibid, 1:85–86.

33. Ibid, 1:87.

34. W. A. Dwiggins, "Color for Bookbindings," in *A Tribute to W. A. Dwiggins*), 14.

35. Dwiggins quoted in Alfred A. Knopf, "Dwig and the Borzoi," in *Portrait of a Publisher,* 1:106.

36. Ibid., 1:107.

37. W. A. Dwiggins, "Color for Bookbindings," 13–14.

38. Quoted in Knopf, "Dwig and the Borzoi," 1:105.

39. Hersey, *The Wall,* 3.

40. Levinson describes this November 1939 regulation in an entry of 12 December 1939, a section that was among the pages sent to Dwiggins: "All of them wore the newly obligatory arm-bands, bearing the Star of David" (Hersey, *The Wall,* 53).

41. Knopf, "Dwig and the Borzoi," 1:113.

42. Ibid., 1:113.

43. Thomas S. Hansen, *Classic Book Jackets: The Design Legacy of George Salter* (New York: Princeton Architectural Press, 2006), 12–26.

44. Hellmut Lehmann-Haupt, *The Book in America: A History of the Making and Selling of Books in the United States* (New York: R. R. Bowker Company, 1952), 296.

45. Steven Heller and Seymour Chwast, *Jackets Required: Illustrated History of the American Book Jacket Design, 1920–1950* (San Francisco: Chronicle Books, 1995), 9.

46. Ibid., 16.

47. Quoted in Heller and Chwast, *Jackets Required,* 9.

48. George Salter, *George Salter: A Third of a Century of Graphic Work* (New York: Gallery 303, 1961), unpag.

49. George Salter, "Designers of Book Jackets: I—George Salter," *Publishers' Weekly*, 1 March 1952, 1096.

50. George Salter, "The History of the Book Jacket," Lecture, George Salter Collection, TS, series 2, box 2, folder 8, The John M. Wing Foundation, The Newberry Library, Chicago.

51. Salter, "Designers of Book Jackets," 1096, 1098.

52. Salter, "Book Jacket Lecture Notes."

53. See John Hersey, "Prisoner 339: Klooga," *Life*, 30 October 1944, 72–83. Hersey explained some of his discontent with the *Life* illustrations in a letter to his wife of 9 February 1945: "But the overwhelming thing is the impression of the Germans. I just do not know what or how to write to get across what those people are capable of doing. I'm positive that American readers simply will not believe those things. Some people right here in Moscow have told me that they had a hard time believing the Weintraub story from Talinn. . . . I've tried to understate what I've written about it, but after LIFE gets through dressing it up with those lurid drawings I'll bet it will seem as if that Hersey had been writing fiction again. Americans ought to hurry up and understand about the Germans: I'm convinced now that they're just as bad as the Japs, if not worse" (John Hersey Collection, Beinecke Library, Yale University).

54. Hansen, *Classic Book Jackets*, 12.

55. In approaching the jacket design for Hersey's book, we are fortunate to have the preserved color separations and test runs, as well as Salter's annotations and specific printer directions. These documents, housed at the Newberry Library, enable us to view Salter's various attempts to translate the world of *The Wall* onto an 8-by-13.5-inch space.

56. Salter, "Designers of Book Jackets," 1096.

57. George Salter, color separation proofs, George Salter Collection, series 4, job 816, box 23, The Wall (1949), The John M. Wing Foundation, The Newberry Library, Chicago.

58. Hansen, *Classic Book Jackets*, 40.

59. Hersey, *The Wall*, 249–51. Although Hersey has his character recite the Milosz poem at a literary gathering on 5 June 1942, a month before the first deportations to Treblinka, the verse was in fact composed in 1943 during the Warsaw Ghetto uprising.

60. Salter, color separation proofs.

61. Hersey, *The Wall*, 5.

62. John Hersey, letter to George Salter, 10 October 1949, George Salter Collection, series 4, job 816, box 23, The Wall (1949), The John M. Wing Foundation, The Newberry Library, Chicago.

63. John Hersey, letter to Harold Strauss, 28 October 1949, Alfred A. Knopf, Inc. Records, box 49, Harry Ransom Humanities Research Center, University of Texas at Austin.

64. Harold Strauss, letter to John Hersey, 28 October 1949, Alfred A. Knopf, Inc. Records, box 49, Harry Ransom Humanities Research Center, University of Texas at Austin.

65. Hersey, letter to Harold Strauss, 24 October 1949, Alfred A. Knopf, Inc. Records, box 49, Harry Ransom Humanities Research Center, University of Texas at Austin.

66. Seeing the ghost images in Salter's design as chalk outlines perhaps illustrates how perceptive a reader he was of Hersey's novel. Early in the opening chapter the archivist Levinson recounts his first meeting with Dolek Berson, who reports on a scene he had witnessed on a Warsaw street: "A small boy darted, as quickly as if he had just committed a theft, from the south to the north side of the street, from the shady to the sunny, stopped abruptly by a high, windowless, brick wall, twisted to one side with the agonized, almost crippled stance of a boy reaching for something in a packed pocket, whipped the something out, and, with four or five bold strokes, used it to draw a picture on the wall" (Hersey, *The Wall*, 17). After the boy flees, Berson sees the image he has left behind: a cartoon of Hitler with, "across the face, insultingly, dismissingly, a huge X."

67. Hilene Flanzbaum, ed., *The Americanization of the Holocaust* (Baltimore: Johns Hopkins University Press, 1999), 6.

68. Hersey, *To Invent a Memory*, 10.

69. Jonathan Dee, "The Art of Fiction XCII: John Hersey," *Paris Review* 100 (1986): 247.

70. Alvin H. Rosenfeld, "The Americanization of the Holocaust," *Commentary* 99 (June 1995): 37.

71. After Salter's death in 1967 Knopf wrote in a letter of condolence on 2 November: "There are some books which, without his help, would have taken a great deal longer to make the public grade. And there were others, like 'The Wall' and 'The Last of the Just' that seem to have been written so that George could design them." (quoted in Hansen, *Classic Book Jackets*, 40). Salter designed the jacket for a 1960 translation of André Schwarz-Bart's *The Last of the Just*, now considered a classic of Holocaust literature.

The Women in Print Movement

History and Implications

Trysh Travis

Writing ten years ago in the newsletter of the Society for the History of Authorship, Reading, and Publishing, Leslie Howsam observed a fascinating tautology shaping the field of book history. Scholars looking to understand the human agency that animates the communications circuit through which books take on life, Howsam noted, had discovered "women at every node of the cycle and at all periods in history, from the printers' widows operating independently of the craft guilds of early modern Europe to the avid readership of romance novels." Unlike older fields, whose entrenched chauvinism meant that their gaze had to be wrenched off of men and onto women, book history had a certain level of gender consciousness built in to it. The result was scholarship that cataloged, even celebrated, "outstanding anomalies in a cultural field dominated by men." But the effect of this attention to exceptional women, Howsam argued, was counterintuitive. Ultimately, it reaffirmed the degree to which "what [Lucien] Febvre and [Henri-Jean] Martin called 'the little world of the book' has been a male domain." Laudable attention to the presence of women had not translated into a feminist book history.[1]

Howsam's brief analysis demonstrates one of the essential insights of feminist scholarship: talk about women is not necessarily talk about gender as a form of power that structures and delimits experience.[2] Some key works of book history, of course, do pay that kind of attention to gender—Janice Radway's *Reading the Romance* (1984), Cathy Davidson's *Revolution and the Word* (1986), Kate Flint's *The Woman Reader, 1837–1814* (1995), Nicola Thompson's *Reviewing Sex: Gender and the Reception of Victorian Novels* (1996), to name just a few, explore the way that reading both reflects and helps to constitute not merely gendered identities, but a whole social order. Similarly, books like Mary Kelley's *Private Woman, Public Stage* (1984), Susan Coultrap-McQuin's *Doing Literary Business* (1990), and

---

Special thanks to Kristen Hogan, Leon Jackson, Kristin Matthews, and Tim Wilson for tactical and conceptual help with this project. Leila Adams and Mark Fenster offered unflagging encouragement and moral support.

Catherine Gallagher's *Nobody's Story: The Vanishing Acts of Women Writers in the Marketplace* (1994) center on questions of gender and power; all explore the ways women authors have negotiated access to the public sphere by toying with the gender roles and expectations that help constitute a fundamentally male-centered world.

Interestingly, however, this canon of what we might call a feminist book history concentrates primarily on women readers and authors, not on the workings of the communications circuit that transforms manuscripts into books and brings them to market. While books by Sharon Harris, Jayne Marek, and Patricia Okker have explored the way ideas about gender informed the work of women periodical editors in the nineteenth and early twentieth centuries, we have yet to see comparable scholarship on how gender norms—for men as well as for women—have shaped editorial practice within book publishing.[3] And while there have been studies of women papermakers, binders, and printers, they have been fairly strict in their historical focus—finding evidence of women's presence, reconstructing their work and relationships, writing them into the record. The desire to document women's presence in the book trades has meant that attention to gender as a form of power has usually been limited to noting that the trades were male-dominated.[4] A review of the literature on women in publishing confirms Leslie Howsam's thoughtful insight: excepting some canonical works on female reading and authorship, book history scholars have done an exemplary job of locating women, but lagged behind when it comes to theorizing gender.

To address this imbalance, this essay offers an account of the Women in Print Movement, a group of late-twentieth-century "bookwomen" whose labor in the realm of print production was intimately connected to their analysis of how gender and power shaped "the little world of the book."[5] A product of Second Wave feminism, the Women in Print Movement was an attempt by a group of allied practitioners to create an alternative communications circuit—a woman-centered network of readers and writers, editors, printers, publishers, distributors, and retailers through which ideas, objects, and practices flowed in a continuous and dynamic loop.[6] The movement's largest goals were nothing short of revolutionary: it aimed to capture women's experiences and insights in durable—even beautiful—printed forms through a communications network free from patriarchal and capitalist control. By doing so, participants believed they would not only create a space of freedom for women, but would also and ultimately change the dominant world outside that space.

Scholars of feminist and lesbian history have documented some aspects of this multifaceted movement, focusing on its most visible and durable institutions, feminist bookstores and publishers.[7] In this essay I build on their work by first tying bookwomen's interest in controlling the means of print production to the larger intellectual history of radical feminism, then fleshing out the picture of the movement as a whole by detailing the workings of two of the small organizations that constituted it: a printing collective, the Women's Press Project/UP Press, and a retailing newsletter, the *Feminist Bookstore News*. These less-than-glamorous institutions linked the publishers and the retailers that authors like Simone Murray, Katheryn Thomas Flannery, Kristen Hogan, and Junko Onosako have written about, and demonstrate the degree to which the various points on the feminist communications circuit were united by common ideological commitments. By way of conclusion, I argue that participants in the Women in Print Movement instantiated the kind of critique of gender and power within "the little world of the book" that Leslie Howsam has argued is lacking within book history—a critical angle of vision that will be increasingly important to book historians as the field moves beyond its original grounding in the modern societies of the West and tries to reckon with the diverse printed materials of both non-Western and postmodern cultures. As such, the movement deserves attention not merely as an important piece of history, but as a reservoir of ideas and practices that may help scholars to grapple with the complex power dynamics of postindustrial global print culture.

Women in Print: Theory and Practice

The Women in Print Movement precipitated directly out of radical agitation for "women's liberation," a variety of feminist activism that flourished in North America and western Europe in the early 1970s. To understand the movement's aims and strategies, therefore, we must situate it in the context of this broader feminist movement. The social and political formation generally referred to as Second Wave feminism (to distinguish it from a First Wave of women's suffrage activism) began in the post–World War II period. Changing economic and social norms in the wake of the war put more women in the U.S. workforce than ever before, and prompted a growing discontent among middle-class white women with the constraints of domestic life—a discontent expressed powerfully in Betty Friedan's 1963 bestseller *The Feminine Mystique*. The success of Friedan's work gave added impetus to a broad-based reform movement focused on issues of gender equity and access—to educational and workplace opportunity, the political process, and the public sphere. The development of this liberal feminist impulse among white middle-class women was paralleled by the growth of a more radical strain of thinking about gender and politics, one informed by the civil rights and New Left movements. Focused on the idea of revolution, rather than reform, activists in this tradition conceptualized the power differential between the genders as a systemic and structural problem. Improved access to the workings of power—via education, workplace, representation in governance, and so forth—would not change the fundamentally unjust nature of "sexual politics," defined by author Kate Millet as "the birthright priority by which males rule females." What was necessary was not merely female enfranchisement but "women's liberation"—a total dismantling of the "sex-class system" through which white, heterosexual, middle-class, First World, capitalist men ensured their enduring dominance.[8]

Until this radical restructuring of the patriarchal world order was achieved, some feminist activists advocated withdrawal from mainstream society into women-only cultural enclaves. These separatist feminists—both sexual and "political" lesbians—believed that women needed to dissociate themselves as completely as possible from the male-dominated world and its structures of "heterosexual privilege," which prompted women to ally with men and against one another in the quest for money, power, and status.[9] Re-centering life within women-centered collectives would enable individual women to "overcome patterns of behavior that reflected . . . their internalized hatred of women."[10] In addition, it would create new economic units, shifting both production and consumption patterns to benefit a women's culture that was artisanal, sustainable, and human-scale—a culture that would challenge and ultimately replace the rapacious global corporate culture created by and associated with men. Simultaneously working to change the economic organization of society and the contents of its culture, separatist feminists and their allies created a variety of institutions—from women's music festivals and art cooperatives to health and legal service clinics.[11] The institutions of the Women in Print Movement were a part of this culture.

Feminist activists had been creating a print culture through broadsides, pamphlets, and other rough-and-ready publications for some years, but Katheryn Thomas Flannery has argued that in 1968 "an identifiably separate feminist press" emerged from the movement, in the form of collectively created and produced journals like *Voices from the Women's Liberation Movement, Lilith,* and *No More Fun and Games.*[12] These pioneering publications generated momentum, and by 1973, 560 feminist periodicals had emerged from the women's movement, including newsletters, newspapers, and magazines and journals.[13] A handful of book publishers—Shameless Hussy (1969) and the Women's Press (1970) in Oakland, California; the Feminist Press (1970) in New York; Diana Press (1972) of Baltimore; and Daughters, Inc. (1972) of Plainfield, Vermont to name just a few—also appeared around this time. As these publishers spread the message of liberation and separatism through both precept and example, women printers, publishers, bookstores, and distributors began to emerge to support them. The appearance across the nation of these like-minded outposts of feminist print culture led participants to begin to see themselves as part of a full-fledged movement, and they gathered to celebrate and strategize that sense of collective purpose at a weeklong get-together in August of 1976, the First National Women in Print Conference. The venue was a Campfire Girl campground near Omaha, Nebraska, chosen in part for its gynocentric resonances, and in part because it was deemed "as close to the center of the country as [was] practical."[14]

The principal organizer and theorizer of the conference was June Arnold, an independently wealthy former debutante, author, and activist, and publisher and founder of Daughters, Inc. Although the conference "was June's baby," she was assisted and informed by several other women who worked in print culture and formed a de facto brain trust for the Women in Print Movement: Charlotte Bunch, founder and editor of *Quest: A Feminist Quarterly*; and Coletta Reid of Baltimore's Diana Press.[15] Bunch and Reid (along with, among others, Daughters, Inc., author Rita Mae Brown) had both been members of the Washington, D.C., radical feminist group The Furies, and the conference bears the distinctive mark of the ideas the collective had propounded—about lesbian vanguardism, women's need for control of media outlets, and the relationship between learning skills and theorizing feminist identity—before it dissolved in 1972.[16] Although they solicited input from would-be conference-goers, Arnold and this post-Furies group defined the theoretical terms that would structure the Nebraska conference and inform the practice that followed from it.

This agenda setting is evident in June Arnold's earliest communications about the conference. After attending the Bay Area women's press meeting in early January of 1976, Arnold sent out a letter to "every known indepent [sic] women's press, journal, bookstore, or distributor in the United States" urging them to come together to "share skills and problems . . . and strengthen our political network of feminist communication." She proposed a highly structured meeting with a set schedule of workshops; each organization could send only two representatives, who had to have been working for them since at least 1 January of 1976. Invitees were advised not to mention the conference to people outside the Women in Print community.[17] As responses to her initial mailing came in, Arnold further refined the terms for inclusion: no white women's publishing concern that included men—either as artists or production workers—would be included, although "Third World feminists working on Third World projects with men" would be allowed to participate.[18] In addition, attendance would be limited strictly to women working in print media, despite the presence of "terrific feminists in radio, video, and various other oral and verbal forms of communication."[19] Authors were also excluded because, as one participant noted later, "we were very influenced by Marxist ideas about laborers controlling their own labor [and] didn't [want] to put writers on a pedestal."[20] The result was a gathering of 132 women, representing 80 organizations from every non-authorial sector of the communications circuit. A *Library Journal* article noted afterward that "a dedication to the printed word and a commitment to publishing the words of women" united the participants.[21]

Beneath this garden-variety "dedication" and "commitment," however, was a quite specific, two-pronged political vision. Its first premise was the assumption (nascent in much radical feminist culture but developed especially within The Furies collective, as Anne Valk has shown), that feminist theory—accurate ideas about what women are and where they are situated within the structures of power and culture—develops in concert with and as a result of women's development of practical skills. Drawing on ideas circulating both within the American New Left and among anti-imperialist struggles for ethnic self-determination abroad, this quasi-Maoist position held that women should learn manual and technical skills in order to empower themselves and, more important, to raise their revolutionary consciousnesses. This knowledge would free them from their dependence on—and hence, exploitation by—the men who typically monopolized the industrial and craft sectors of the economy; taking literal control of the means of production was one more way for women to gain control of their identities and claim their places in the world. From this premise followed the belief that the simultaneous development of women's heads and hands was necessary to prevent a divisive split between radical theory and practice. Without a conscious blurring of the lines between manual and mental labor, feminists risked recreating among themselves the hierarchies of class, intellect, power, and so forth, that they were committed to eradicating.

Memoirs and biographies suggest that many of the skilled printers involved in the Women in Print Movement originally entered the trade for bread-and-butter reasons, and the fact that print shop work paid better than many "pink collar" jobs remained an important motivator, as the case of the Women's Press Project, described below, makes plain.[22] But the Nebraska conference included workshops on such topics as "Style Sheets Used," "General Ledger Bookkeeping," "Setting Up a Shipping Room," and "Building Our Own Light Tables" in part to forestall intellectualization and specialization. It was with this theoretical aim in mind that Arnold constructed a schedule routing conference participants to "skills" sessions in the mornings and "politics" sessions in the afternoons.[23]

This vision of a dialectical relationship between skills and politics was the "how" of the Women in Print Movement: by embracing and working the dialectic, movement participants would create both a revolutionary women's culture—one that made all women theorizers of gender—and a revolutionary print culture—one that undid the specialization and professionalization that had characterized printing and publishing since the early modern period. The movement's "why"—implicit in the conference sessions and articulated in writing leading up to it—was the belief that feminists needed to create their own print networks because the traditional, male-dominated media were at best untrustworthy and, more likely, were engaged in active attempts to undermine women's interests. The same belief had prompted the founding of the feminist periodical press in the late '60s. As women's media activist Donna Allen explained, a mainstream media looking to maximize shock value and hence sales purveyed an *"image* of women that too often is derogatory, restrictive, and inaccurate."[24] It is ironic, then, that Women in Print activists sought a separatist book culture for precisely the opposite reason—the fact that trade publishers had begun to take feminism more seriously.

The early '70s had seen a flurry of feminist bestsellers. Robin Morgan's anthology *Sisterhood Is Powerful,* a mass-market paperback brought out by Random House in 1970, sold three hundred thousand copies its first year and was named "one of the hundred most influential books of the 20th century" by the American Library Association.[25] Closer to home, Rita Mae Brown's *Rubyfruit Jungle* (1973), originally published by June Arnold's own Daughters, Inc., had sold "close to 100,000 copies" before the press sold the rights to mass-market house Bantam Books. The novel went on to become a national bestseller.[26] In 1975 author and activist Susan Brownmiller scandalized the radical feminist community by accepting $250,000 from Simon and Schuster for the paperback rights to her bestselling *Against Our Will: Men, Women, and Rape.*[27] To radical eyes, authors like these, whose books and business dealings crossed over into the commercial mainstream, were sell-outs, and the established houses that bought and promoted their works mere cynical trend mongers. Together, they seemed poised to destroy the nascent feminist print culture just coming into being across the country and, in so doing, to roll back the social changes that it both argued for and embodied.[28]

In the feminist periodical press, Women in Print activists stated these beliefs in the most emphatic terms. Feminist media were important, Charlotte Bunch pointed out in *Heresies,* "not 'just because the boys won't print us.'" Quite the contrary, she explained, "today they will print us [but] for money, *not* to advance feminism."[29] Writers who ignored this fact were guilty, the publishers of the journal *Sinister Wisdom* argued, of "seduction and betrayal." "*Every genuinely feminist work of art is a blow at the heart of patriarchal reality.* When lesbians control our own publishing and our own printing and our own distributing of our own words, we're directing those blows to the target."[30] Conversely, when they did not exercise that control, they allowed patriarchal reality to thrive.

In an article leading up to the Nebraska conference, June Arnold made a similar argument, fusing the maleness of traditional publishing with the industry's move toward international multimedia conglomeration to create a monolithic patriarchal-global-capitalist bogeyman. Writing in Bunch's journal *Quest: A Feminist Quarterly*, she described the "Madison Avenue publishers [who are] now owned by . . . Kinney Rent-a-Car, Gulf and Western, and RCA," as "the hard-cover of corporate America, the intellectuals who put the finishing touches on patriarchal politics to make it sell." Comparing the creation of a viable feminist print culture with women's fight to gain legal access to abortion, she proclaimed, "in 1970 we marched wearing aprons which read: Is this uterus the property of New York State? In 1976 we should wear headbands which state: My words will not be sold to 'his master's voice.'" Would-be authors had a special duty to avoid cooptation by mainstream publishers, which Arnold referred to as "the finishing press" because "it is our movement they intend to finish."[31] The depth and breadth of this hostile environment, Women in Print activists argued, meant that feminists needed not merely a room, but an entire print culture of their own if they hoped to communicate among themselves and spread their ideas to a larger public.

Women in Print activists, then, were motivated by more than a simple "dedication to the printed word and a commitment to publishing the words of women." While organizations like Donna Allen's Women's Institute for Freedom of the Press worked to open the mainstream media to women, the denizens of the Women in Print movement had little interest in such reformist schemes. Their interests lay not merely in women, but in gender politics and the modes of capitalist production that underpinned them. Women would never be truly free unless they first seized ownership of the means of cultural production and then restructured and de-hierarchicalized that production, liberating the written word from the material regime that had grown up to enforce the oppressive epistemological and moral structures of capitalist patriarchy. Achieving those goals at the base was a necessary part of creating a liberatory superstructure—a writing and culture that would represent, interpellate, and liberate *all* women. The creation of such institutions was underway, and the Nebraska conference celebrated the fact that their growth and ultimate triumph were practically assured—provided they were not diluted by "seduction" or "betrayal."

Such was the position theorized by participants in the Omaha Women in Print conference of 1976; memoirs, biographies, and archival materials reveal the ways that the women who attended identified themselves with these high-minded goals. Even as they embraced the theory, however, they struggled to put it into practice. The ways in which they negotiated the gap between separatist feminism's utopian vision and the workaday routines of print practice testify to the diversity and creativity that thrived within the larger movement—even as they demonstrate the stubbornness of the patriarchal capitalist enemy that it sought to unseat.

The Women's Press Project and UP Press

The organization that came to be known as the Women's Press actually predates the Nebraska Women in Print Conference by some years.[32] It began as two distinct entities, UP Press and The Women's Press Project (WPP), each located in the San Francisco Bay Area and founded in the early 1970s; UP and the WPP merged into the Women's Press in 1984 before folding in 1987.[33] Both institutions (and the later, merged entity) embodied and enacted the lesbian separatist impulse described above: collaboratively owned and operated by women only, they prioritized printing women's work; flattening of workplace hierarchies; partnership with, rather than exploitation of their clients; and a break-even financial model. They came to this embrace of Women in Print ideology, however, in different ways. In their archival materials, at least, neither group has much to say about lesbian identity or community as such; rather, they focused primarily on economic critique and empowerment, elaborating different strains of the expansive anti-capitalism common among '60s-era radical organizations. Their focus was less on securing the means of lesbian/feminist cultural production than on making the printed word accessible to a variety of people—including, but not limited to women—whose access to it had historically been limited by race, class, and educational background.

UP Press was an offshoot of the Bay Area People's Union (the name "UP" inverts the initials of "People's Union") founded in 1972 as a "movement press," a collective, no-profit endeavor dedicated to providing low-cost, high-quality printing to progressive organizations "at a time when the need for propaganda [is] growing."[34] Originally located on "The Land," a countercultural community in the Palo Alto Hills, the press moved first to Redwood City and then to East Palo Alto in 1974. The collective originally consisted of both men and women and defined itself against the "straight press" of mainstream capitalist America, which, they believed, "prints anything . . . has no interest or personal connection with the movement. . . . Must keep up the wages, the front. Has no incentive to cut corners for movement work . . . [and] only perpetuates what has existed in the past.

Will not lead to new solutions to old problems." By contrast, a movement press "prints work it is committed to politically; encourages rather than discourages political action [and makes] the staff . . . an integral part of the movement." Shared political commitment, the UP collective hypothesized, would make the movement press economically as well as ideologically viable: "The staff works for subsistence wage. By concentrating on movement work, expensive sales promotion activities and 'front' can be avoided."[35]

After a split within the collective "in which two men left and took quite a bit of valuable equipemtn [sic] with them," UP became a "women's shop" in 1974; representatives attended the Nebraska conference.[36] In addition to "business cards, leaflets, small books, and posters up to 17 x 22", they printed the nonracist and nonsexist children's books of New Seed Press, a women's publishing collective; *Gaia's Guide,* a lesbian travel guide compiled by Sandy Horn; and the instruction manual/erotica guide *Loving Women,* by the Nomadic Sisters collective of Sonora, California.[37] UP preferred printing women-centered work, and hoped "to see more feminist work coming into our shop," but framed its mission more broadly. A flyer from 1979 explained that "our first priority is to print for political groups." Moreover, they admitted that "in order to remain self-sustaining we do a lot of work for alternative groups and non-offensive commercial businesses."[38]

Further north, the Women's Press Project began as a vocational class offered through the Women's Skills Center in San Francisco's Mission District in 1975. The Skills Center closed in 1976, but the printers (all women) continued to teach as volunteers; over the next several years, funded by a federal CETA grant, they formed a volunteer collective that aimed to teach women the skills of the printing trade in a supportive environment.[39] All the collective members had full-time jobs elsewhere but saw their teaching as an important form of feminist activism, especially because it served as a form of outreach to minority, working-class, and previously incarcerated women.[40]

Originally, the WPP took on printing jobs simply to underwrite the costs of their educational mission, but in 1980 they became a business as well as a school. The shift toward full-time printing, collective members believed, would help to further the political agenda embodied in their skills teaching, and they focused on printing material for feminist and progressive community groups. At a meeting intended to prompt critical self-reflection, Project members noted that "in contrast to an ice cream parlor or hair cutting place, printing is a media device which can potentially be used as a political tool, i.e., getting out the message."[41] By offering reasonably priced, high-quality work to the people of the Mission (in the early '80s a low-income, predominately Latin and African American neighborhood) as well as to lesbian/feminist organizations, the project sought to further its broad-based progressive agenda. A document circulated at the board meeting laid the issue out plainly:

> Getting the message out is an integral part of any political effort. There have been instances of commercial shops refusing to print lesbian and feminist publications. We must maintain control over this area of our lives. Further there is the issue of providing quality work for people irrespective of their material resources.... At the Women's Press Project the staff takes the time to discuss peoples' jobs with them; to correct copy and layout and figure out the cheapest way to produce attractive materials. Additionally, people are not put in the vulnerable position of presenting their work to a commercial enterprise which is not supportive of their efforts. This involves labor which often goes unnoticed and a sense of security upon which a dollar value cannot be placed.[42]

While they expressed themselves in a slightly different language than the revolutionary patois of UP Press, the WPP also saw themselves working in conscious opposition to an exploitative mainstream—one characterized by class and race divisions as much as by gender inequity.

Both UP and the WPP members worked from the assumption that a matrix of "interlocking systems of oppression," not a monolithic and all-powerful patriarchy, was responsible for the inegalitarian system in which they lived and worked.[43] Their institutional histories—UP's association with the People's Union and the WPP's origins in adult education—informed this belief, as did their day-to-day practice. Workers saw themselves as the allies and teachers, the partners and servants of their diverse communities—and they acknowledged that without connections to such heterogeneous communities they would lack sufficient revenue to stay afloat. In these ways, both organizations diverged from the pure version of lesbian separatism that formed the theoretical heart of the Nebraska conference.

Despite this key difference, however, the Bay Area print shops clearly saw themselves as part of a dedicated and oppositional lesbian feminist world. The all-woman shop was the most visible embodiment of that oppositional identity, as it "raises the consciousness of the community at large [when] a man ... walks into the shop and asks, 'where's the boss?'"[44] Not merely women's workplaces, the shops were feminist public spaces structured to be free from the discrimination and harassment that many members had suffered in male-owned and operated businesses in the past. Perhaps most important, collective members worked consciously to reject what they deemed to be the masculinist values and logics of the market, and to replace them with tolerant, flexible, non-hierarchical, and hence empowering labor practices.

Thus the collective aimed to reward its members with the pleasure of collaboration and commitment, not the increased authority or money that were hallmarks of the capitalist economy. Subsistence wages were the norm, and while some division of labor and specialization took place over time, the principles of "worker control [and] skills sharing" remained a bedrock value, as did explaining to community members how to print things more cheaply or even do some aspects (stripping, paste-up) of a job themselves.[45] Workplaces were structured to tolerate high degrees of personal idiosyncrasy and the collective members' varied schedules. UP Press noted in a 1977 advertisement seeking a new collective member that "work days are flexible, both as to days and hours [and] vacations, and sick days are taken pretty much at will, (but not with pay)."[46] Two years later, a similar advertisement noted that "we pay ourselves $300/month, negotiable. We plan to increase this, but haven't gotten around to it yet."[47] Such labor practices were intended to counter the fact that, as Women's Press collective members ruefully noted, "trying to operate a business within the context of a capitalist system will require us to plug into that system to a large extent." But "experimenting with and implementing alternative working relationships," they continued, "AS IF we were living in an egalitarian society is part of the revolutionary process."[48]

Living "as if," however, proved challenging. One UP Press collective member captured the difficulty of maintaining a non-hierarchical, skills-sharing workplace when she told an interviewer that "it is often difficult to maintain the balance between teaching someone the trade and keeping the business open at the same time."[49] Similarly, a 1981 application for assistance from San Francisco's Community Training and Development Project noted that collective members were frustrated by the fact that "it takes more time to show a volunteer how to do something than to do it themselves." The flexible and anti-hierarchical approach to workplace participation resulted in wildly varying levels of commitment and professionalism, which in turn created "tension and resentment."[50]

Those feelings were exacerbated during the 1980s by changing external circumstances. UP and the WPP merged in 1984 with the hope of reducing operating costs and expanding output, but their plan coincided not only with an increasingly chilly political climate and rising rents brought on by gentrification, but also with the growth of low-cost, high-quality photocopy shops, which drained away the market for traditional offset printing. As the economy constricted, tensions escalated. Members met in 1985 to try to address "how to deal with differences in power and trust created by some workers choosing to have a more limited role in running the shop and by others assuming more overall responsibility."[51] The result was a compromise with capitalism—a tiered structure, with different levels of pay, responsibility, and decision-making power, at the top of which workers would become "full-fledged collective partner[s] and [get] paid the same as everyone else."[52] But this attempt to systematize the workplace did not resolve underlying problems, and in April of 1987 the Women's Press announced it was "permanently closing shop." A letter to potential buyers of the shop's machinery explained that it was closing because "people are tired and decided to leave" and "the collective wasn't cost efficient."[53]

Neither UP nor the WPP desired, or could afford, to adhere to the full-on separatist feminism that formed the theoretical heart of the Women in Print Movement. From the start, both organizations' attention to gender, and to women's differential access to the material means of public expression, were interwoven with and influenced by their concerns about class, ethnicity and race, age, social location within the cityscape, and so on. But their nuanced take on gender politics did not translate into an equally subtle negotiation of capitalism. When it came to thinking about financing and labor, the Bay Area print shops hewed closely to Women in Print's anti-capitalist ideals—and thus ensured that their business foundations would give way under the pressures of the 1980s. In this, they were not unusual.

The Feminist Bookstore News

The Bay Area feminist print shops described above sprang up organically—the products of the area's vibrant and varied radical culture. By contrast, the publication originally called *Feminist Bookstores Newsletter* and, after 1984, *Feminist Bookstore News* (*FBN*), grew directly out of the Nebraska conference of 1976. In Omaha, conference-goers met in different work groups based on their places in the communications circuit—printers with printers, publishers with publishers, and so forth—and each group planned a newsletter that would keep them in touch and facilitate information sharing and community.[54] In addition to a newsletter, the twenty bookstore representatives present called for the creation of a feminist analogue to the American Booksellers Association *Handbook* and to the standard *Books in Print*.[55] Together, the retailers argued, these book and serial publications would allow them to "share information to help create a communications network based on cooperation," "help develop our politics as well as our service functions," "develop ways of working together that make us more accountable to our communities and to each other," and "support the feminist media and . . . increase its effectiveness."[56] Neither an alternative *Hand-*

book nor a *Books in Print* ever materialized, in part because the newsletter so successfully performed the functions of each (as well as a host of purposes that the ABA and R. R. Bowker never imagined). Circulating among the various nodes of the feminist communications circuit from its headquarters in San Francisco, *FBN* united not only booksellers, but Women in Print activists from every part of the communications circuit for nearly twenty-five years.

Underwritten by funds from three relatively well-established feminist bookstores (Womanbooks of New York City [founded 1975], Amazon Bookstore of Minneapolis [founded 1970], and New Words Bookstore of Somerville, Massachusetts [founded 1976]), *FBN* first appeared in the fall of 1976 as a six-page mimeographed newsletter that circulated only to feminist bookstores. By its tenth anniversary, it was a forty-eight-page professionally printed journal published about six times a year. Its nearly five hundred subscribers included not only feminist bookstores, but also publishers, writers, librarians and "non-feminist bookstores that were serving feminist communities in towns where there wasn't a feminist store."[57] Every issue contained an extensive "Letters" column that acted as a collective bulletin board on which subscribers shared news and information. Other features included articles about trends and developments in the book trade and publishing world, a "Writing Wanted" column where periodicals and presses solicited contributions, and an overview of forthcoming titles of interest to feminists—including books "From Our Own Presses" (as a special section header proclaimed) as well as from mainstream publishers.

As Kristen Hogan has argued in her insightful dissertation on feminist bookselling, *FBN* aimed both to provide information and to instantiate community; one document Hogan cites describes *FBN* as a "support system masquerading as a magazine."[58] This formula proved successful until the changing economics of the book trade in the mid- to late '90s put the squeeze on small scale/special interest publishers and retailers. As first chain stores and then internet retailing began to take business away, the number of feminist bookstores in North America declined, from 175 in 1998 to 45 in 2003.[59] With its subscriber base in freefall, *FBN* ceased publication in 2000.

The *FBN* was primarily the work of Carol Seajay, a young lesbian booklover from Kalamazoo, Michigan. Like many lesbians growing up in the 1950s and '60s, Seajay had devoured midcentury lesbian classics like Anne Aldrich's Beebo Brinker novels and Patricia Highsmith's *The Price of Salt*, but been angered by their refusal to allow their characters a happy ending.[60] As she traveled around the country in the early 1970s, exchanging books hand-to-hand with other lesbians searching for richer reading material, she began to see the ways that book distribution and marketing structures, as well as editorial policy, had helped to create the community's impoverished canon.[61]

Seajay first thought to remedy this situation by going into bookselling; upon her arrival in San Francisco in early 1976, she joined the Full Moon cooperative bookstore/café in the Mission district and also worked at Oakland's ICI: A Woman's Place. In the fall of that year, with partner Paula Wallace, she opened Old Wives Tales books in the Mission.[62] After attending the Nebraska conference, Seajay began the *FBN*, which she originally intended as a simple sideline to bookselling. By 1983, however, she had left the retail world to devote herself fully to the newsletter.[63]

Even more than the Bay Area print shops, with their roots in class-based politics, Seajay's work articulated and promoted a version of lesbian separatism. She shared with June Arnold a vision of a "finishing press" whose relationship to the women's/feminist publishing world was innately antagonistic. *FBN* routinely referred to mainstream book culture as "the Literary Industrial Corporate Establishment," which it pointedly condensed to the acronym LICE.[64] In a 1987 article Seajay stated flatly that "most of the mainstream publishers didn't get into feminist publishing until after feminist publishers [and] booksellers proved that there was a market for the work. . . . If we ever let the feminist presses in this country fade away . . . most of the mainstream published [feminist] books will fade out right behind them."[65]

But, like the members of the Women's Press Project quoted above, Seajay came to recognize that "trying to operate a business" required "plug[ging] into th[e] system to a large extent." Her ability and willingness not merely to plug into, but really to *work* that system over the course of two decades made *FBN* a particularly noteworthy Women in Print institution. Temperament and personality may have contributed to Seajay's pragmatic engagement with the mainstream, but it is important to note as well that, while she had various collaborators over the years, *FBN* was largely a one-woman operation, which afforded her a good deal of institutional flexibility.[66] Letters in the *FBN* archive attest to the fact that producing the magazine alone was an exhausting and unprofitable ordeal. Until she shifted to a word-processing platform in the mid-1980s, Seajay typed all the copy herself on stencils; she also did the layout and paste-up, delivered the copy to the printer ("two buses [each way] unless I can get someone to loan me a car"), and addressed and stamped every issue by hand.[67] Beginning in the early '80s, she drove a FedEx truck part-time to support herself and underwrite her costs.[68] But while working alone took a toll, it also meant Seajay did not expend energy on the theoretical and practical struggles around job descriptions and the division of labor that seem to have sucked the energy out of so many Women in Print collectives—not only the Women's Press, described above, but also the stores Seajay herself had worked at, ICI: A Woman's Place and Old Wives Tales.[69] As a solo operator, she did not have to theorize or implement a non-hierarchical, empowering division of labor (that nevertheless got the job done) nor did she have to grapple with race or class politics in the workplace. Given the degree to which these related issues taxed the energies of many movement institutions, the ability to avoid them may have been worth the strain of working alone.[70]

Seajay's ability cannily to negotiate the space between the margin and the mainstream manifested itself early in *FBN*'s history, when debates over the journal's circulation policy crowded onto the "Letters" page. Store owners in Eugene, Oregon, took one side, asserting that they "would prefer that you restrict distribution to feminist bookstores + women-owned publishers." Allowing *FBN*'s rich listings and discussions of books of interest to women to circulate outside the feminist community, they argued, "would help . . . other stores compete with us in the major area in which we have an 'advantage.'"[71] Members of an East Lansing, Michigan, book co-op with one male member/owner countered the Oregon letter with their own communiqué, which noted that the all-women bookstore in their area had failed, despite being "as commercial, apolitical, and unoffensive as a women's bookstore could be." They, on the other hand, had tapped into the male community and "'the Man's' money" and "come out with a bookstore that is much more fundamentally and overtly feminist and political." Having done so, they resented being shut out of the *FBN* loop.[72]

Seajay solved this potentially divisive issue with a compromise, inviting all interested parties to subscribe to *FBN* itself, while creating supplementary publications (a catalog and a shorter newsletter entitled *Hot Flashes*) that circulated to feminist bookstores only. This increased her subscriber base—which helped cover operating costs and kept *FBN* circulating at the grassroots—while also giving her a purchase in the mainstream publishing world. Her correspondence shows that Seajay cultivated relationships with women (and gay men) throughout "LICE"—at major houses, as well as in the ABA and at *Publishers Weekly*. While she deplored the capitalist culture that assigned market value to feminist community, she acknowledged that it existed; as *FBN* grew, it became a tool with which to leverage that value on behalf of folks in the family, and Seajay recognized that the efficacy of that tool was predicated on a functional relationship with "LICE," not an antagonistic withdrawal from it. She established a sliding rate scale for advertisements, with pricing based on overall annual sales; by the early 1990s, 70 percent of *FBN*'s revenue came from ads, so that mainstream trade publishers effectively subsidized their smaller feminist counterparts.[73]

FBN's partnership with the non-feminist mainstream grew increasingly close over the years. In 1992 Seajay organized subscribers into the "Feminist

Bookstore Network," a lobbying and PR group within the ABA that, ironically, became the voice of independent booksellers. As a set of mergers and acquisitions among publishing houses, coupled with the rise of chain stores, changed the scale on which the publishing business was conducted, the definitions of mainstream and margin shifted, and feminist and non-feminist independent retailers felt a sudden need to unite against a common enemy. As "the only formal organization of specialty bookstores" within the ABA, the Feminist Bookstore Network provided what Kristen Hogan calls "a singular and collective voice" for all independents, and led the charge to demand that the ABA sue several multinational publishing conglomerates and a group of chain superstores for anti-competitive practices, including co-op advertising deals and differential discount rates.[74]

Within the pages of *FBN* Seajay retained a critical edge about the antics of "LICE"—but the journal's sense of what, precisely, constituted the literary corporate establishment had changed somewhat since Seajay had originally coined the term. When the ABA's lawsuits resulted in a settlement in 1997, she observed bitterly that "Penguin acknowledges that, over six years, it gave $77M in discounts to a handful of accounts, presumably superchains. Independents will get a $25M settlement. Superchains and independents did roughly the same amount of business during the period covered, but the chains got $77M—three times as much as the indies. . . . Do the math, then be angry." Anger had fueled *FBN*—like many other Women in Print institutions—from its founding, but the anger here was directed not at the patriarchal capitalist enemy of the mid-'70s, but at its late-twentieth-century inheritor, a global hypercapitalism of non-specific gender. That *FBN* had traveled some distance from its origins was also evident in its endorsement of coalition politics. After reminding her readers to "be angry," Seajay concluded her editorial with an additional prompt: "take time to cheer ABA and its lawyers. Renew your membership."[75] That injunction suggests that the original revolution the Women in Print Movement suborned had, if not quite collapsed into a struggle of small-scale entrepreneurs against capitalist behemoths, at least merged with it for the purpose of fighting the good fight.

FBN's partnership with the broader independent bookselling culture, ultimately, proved insufficient: the continued decline of both feminist and generalist independent bookstores, combined with the merger-mania in publishing, spelled the end of the *FBN* in 2000. Unlike some of her subscribers, however, Seajay adapted successfully to changed market conditions. Beginning in 2004, she began to publish an electronic newsletter called "Books to Watch Out For" (BTWOF). Appearing every six weeks or so, it catalogs forthcoming titles of interest for the feminist and LGBTQ market. Available in three separate editions, Feminist, Lesbian, and Gay Men's (compiled by longtime *FBN* contributor Richard Labonte), BTWOF targets readers who

- don't have a good bookstore in their town
- don't have time to search through a zillion web pages to find the books they want to read
- or just want to know what's going on in the worlds of lesbian and gay books.[76]

The BTWOF website preserves some of the community-building functions of *FBN*, with a page hosting links to the individual sites of feminist and lesbian/gay publishers, book clubs, journals, and bookstores. But like many of the gay/lesbian organizations of the 1970s, its focus has shifted from advocating revolutionary social change to promoting a lifestyle.[77] Indeed, BTWOF strikes a recognizably middlebrow tone on its website, promising readers of the newsletter "a bit of publishing news" in each issue, along with "short reviews of 20 to 30 (or more) new books . . . detailed enough to help you decide which books you want to read but short enough to scan on your lunch break."[78] By modulating its politics and harnessing electronic technology, BTWOF has positioned itself to continue spreading lesbian feminist (and gay male) culture, in terms that reflect both the changed economic conditions of twenty-first-century publishing and the "postfeminist" political climate.

Conclusion: Women in Print and the Practice of Book History

In her groundbreaking 2004 work *Mixed Media: Feminist Presses and Publishing Politics,* Simone Murray called for scholars to "fill the gaps" in book history by restoring to visibility the efforts of women in publishing.[79] The Women in Print Movement offers a wealth of case studies like those I have presented here—fascinating, complex histories of small-scale organizations and individuals who, with abiding passion and self-consciousness, engaged in the production and circulation of printed materials that they believed could transform the world. The archive left by Women in Print is enormous and enormously rich—and largely untouched. It awaits the attention of scholars eager to document the nuances of women's evolution from "fascinating anomalies in a field dominated by men" to visible and equal participants in the book trades.[80]

Not every book historian, however, has a clear stake in that archive. It is resolutely contemporary; skewed toward (though not exclusively about) middle-class, white, Western experience; and offers little in the way of insight into traditional "literary" culture. Beyond satisfying the field's desire for the enumeration and description of the varieties of print culture experience, then, what does a reckoning with the Women in Print Movement do for book history as a whole? The answer to this question lies less in the individual histories of the movement's constituent institutions than in the critical discourse that united them, which was the first sustained attempt to draw attention to gender as a form of power that structures the workplaces, professional practices, and amorphous but powerful "culture" of publishing.[81] Scholars need not share Women in Print Movement activists' beliefs in the virtues of feminist separatism to profit by their exemplary inquiries into the flows of power within the book trade.

The movement's castigations of mainstream, male-dominated print culture—"the finishing press," "the straight press," "LICE"—should prompt book historians to inquire into both the gender and the gender politics of trade publishing in the years leading up to the Women in Print Movement. Women in Print activists correctly pointed out the domination of the industry by men; they were less adroit at capturing the nuances of its masculinity. In what, precisely, did the patriarchalism of publishing inhere? Such an inquiry might touch on issues of routine sexism and the ghettoization of talented women in "appropriate" divisions like the secretarial pool and juvenile publishing.[82] Its real focus, however, would be less the enumeration of chauvinist sins than an exploration of the nature of the masculinity that prevailed within mainstream houses—a set of unexamined gender norms and expectations that shaped both the profession and, by extension, literary culture writ large. Michael Warner has plumbed the deep structures of the elite white male "negativity" that defined the world of print culture in the early republic, and Susan Coultrap-McQuinn has examined the paternalistic culture of nineteenth-century "Gentleman Publishers"; these works lay a foundation—both historical and conceptual—for thinking about masculinity as a structuring feature of publishing culture.[83] But beyond the insights offered in scattered biographies and memoirs, we know little about the masculine world of the twentieth-century "bookman." Was trade publishing, up to a certain point in history, the monolithic patriarchy that Women in Print theorists like June Arnold made it out to be? Or did some residual gentility create gaps in the system—either instances of what the UP collective called "non-offensive businesses" with whom women might usefully collaborate, or individual men who disavowed their own patriarchal privilege in order to ally with women? The Women in Print Movement's emphasis on gender reminds book historians who would grapple with the complexities of the field of literary production to take into account what Pierre Bourdieu calls the "habitus" of those who labor in it—the "practice-generating schemes" that organize their world. A gendered sense of self—for men as well as for women—is one such scheme.[84]

Patriarchy is the most obvious framework that Women in Print activists used to interpret and engage with the publishing world, but their Marxist cultural analysis (admittedly employed somewhat loosely) was nearly as significant. Their investment in the critical lens of political economy, like that in gender, should draw book historians' attention. Women in Print participants came at the question of publishing with an ideological bent similar to that which Kristin Matthews has argued animated the American New Left writ large. Print, for these activists, was not a neutral medium through which a variety of political opinions might be conveyed, but a part of an existing and self-replicating economic and cultural system that, for its entire history, had taken the disenfranchisement and oppression of women as its goal. Yet paradoxically, publishing was also a means to break free from that system. Once the printed word was extricated from its historical partnership with industrial capitalism, it would express an alternate and beneficent reality.[85]

Just as they might quarrel with Women in Print activists over the degree to which the book trade was a masculinist bastion, reasonable people might disagree with this characterization of publishing as a capitalist tool. But by raising the question of power in this way, mid-twentieth-century radicals (whether agitated over U.S. aggression overseas, gender and sexuality, race, or decolonization) call on book historians to engage more forthrightly with the power of institutions and the political economy that supports them. June Arnold and Carol Seajay were not the only ones to argue that, in the late twentieth century at least, it was naïve to view contemporary mainstream publishing as a quaint cottage industry. Individuals and communities who had long been at the margins of polite print culture were in many ways positioned best to recognize its absorption into a global communications market characterized by rapid change, shifting boundaries, and an insatiable appetite for profit.

Against this monstrosity the Women in Print Movement—like its coevals, Afrocentric publishers across the U.S. and indigenous publishing collectives in postcolonial nations—posited a utopia based on changed ownership patterns and institutional practices, out of which would naturally precipitate a better culture.[86] A new base, in short, would yield a new superstructure. As the 1980s and '90s wore on, many such print revolutionaries, including Women in Print activists, discovered that the structuring power of capitalism ran deeper than they had imagined. But if their plans for the creation of a utopian print counterculture were unsuccessful, it was not because their analysis of the economics of publishing was wrong. On the contrary, as both the Women's Press and, eventually, the *Feminist Bookstore News* discovered, it was all too right. The Women in Print Movement's insight into political economy's central role in defining a mainstream, hegemonic print culture—as well as their relative blindness about what it might take to craft a margin that could resist incorporation by that mainstream—is a critical legacy that book historians of the present day can employ to good effect.

The account of the Women in Print Movement I have given here, then, is important at bottom because it offers a set of theoretical tools upon which book historians—particularly, though not exclusively, those working on contemporary topics—can and should draw. The movement's members (to greater and lesser degrees) were steeped in a radical leftist tradition that shaped their thinking not only about gender, but also about media institutions, political economy, and power. Incorporating this angle of vision—which owes as much to critical media or mass communications studies as to traditional *histoire du livre* or analytical bibliography—into the practice of book history is important if the field hopes to grapple with the complexities of a postindustrial, postcolonial, postmodern print culture. Schematically, somewhat ham-handedly, and in some cases simply as a by-product of lives focused on production, Women in Print activists took it upon themselves to be book historians of the present, analyzing late-twentieth-century publishing institutions, the political economy that supported them, and the identitarian norms—in this case, norms of gender and sexuality—that inflected their workings.

The alternative print culture that arose out of their analysis was relatively short-lived, and the answers they provided to the questions they asked may have been wrong. But the questions themselves—about the intersections of identity, ownership, and the deep structures of global capitalism—may be the most appropriate ones with which to grapple with the book history of our time. As such, we should not be surprised if they revise, or even displace, traditional questions about aesthetic value, knowledge transmission, and cultural capital as the field comes to reckon more fully with the print culture of the recent past and the present day.

Notes

1. Leslie Howsam, "In My View: Women and Book History," *SHARP News* 7 (Autumn 1998): 1–2.

2. This distinction, and the institutional dynamics that support it, is explored at length in Ellen Messer-Davidow's *Disciplining Feminism: From Social Activism to Academic Discourse* (Durham: Duke University Press, 2002).

3. *Blue Pencils and Hidden Hands: Women Editing Periodicals, 1830–1910* (Boston: Northeastern University Press, 2004); *Women Editing Modernism: "Little" Magazines & Literary History* (Lexington: University Press of Kentucky, 1995); *Our Sister Editors: Sarah J.*

Hale and the Tradition of Nineteenth-Century American Women Editors (Athens: University of Georgia Press, 1995).

4. See, for example, Ava Baron, "Questions of Gender: Deskilling and Demasculinization in the U.S. Printing Industry, 1830–1915," *Gender and History* 1 (Summer 1989): 178–99; Marjorie Barlow, ed. *Notes on Women Printers in Colonial America and the United States, 1639–1975* (Charlottesville: University Press of Virginia, 1976); Leona Hudak, *Early American Women Printers and Publishers, 1639–1820* (Metuchen, N.J.: Scarecrow Press, 1978); Roger Levinson, *Women in Printing: Northern California, 1857–1890* (Santa Barbara, Calif.: Capra Press, 1994); Madelon Golden Schlipp and Sharon Murphy, *Great Women of the Press* (Carbondale: Southern Illinois University Press, 1983). Notable exceptions to this trend, in addition to works cited in the body of this essay, include some of the pieces in James Danky and Wayne Wiegand's anthology *Women in Print* (Madison: University of Wisconsin Press, 2006), and Paula McDowell's *The Women of Grub Street: Press, Politics, and Gender in the London Literary Marketplace 1678–1730* (Oxford: Oxford University Press, 1998).

5. In "Reading at Feminist Bookstores: Women's Literature, Women's Studies, and the Feminist Bookstore Network" (Ph.D. diss., University of Texas, 2006), Kristen Hogan self-consciously uses the term "bookwomen" to describe the feminist bookstore workers she chronicles, using the term to play on the (imagined) genteel past in which male book trade workers described themselves as "bookmen." "Referring to the women of the feminist bookstores as feminist bookwomen," Hogan argues, "both recuperates the power of the plural title and establishes the feminist bookseller as a particular political identity" (43n.75). In this article, I extend her use of the term to include feminists in all sectors of the book trade.

6. Robert Darnton originated the idea of the "communications circuit" in "What Is the History of Books?" in *Reading in America: Literature and Social History*, ed. Cathy Davidson (Baltimore: Johns Hopkins University Press, 1989), 31.

7. On feminist bookstores, see not only Hogan, "Reading at Feminist Bookstores," but also Saralyn Chesnut and Amanda C. Gable, "'Women Ran It': Charis Books and More and Atlanta's Lesbian-Feminist Community, 1971–1981," in *Carryin' On in the Lesbian and Gay South*, ed. John Howard (New York: New York University Press, 1997), 241–84; Kathleen Liddle, "More Than a Bookstore: The Continuing Relevance of Feminist Bookstores for the Lesbian Community," *Journal of Lesbian Studies* 9, no. 1/2 (2005): 145–59; and Junko Onosaka, *Feminist Revolution in Literacy: Women's Bookstores in the United States* (New York: Routledge, 2006). On feminist book publishers, see Simone Murray, *Mixed Media: Feminist Presses and Publishing Politics* (London: Pluto Press, 2004), and Katheryn Thomas Flannery, *Feminist Literacies, 1968–1975* (Urbana: University of Illinois Press, 2005). On the feminist periodical press, see Kate Adams, "Built Out of Books: Lesbian Energy and Feminist Ideology in Alternative Publishing," *Journal of Homosexuality* 34, no. 3/4 (1998): 113–41; and Jan Witt, "A 'Labor from the Heart': Lesbian Magazines from 1947–1994," *Journal of Lesbian Studies* 5, no. 1/2 (2001): 229–51. A slightly different approach to feminist periodical publishing can be found in Amy Erdman Farrell's *Yours in Sisterhood: Ms. Magazine and the Promise of Popular Feminism* (Chapel Hill: University of North Carolina Press, 1998).

8. Kate Millet, "Theory of Sexual Politics from *Sexual Politics*" in *Feminist Theory: A Reader*, ed. Wendy Kolmar and Frances Bartkowski (Boston: McGraw-Hill, 2005), 219.

9. The term "heterosexual privilege" is Charlotte Bunch's, found in "Not for Lesbians Only" (1975), in *Passionate Politics* (New York: St. Martin's, 1987), 177. Being a "political lesbian" meant, in Sheila Jeffries piquant formulation, being "a woman-identified woman who does not fuck men. It does not mean compulsory sexual activity with women" (Jeffries, *Love Your Enemy?: The Debate between Heterosexual Feminism and Political Lesbianism* [London: Onlywomen Press, 1981]). See also Jill Johnston, *Lesbian Nation: The Feminist Solution* (New York: Simon and Schuster, 1974).

10. Anne M. Valk, "Living a Feminist Lifestyle: The Intersection of Theory and Action in a Lesbian Feminist Collective," *Feminist Studies* 28 (Summer 2002): 321.

11. Myra Marx Ferree and Patricia Yancey Martin, eds., *Feminist Organizations: Harvest of the New Women's Movement* (Philadelphia: Temple University Press, 1995).

12. Flannery, *Feminist Literacies*, 27.

13. Flannery, *Feminist Literacies*, 23.

14. Arnold, "Dear Sisters." Mass mailing, January, 1976, Charlotte Bunch Papers, box 93, Schlesinger Library, Radcliffe Institute, Cambridge, Massachusetts (hereafter, "CB Papers").

15. Mary Lowry of New Words bookstore in Cambridge, Mass., was originally an organizer but dropped out; Nancy Stockwell of Plexus and the Bright Medusa took her place fairly late in the organizing process. See "Simplified Workshop Schedule," 3, CB Papers, box 93. Junko Onosako's account of the conference credits this whole group with organizing it, but Bertha Harris's treatment of the event ("Introduction," *Lover*, 2nd ed. [New York: New York University Press, 1993]) puts Arnold squarely at the center. Harris's perspective is confirmed by Charlotte Bunch's interview with the author, 27 September 2007.

16. Valk, "Living a Feminist Lifestyle."

17. Arnold, "Dear Sisters."

18. "Second Mailing: 1976 Conference Women in Print," CB Papers, box 93. These limits on participation meant about twenty requests to attend were refused. Evidence of the difficulty the organizing committee had in specifying meaningful boundaries is evident in a letter from Arnold to the Feminist Poetry and Graphics Center of San Diego, which "help[ed] out men poets" in addition to women. Arnold's typing was hesitant as she tried to explain why they could not attend, and the letter reads "only women should come, with an exception to be made for ~~Thri~~ Third World ~~women~~ feminists working on Third World projects with men ~~who were feminist identified and not the~~ [blank space]. The job of the conference planners . . ." Arnold to Vicky, Mary, Joyce, and Shelley, n.d., CB Papers, box 93.

19. Arnold to Vicky et al.

20. Elizabeth Sullivan, "Old Wife's [sic] Tales and Feminist Bookstore Network," http://www.shapingsf.org/ezine/gay/files/oldwifes.html (accessed 30 August 2007).

21. Kay Ann Cassell, "Women in Print an Update," *Library Journal* 102 (June 1977): 1352.

22. "WPP Interview with Juanita Owens" 13 July 1982, typescript, Women's Press/UP Press Records, box 1. Gay, Lesbian, Bisexual, Transgender History Society of Northern California, San Francisco (hereafter "WPUP"); Sandra Marilyn and Joss Eldredge, "Women in Print: The Women's Press Project," and Joss Eldredge, "Women in Print: Slowly, but Surely," *Tradeswomen* 4 (1985), 20–29, 30–36, WPUP, box 2.

23. Draft of Schedule, typescript with comments in hand, CB Papers, box 93.

24. Donna Allen and Martha Leslie Allen, "Three Principles of Feminist Journalism," in *Women in Media: A Documentary Sourcebook,* ed. Maurine Beasley and Sheila Silver (Washington, D.C.: Women's Institute for Freedom of the Press, 1977), 178 (original emphasis).

25. Sales figures from Carol Newton, e-mail to the author, 23 August 2007; ALA citation from http://www.robinmorgan.us/robin_morgan_bookDetails.asp?ProductID=6 (accessed 17 August 2007).

26. Rita Mae Brown, *Rita Will: Memoir of a Literary Rabble-Rouser* (New York: Bantam, 1997), 281.

27. Harriet Desmoines and Catherine Nicholson, "Dear Beth," *Sinister Wisdom* 1 (October 1976): 128.

28. This dynamic is treated in detail by Murray, *Mixed Media,* 126–66, using the British feminist presses as examples.

29. "Feminist Publishing: An Antiquated Form?" *Heresies* 3 (1977): 25.
30. Desmoines and Nicholson, "Dear Beth," 128, 127 (original emphasis).
31. "Feminist Press and Feminist Politics," *Quest* 3 (Summer 1976): 19.
32. "The Women's Press" was, not surprisingly, a common name for feminist publishers and print shops. It is important to note that the entity under discussion here was not the better-known Women's Press Collective founded in Oakland in 1969 by members of the Gay Women's Liberation Group, nor the Women's Press of Toronto, founded in 1972.
33. At the time of the collective's closing, members included Julie Twichell, Lisa Mischke, Josie Brown, Lee Mosswood, Cheryl DeYoung, Bo Brown, and Annie Armstrong. "SF Women's Press Closes," *Feminist Bookstore News* 9, no. 3 (1987): 7.
34. "SF Co-Op: Notes toward a Draft Summation of Practice," typescript, 11 May 1975, WPUP, box 1.
35. "Dear Friends," undated typescript signed by Karen [Townsend] and Casey [McCarthy] WPUP, box 1.
36. "Listing of Alternative Print Shops in Bay Area" undated typescript, WPUP, box 3; "Dear People" undated typescript [1976], WPUP, box 1.
37. "Dear People," contribution of UP Press to unpaginated *Women in Print Newsletter*, signed by Judith, Peggy, and Jesse, April 1977, WPUP, box 3.
38. Typescript mailing on UP Press letterhead, no signature, 9 February 1979. WPUP, box 1.
39. The Comprehensive Education and Training Act, passed in 1973, was a central piece of Lyndon Johnson's War on Poverty. For discussion of its impact, see Grace A. Franklin and Randall B. Ripley, *CETA: Politics and Policy, 1973–1982* (Knoxville: University of Tennessee Press, 1984).
40. Marilyn and Eldredge, "Women in Print," 21; "CTDP [Community Training and Development Project]: Problem Statement," 12 May 1981, unpag., WPUP, box 1.
41. "Notes from May 16, 1982 Women's Press Project Board Meeting re: 'Why Print?'" unpag., WPUP, box 1.
42. Untitled, unpaginated, unsigned typescript beginning "Some time last spring . . . ," ca. 1983, WPUP, box 1.
43. Combahee River Collective, "A Black Feminist Statement" (1977), in *Feminist Theory*, eds. Kolmar and Bartkowski, 312.
44. "Why Print?"
45. "Some time last spring. . . ."
46. "Dear People" from *Women in Print Newsletter*.
47. Typescript mailing of 9 February 1979.
48. "Some time last spring. . . ." (original emphasis).
49. Mary Ann Seawell, "Making an Imprint in Business," *Palo Alto Times*, c-1, clipping in WPUP, box 1.
50. "CTDP Problem Statement."
51. "Questions for Mobilization Support Network," handwritten notes dated 1985–86, WPUP, box 2.
52. "The Women's Press Hiring Policies," WPUP, box 1.
53. "Dear Customers," 11 April 1987, WPUP, box 1.
54. Several women's print shops—including UP Press—collaborated to produce a few issues of a newsletter, but production and mailing were very cumbersome, rotating from shop to shop, and it seems only to have lasted a few issues. See *Womyn Who Print* (October 1976), *Women in Print Newsletter* (April 1977), and *Dear Print-hers* (n.d.), all WPUP, box 3.
55. "Feminist Books in Print: Supplementary Information," undated typescript, unpag.,

Feminist Bookstore News Records, box 1. James C. Hormel Gay and Lesbian Center, San Francisco Public Library (hereafter, "FBN Records").

56. *FBN* 1, no. 1 (14 October 1976): 2. FBN Records, Box Label "Original Copy."

57. Carol Seajay, "The Feminist Bookstore News Celebrates 10 Years of Publishing," *Feminist Writers Guild National Newsletter,* February 1987, 18. Clipping in box 1, FBN Records.

58. Hogan, "Reading at Feminist Bookstores," 79.

59. Claire Kirch, "The Struggle Continues," *Publishers Weekly,* 13 October 2003, 20.

60. Discussed in Adams, "Built out of Books." See also Yvonne Keller, "'Was It Right to Love Her Brother's Wife So Passionately?': Lesbian Pulp Novels and U.S. Lesbian Identity, 1950–1965," *American Quarterly* 57, no. 2 (2005): 385–410.

61. Sullivan, "Old Wife's Tales," 1.

62. Adams, "Built out of Books," 126–27.

63. Lisa C. Moore "Start Spreading the News," *Lambda Book Report,* 1 May 2004, 42–44. http://www.proquest.com.lp.hscl.ufl.edu/ (accessed 29 August 2007).

64. Adams, "Built out of Books," 131.

65. Seajay, "Feminist Bookstore News," 16.

66. *FBN* had no masthead until the mid-'80s. Gradually, as the magazine expanded (taking on advertising and automating production via computer systems) during the 1990s, Seajay acquired collaborators—both columnists who focused on special subject areas and assistants focused on editorial and advertising tasks.

67. Adams, "Built out of Books," 130.

68. Moore, "Start Spreading the News," 42.

69. Problems within Old Wives Tales are discussed in Sullivan, "Old Wife's Tales"; strife at ICI, which ended in a "lockout" of several original collective members, is described in Hogan, "Reading at Feminist Bookstores," 69, and Onosaka, *Feminist Revolution in Literacy,* 96–97.

70. Flannery, *Feminist Literacies,* 50–59, Murray, *Mixed Media,* 66–96 and passim, and Onosaka, *Feminist Revolution in Literacy,* 76–84, all treat these issues, the centrality of which cannot be overstated. Carol Seajay's correspondence files are filled with letters—specified as not for publication—describing the way various collectives were wrestling with these issues. For an extended treatment of one institution's experience, see Thaba Niedzwiecki, "Print Politics: Conflict and Community-Building at Toronto's Women' Press" (MA Thesis, University of Guelph, 1997).

71. Hogan, "Reading at Feminist Bookstores," 80.

72. Carolyn Shafer to Seajay, 1 November 1979, FBN Records, group 3, box label "FBN Misc. Archives 1976–1985."

73. Onosaka, *Feminist Revolution in Literacy,* 153–54.

74. Hogan, "Reading at Feminist Bookstores," 97–127.

75. Quoted in Hogan, "Reading at Feminist Bookstores," 113. Hogan also notes that FBN's public statements during the lawsuits were more politically charged than those of the ABA, with FBN arguing that anti-competitive practices threatened "rights" and "diversity," and ABA spokesmen framing the issues less contentiously, in terms of the need for a "level playing field" for all booksellers (103).

76. See http://www.bookstowatchoutfor.com/ (accessed 14 September 2007).

77. On this dynamic, see John D'Emilio, "Placing Gay in the '60s," in *Long Time Gone: '60s America Then and Now,* ed. Alexander Bloom (New York: Oxford University Press, 2001), 209–29, and Alexandra Chasin, *Selling Out: The Gay and Lesbian Movement Goes to Market* (New York: Palgrave Macmillan, 2001).

78. See http://www.bookstowatchoutfor.com/.

79. Murray, *Mixed Media*, 10.
80. Howsam, "In My View," 1.
81. Lewis Coser et al. explore the culture of the industry via a contrast of its "cottage" and "corporate" features in *Books: The Culture and Commerce of Publishing* (New York: Basic Books, 1982; repr., Chicago: University of Chicago Press, 1985), 175–99. See also Thomas Bonn, *Heavy Traffic and High Culture: New American Library as Literary Gatekeeper in the Paperback Revolution* (Carbondale: University of Southern Illinois Press, 1989; repr., New York: Penguin, 1990).
82. Michele Caplette in Coser et al., *Books*, 148–74. Jacalyn Eddy discusses this phenomenon, and women's successful negotiations within it, in *Bookwomen: Creating an Empire in Children's Book Publishing, 1919–1939* (Madison: University of Wisconsin Press, 2006).
83. Warner defines "negativity" as a political as well as a social position, attendant on being white, male, able-bodied, and with access to capital. This power is "negative" because those qualities are coded not as attributes themselves so much as a *lack* of the attributes that undermine power, for instance, race/ethnicity, femaleness, disability, or lack of access to capital. Entrance into public discourse and the publishing culture that shaped it in the early republic, Warner argues, was permissible only for those whose negativity allowed them to voice the "abstract and universal" and "rational and disinterested concern for the public good." See Michael Warner, *Letters of the Republic: Publication and the Public Sphere in 18th-Century America* (Cambridge: Harvard University Press, 1990), 42. On "Gentleman Publishers," see Susan Coultrap-McQuinn, *Doing Literary Business: American Women Writers in the Nineteenth Century* (Chapel Hill: University of North Carolina Press, 1990), 28–48. Donald Sheehan's *This Was Publishing: A Chronicle of the Book Trade in the Gilded Age* (Bloomington: Indiana University Press, 1952) describes the same behavioral and cultural norms, though Sheehan never discusses it as an explicitly gendered world.
84. Pierre Bourdieu, *Distinction: A Social Critique of the Judgment of Taste*, trans. Richard Nice (Cambridge: Harvard University Press, 1984) 172.
85. Kristin Matthews, "The Medium, the Message, the Movement: Print Culture and New Left Politics," in *Print Culture in the Cold War*, ed. Greg Barnhisel and Cathy Turner (Amherst: University of Massachusetts Press, forthcoming).
86. On Afrocentric publishing in the United States, see Julius E. Thompson, *Dudley Randall, Broadside Press, and the Black Arts Movement in Detroit, 1960–1995* (Jefferson, N.C.: McFarland, 1999), and Melba Joyce Boyd, *Wrestling with the Muse: Dudley Randall and the Broadside Press* (New York: Columbia University Press, 2004). Third World Press, founded by Haki Madhubuti (Don Lee) in 1965 and one of the longest-lived Afrocentric publishers in the United States, has yet to receive the scholarly attention it merits. Thompson, above, discusses it briefly (212–27), as does Donald Joyce, *Black Book Publishers: A Historical Dictionary of the Presses, 1817–1980* (New York: Greenwood Press, 1991), 207–11. For discussion of the work of indigenous presses in decolonizing nations—and of the still-powerful Western publishers' role in the developing world's print cultures—see, for example, Per Gedin, "Cultural Pride: the Necessity of Indigenous Publishing," in *Publishing and Development in the Third World*, ed. Philip Altbach (London: Hans Zell, 1992), 43–54, and Dick Cloete, "Alternative Publishing in South Africa in the 1970s and 1980s," in *The Politics of Publishing in South Africa*, ed. Nicholas Evans and Monica Seeber (London: Holger Ehling Publishing, 2000), 43–72. On the intersection between feminist and indigenous publishing, see Urvashi Butalia, *Making a Difference: Feminist Publishing in the South* (Chesnut Hill, Mass.: Bellagio Publishing Network, 2005).

THE HISTORY OF THE BOOK IN NEW ENGLAND

The State of the Discipline

Matt Cohen

The region of New England has been fertile ground for the study of what has been termed "print culture." Such work has been remarkable for its impact beyond the field of American book history. Work by David D. Hall, Robert A. Gross, Michael Warner, and Cathy N. Davidson, to name just a few, appears in debates in political science, religious studies, and postcolonial theory, in addition to the usual homes to book history, literary and historical studies. David Finkelstein and Alistair McCleery's *Book History Reader* (2001) includes essays by Jane Tompkins on Nathaniel Hawthorne and by E. Jennifer Monaghan on literacy instruction and gender in New England. Studies of New England's media history have also persistently troubled the boundaries of book history, asking definitional questions about literacy, the relationship between orality and literacy, the existence of a "public sphere"—even the definition of the "book" and of "culture." Institutionally, too, New England has been an epicenter for Anglo-American book studies. The American Antiquarian Society (AAS), founded in 1812 in Worcester, Massachusetts, launched its influential Program for the History of the Book in American Culture in 1983.[1]

The mulling over of books, society, consciousness, and power has a long pedigree in New England. Two years before he helped found the AAS, Isaiah Thomas, one of the republic's most successful printers, published his *History of Printing in America* (1810), which is to this day the starting point for most historians of the book in North America. A little over a decade later, Lydia Maria Child's *Hobomok* (1824) asked its readers to think about the connections among textual media, meaning, and sociopolitical power in colonial New England. Child's audiences are expected to know that *Hobo-*

For their assistance in improving this essay, the author would like to thank Robert A. Gross, Christopher Labarthe, Socorro Finn, and Kinohi Nishikawa. This essay was researched under fellowship support from the Newberry Library (via the National Endowment for the Humanities) and the American Council of Learned Societies.

mok's young heroine, Mary Conant, is in for trouble when she unwraps a package from her lover and finds a "prayer book, bound in the utmost elegance of the times," which is "ornamented with gold clasps, richly chased; the one representing the head of king Charles, the other the handsome features of his French queen; and the inside of both adorned with the arms of England." Her nonconformist father's lectures on the evils of the Book of Common Prayer and the sins of adornment jar with her lover's romantic binding, inducing a readerly reflection on the place of the physical book in the moral and intellectual worlds.[2]

Child's work was part of a wave of fictional writing that helped promote a notion that underwrote much of the early attention to New England: In that region and its Puritan culture were to be found the national origins of the United States. Providentially guided on a special path to political self-determination and economic success, it was imagined, the United States was incubated in New England's complex mix of financial ambition, religious perfectionism, and English sociopolitical inheritance. In the wake of decades of American Studies scholarship interrogating this sort of exceptionalism, a host of assumptions embedded in that approach have given way to a new spectrum of questions. Scholars across the humanities have emphasized border-crossing, transnational, and transregional approaches. The study of the writing, publishing, distributing, and reading of books remains central to this new research. But if New England is no longer, as Philip Gura puts it, "the *omphalos*" of the United States, why organize an essay around its print culture?[3] In this essay I will outline the exciting work that has been done to pull New England book history out of its regional comfort zone. But I will also suggest why book historical studies delimited by the region are still productive when performed in ways that attend to the cross-cultural communications environment of colonial New England. Such studies can show how book culture has been used to construct "New England" as a region, while interrogating the connections between print and region reveals an occluded media sphere that nonetheless gave shape to the history of the New English book.

The chronological parameters here are necessarily constrained for lack of space. Even focusing on the colonial period as I do won't allow me to illuminate every corner of a rich, rigorous part of the discipline. Certainly I can do no more than gesture beyond the period of the early Republic. There is a great richness in pursuing the question of New England's regional significance in the print world, or the question of "print culture" as an ideology, beyond that time. William Charvat famously argued that New England's significance in the American print world declined as the centers of book production and distribution shifted out of Boston to Philadelphia and New York. Important work by Robert Gross on the relationship between local and extra-local material and conceptual networks in Concord, Massachusetts, suggests a more complex story, as does the vast work on New England regionalism.[4] Amy Kaplan and Richard Brodhead have argued that the imagination of the United States as nation and the nostalgia taking place in stories set in New England were routed, in material terms, through urban centers and audiences, resulting in a national mindset rather than a sustained, tense negotiation between local or regional needs and longer-distance relationships. Nancy Glazener argues that the cultural capital developed by Boston's Brahmins in the mid-nineteenth century gave that city lasting power in the print market, even if the region was not the major distribution source.[5] Recent scholarship has begun to look more closely at local print production and to question the determining power of nationalism, offering new ways of thinking about the uses of print both by regional writers and publishers and by "subaltern" populations such as Native Americans, African Americans, and recent immigrants.[6] And New England continued to innovate in the area of the mechanization of print into the twentieth century, while book artistry flourishes there to this day in the work of artists such as Rosamond Purcell.[7]

For many scholars, it was the work of David D. Hall that catalyzed the study of *histoire du livre* in America. To a field still dominated by Perry Miller's magisterial study of seventeenth-century American Puritanism, *The New England Mind* (1954), Hall offered a new approach to the history of the life of the mind. Certainly many settlers lived a life deeply engaged with pietistic Calvinism and its conceptual world, as Miller had brilliantly shown. But New England's colonists could not, Hall argued, be characterized only by their theologians or their ministers' sermons; nor could they be studied without attention to the way popular culture—a world of wonders, magical events, divine providences—was interwoven with theology in daily life. This revision of the accepted picture of Puritan *mentalité* owed much to the Annales school approach to social history. But it drew specifically on detailed attention to the print world of England and New England and the readers who participated in it. The argument drew on literacy studies, descriptive bibliography, and close readings of archival documents that reported colonists' reading experiences. Borrowing Richard Hoggart's phrase, Hall set out to track "the uses of literacy . . . predominant in the first two centuries of New England life," concluding that "reading functioned as a cultural style" and fueled a rich life of the mind for the settlers.[8] To accomplish this was also to push the field of book history into the realm of social history, widening its appeal and putting the question of how information was produced, circulated, and read at the heart of historical studies.[9]

A sophisticated picture of New England's early information culture emerged in Hall's work and that which followed closely upon it. Settlers from England crossed the Atlantic to live in what they thought of as a "wilderness," but they never completely left the information realm of the old country. Even after the first printing press in North America was established at Cambridge in 1638, most books were imported from England, and most of them were "steady sellers": almanacs, advice books, and Bibles. (*Hobomok*'s depiction of Charles Brown's gift to Mary of a fancy-bound steady seller, together with a letter and locket, would have been a demonstration of economic promise and of long-distance intimacy.) As was the case with other Protestants, for New England's settlers print stood for the Word of sacred scripture, language was tied intimately to an original divine tongue, and writing was understood in a deep, structural way as a source of power, history, even identity.

"Publication" in America, as in Europe, had a broader definition than it does today, including all kinds of public speaking or performances as well as the posting and circulation of printed and manuscript texts. The theater was banned by colonial governments, but marketplaces, public religious events, and letter writing kept settlers in contact with one another, their relatives, and their business partners in England. Wonder tales were popular, and, like other information, circulated both orally and in print and manuscript. In all its forms that circulation was regulated by both civil and church authorities in both England and America—and religious leaders had particularly strict control over the productions of the press. Per capita English language literacy rates in America quickly exceeded those in England, and continued to rise throughout the colonial period. E. Jennifer Monaghan showed that this was true for women as well as men, at least when it came to reading, though women's public speech was deprecated and strictly controlled. Massachusetts Bay's harsh response to Anne Hutchinson in the Antinomian Crisis showed that women's acts of interpretation and their potential to create networks of spiritual believers brought out a deep-seated fear of women's power, even as it revealed the presence of such networks of dissent alongside orthodox expressions.[10]

The eighteenth century saw major shifts in information practices in New England. Richard Brown's *Knowledge Is Power* (1991) showed the processes by which information strictly controlled by the elite in the seventeenth century began to be accessible to a broader social spectrum. Benjamin Franklin's rise to authority—built on a rhetorical mastery of public discourse in new venues such as newspapers, a material system of printing businesses, and the holding of public offices such as postmaster general—is considered a paradigmatic example of such shifts. But the appearance of writers such as Phillis Wheatley, the preaching and writings of Native ministers such as the Mohegan Samson Occom, and the rise of the novel in the wake of the American Revolution also signal tectonic changes. As ministerial authority waned after the Great Awakening, merchants and lawyers began to take a larger part in policy determinations and the shaping of public opinion through professional organizations (both local and transatlantic) and newspapers. For Brown, such shifts in the accessibility of information and, to an extent, in access to public discourse, had the effect of opening up possibilities for personal transformation, including self-improvement and class mobility, that had not existed for seventeenth-century colonists. Hall argued that important changes in cultural attitudes accompanied a shift, around 1800, from what he termed "intensive reading," in which the average reader engaged deeply with a small number of texts such as the Bible, to "extensive reading," in which a large number of print sources were consulted and collated by readers.[11]

Despite these changes, there were equally powerful continuities. Some of these were rooted in the desire by male elites to retain authority over the Native Americans, African slaves, women, and unpropertied men who constituted the majority of their world. While emergent forms of public and private expression and organization such as fraternal, philanthropic, and political associations created opportunities for subaltern discourses to expand, elites created new laws and new systems of control of information flow—new means, one might say, of transforming "information" into "knowledge." Other continuities were rooted in the way media practices and marketplaces functioned. Imports still dominated the print marketplace. The vernacular tradition described by Hall continued even as it was superficially transformed. Crime literature and other popular forms entered the scene, and new "steady sellers" came along, such as Mary Rowlandson's narrative of her captivity in King Philip's War. As literacy rates steadily increased (and as women's writing instruction began to be de rigueur), the potential for participation in a range of discourses increased.[12]

The question of what sociocultural effects resulted from these shifts and continuities drove a series of influential analyses of the eighteenth-century culture of writing in America in the late 1980s and early 1990s. At the same time, such inquiries were fueled by the profound theoretical questions that book historical methodology opened up, particularly at a moment when the "linguistic turn" was putting pressure on historical method.[13] What is the relationship between literacy and power—and by extension, between print culture and historical change? Hall's focus on steady sellers offered a new methodology for the history of ideas; his notion of intensive and extensive reading practices, while controversial, has shaped countless inquiries into the connections between reading and subjectivity. Just as influential has been Michael Warner's *The Letters of the Republic* (1990), which focused on the revolutionary era.

Warner, like Hall and Brown, rejected technological determinist narratives that claimed that alphabetic literacy and print culture naturally led to higher consciousness and more democratic governance. He insisted, however, that a public print sphere—an imagined "republic of letters" in which disembodied actors deliberated policy through printed public media—was not preceded by the United States as a nation or the adoption of republican ideology, but was in fact integral to the generation of such notions. The encoding of limited participatory governance in the U.S. Constitution was, for Warner, a product of new imaginations of the reach of print and new forms of public discourse through that medium no less than it was a product of discussions about republicanism, economics, and English political heritage. In a sophisticated application (and modification) of Jürgen Habermas's theory of the public sphere, Warner argued that "republican ideology was also an ideology of print in that its central categories—at least in the colonial American version of republicanism—were articulated in, and thus given meaning within, the symbolic practices of publication."[14] At the root of this political shift was, for Warner, a basic secularization. "No longer a technology of privacy underwritten by divine authority," he writes of eighteenth-century reading and writing, "letters have become a technology of publicity whose meaning in the last analysis is civic and emancipatory."[15]

Cathy Davidson, in an equally influential study, *Revolution and the Word* (1986), also argued for the civic and emancipatory quality of print publicity, using the early American novel and its reception as her archival focus. Before Davidson's study, the eighteenth-century American novel had been deprecated; *Revolution and the Word* made clear that the flowering of long narrative fiction in the early Republic was a window onto an important cultural shift and an opportunity to develop a powerful methodological collusion between the history of the book and approaches based in literary analysis—a synthesis Davidson termed "a history of texts."[16] Like Hall, Davidson used descriptive bibliography and techniques inspired by the Annales school to offer a social history of the first novels produced in America, beginning with William Hill Brown's *The Power of Sympathy* (1789). But she also employed poststructuralist and feminist reading techniques, ideological analysis, and (from an Americanist's perspective of the time) daring methodological moves such as using readers' marginalia to sketch reception.

Early American novels, Davidson found, served as key sites for theorizing and contesting politics, education, and social mores at a formative moment in the experience of nationhood in North America. Thus, even though issuing a novel was a risky financial and moral venture, writers, printers, and booksellers did so because such works were hotspots of public interest. While men's names tended to dominate subscription lists, Davidson demonstrated that gender did not function as a boundary in the circulation and reading of novels. Novels like Hannah Webster Foster's *The Coquette*

(1797) offered titillation and a glimpse into scandals of the day, but they also theorized women's relationship to law, property, and political representation. Men were cautioned about arbitrary claims to social preeminence and offered models of moral, republican masculine behavior in fictions like *The Power of Sympathy*. The radical potential of the post-Revolution novel, with its everyday language, broad appeal, and morally questionable scenarios, was inseparable, Davidson argued, from the difficult subjective position into which it put its readers. "The woman reader was . . . caught in the middle," she emphasizes, "with no socially sanctioned rationale for her novel reading, while the male novel-reader must have felt somewhat defensive about enjoying a form often implicitly and explicitly feminine."[17] The picture Davidson offered of the conditions under which men and women read in the early Republic has opened an archive and spurred study of the intersections of politics and literary production across the humanities and around the world.[18]

The foundational work on New England's book history from the 1970s to the early 1990s provoked a flowering of scholarship both extending and challenging this newly complex understanding of the history of American print culture. David Shields's study of manuscript-based literary coteries, *Civil Tongues and Polite Letters* (1997), showed the complex relationship between public and private discourse in the establishment and maintenance of social and political power and proved dramatically that manuscript, not just print, continued to be a crucial medium. In coffeehouses, taverns, and parlors, civil discourses—different "cultural styles" of literacy, to pluralize Hall's phrase—were maintained in conversation and through writing that, while in touch with print culture, permitted a range of expressions that were key to shaping republicanism during the Revolution. Women and unpropertied men, in Shields's analysis, participated in discursive realms that gave them a degree of social power. Contesting the link implied in Warner's argument (and to an extent Shields's) between free discourse and a free state, Grantland Rice argued that if the end of censorship and the expansion of print opened new possibilities for authorship in the eighteenth century, "they did so only by transforming printed texts from a practical means for assertive sociopolitical commentary into the more inert medium of property and commodity."[19]

Brown, Shields, Warner, and Davidson all situate New England reading practices in the wider sphere of English settler colonial information culture. By implication, in their studies New England begins to look less exceptional, as the social practices of literacy transcend geographic limitations and increasingly, as the eighteenth century progressed, social boundaries. More recent work has extended this perspective, asking what happens to the picture of New England's information culture if the implicit understanding of its isolationism is interrogated? Thinking back on the finely bound prayer book in Child's *Hobomok*, we recall not only that the text is a transatlantic gift, but that it situates Mary's lover's faith geopolitically through its depiction of Charles and his handsome (and dangerously Catholic) "French queen." That these figures are depicted on the "clasps" of the book metaphorically binds the intimacy of the gift and its spiritual contents to an interimperial history of political theology. The contests over souls and subjects are inseparable. Whether inspired by work emerging from institutions such as Harvard's Atlantic History seminar or by race and postcolonial studies (such as Paul Gilroy's influential *The Black Atlantic*), book studies have begun to situate North America's information culture within a wider frame—hemispheric, circum-Atlantic, even to an extent global. The disciplinary gravity of this approach is signaled in the title to the first volume of the ambitious series "A History of the Book in America," edited by Hall and Hugh Amory: *The Colonial Book in the Atlantic World* (2000). This volume, perhaps second in importance to the history of the book in America only to Isaiah Thomas's, expands on Hall's story, offering a bibliographic history of the colonies as an internationally variegated print world.[20]

Phillip H. Round's *By Nature and by Custom Cursed* (1999) and Ralph Bauer's *The Cultural Geography of Colonial American Literatures* (2003) demonstrate some of the complex results of such new wide-frame approaches. On one hand, considering colonial print culture in a broader spatial context shows how continuous the information experiences of the American colonists were with those of England's denizens. On the other hand, telling about New World experience transformed the way Europeans talked about their own worlds and about each other. Round's book looks at New England narratives as works with both a local audience in the colonies and a metropolitan one in London. Inspired equally by book historical approaches and by sociolinguistics, and in particular by the theories of sociologist Pierre Bourdieu, Round sees such narratives in terms of contests for social power. "New England culture," he writes, was "the product of social agents (rather than of a 'New England mind,' an 'American self,' or a 'Protestant vernacular') whose reputations and talents allowed them to take part in the highly elaborated field of *English* cultural production" that in the seventeenth century was taking on its own distinct identity.[21] Narratives about New England were designed to create cultural authority for colonists not by establishing a separate world but by participating in crucial English political, social, and religious conflicts of the time. Bauer's approach, which uses book historical methods guided by Fredric Jameson's theories about the politics of literary form, compares English and Spanish colonial literary fields. Writers in both spheres had to establish their authority; both used a new language of empirical vision to perform long-distance truth-telling in a context shaped profoundly by the power politics of European metropoles. But at the same time, inter-imperial competition, perhaps best exemplified by the cultural power of the Black Legend, profoundly shaped both the material circuits of print and the discourses that it carried.[22] "Thus," Bauer concludes, "a 'British' American discourse evolved in large part in a dialectical process of translation, editing, and commentating 'Spanish' American discourses."[23]

Jonathan Beecher Field and Douglas Anderson also resituate important colonial writers in transatlantic context, Field by looking at writers with substantial and controversial careers in the London print market and Anderson by turning to a seventeenth writer who didn't see print until the nineteenth century. Field's work suggests that mid-seventeenth-century print performances of writers like Roger Williams, often read principally for their place in American intellectual history, played important political roles during the English Civil War and Interregnum. Anderson zooms in on William Bradford's *Of Plimmoth Plantation* (1630–ca. 1650; first printed 1856), richly situating it within the reading realm of transatlantic Protestantism. Bradford's struggle to represent the history of the Separatist settlement of Plymouth Colony emerges as simultaneously a matter of information management, rhetorical mastery, and faith, as Bradford wielded the genres of the letter, the history, the providential tale, and biography from day to day. In many trans-Atlanticist studies the Dutch print market takes an important role as a sphere in which unauthorized texts of all kinds could see print and be smuggled back into England. American nonconformists' nemesis Thomas Morton, for example, had his *New English Canaan* (1637) printed by a shop in Amsterdam that also issued tracts by Puritans and other dissenters. The print culture imagination of New England in the seventeenth century, these studies suggest, included Spanish competitors, the possibility of Dutch printing, and metropolitan politics no less than local theological and social conflicts.[24]

Native Americans are conspicuously absent from, or at most symbolic in, many of the foregoing works. Hall suggested that one of the advantages of studying the northern colonies was that "the whole of New England constituted a reasonably uniform language field, a circumstance that helps us understand how deeply the culture was bound up with print as a medium of communication."[25] Yet there were dozens of Algonquian dialects, to say nothing of the other European languages heard in the region from time to time throughout the colonial period. (To give just one early example, many Plymouth colonists spoke Dutch; part of *Of Plimmoth Plantation* is written in it.) One of the most dynamic elements of recent work on New England's information world is its pursuit of the question of Native American and

African American participation in the cultures of print and European literacy sketched by earlier scholars.[26]

Hilary Wyss, Kristina Bross, and Jill Lepore have described Native participation in European print culture spheres. English missionary efforts, and in particular those of John Eliot, have been the focus of most inquiries into the relationship between early indigenous and settler communication worlds. Eliot's Massachusett-language Bible was the first Bible printed in New England, and his "Praying Towns" of Native Christians were sites of both conversion and contest. Jill Lepore's prize-winning *The Name of War* (1998) retells the story of King Philip's war as a contest of cultures of communication. Literacy emerges here in its fully paradoxical form. It could be a pathway to power (and perhaps salvation) for American Indians; it could also be a threat to cultural and, as in the dramatic case of the murder of translator John Sassamon, literal existence. Lepore argues that English chroniclers of the conflict such as William Hubbard and Cotton Mather, "[l]ike all literate Europeans in the New World," had "a veritable monopoly on making meaning, or at least on translating and *recording* the meaning of what they saw and did."[27] The many Natives who learned to read and write in English, and the many more who learned about settler religion and culture, nonetheless lacked access to the print sphere—a key technology of war. Lepore's surveys of Native literacy, the history of the print culture of the war, and the rhetoric surrounding it both at the time and in the ensuing centuries, demonstrate the war's lasting significance to racial conceptions of American identity. In doing so, they reveal implications of literacy hitherto left out of the story of New England.[28]

Still, there is a big difference between the two sides of Lepore's "or at least" in the passage just quoted. Postcolonial studies points to the difference between "recording" and "making meaning" as a key site for the study of resistance. Wyss takes up just this question of Native uses of European literacy in *Writing Indians* (2000). She emphasizes that Native Americans began to use writing as early as the 1640s and shows that they subjected alphabetic writing to their own expectations and practices. Instead of being merely shadows of English expressions of faith, Native uses of literacy suggest an adaptation of English beliefs to indigenous ways. Wyss offers a newly complex picture of New England literacy by looking at, among other evidence, marginal comments written by Indian readers in books, Indian voices appearing in accounts of proselytizing ventures such as the Mayhew family's on Martha's Vineyard, and the writings of Samson Occom and William Apess. In these sources, Wyss finds, "Natives struggle to reconcile the experience of Nativeness with the concept of salvation."[29] Such a process involves both a sustained resistance against profoundly alien concepts (such as the idea of sin) and a dynamic adaptation and hybridization of ideas with analogs in Algonquian thought. For example, expressions of self-loathing common in conversion narratives articulated by Martha's Vineyard's natives are shaped simultaneously by "Christian expressions of humility and devotion" and by "the system of Wampanoag reciprocation, in which the supplicant ensures the favor of the benefactor by setting off a series of cultural obligations."[30]

In *Dry Bones and Indian Sermons* (2004), Bross focuses on one genre of evidence, the missionary tracts published in England by John Eliot, Edward Winslow, and others working for the establishment and support of the Society for the Propagation of the Gospel. Bross uses tactics similar to Wyss's to probe the dynamics of the interactions between Eliot and local indigenous people. At the same time, she uses approaches similar to those of Field and Round to understand the representation of Indian conversion in the context of English politics. Indian mission publications were shaped by the English Civil War and its aftermath, the "pamphlet wars" (making the Antinomian Crisis an important context for understanding how Native converts are depicted in Eliot's works of that period), and by the shifting relationship of authority between the colonies and the English government. Bross's argument, crucially, understands Natives to be an audience: missionary writers had listener- and readerships that included London politicos, New England settlers, *and* local Algonquians, and their works must be analyzed in the context of this multiplicity of receivers. The substantial implications of this last point are only beginning to be taken up by scholars.[31]

Joanna Brooks uncovers the generation of semi-independent print cultures of critique among African Americans in the eighteenth century in her essay "The Early American Public Sphere and the Emergence of a Black Print Counterpublic" (2005). Where Warner argued that "print and writing could only be alien to the entirely or even partially illiterate, including almost all Native Americans and the enslaved blacks,"[32] Brooks argues that black authors, individually and collaboratively, actively manipulated print conventions to criticize public policies and social prejudices. Brooks, like feminist critics of Habermas before her, takes her theory of counterpublics from the work of Oskar Negt and Alexander Kluge on working-class print environments as sites of critique. She finds that, while Phillis Wheatley's use of white evangelical associations in England and America to publish her poetry offers a famous example of black participation in public discourse, black counterpublics more often emerged out of black fraternal and religious associations. "Given this new knowledge," Brooks insists, "it is no longer possible to theorize about the eighteenth-century American public print sphere without acknowledging the emergence in this era of a distinctly black tradition of publication informed by black experiences of slavery and postslavery, premised on principles of self-determination and structured by black criticisms of white political and economic dominance."[33]

Sandra Gustafson's book *Eloquence Is Power* (2000) pushes the question of indigenous participation in settler communications worlds further by questioning the centrality of print to European settlers. As its revision of Richard Brown's title suggests, *Eloquence Is Power* argues that writing was only one part, and not always the most important one, of a culture of performances that were bodily, linguistic, textual, and aural—often all at once. Gustafson's extraordinary work suggests that print, gesture, and speech must be considered together, necessarily pointing to new archival sources. Moreover, since East Coast indigenous societies had profoundly performative understandings of the relationships among media, it is possible to read the colonial record for rich accounts of power struggles taking place through interactions involving many media articulated together.[34]

With Christopher Looby, Gustafson finds oratorical performance to be the principal means to public power in early America, whether in diplomatic, religious, or political situations. Such a way of looking at early American public culture has wide-ranging implications. "The forms of state power that white men designed in the early republic," Gustafson points out, "were shaped in crucial ways by their proximity and resistance to the speech of white women, native Americans, and African Americans."[35] Tracing the use of eloquence into the time of the early Republic, Gustafson demonstrates shifts in public performances of eloquence, but also the rise of other, nonverbal performances used to maintain distinctions: "Gambling, horse racing, dancing, and other displays of elite power concentrated on the heroic or elegant body," reinforcing other icons of the gentry's power.[36]

Gustafson shares with Wyss, Bauer, and Round an interest in the problematics of "authenticity," which persist out of the colonial period into our own moment. Indeed, our own desires to distinguish "authentic" records by, say, Native American writers of the early settlement period stem from struggles over media and authenticity brought on by long-distance colonization itself. American colonization spurred attempts to attach cultures to media use and, reflexively, to establish cultural and medial hierarchies. An emphasis on written forms of evidence still predominates in historical method; thus the scholar of early America faces nested problems of authenticity and source analysis. Gustafson, in response, uses visual and anthropological evidence in addition to more traditional historical sources. The imagined instrumental power of the written word is denaturalized in Gustafson's readings, as writing emerges as a source of both liberation and control: "The textual prophylaxis that Puritan leaders employed to control the internal threat of multiplicity that women's oppositional speech represented was matched by their use of text to distinguish English eloquence from native speech traditions and thus to contain a threat of multiplicity from outside their speech community."[37]

Gustafson's embrace of Native speech traditions was enabled and accompanied by the publication of a number of important works in Native American studies. This thickening evidentiary and interpretive milieu of indigenous studies in New England has led to an important line of interrogation at a different level of the discipline.[38] What happens if we open up the question of what constitutes a book, or even of what "literacy" means? Anthropologists such as Brian Street were contesting work by Walter Ong and Jack Goody that linked consciousness, civilization, and literacy even as David Hall was setting aside such hierarchies in his formative work. Studies of Amerindian cultures in central and South America by Walter Mignolo and Gordon Brotherston redefined the concept of a "book" within indigenous communities by turning close attention to issues such as format, portability, and language.[39]

In this vein, in an important essay in *Book History* (1999) Germaine Warkentin asks, what if Native American wampum is a book? Wampum, beaded belts made from two kinds of shells, served northeastern woodlands societies as money, clothing, and emblemata. But it was also used in conjunction with the kinds of diplomatic oratory studied by Gustafson (usually to mark an important item in a negotiation or to symbolize past interactions). As both ritual gift and mnemonic device, wampum gave material heft to a social exchange. "The book historian is grounded in . . . solid materiality," Warkentin asserted, and "book history assumes the basic bibliographical requirement of *marks made upon a material base for the purpose of recording, storing, and communicating information.*"[40] But "many Native sign systems are distinguished from alphabetic ones by their character as process rather than as representation."[41] Consequently, a focus on the social performances surrounding an object is required. In one of my essays, inspired by the work of Hall and Warkentin, I suggested that Thomas Morton's famous Maypole ceremony drew fire from nonconformist colonial governments as much because it established a center of communications power as because its owner threatened religious or economic disaster. Key to my argument was that the Maypole could serve as a publishing venue in part because, much like an Algonquian ceremonial pole, Morton used it to link local indigenous and English communications systems. Native American inscription practices in the earliest days were not based in alphabetic literacy, but they were clearly systematized, widespread communication networks with which settlers had to contend.[42]

Matthew P. Brown, in a series of articles, but most eloquently in *The Pilgrim and the Bee* (2007), pursues the implications of performance, indigeneity, and the materiality of the book for the historiography of "print culture" in New England. Brown agrees with Lepore, Wyss, and others who have argued that "cross-cultural contact and conflict is inescapable when writing a literary history of early American expression."[43] While *The Pilgrim and the Bee* focuses more on English than on Native reading practices, it emphasizes the materiality of the text "as a prop circulating in society, with ceremonial presence—tactility, visibility, heft—that recognizes its ontological difference from speech." Books socialize readers, who in turn socialize texts and textuality through performances of reading (often out loud), writing, and distribution.[44]

For all his emphasis on performance, Brown understands the book's difference from other media to reside in its materiality, its "heft." Brown's analysis is relentlessly subtle, sensitive to reception as a performance that must be studied in multiple contexts and by different means in order to breathe again in our histories of books. On his way to performing what he terms *"interpretive bibliography,"* which brings together the analysis of content with that of morphology, Brown qualifies a number of important book historical frameworks that have been influenced by scholarship on New England.[45] We should, he argues, leave behind the rubrics of "intensive" and "extensive" reading for "continuous" and "discontinuous" paths through a text; substitute an attention to format for the generalization of "print culture"; and question the notion of readers "appropriating" texts as a principally conceptual, not also bodily, habit.

Others go farther in questioning "format"—and this goes for both traditional descriptive bibliographers of New England and for those pushing toward more attention to media that would have been meaningful to both Native Americans and European settlers. Hugh Amory, for example, argues for the sheet, rather than the book, as the basic unit of book analysis, since books were often sold unbound in the colonial era and since textual variants emerge out of changes to formes, not some larger unit.[46] Among those exploring the materiality of communication more broadly, an extraordinary range of new studies has recently emerged. Richard Cullen Rath explores the sonic realms of colonial settlements, from church bells to the sounds of the forest; Peter Charles Hoffer looks more broadly at the "sensory" aspects of colonial history. Bruce R. Smith studies the relationships between American sounds—including indigenous languages—and the audio dynamics of English theater. For Robert Blair St. George, New England architecture itself becomes a mode of communication in space, across time, and into the spirit realm. In a surprising but revelatory section of his book *Vicious* (2004), Jon Coleman explores the ways wolf communications systems in the Northeast interfaced with (and served as an interface for) indigenous and English communicative modes in the early colonial era.[47]

The methodological implications of such studies are important, in turning from books to systems and from single to multiple networks of signification. Communications systems have usually been studied by attention to a limited number of physical and social networks. In the early colonial period, messages ran through heterogeneous networks, in the sense that information and narratives often moved through different pathways of circulation and reception than intended by their creators. Fragments of English Bible text appear in Indian burial bundles; in nearby New England Native graves, Jesuit rings are found; dogs and birds signal the presence of humans about to attack, saving lives; rumors about the whereabouts of English and Indian warriors run through both Algonquian and English oral networks; and, as Gustafson and Daniel K. Richter demonstrate in different ways, English and Indians unevenly learn and employ each other's negotiating protocols in political encounters over the course of colonization.[48]

My inclusion of such work in this context raises again a question long ago put by Robert Darnton: Does opening up book history to so many topics, such different approaches, weaken its specific utility or explanatory power?[49] I think these studies invigorate book history by pushing it to reflect on the definitions of "culture" and "history" and to interrogate the materiality of the book as the sine qua non of consciousness-manufacturing. Wyss points out that the evidentiary difficulties involved in such a project—the incapacity of extant history of the book or comparative literary approaches to get at indigenous signifying cultures—are deeply rooted and politically touchy. "There are no written records of 'authentic Native communities,'" she warns, "because the act of writing and the possibility of recording the authenticity of nonliterate peoples ultimately contradict each other."[50] Andrew Newman's work on northeastern indigenous cultures' interactions with Europeans and the ways in which scholars have written about those interactions provokes him to call the categorical usefulness of "literacy" itself into question.[51]

The utility of New England as a region may be that it offers not a unified linguistic field, or even a unified communicative field, in which to study print culture, but in fact that it was so heterogeneous; that it challenges the methods of book history to account for the materiality of communication in a place where multiple modes of communication operated (and still operate) simultaneously.[52] It offers a specific historical space for pursuing a question posed by Jacques Derrida: "What then do we have the right to call 'book' and in what way is the question of *right,* far from being preliminary or accessory, here lodged at the very heart of the question of the book?"[53] For many Native Americans, this is precisely the question: literacy has not unequivocally meant freedom; when taken as an ideal communication form, books can do as much harm as good. To return one final time to Mary's prayer book in *Hobomok:* the gift of that book by Charles Brown contributes to the displacement of Mary's Native husband, Hobomok. In this narrative, the scene exemplifies a kind of "binding" that Hobomok, for all his fluency and persuasive power, cannot perform. The same year Child published her novel, New England-educated Cherokee Elias Boudinot married a Yankee woman, Harriet Gold, provoking public outrage. Having acquired precisely the substance of literacy idealized by New Englanders, Boudinot was rejected for daring to act on his acculturation by crossing racial lines.[54]

Work on New England that questions the definitions of the chief terms of book history has been profoundly generative of new understandings of settlement, the extension and contestation of colonial power, the movement of ideas across the Atlantic, and the confrontation of European and indigenous American societies and economies. It rather extends than overturns the foundational research that has made such forays possible. Questions remain, however: How can we picture New England's book history in the early colonial age in a larger imperial contest—and in the context of widespread Native resistance to, collaboration in, or avoidance of, that contest—while still depicting the intimacies and complexities of local reading and writing? Can we extend the rich interrogations of the relationships among media, time, and language initiated among historians of the book in Latin America? In what terms can we, or should we, imagine a Native American history of communication? To what extent do identifications such as gender and race cut across roughly "national" practices of media use? As Davidson points out, the complexities of studying the writing, circulation, printing, distribution, and reading of books make it an undertaking that "cannot be comprehended by one field alone and, indeed, rarely by one person."[55] Collaborative work may be increasingly called for, and in the case of the study of indigenous information practices, ethically necessary as a methodological principle.

The theoretical provocativeness of early American communications cultures gives continued significance to regionally organized studies.[56] In New England, the dynamics of long-distance communication, a multilingual environment, cross-cultural *and* same-language communications protocol diversities offer productive challenges. But it is also *what happened* that matters, a colonial legacy of violence and displacement that calls print culture's role to court for its fusion of the printed word with the logics of dispossession.[57] The idea of New England as region was fashioned by English settlers in the very crucible of the multi-cultural encounters it sought to deny. That relationship gave shape to a long subsequent history of media contest, one that endures to this day. Given the increasing use of non-textual media on the internet and in other environments, and perhaps particularly given the powerful use of all of these media by many of New England's

Native people during their recent political resurgence, studying the history of the book in New England may gesture to a different way of doing history. That way would necessarily look backwards and forwards at the same time and would acknowledge that judgments about literacy and power in the past have an effect on struggles for sovereignty today.

After all, if you want to study the print documents of the past in New England in person, you can go to the American Antiquarian Society in Worcester, or the John Carter Brown Library in Providence, both bastions of historical authority. But you could also go a little farther south, to the Mashantucket Pequot Museum and Research Center on the Pequot Reservation in Connecticut. With its substantial support—the Pequots' Foxwoods Casino and related businesses bring in an estimated $1.4 billion annually—the MPMRC has been able to amass an impressive collection of documents from early colonial New England.[58] The history of the book itself teaches us that none of these institutions is apolitical; that all are guided by expectations of their researchers and convey authority with certain publishing venues and institutions—and not with others. An archive is connected to place, even as it gives meaning to time. New England's terrain is still one of fascinating and instructive contest over books and over history.

Notes

1. This scholarship has been important to the larger book history world but also within American Studies, because of its sophisticated, integrative studies of religion, politics, and representation, at a time when religion often receives short methodological shrift (however much current politics might seem to cry out for its study). In New England print culture studies, religion is epistemologically central, whether focused on "print culture" strictly materially defined or on Native American, African American, or other signifying realms with complex relationships to European ideologies of the book. Michael Warner, *The Letters of the Republic: Publication and the Public Sphere in Eighteenth-Century America* (Cambridge: Harvard University Press, 1990); Robert A. Gross, *Printing, Politics, and the People: The 1989 James Russell Wiggins Lecture in the History of the Book in American Culture* (Worcester, Mass.: American Antiquarian Society, 1989), and *Books and Libraries in Thoreau's Concord: Two Essays* (Worcester, Mass.: American Antiquarian Society, 1988); David D. Hall, *Cultures of Print: Essays in the History of the Book* (Amherst: University of Massachusetts Press, 1996); Cathy N. Davidson, *Revolution and the Word: The Rise of the Novel in America* (Oxford: Oxford University Press, 2004); David Finkelstein and Alistair McCleery, eds., *The Book History Reader* (London: Routledge, 2001).

2. Isaiah Thomas, *The History of Printing in America* (New York: Weathervane, 1970); Lydia Maria Child, *Hobomok: A Tale of Early Times* (Boston: Cummings, Hilliard & Co., 1824), 128.

3. Philip Gura, "Early American Literature at the New Century," *William and Mary Quarterly* 3rd ser., 57, no. 3 (2000): 599–620 (quote at 600); and see Ivy Schweitzer, "Salutary Decouplings: The Newest New England Studies," *American Literary History* 13, no. 3 (2001): 578–91; and Robert A. Gross, "Books, Nationalism, and History," *Papers of the Bibliographi-*

cal Society of Canada/Cahiers de la Société bibliographique du Canada 16 (1998): 107–23. Michael Zuckerman rejects the significance of regionalism entirely in reference to the colonial era in his essay "Regionalism," in *A Companion to Colonial America*, ed. Daniel Vickers (London: Blackwell, 2003), 311–33.

4. William Charvat, *Literary Publishing in America, 1790–1850* (Amherst: University of Massachusetts Press, 1993); for a recent account of northeastern audiences in this period, see Ronald J. Zboray and Mary Saracino Zboray, *Everyday Ideas: Socio-Literary Experience among Antebellum New Englanders* (Knoxville: University of Tennessee Press, 2006). See Robert A. Gross, *The Minutemen and Their World* (New York: Hill and Wang, 1976), and "The Transcendentalists and Their World" (forthcoming). For exemplary new approaches to regionalism see Stephanie Foote, *Regional Fictions: Culture and Identity in Nineteenth-Century American Literature* (Madison: University of Wisconsin Press, 2001); and Hsuan Hsu, "Literature and Regional Production," *American Literary History* 17, no. 2 (2005): 36–69.

5. Richard Brodhead, *Cultures of Letters: Scenes of Reading and Writing in Nineteenth-Century America* (Chicago: University of Chicago Press, 1993); Amy Kaplan, "Nation, Region, and Empire," in *The Columbia History of the American Novel*, ed. Emory Elliott et al. (New York: Columbia University Press, 1991), 256–66; Nancy Glazener, *Reading for Realism: The History of a U.S. Literary Institution, 1850–1910* (Durham: Duke University Press, 1997); see also Ronald J. Zboray, *A Fictive People: Antebellum Economic Development and the American Reading Public* (New York: Oxford University Press, 1993).

6. See, for example, Elizabeth McHenry, *Forgotten Readers: Recovering the Lost History of African American Literary Societies* (Durham: Duke University Press, 2002); Robert Warrior, *The People and the Word: Reading Native Nonfiction* (Minneapolis: University of Minnesota Press, 2005), esp. 1–47; Marc Shell and Werner Sollors, eds., *The Multilingual Anthology of American Literature: A Reader of Original Texts with English Translations* (New York: New York University Press, 2000); Patrick Michael Erben, "Writing and Reading a 'New English World': Literacy, Multilingualism, and the Formation of Community in Early America," Ph.D. diss., Emory University, 2003; and Phillip Round's forthcoming history of the book in Indian country. On the persistence of religion as a major force in publishing and a source of innovation in book distribution and marketing, see David Paul Nord, *Faith in Reading: Religious Publishing and the Birth of Mass Media in America* (New York: Oxford University Press, 2004); and Candy Gunther Brown, *The Word in the World: Evangelical Writing, Publishing, and Reading in America, 1789–1880* (Chapel Hill: University of North Carolina Press, 2004).

7. See, for example, the Museum of Printing in North Andover, Massachusetts, http://museumofprinting.org/; Rosamund Purcell, *Bookworm* (New York: Quantuck Lane Press, 2006).

8. Hall, *Cultures of Print*, 41.

9. Perry Miller, *The New England Mind: The Seventeenth Century* (Cambridge: Harvard University Press, 1954); Richard Hoggart, *The Uses of Literacy: Aspects of Working-class Life, with Special Reference to Publications and Entertainments* (1957; repr., New York: Oxford University Press, 1970); David D. Hall, *Worlds of Wonder, Days of Judgment: Popular Religious Belief in Early New England* (Cambridge: Harvard University Press, 1990).

10. See Lawrence C. Wroth, *The Colonial Printer* (Portland, Maine: Southworth-Anthoensen, 1938); Kenneth Lockridge, *Literacy in Colonial New England: An Enquiry into the Social Context of Literacy in the Early Modern West* (New York: W. W. Norton, 1974); Stephen Botein, "'Meer Mechanics' and an Open Press: The Business and Political Strategies of Colonial American Printers," *Perspectives in American History* 9 (1975): 127–225; David Cressy, *Coming Over: Migration and Communication between England and New England in the Seventeenth Century* (New York: Cambridge University Press, 1987); Hall, *Worlds of Won-*

der; Amy Schrager Lang, *Prophetic Woman: Anne Hutchinson and the Problem of Dissent in the Literature of New England* (Berkeley and Los Angeles: University of California Press, 1987); E. Jennifer Monaghan, "Literacy Instruction and Gender in Colonial New England," *American Quarterly* 40, no. 1 (1988): 18–41, and her rich treatment in *Learning to Read and Write in Colonial America* (Amherst: University of Massachusetts Press, 2005).

11. Richard Brown, *Knowledge Is Power: The Diffusion of Information in Early America, 1700–1865* (New York: Oxford University Press, 1991). The scholarly literature on Phillis Wheatley is vast; for good summaries and examples of print history approaches see Wheatley, *Complete Writings: Phillis Wheatley*, ed. Vincent Carretta (New York: Penguin Classics, 2001); Kirstin Wilcox, "The Body into Print: Marketing Phillis Wheatley," *American Literature* 71, no. 1 (1999): 1–29; and Hall, *Cultures of Print*, 11, 91–92.

12. Daniel A. Cohen, *Pillars of Salt, Monuments of Grace: New England Crime Literature and the Origins of American Popular Culture, 1674–1860* (New York: Oxford University Press, 1993); Charles E. Clark, *The Public Prints: The Newspaper in Anglo-American Culture, 1665–1740* (New York: Oxford University Press, 1993). Mary Rowlandson, *The Sovereignty and Goodness of God* (1682).

13. See, for example, Jerome J. McGann, *The Textual Condition* (Princeton: Princeton University Press, 1991); Fredric Jameson, *The Political Unconscious: Narrative as a Socially Symbolic Act* (Ithaca: Cornell University Press, 1982); and Hayden White, *Tropics of Discourse: Essays in Cultural Criticism* (Baltimore: Johns Hopkins University Press, 1986). Hall, like D. F. McKenzie (*Bibliography and the Sociology of Texts* [Cambridge: Cambridge University Press, 1999]), saw book historical method as a kind of disciplinary mediator, one that called scholars to bring together discourse analysis and social history. "Can we hope," Hall wrote (*Cultures of Print*, 187), "that some day [literary] critics will interest themselves in the social history of production and consumption, and, conversely, that social historians will acknowledge the power of texts?"

14. Warner, *Letters of the Republic*, 64. Robert A. Gross cautions that Warner's "incisive account of ideology has been taken for a description of social fact," a tendency that reduces attention to the range of historically specific ways in which text was actually used and produced in America. Despite its idealization, the print sphere in the early years of the United States "was not always or everywhere an 'age of print'"; supposedly disinterested public discourse could rapidly collapse into petty name-calling when reputations were on the line; and participants in the public sphere worked hard to exclude or denigrate elements of the population that threatened extant social hierarchies. Gross, "Print and the Public Sphere in Early America," in *The State of U.S. History*, ed. Melvin Stokes (New York: Berg, 2002), 245–64 (quotes on 252, 259). On the relationship between early American evangelism and the print sphere, see Frank Lambert, *Inventing the "Great Awakening"* (Princeton: Princeton University Press, 2001), 3–56.

15. Warner, *Letters of the Republic*, 3. Warner's book moves geographically from New England to Philadelphia and New York as it progresses, beginning with John Adams and the Puritan tradition, taking up Benjamin Franklin as a key case study in the middle, and concluding with a reading of Charles Brockden Brown's *Arthur Mervyn*. In this it implicitly follows Charvat's arguments about print infrastructure and historical change. Other scholars have argued that the widespread print realm of eighteenth-century America included not only southern colonies but the imperial Atlantic world, calling for a reframing of Warner's argument.
The major exemplar of the "great divide" theory of literacy, orality, and consciousness is Walter J. Ong, *Orality and Literacy: The Technologizing of the Word* (New York: Methuen, 1982); see also Jack Goody and Ian Watt, "The Consequences of Literacy," in *Perspectives on Literacy*, ed. Eugene R. Kintgen et al. (Carbondale: Southern Illinois University Press, 1988), 3–27.

16. Davidson, *Revolution and the Word*, 59–72.

17. Ibid., 170.

18. For a panoptic and elegantly self-reflexive précis of the effects of *Revolution and the Word*, see Davidson's introduction to the expanded edition of her text (3–56).

19. David Shields, *Civil Tongues and Polite Letters in British America* (Chapel Hill: University of North Carolina Press, 1997), 4; Grantland S. Rice, *The Transformation of Authorship in America* (Chicago: University of Chicago Press, 1997). See also Eric Slauter's "Reading and Radicalization: Print, Causality, and the American Revolution," in *The Atlantic World of Print in the Age of Franklin*, ed. James N. Green and Rosalind Remer (Philadelphia: University of Pennsylvania Press, forthcoming), and his *The State as a Work of Art: The Cultural Origins of the Constitution* (Chicago: University of Chicago Press, 2008); and David Conroy, *In Public Houses: Drink and the Revolution in Authority in Colonial Massachusetts* (Chapel Hill: University of North Carolina Press, 1995).

20. Paul Gilroy, *The Black Atlantic: Modernity and Double Consciousness* (Cambridge: Harvard University Press, 1993); Hugh Amory and David D. Hall, eds., *A History of the Book in America*, vol. 1, *The Colonial Book in the Atlantic World* (New York: Cambridge University Press, 2000).

21. Phillip H. Round, *By Nature and By Custom Cursed: Transatlantic Civil Discourse and New England Cultural Production, 1620–1660* (Amherst: University of Massachusetts Press, 1999), 6–7.

22. See most recently Margaret Greer et al., eds., *Rereading the Black Legend: The Discourses of Religious and Racial Difference in the Renaissance Empires* (Chicago: University of Chicago Press, 2007).

23. Ralph Bauer, *The Cultural Geography of Colonial American Literatures: Empire, Travel, Modernity* (New York: Cambridge University Press, 2003), 13. Bauer was also the organizer of an important summit between early Americanists and colonial Latin Americanists in Tucson, Arizona, in 2002. Book historical approaches emerged at that conference as a kind of methodological lingua franca; most of the presentations, which offered summaries of scholarly conversations around key colonial documents, began with a history of the production, distribution, and reception of the text in question. A collection of essays emerging from that summit is forthcoming from the Omohundro Institute of Early American History and Culture's series at the University of North Carolina Press. For similar approaches, see Teresa Toulouse, *The Captive's Position: Female Narrative, Male Identity, and Royal Authority in Colonial New England* (Philadelphia: University of Pennsylvania Press, 2007); and Rebecca Ann Bach, *Colonial Transformations: The Cultural Production of the New Atlantic World, 1580–1640* (New York: Palgrave, 2000).

24. Jonathan Beecher Field, "The Grounds of Dissent: Heresies and Colonies in New England, 1636–1663," Ph.D. diss., University of Chicago, 2004; Douglas Anderson, *William Bradford's Books: Of Plimmoth Plantation and the Printed Word* (Baltimore: Johns Hopkins University Press, 2003); see also Jeffrey Glover, "Thomas Lechford's *Plain Dealing*: Censorship and Cosmopolitan Print Culture in the English Atlantic," *Book History* 10 (2007): 29–46.

25. Hall, *Cultures of Print*, 93.

26. Eighteenth-century indigenous New England communities were often significantly or predominantly Afro-Native. Scholars are only beginning to think about the implications of the information culture inheritances of these communities, but it is clear that a lack of understanding of such heritages, combined with racism, has shaped some of the best-known tribal recognition decisions in U.S. courts. See James Clifford, *The Predicament of Culture: Twentieth-Century Ethnography, Literature, and Art* (Cambridge: Harvard University Press, 1988), 277–346 ("Identity in Mashpee"); Jean M. O'Brien, *Dispossession by Degrees: Indian Land and Identity in Natick, Massachusetts, 1650–1790* (New York: Cambridge University Press, 1997);

Tiya Miles and Sharon P. Holland, eds., *Crossing Waters, Crossing Worlds: The African Diaspora in Indian Country* (Durham: Duke University Press, 2006).

27. Lepore, *The Name of War: King Philip's War and the Origins of American Identity* (New York: Knopf, 1998), xviii.

28. For other important accounts of Native literacy and the controversy over Native attitudes toward books as objects, see the work of James Axtell, most recently his article "Babel of Tongues: Communicating with the Indians in Eastern North America," in *The Language Encounter in the Americas, 1492–1800*, ed. Edward G. Gray and Norman Fiering (New York: Berghan, 2000), 15–60; Peter Wogan, "Perceptions of European Literacy in Early Contact Situations," *Ethnohistory* 41, no. 3 (1994): 407–29; and Edward G. Gray, *New World Babel: Languages and Nations in Early America* (Princeton: Princeton University Press, 1999).

29. Hilary Wyss, *Writing Indians: Literacy, Christianity, and Native Community in Early America* (Amherst: University of Massachusetts Press, 2000), 76.

30. Ibid., 76. See also Wyss's forthcoming collection of documents with critical introductions, edited with Kristina Bross, *Early Native Literacies in New England: A Documentary and Critical Anthology* (Amherst: University of Massachusetts Press); Ives Goddard and Kathleen Bragdon, eds., *Native Writings in Massachusett* (Philadelphia: American Philosophical Society, 1988); and Apess, *On Our Own Ground: The Complete Writings of William Apess, A Pequot*, ed. Barry O'Connell (Amherst: University of Massachusetts Press, 1992).

31. Kristina Bross, *Dry Bones and Indian Sermons: Praying Indians in Colonial America* (Ithaca: Cornell University Press, 2004). See also James P. Ronda, "'We Are Well As We Are': An Indian Critique of Seventeenth-Century Christian Missions," *William and Mary Quarterly* 3rd ser., 34, no. 1 (1977): 66–82; and Craig White, "The Praying Indians' Speeches as Texts of Massachusett Oral Culture," *Early American Literature* 38, no. 3 (2003): 437–66.

32. Warner, *Letters of the Republic*, 11.

33. Joanna Brooks, "The Early American Public Sphere and the Emergence of a Black Print Counterpublic," *William and Mary Quarterly* 62, no. 1 (2005): 67–92 (quote on 67–68), and *American Lazarus: Religion and the Rise of African-American and Native American Literatures* (New York: Oxford University Press, 2007). See also Julius Scott, "The Common Wind: Currents of Afro-American Communication in the Era of the Haitian Revolution," Ph.D. diss., Duke University, 1986; and Frances Smith Foster, "A Narrative of the Interesting Origins and (Somewhat) Surprising Developments of African-American Print Culture," *American Literary History* 17, no. 4 (2005): 714–40.

34. Sandra Gustafson, *Eloquence Is Power: Oratory and Performance in Early America* (Chapel Hill: University of North Carolina Press, 2000). See also for the early colonial period Jane Kamensky, *Governing the Tongue: The Politics of Speech in Early New England* (New York: Oxford University Press, 1997); and the multimedia approach to the postrevolutionary era taken in Laura Rigal, *The American Manufactory: Art, Labor, and the World of Things in the Early Republic* (Princeton: Princeton University Press, 1998).

35. Gustafson, *Eloquence Is Power*, xix.

36. Ibid., 158. Christopher Looby, *Voicing America: Language, Literary Form, and the Origins of the United States* (Chicago: University of Chicago Press, 1996); see also Christopher Grasso, *A Speaking Aristocracy: Transforming Public Discourse in Eighteenth-Century Connecticut* (Chapel Hill: University of North Carolina Press, 1999).

37. Gustafson, *Eloquence Is Power*, 33. On performances of authority in New England and the problems of historical evidence, studied from quite different, but book history–informed perspectives, see Jim Egan, *Authorizing Experience: Refigurations of the Body Politic in Seventeenth-Century New England Writing* (Princeton: Princeton University Press, 1999); Jay Fliegelman, *Declaring Independence: Jefferson, Natural Language, and the Culture of Performance* (Stanford: Stanford University Press, 1994); Matthew P. Brown, "'BOSTON SOB/

NOT': Elegiac Performance in Early New England and Materialist Studies of the Book," *American Quarterly* 50, no. 2 (1998): 306–39; and David Murray, *Forked Tongues: Speech, Writing, and Representation in North American Indian Texts* (Bloomington: Indiana University Press, 1991).

38. Major histories of Native culture in the Northeast that have informed book history approaches include Neal Salisbury, *Manitou and Providence: Indians, Europeans, and the Making of New England, 1500–1643* (New York: Oxford University Press, 1982); Richard White, *The Middle Ground: Indians, Empires, and Republics in the Great Lakes Region, 1650–1815* (New York: Cambridge University Press, 1991); Kathleen J. Bragdon, *Native People of Southern New England, 1500–1650* (Norman: University of Oklahoma Press, 1996); and Karen Kupperman, *Indians and English: Facing Off in Early America* (Ithaca: Cornell University Press, 2000).

39. Brian Street, *Literacy in Theory and Practice* (New York: Cambridge University Press, 1984); Walter Mignolo, *The Darker Side of the Renaissance: Literacy, Territoriality, and Colonization* (Ann Arbor: University of Michigan Press, 1995); and Gordon Brotherston, *Book of the Fourth World: Reading the Americas through Their Literature* (New York: Cambridge University Press, 1992).

40. Germaine Warkentin, "In Search of 'The Word of the Other': Aboriginal Sign Systems and the History of the Book in Canada," *Book History* 2 (1999): 1–27 (quote on 3; emphasis in original). On the ways wampum satisfies basic definitions of writing, see also Nancy Shoemaker, *A Strange Likeness: Becoming Red and White in Eighteenth-Century North America* (New York: Oxford University Press, 2004), 61–81.

41. Warkentin, "In Search of 'The Word of the Other,'" 6.

42. Matt Cohen, "Morton's Maypole and the Indians: Publishing in Early New England," *Book History* 5 (2002): 1–18. See also Gordon Sayre, *Les sauvages américains: Representations of Native Americans in French and English Colonial Literature* (Chapel Hill: University of North Carolina Press, 1997).

43. Matthew P. Brown, *The Pilgrim and the Bee: Reading Rituals and Book Culture in Early New England* (Philadelphia: University of Pennsylvania Press, 2007), 11.

44. Ibid., 13. Brown argues, in his final chapter, that the archive of printed documents from early New England was shaped profoundly by John Eliot's mission publications. As a result, the evidentiary archives of such influential scholars of Puritanism as Miller and Bercovitch are "a product of publication technologies in the seventeenth century, technologies that were predicated on the use value of indigenous peoples" (206). See also Brown, "Cultural Studies, Materialist Bibliography and the New England Archive: Editing an Elegy from King Philip's War," *Studies in the Literary Imagination* 32, no. 1 (1999): 81–89, and "The Study and Story of Books in Early America," *Papers of the Bibliographical Society of America* 98, no. 4 (2004): 522–30.

45. Brown, *The Pilgrim and the Bee*, 15.

46. See Hugh Amory, *Bibliography and the Book Trades: Studies in the Print Culture of Early New England*, ed. David D. Hall (Philadelphia: University of Pennsylvania Press, 2005). Amory's chief influence has been on the large-scale story of bookselling and distribution. Focusing on London print market conditions, the physical properties of books themselves (in particular their differential fungibility in sheets or bound), and the range of comparative methods that can be brought to the study of the book culture of early New England, Amory argues for an appreciation of what might be called the zonal quality of book distribution there. Rethinking the major categorizations—literacy, cultural insularity, creole anxieties—that book data have been used to produce also led Amory to an important attempt to bring together Native American studies and bibliography. As a result, with a nod to Axtell, he terms his overall project "ethnobibliography."

47. Richard Cullen Rath, *How Early America Sounded* (Ithaca: Cornell University Press, 2003); Peter Charles Hoffer, *Sensory Worlds in Early America* (Baltimore: Johns Hopkins University Press, 2003); Bruce R. Smith, *The Acoustic World of Early Modern England: Attending to the O-Factor* (Chicago: University of Chicago Press, 1999), 287–341; Robert Blair St. George, *Conversing by Signs: Poetics of Implication in Colonial New England Culture* (Chapel Hill: University of North Carolina Press, 1998); Jon Coleman, *Vicious: Wolves and Men in America* (New Haven: Yale University Press, 2004), esp. 1–68.

48. Daniel K. Richter, *Facing East from Indian Country: A Native History of Early America* (Cambridge: Harvard University Press, 2001). For the study of a Pequot medicine bundle containing a page from a Dutch-printed English Bible, see Amory, *Bibliography and the Book Trades*, 11–33.

49. Darnton, "What Is the History of Books?" in *Books and Society in History*, ed. Kenneth E. Carpenter (New York: Bowker, 1983), 3–26.

50. Wyss, *Writing Indians*, 10.

51. Andrew Newman, "The *Walam Olum* and Indigenous Apocrypha," *American Literary History* (forthcoming), and "On the Literacy Frontier: Early American Letters at their Limits," Ph.D. diss., University of California Irvine, 2004.

52. In her James Russell Wiggins Lecture to the American Antiquarian Society in 2005, Gustafson pointed out that the influence of New England on book history is also in part rooted in a wealth of bibliographical foreground—work by William S. Reese, Charles Evans, G. Thomas Tanselle, Clifford K. Shipton, Charles Heartman, and many others—much of the fruits of which is now available electronically. Her reflections on the long history of what she terms "emergent media" in America are spurred in part by the changes electronic access are bringing to the field. See Sandra Gustafson, "The Emerging Media of Early America," *Proceedings of the American Antiquarian Society* 115, no. 2 (2005): 205–50.

53. Jacques Derrida, *Paper Machine* (Stanford: Stanford University Press, 2005), 5.

54. My thanks to Robert Gross for pointing out this revealing coincidence. On the contradictory politics of assimilation in this era, see John Wood Sweet, *Bodies Politic: Negotiating Race in the American North, 1730–1830* (Baltimore: Johns Hopkins University Press, 2003).

55. Davidson, *Revolution and the Word*, 42.

56. In Scott Casper, Joanne Chaison, and Jeffrey Groves's anthology *Perspectives on Book History,* the teleology of nation is deprecated, but region is still an organizing factor, in part because of the importance of geography in early distribution networks. But other categories, such as class, race, and religion, are just as significant in organizing the topics. Lepore's contribution, "Literacy and Reading in Puritan New England," is specifically titled with reference to religion and does not claim to embrace information systems as a "culture." Alice Fahs writes about "Northern and Southern Worlds of Print," while Ann Fabian synopsizes "Laboring Classes, New Readers, and Print Cultures." See Casper et al., eds., *Perspectives on American Book History: Artifacts and Commentary* (Amherst: University of Massachusetts Press, 2002).

57. Gross points out that the *ideology* of regionalism has had a long history as well, which makes the history of the uses of the concept of New England an important analytical factor. See Robert Gross, "Where IS New England?" *Uncommon Sense* 119 (Fall 2004), http://oieahc.wm.edu/uncommon/119/NewEngland.htm.

58. See the description at the MPMRC's website, http://www.pequotmuseum.org/Home/LibrariesArchives/.

CONTRIBUTORS

Ross Alloway completed his PhD at the University of Edinburgh on the topic of F. R. Leavis and the publishing market, which will be published by Ashgate in 2009 as *The Leavises and the Marketplace: The Economics of Literary Criticism*. After completing his PhD he held a two-year AHRC research post as editorial assistant for *The Edinburgh History of the Book in Scotland*, vol. 3, *Industry and Ambition 1800–1880*, ed. Bill Bell (Edinburgh University Press, 2007), to which he contributed. In 2006 he received a three-year British Academy Postdoctoral Fellowship to work on the diaries of the nineteenth- century publisher Robert Cadell. He has published on the history of the book and is associate director for the Scottish Book Trade Archive Inventory (http://www.hss.ed.ac.uk/chb/sbtai.htm).

Janice Cavell is an adjunct research professor of history at Carleton University. She is the author of *Tracing the Connected Narrative: Arctic Exploration in British Print Culture, 1818–1860* (University of Toronto Press, 2008). She has published articles in journals including the *Canadian Historical Review*, the *Journal of Imperial and Commonwealth History*, and *Polar Record*, and in the collection *Canadas of the Mind*, edited by Norman Hillmer and Adam Chapnick (McGill-Queen's University Press, 2007).

Matt Cohen is an assistant professor in the Department of English at Duke University. He is the author of several articles in the field of book history and of *Native Audiences: Communicating in Early New England* (University of Minnesota Press, forthcoming). He is the editor of *Brother Men: The Correspondence of Edgar Rice Burroughs and Herbert T. Weston* (Duke University Press, 2005) and a contributing editor at the online Walt Whitman Archive.

David Faflik is an assistant professor in the Department of American Culture and Literature at Bilkent University in Ankara, Turkey. A specialist on the city in literature, he currently is completing his first book project, titled "Boarding Out: Inhabiting the American Urban Literary Imagination, 1840–1860," which addresses U.S. writers' response to the problems of metropolitan habitation during the middle decades of the nineteenth century. He also is the editor of Thomas Butler Gunn's *The Physiology of New York Boarding-Houses* (1857; critical reprint edition Rutgers University Press, 2008).

Robert Franciosi is Professor of English and Honors at Grand Valley State University. He edited *Elie Wiesel: Conversations* (University Press of Mississippi, 2002) and has published articles and chapters on a range of Holocaust texts. His article is part of a book manuscript in progress, "Imagining The Ghetto: John Hersey's *The Wall* and American Holocaust Memory."

Nicole Howard is an assistant professor of history at California State University, East Bay, and the author of *The Book: The Life Story of a Technology* (Greenwood Press, 2005). Her research centers on the intersection of early modern science and print culture.

Lize Kriel teaches African history and cultural history at the University of Pretoria, South Africa. She is interested in missionary writings and publications for what they reveal about understandings of gender, race, and religion in colonial encounters.

Mary A. Nicholas is an associate professor of Russian language and literature at Lehigh University, Bethlehem, Pennsylvania. She has published widely on Russian prose of the 1920s and 1930s and on poetry of the late Soviet period. She is currently at work on a project devoted to the role of text in Russian visual art of the late Soviet and early post-Soviet period.

Joanne Filippone Overty, a PhD candidate in the Department of History at Fordham University, is currently working on her dissertation examining fifteenth-century monastic choir book production in Northern Italy. She received a BA in Economics from New York University and an MA in Medieval Studies from Fordham University. She and her husband, Darren, own Clouds Hill Books, a rare book and manuscript company in Manhattan's West Village.

Cynthia A. Ruder is an associate professor of Russian language and literature at the University of Kentucky. Her work includes publications on Soviet literature in the 1930s and on Russian language pedagogy. Her current project examines the notions of space and place in connection with the construction of the Moscow Canal, 1932–37.

Margaret Schotte is a doctoral candidate in the History of Science program at Princeton University. Her interest in William London developed while participating in the Book History and Print Culture program at the University of Toronto.

Mark R. M. Towsey held a Past and Present Postdoctoral Fellowship for 2007–8 at the Institute of Historical Research in London, having completed a PhD in Scottish History at the University of St. Andrews. He has numerous papers forthcoming on the history of libraries, reading, and intellectual culture in Scotland in the long eighteenth century. He won the Economic and Social History Society of Scotland Research Essay Prize in 2007.

Trysh Travis is an assistant professor of women's studies at the University of Florida, where she teaches twentieth-century U.S. literary and cultural history, with a focus on the gendered history of books and reading. She holds an MA from the Bread Loaf School of English at Middlebury College, and a PhD in American Studies from Yale. Her work has appeared in such venues as *American Literary History, The Journal of Modern Literature,* and *American Quarterly.* Her book *The Language of the Heart: Reading, Writing, and the Culture of 12-Step Recovery,* is forthcoming in 2009 from the University of North Carolina Press.

NEW from NORTH CAROLINA

A HISTORY OF THE BOOK IN AMERICA
PUBLISHED IN ASSOCIATION WITH
THE AMERICAN ANTIQUARIAN SOCIETY

The five-volume *A History of the Book in America* is a sweeping chronicle of our country's print production and culture from colonial times to the end of the twentieth century. This inter-disciplinary, collaborative work of scholarship examines the book trades as they have developed and spread throughout the United States; provides a history of U.S. literary cultures; investigates the practice of reading and, more broadly, the uses of literacy; and links literary culture with larger themes in American history.

VOLUME 1: THE COLONIAL BOOK IN THE ATLANTIC
Edited by Hugh Amory and David D. Hall
664 pages $34.95 paper

VOLUME 3: THE INDUSTRIAL BOOK, 1840-1880
Edited by Scott E. Casper, Jeffrey D. Groves, Stephen W. Nissenbaum, and Michael Winship
560 pages $60.00 cloth

VOLUME 4: PRINT IN MOTION: THE EXPANSION OF PUBLISHING AND READING IN THE UNITED STATES, 1880-1940
Edited by Carl F. Kaestle and Janice A. Radway
Available January 2009 640 pages $60.00 cloth

VOLUME 5: THE ENDURING BOOK, 1945-1995
Edited by David Paul Nord, Joan Shelley Rubin, and Michael Schudson
Coming Spring 2009

VOLUME 2: AN EXTENSIVE REPUBLIC: PRINT, CULTURE, AND SOCIETY IN THE NEW NATION
Edited by Robert A. Gross and Mary Kelley
Coming Fall 2009

ALSO AVAILABLE

What America Read
Taste, Class, and the Novel, 1920-1960
GORDON HUTNER
"For more than twenty years, Gordon Hutner has been a leader in transforming the field of American literature studies. In *What America Read*, he makes a distinctive and original undertaking: to diagnose the soul of the American literate middle class over a crucial forty-year period by examining quality realist fiction and the critical conversations in which this fiction took part."
—**Jonathan Arac**, University of Pittsburgh
Available January 2009
432 pages $39.95 cloth

The Rise of Multicultural America
Economy and Print Culture, 1865-1915
SUSAN L. MIZRUCHI
Between the Civil War and World War I the United States underwent the most rapid economic expansion in history. At the same time, the country experienced unparalleled rates of immigration. This era marked the emergence of Americans' self-consciousness about what we today call multiculturalism. Mizruchi approaches this complex development from the perspective of print culture, demonstrating how both popular and elite writers played pivotal roles in articulating the stakes of this national metamorphosis.
Available January 2009
352 pages
$65.00 cloth / $24.95 paper

THE UNIVERSITY of NORTH CAROLINA PRESS
at bookstores or 800-848-6224 | www.uncpress.unc.edu | visit uncpressblog.com